Adobe®
InDesign® CS6
Digital
Classroom

D1337827

Adobe®
InDesign® CS6
Digital
Classroom

Christopher Smith and the AGI Creative Team

WILEY

John Wiley & Sons, Inc.

Adobe® InDesign® CS6 Digital Classroom

Published by
John Wiley & Sons, Inc.
10475 Crosspoint Blvd.
Indianapolis, IN 46256

Published simultaneously in Canada

ISBN: 978-1-118-12406-2

Manufactured in the United States of America

10 9 8 7 6 5 4 3 2 1

For general information on our other products and services or to obtain technical support, please contact our Customer Care Department within the U.S. at (877) 762-2974, outside the U.S. at (317) 572-3993 or fax (317) 572-4002.

Wiley publishes in a variety of print and electronic formats and by print-on-demand. Some material included with standard print versions of this book may not be included in e-books or in print-on-demand. If this book refers to media such as a CD or DVD that is not included in the version you purchased, you may download this material after registering your book at *www.digitalclassroombooks.com/CS6/InDesign*. For more information about Wiley products, visit *www.wiley.com*.

Please report any errors by sending a message to *errata@agitraining.com*.

Library of Congress Control Number: 2012935800

About the Authors

Christopher Smith is the president of American Graphics Institute (AGI). He provides business strategy and technology-related consulting services to creative, marketing, and publishing organizations. Educated as a journalist, he works extensively with marketing and corporate communications departments, advertising agencies, along with magazine and newspaper clients who are migrating to InDesign and InCopy. Christopher regularly speaks at events and conferences around the world, and has delivered InDesign seminars, lectures, and classes in Europe, North America, Australia, and New Zealand. He helped develop the Adobe Certified Expert and Adobe Certified Instructor exams for InDesign and was hired by Adobe to help promote InDesign prior to the launch of the first version of the product, and has been working with the software ever since. He is also the co-author of the *Adobe Creative Suite for Dummies*, also published by Wiley.

Outside of AGI, he has served as an elected member of the school board in his hometown in suburban Boston, Massachusetts and has served as a board member for a private K–8 Montessori school. Prior to founding AGI, Christopher worked for Quark, Inc.

Chad Chelius is an instructor with AGI Training. His formal education is in publishing technology, but it is his trial-by-fire production experience working with the Mac OS and many creative software programs that makes him such a valuable contributor to every project on which he works. He has served as the lead consultant for major publishing technology migrations at leading book and magazine publishers. In his work with AGI Training, he has assisted such clients such as Rodale Press (publishers of Prevention Magazine, Runner's World, and multiple other magazine titles), and the publishing group of the National Geographic Society. Chad holds professional certifications from both Adobe and Apple.

The **AGI Creative Team** is composed of Adobe Certified Experts and Adobe Certified Instructors from American Graphics Institute (AGI). The AGI Creative Team has authored more than 10 Digital Classroom books, and previously created many of Adobe's official training guides. They work with many of the world's most prominent companies, helping them to use creative software to communicate more effectively and creatively. They work with marketing, creative, and communications teams around the world delivering private customized training programs, and teach regularly scheduled classes at AGI's locations. They are available for professional development sessions at schools and universities. More information at *agitraining.com*.

Acknowledgments

A special thanks and shout-out to our many friends at Adobe Systems, Inc. who made this book possible and assisted with questions and feedback during the writing process. To the many clients of AGI who have helped us better understand how they use InDesign and provided us with many of the tips and suggestions found in this book. A special thanks to the instructional team at AGI for their input and assistance in the review process and for making this book such a team effort.

Credits

Additional Writing
Chad Chelius

President, American Graphics Institute and Digital Classroom Series Publisher
Christopher Smith

Executive Editor
Jody Lefevere

Technical Editors
Cathy Auclair, Haziel Olivera

Editor
Karla E. Melendez

Editorial Director
Robyn Siesky

Business Manager
Amy Knies

Senior Marketing Manager
Sandy Smith

Vice President and Executive Group Publisher
Richard Swadley

Vice President and Executive Publisher
Barry Pruett

Senior Project Coordinator
Katherine Crocker

Project Manager
Cheri White

Graphics and Production Specialist
Jason Miranda, Spoke & Wheel

Media Development Project Supervisor
Chris Leavey

Proofreading
Jay Donahue, Barn Owl Publishing

Indexing
Michael Ferreira

Register your Digital Classroom book for exclusive benefits

Registered owners receive access to:

 The most current lesson files

 Technical resources and customer support

 Notifications of updates

 On-line access to video tutorials

 Downloadable lesson files

 Samples from other Digital Classroom books

Register at *DigitalClassroomBooks.com/CS6/InDesign*

DigitalClassroom

Register your book today at
DigitalClassroomBooks.com/CS6/InDesign

Contents

Starting up

Prerequisites 1

System requirements 2

Starting Adobe InDesign CS6 3

Resetting the InDesign workspace and preferences........... 4

Loading lesson files... 4

Working with the video tutorials 6

Setting up for viewing the video tutorials 6

Viewing the video tutorials
with the Adobe Flash Player.. 6

Additional resources... 7

Lesson 1: InDesign CS6 Essential Skills

Starting up 9

InDesign tools..10

The InDesign workspace...11

The document window 11

Using guides..13

Viewing modes...14

Working with panels 15

The Tools panel..15

Managing panels 17

Saving your workspace...19

Working with the Control panel 20

Navigating through an InDesign document 20

Using the Pages panel 20

Changing the magnification of your document...............22

Working with type 24

Entering and formatting type 24

Placing and formatting type 26

Flowing type..27

Using styles 29

Applying paragraph styles...29

Applying character styles 30

Apply styles across a story using Find/Change 30

Applying object styles..32

Working with graphics 34

Placing graphics..34

Positioning graphics within a frame 36

Applying text wrap 39

Understanding layers 40

Applying effects..42

Resources for additional help....................................44

Self study...46

Review 46

Lesson 2: Building Documents with Master Pages

Starting up 47

Planning your document 48

Creating custom page sizes.......................................48

Creating a new custom-sized document......................48

Creating and formatting master pages 51

Formatting master pages 52

Adding automatic page numbers.................................53

Using text variables...55

Basing master pages on other master pages.................59

Overriding master page items....................................60

Adding layout pages 64

Placing formatted text..69

Creating the classified page 71

Adding images and text to the master frames...............73

Applying master pages to multiple pages.....................75

Self study...76

Review 76

Lesson 3: Working with Text and Type

Starting up 77
Adding text to your document.................................78
Creating a text frame..78
Changing character attributes.................................80
Changing font and type styles 80
Adjusting size 81
Adjusting line spacing 82
Adjusting character spacing: kerning and tracking 82
Using a baseline shift..83
Changing paragraph attributes................................84
Horizontally aligning text 84
Changing the spacing before and after paragraphs........84
Using tabs..85
Adding rules above or below paragraphs.......................89
Changing text color...90
Creating drop caps 92
Finding and changing text.......................................92
Finding and changing text and text attributes 92
Finding and changing text using GREP 94
Checking and correcting spelling 98
Checking spelling..98
Adding words to the dictionary...............................99
Checking spelling as you type.................................100
Automatically correcting spelling.............................102
Editing text using the Story Editor...........................103
Using Track Changes..104
Drag-and-drop text editing 106
Special characters and glyphs..................................107
Using the Glyphs panel and glyph sets 109
Text frame options 110
Adjusting text inset..110
Vertically aligning text...111
Importing text 112
Flowing text manually..113
Threading text between frames................................114
Using semi-autoflow to link several text frames 115

Changing the number of columns in a text frame 117

Baseline grid 120

Viewing and changing the baseline grid 120

Adding story jumps 122

Using styles to format text 123

Creating a headline and applying a style 123

Importing styles from other documents 125

Redefining styles 125

Placing text on a path 127

Importing text from Microsoft Word 129

Missing fonts 133

Finding and fixing missing fonts 133

Self study 135

Review 135

Lesson 4: Working with Styles

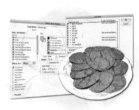

Starting up 137

Style types 138

Paragraph styles 139

Defining paragraph styles 139

Applying paragraph styles 141

Character styles 142

Defining character styles 142

Applying character styles 143

Using nested styles 144

Updating styles 146

Loading styles from another InDesign document 147

Quick Apply 149

Organizing styles into groups 151

Object styles 152

Creating object styles 152

Applying an object style 154

Changing an object style 155

Finishing up 156

GREP Styles 157

Self study 159

Review 159

Lesson 5: Working with Graphics

Starting up 161
Understanding how InDesign handles graphics 162
Locating missing images 162
Working with the Links panel and the Link badge 163
Customizing the Links panel 167
Adding graphics to your layout 168
Fitting an image within an existing frame.................... 172
Auto Fitting 175
Using Adobe Bridge to import graphics....................... 176
Placing multiple graphics using Mini Bridge................. 178
Using object styles for images.................................... 181
Wrapping text around images 185
Wrapping text around the bounding box 185
Using graphics with clipping paths and
alpha channels.. 186
Removing an image background using InDesign........... 189
Using anchored objects... 191
Advanced importing 196
Importing layered Photoshop files 196
Importing InDesign layouts as graphics....................... 198
Self study..200
Review 200

Lesson 6: Creating and Using Tables

Starting up..201
Creating a table..202
Creating new tables 203
Copying and pasting table information 204
Converting text to a table and a table to text..............208
Importing a table..209
Editing tables and table options................................. 211
Changing row height... 211
Editing the border.. 213
Formatting rows and columns 214
Using fills.. 217

Formatting cells and text...219

Resetting the cell styles within a table.........................219

Text alignment and inset within a cell..........................221

Formatting text within a cell and saving
paragraph styles 222

Formatting text in tables by column............................227

Working with tables in Story Editor 229

Merging cells 230

Defining a header cell...230

Setting column and row dimensions 236

Setting a fixed row height 236

Setting column width..238

Using graphics in tables..239

Placing graphics in cells..239

Cell styles and table styles 243

Cell styles 243

Applying cell styles 246

Creating table styles...247

Applying table styles..249

Self study..251

Review 251

Lesson 7: Using Color in Your Documents

Starting up 253

Applying colors to frames and text..............................254

Applying color to text...255

Applying color to frames 256

Applying Live Corner Effects......................................257

Creating and saving a new swatch 260

Applying strokes to text..262

Creating a tint reduction...265

Making a dashed stroke...267

Creating and saving gradients....................................269

Linear gradients 270

Saving a gradient 272

Adjusting fill opacity 273

Radial gradient 274

Adjusting the direction of a radial gradient 274

One-click edits 276

Using the Eyedropper tool to copy frame attributes 276

Applying colors to multiple objects 277

Updating and editing colors 278

Using and saving spot colors 280

Colorizing a grayscale image 281

Self study 283

Review 283

Lesson 8: Using Effects

Starting up 285

Creative effects 286

Applying opacity to objects 287

Apply effects to stroke or fill only 289

Drop shadow 290

Adjusting effects for objects 293

Bevel and Emboss 294

Object styles with effects 296

Using Find/Change to apply object styles 297

Basic Feather 298

The Gradient Feather tool 301

Converting text to a path 302

Applying blending modes to objects 305

The Screen blending mode 306

The Multiply blending mode 307

Working with imported files that use transparency 309

Applying an alpha channel selection 311

Applying a path selection 314

Self study 316

Review 316

Lesson 9: Advanced Document Features

Starting up 317
Adding text variables 318
Creating a book from multiple files 321
Defining pagination and document order.................... 322
Synchronizing attributes across a book file 325
Creating Captions.. 330
Creating a Table of Contents 333
Building an index.. 338
Adding topics 339
Adding cross-references 342
Generating the index... 343
Creating PDFs and printing from the Book panel........... 344
Creating PDFs 344
Printing 345
Self study... 346
Review 346

Lesson 10: Preflighting, Printing and Creating PDFs from InDesign

Starting up 347
Package inventory.. 348
Preflight checks 351
Packaging your document... 355
Creating an Adobe PDF.. 359
Separation preview 363
Printing a proof... 366
Self study... 368
Review 368

Lesson 11: Introduction to Digital Documents

Starting up 369

InDesign as your Digital Publication Hub 370

Interactive design considerations 370

Importing multimedia content...................................... 371

Adding a Hyperlink 374

Creating a Multi-State Object.. 375

Creating buttons to control multimedia content 377

Adding buttons to control a multi-state object 378

Creating page transitions.. 381

Creating animations... 383

Previewing your document... 385

Exporting your document.. 386

Creating an interactive PDF... 386

Creating a SWF file 388

New layout features 391

Auto-Size Text Frames 392

Flexible Width Text Frames... 393

Layout adjustments.. 395

Liquid Layout.. 395

Alternate Layouts... 397

Linked Content 400

The Content tools.. 404

Creating PDF Forms.. 406

Adding a Combo Box.. 408

Creating a Submit button 409

Creating the PDF Form 411

Self study... 413

Review 413

Lesson 12: Creating Digital Books

Starting up 415

Preparing your InDesign document
for ePub conversion 417

Using styles 417

Controlling Object Export Settings 418

Adding interactive links 419

Adding hyperlinks 419

Creating an interactive Table of Contents 420

Adding document metadata 423

Creating an ePub 424

Specifying Object Export Order 424

Using anchored objects to control
object placement 425

Specifying the cover 426

ePub export settings 427

Testing your ePub 432

ePub viewers 432

Distributing ePub files 434

Self study 435

Review 435

Lesson 13: Adobe InDesign CS6 New Features

Starting up 437

About the new features in InDesign CS6 438

Content Collector 439

Linked content 440

Liquid layouts 441

Alternate layouts 443

PDF forms 445

Primary text frame 446

ePub enhancements 447

Starting up

About InDesign Digital Classroom

Adobe® InDesign® CS6 lets you create layouts for brochures, magazines, books, flyers, marketing and sales sheets. InDesign was originally conceived for creating print and PDF documents, but it is evolving into a tool for creating interactive and digital documents as well. With the *Adobe InDesign CS6 Digital Classroom* you will discover how to integrate InDesign CS6 with other Adobe Creative Suite products and how you can create InDesign projects and export them for use on the nook, Kindle, or iPad or as interactive projects that can be edited using Adobe® Flash®. The *Adobe InDesign CS6 Digital Classroom* helps you to understand all the essential capabilities of Adobe InDesign and to get the most out of InDesign. The goal of the *Adobe InDesign CS6 Digital Classroom* is to get you up-and-running right away, creating documents for print and digital environments. You can work through all the lessons in this book, or complete only specific lessons. Each lesson includes detailed, step-by-step instructions, along with lesson files, useful background information, and video tutorials.

Adobe InDesign CS6 Digital Classroom is like having your own expert instructor guiding you through each lesson while you work at your own pace. This book includes 13 self-paced lessons that let you discover essential skills, explore new ones, and pick up tips that will save you time. You'll be productive right away, with real-world exercises and simple explanations. Each lesson includes step-by-step instructions, lesson files, and video tutorials, all of which are available on the included DVD. The *Adobe InDesign CS6 Digital Classroom* lessons are developed by the same team of Adobe Certified Experts who have created many of the official training titles for Adobe Systems, participated in development of Adobe Certified Expert exams, and have more than a decade of experience teaching InDesign so you can be confident that you will discover useful skills quickly and easily.

Prerequisites

Before you start the *Adobe InDesign CS6 Digital Classroom* lessons, you should have a working knowledge of your computer and its operating system. You should know how to use the directory system of your computer so that you can navigate through folders. You also need to understand how to locate, save, and open files, and you should also know how to use your mouse to access menus and commands.

Make sure that you have installed Adobe InDesign CS6. The software is sold separately, and not included with this book. You may use the free 30-day trial version of Adobe InDesign CS6 available at the *adobe.com* web site, subject to the terms of its license agreement.

System requirements

Before starting the lessons in the *Adobe InDesign CS6 Digital Classroom*, make sure that your computer is equipped for running Adobe InDesign CS6, which you must purchase separately. The minimum system requirements for your computer to effectively use the software are listed on the following page.

System requirements for Adobe InDesign CS6

These are the minimum system requirements for using the InDesign CS6 software. Your computer will need to meet these requirements to use the software and the lessons in this book:

Windows

- Intel® Pentium® 4 or AMD Athlon® 64 processor
- Microsoft® Windows® XP with Service Pack 3 or Windows 7
- 1GB of RAM (with 2GB or more recommended)
- 1.6GB of available hard-disk space for installation; although additional free space is required during installation. The software cannot be installed on removable flash storage devices
- 1024 × 768 display (1280 × 800 recommended) with 16-bit video card
- DVD-ROM drive
- Adobe® Flash® Player 10 software required to export SWF files
- InDesign CS6 requires activation. Broadband Internet connection and registration are required for software activation

Mac OS

- Multicore Intel processor
- Mac OS X v10.6.8 or v10.7
- 1GB of RAM (with 2GB or more recommended)
- 2.6GB of available hard-disk space for installation; additional free space required during installation. The software cannot be installed on removable flash storage devices and cannot be installed on a hard drive volume that uses a case-sensitive file system.
- 1024 × 768 display (1280 × 800 recommended) with 16-bit video card
- DVD-ROM drive
- Adobe Flash Player 10 software required to export SWF files
- InDesign CS6 requires activation. Broadband Internet connection and registration are required for software activation

Menus and commands are identified throughout the book by using the greater-than symbol (>). For example, the command to print a document appears as File > Print. This indicates that you should click the File menu at the top of your screen and choose Print from the resulting menu.

Starting Adobe InDesign CS6

As with most software, Adobe InDesign CS6 is launched by locating the application in your Programs folder (Windows) or Applications folder (Mac OS). If you are not familiar with starting the program, follow these steps to start the Adobe InDesign CS6 application:

Windows

1 Choose Start > All Programs > Adobe InDesign CS6.

2 Close the Welcome Screen when it appears. You are now ready to use Adobe InDesign CS6.

Mac OS

1 Open the Applications folder, and then open the Adobe InDesign CS6 folder.

2 Double-click on the Adobe InDesign CS6 application icon.

3 Close the Welcome Screen when it appears. You are now ready to use Adobe InDesign CS6.

Fonts used in this book

Adobe InDesign CS6 Digital Classroom includes lessons that refer to fonts that were installed with your copy of Adobe InDesign CS6. If you did not install the fonts, or have removed them from your computer, you may substitute different fonts for the exercises or reinstall the software to access the fonts.

If you receive a Missing Font warning, replace the font with one available on your computer and proceed with the lesson.

Access lesson files & videos any time

Register your book at *www.digitalclassroombooks.com/CS6/InDesign* to download the lesson files onto any computer, or watch the videos on your Internet connected tablet, smartphone, or computer. You'll be able to watch the Digital Classroom videos anywhere you have an Internet connection. Registering your book also provides you access to lesson files and videos even if you misplace your DVD.

Checking for updated lesson files

Make sure you have the most up-to-date lesson files and learn about any updates to your InDesign CS6 Digital Classroom book by registering your book at *www.digitalclassroombooks.com/CS6/InDesign*.

Resetting the InDesign workspace and preferences

To make certain that your panels and working environment are consistent, you should reset your workspace at the start of each lesson. To reset your workspace, choose Window > Workspace > Typography. The selected workspace determines which menu items display, which panels display, and which options display within the panels. If menu items that are identified in the book are not displaying, choose Show All Menu Items from the menu in which you are working to locate them, or choose Window > Workspace > Advanced to show all panel options.

You can reset the settings for InDesign at the start of each lesson to make certain you match the instructions used in this book. To reset the InDesign preferences, start Adobe InDesign, and immediately press Shift+Alt+Ctrl (Windows) or Shift+Option+Command+Control (Mac OS). In the dialog box that appears, press OK to reset the preferences.

Loading lesson files

The *InDesign CS6 Digital Classroom* DVD includes files that accompany the exercises for each of the lessons. You may copy the entire lessons folder from the supplied DVD to your hard drive, or copy only the lesson folders for the individual lessons you wish to complete.

For each lesson in the book, the files are referenced by the name of each file. The exact location of each file on your computer is not used, as you may have placed the files in a unique location on your hard drive. We suggest placing the lesson files in the My Documents folder (Windows) or at the top level of your hard drive (Mac OS).

Copying the lesson files to your hard drive:

1 Insert the *InDesign CS6 Digital Classroom* DVD supplied with this book.

2 On your computer desktop, navigate to the DVD and locate the folder named idlessons.

3 You can install all the files, or just specific lesson files. Do one of the following:

- Install all lesson files by dragging the idlessons folder to your hard drive.

- Install only some of the files by creating a new folder on your hard drive named idlessons. Open the idlessons folder on the supplied DVD, select the lesson(s) you wish to complete, and drag the folder(s) to the idlessons folder you created on your hard drive.

Unlocking Mac OS files

Mac users may need to unlock the files after they are copied from the accompanying disc. This only applies to Mac OS computers and is because the Mac OS may view files that are copied from a DVD or CD as being locked for writing.

If you are a Mac OS user and have difficulty saving over the existing files in this book, you can use these instructions so that you can update the lesson files as you work on them and also add new files to the lessons folder

Note that you only need to follow these instructions if you are unable to save over the existing lesson files, or if you are unable to save files into the lesson folder.

1 After copying the files to your computer, click once to select the idlessons folder, then choose File > Get Info from within the Finder (not InDesign).

2 In the idlessons info window, click the triangle to the left of Sharing and Permissions to reveal the details of this section.

3 In the Sharing and Permissions section, click the lock icon, if necessary, in the lower-right corner so that you can make changes to the permissions.

4 Click to select a specific user or select everyone, then change the Privileges section to Read & Write.

5 Click the lock icon to prevent further changes, and then close the window.

Working with the video tutorials

Your *InDesign CS6 Digital Classroom* DVD comes with video tutorials developed by the authors to help you understand the concepts explored in each lesson. Each tutorial is approximately five minutes long and demonstrates and explains the concepts and features covered in the lesson.

The videos are designed to supplement your understanding of the material in the chapter. We have selected exercises and examples that we feel will be most useful to you. You may want to view the entire video for a lesson before you begin. The DVD icon, with appropriate lesson number, indicates that an overview of the exercise being described can be found in the accompanying video.

DVD video icon.

Setting up for viewing the video tutorials

The DVD included with this book includes video tutorials for each lesson. Although you can view the lessons on your computer directly from the DVD, we recommend copying the folder labeled videos from the *InDesign CS6 Digital Classroom* DVD to your hard drive.

Copying the video tutorials to your hard drive:

1   Insert the *InDesign CS6 Digital Classroom* DVD supplied with this book.

2   On your computer desktop, navigate to the DVD and locate the folder named videos.

3   Drag the videos folder to a location on your hard drive.

Viewing the video tutorials with the Adobe Flash Player

To view the video tutorials on the DVD, you need the Adobe Flash Player 8 or later. Earlier versions of the Flash Player will not play the videos correctly. If you're not sure that you have the latest version of the Flash Player, you can download it for free from the Adobe web site: *http://www.adobe.com/support/flashplayer/downloads.html*

Playing the video tutorials on your computer

1   On your computer, navigate to the videos folder you copied to your hard drive from the DVD. Playing the videos directly from the DVD may result in poor quality playback.

2   Open the videos folder and double-click the Flash file named PLAY_IDCS6 to view the video tutorials.

3   After the Flash player launches, press the Play button to view the videos.

The Flash Player has a simple user interface that allows you to control the viewing experience, including stopping, pausing, playing, and restarting the video. You can also rewind or fast-forward, and adjust the playback volume.

Lesson 06: Creating a Good Image

A. Go to beginning. B. Play/Pause. C. Fast-forward/rewind. D. Stop. E. Volume Off/On. F. Volume control.

Playback volume is also affected by the settings in your operating system. Be certain to adjust the sound volume for your computer, in addition to the sound controls in the Player window.

If you prefer to watch the videos on a tablet device or another computer, you can register your book at *www.digitalclassroombooks.com/CS6/InDesign to gain access to the videos online and view them on another device.*

Additional resources

The Digital Classroom series goes beyond the training books. You can continue your learning online, with training videos, at seminars and conferences, and in-person training events.

Training from the Authors

The authors are available for professional development training workshops for schools and companies. They also teach classes at American Graphics Institute including training classes and online workshops. Visit *agitraining.com* for more information about Digital Classroom author-led training classes or workshops.

Book series

Expand your knowledge of creative software applications with the Digital Classroom training series. Books are available for most creative software applications as well as web design and development tools and technologies. Learn more at *DigitalClassroom.com.*

Seminars and conferences

The authors of the Digital Classroom seminar series frequently conduct in-person seminars and speak at conferences, including the annual CRE8 Conference. Learn more at *agitraining.com* and *CRE8summit.com.*

Resources for educators

Visit *DigitalClassroom.com* to request access to resources for educators, including an instructors' guide for incorporating this Digital Classroom book into your curriculum.

What you'll learn in this lesson:

- Understanding the InDesign CS6 Workspace

- Working with panels and tools

- Navigating through InDesign documents

- Importing text and images

- Using styles to quickly format text and objects

InDesign CS6 Essential Skills

This lesson gets you started with InDesign CS6, covering essential skills necessary for working efficiently with InDesign documents. It provides a high-level overview of key concepts associated with creating layouts using InDesign. You'll work with an existing document to understand how to navigate, place graphics, and add formatting to text, creating a finished newsletter that can be printed or distributed as a digital document.

Starting up

Before you begin, make sure that your tools and panels are consistent by resetting your preferences. (For more information, see "Resetting the InDesign workspace and preferences" in the Starting up section of this book.)

In this lesson, you will work with several files from the id01lessons folder. Make sure that you have copied the id01lessons folder onto your hard drive from the DVD. For more information, see "Loading lesson files" in the Starting up section of this book. If you are completely new to InDesign and don't have much computer experience, it may be easier to follow the lesson if the id01lessons folder is placed on the desktop of your computer. This lesson provides an overview of InDesign concepts. After completing this lesson, you'll then examine individual capabilities and features in more details in each of the remaining lessons. It may be helpful to view this lesson as a broad survey, providing you with a general understanding of the InDesign landscape, while the remaining lessons provide much more detail about specific InDesign capabilities.

See Lesson 1 in action!

Use the accompanying video to gain a better understanding of how to use some of the features shown in this lesson. The video tutorial for this lesson can be found on the supplied DVD.

InDesign tools

You'll use InDesign's tools for creating or modifying everything that appears in your documents, including text, images, and multimedia elements for digital documents. You'll also use InDesign's tools for navigating around the document. All tools are found in the Tools panel, located along the left side of your screen.

Many tools displayed in the tools panel have related tools that provide additional functionality, and you can select these related tools by clicking and holding the tool that is displayed in the tools panel. You can identify the tools with additional functionality by the small arrow in the lower-right corner. You can also right-click (Windows) or Ctrl-click (Mac OS) on a tool to access any related tools.

If you place your cursor over any tool in the Tools panel without clicking, a tooltip appears, displaying the tool's name and a keyboard shortcut in parentheses. You can use the keyboard shortcut to access a tool from your keyboard, instead of clicking on it with your mouse.

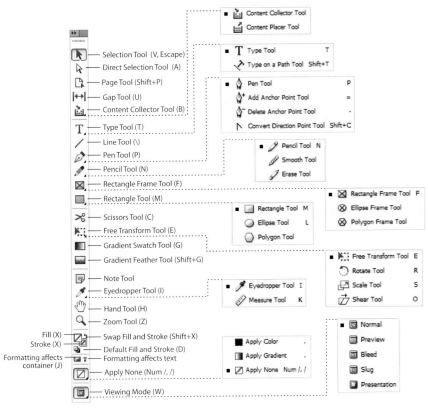

Use the InDesign CS6 Tools panel to create objects, make selections, and modify objects and pages.

The InDesign workspace

InDesign documents are displayed in the center of the work area, while panels that let you control objects or perform specific tasks are displayed along the right side of the workspace in the panel docking area. InDesign uses many panels, and many are critical for editing and design work you perform. InDesign includes various workspaces that provide easy access to the panels and tools you'll use for specific tasks. Let's take a closer look at the InDesign workspace, including the document window and panels.

The document window

InDesign pages are displayed within a black border. Anything positioned within this area appears when the page is finished. The area outside of the black border is referred to as the pasteboard. Anything that is placed completely outside this black border on the pasteboard is generally not visible when the final document is distributed.

You can use the pasteboard to temporarily hold elements while designing your project. You can move design elements such as images from the pasteboard to the page, trying different layout variations. The pasteboard can also be useful for placing notes to colleagues—or even yourself—regarding the project. To get a better understanding of the InDesign workspace, you'll open up the completed project, reset the workspace, and look at the work area.

1   Choose File > Open. In the Open a File dialog box, navigate to the id01lessons folder and select the id01_done.indd file. Click Open.

2   Choose Window > Workspace > Typography. Panels containing controls that help you work with type are now displayed.

You can also use the dedicated Workspace switcher to switch to a specific workspace. The Workspace switcher is located in the Application bar above the Control panel. The Workspace switcher displays the name of the current workspace and can also be used to change between workspaces or to reset the current workspace. The selected workspace determines which panels display and which menu items are available. The number of available panels and menu choices is based upon the selected workspace.

The workspace switcher makes it easy to display specific panels and menus depending upon your needs.

3   Choose Window > Workspace > Reset Typography to reset the InDesign panels to their default positions for the Typography workspace. This ensures that your panels are in position, making them easier to locate during this lesson.

A. The document window. B. The page border (black lines). C. Bleed guides. D. Margin guides. E. Column guides. F. The pasteboard.

Using guides

Non-printing guides help you align content on your page and create an organized layout. There are several types of guides, but the essential guides for starting to work with InDesign are margin guides and ruler guides. Margin guides define the space around the edge of your document—a space you generally want to keep free from objects. White space around the edge of your document creates good design, and also eliminates the risk of content being cut off if your document is printed and trimmed to a specific size at a printing plant. Margin guides are displayed in magenta by default, immediately inside the page border. By default, they display one-half inch inside of the page edge, but you can adjust them, as you will learn in Lesson 2, "Building Documents with Master Pages."

Ruler guides are the other type of guide you may want to add to your document layout. Ruler guides are created manually by dragging them from the rulers onto the page. Both ruler guides and margin guides are useful, but they can also be distracting when you want to see the elements of your page design. In this case, you can hide the guides.

1   Choose View > Grids & Guides > Hide Guides, or use the keyboard shortcut Ctrl+; (Windows) or Command+; (Mac OS), to hide all the guides in the open document.

2   Choose View > Grids & Guides > Show Guides, or use the keyboard shortcut Ctrl+; (Windows) or Command+; (Mac OS), to show all the guides in the open document.

3   You can show or hide guides by toggling back and forth using these commands.

Another type of guide is the liquid guide, which is used to help adjust the layout of an InDesign page when it is displayed as a digital document. Liquid Guides are a more advanced topic and are covered in the Creating Digital Documents lesson of the *InDesign CS6 Digital Classroom* book.

Viewing modes

You can use viewing modes to hide guides and other items that will not display when the final document is printed or distributed. This provides a fast-and-easy way to preview your document. You can even turn your document into a presentation.

The viewing modes option lets you choose whether all content and guides display on your monitor, or whether InDesign displays only content that is positioned on the page and will print. Here you will explore the various viewing modes.

1   At the bottom of the Tools panel, click and hold the Mode button (▣), and choose Preview from the available modes. Notice that the entire pasteboard appears gray and all elements located on the pasteboard are hidden. The borders do not display around any items on the page if they are not selected.

Click the display mode button at the bottom of the Tools panel to change how a page is displayed using InDesign.

2   Click and hold the Mode button again and choose Bleed from the menu. This shows the allowable bleed area that was specified when the document was created. Bleed is an area outside of the page that is intentionally used by designers so that any inaccuracies in the cutting, trimming, and binding process do not create a visible white space along the edge of an object that is intended to print all the way to the edge of a document. This mode is useful when you need to make sure that all the elements on your page extend to a specific bleed value. In this document, the bleed is set to 1/8 inch, which is a standard bleed value in the printing industry.

3   Click and hold the Mode button again and choose Presentation from the menu. This mode presents your document on a black background with no distracting interface elements. This is great for viewing your document or showing it to a client. When in this mode, you can navigate through the pages of your document by using the up and down or left- and right-arrow keys on your keyboard. To exit Presentation mode, simply press the Escape key on your keyboard.

4   Click and hold the Mode button again and choose Normal.

You can also use the shortcut key W on your keyboard to switch between Preview and Normal modes, and Shift+W to activate Presentation mode, or you can use the Screen Mode button in the Application bar. Keep in mind that keyboard shortcuts do not work if you are using the Type tool and working with text inside a text frame.

Working with panels

Another important part of the InDesign workspace are the panels used to modify and create objects. You can access panels by clicking on their name in the panel docking area, or choose the panel you want to access from the Window menu.

The Tools panel

The Tools panel is located on the left side of your screen and contains all the tools necessary to draw, add, or edit type, and edit items in your document. The Tools panel appears as a single column attached to the left side of your screen. You can modify the appearance and location of the Tools panel to accommodate your needs.

1   Click on the double-arrow icon (↔) at the top of the Tools panel. The Tools panel changes from a single column to a double column. If the Tools panel is not docked, you have a third option when you click the double-arrow; it changes to a horizontal layout, then to a single column, and then a double column each time you click. Go to step 2 to learn how to dock and undock panels in InDesign.

Clicking on the Double-arrow icon at the top of the Tools panel changes its appearance between a one-column, two-column, or horizontal layout.

2   Click the gray bar at the top of the Tools panel, and while holding down the mouse button, drag the panel to the right, into the document area. Release the mouse button when over the document area. The Tools panel is repositioned as a free-floating panel at the location where you released the mouse button. You can position the panel anywhere on your display, or return it to the docking area on the side of the workspace.

3 Click the gray bar at the top of the Tools panel and drag the panel to the right so that it is positioned just to the left of the panels. A blue, vertical bar appears. Release the mouse button, and the Tools panel is docked to the right of your screen. If you have trouble moving the panel by clicking on the gray bar, click on the dotted area just below the gray bar at the top of the Tools panel to reposition and dock the panel.

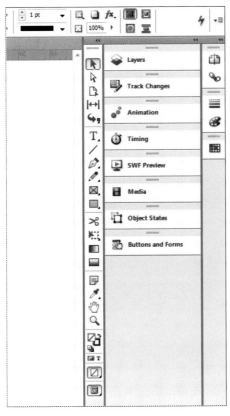

The tools panel can be docked along either the left or the right side of the InDesign workspace by dragging it into position using the gray dotted line near the top of the panel. Here the tools panel has been docked along the right side of the workspace.

Managing panels

InDesign's panels are essential for your design work. They help you create new objects, edit existing objects, and work more efficiently as you design your documents. The various workspaces include different panels that are docked at the right side of the document window. The available panels change based upon the selected workspace. You can add panels to the workspace as you need them, or remove panels. When the panels display only their name or icon, they are in collapsed mode. Collapsed mode saves screen space by providing you with easy access to many panels, and only displaying the full panel when you need to access all the controls. Here you will work with the various display modes available for panels.

1 Click the double-arrow icon (◄◄) at the top-right corner of the docked panels that are in collapsed mode along the right side of the document window. Notice how all the docked panels expand to reveal their options.

2 Click the double-arrow icon again to collapse the dock and return the panels to their previous state.

3 Click the Pages button in the dock. This reveals the entire contents of the Pages panel. When you click a panel button, only the individual panel expands.

4 Click the Pages button again, and the panel closes and is displayed only as a button.

5 Place your cursor along the left edge of the panel docking area, where the panels meet the page area. When the cursor changes to a double-arrow (↔), drag the panels to the right until the panels display only as icons. Click and drag back to the left so the panels display as icons along with their name.

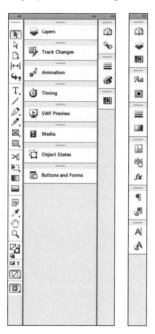

Click and drag the panel docking area to the right so the panels take up less space and display only their icons.

6 Click and drag the Pages button, moving it to the far-left side of the document window. When a vertical bar appears, release the mouse button. The Pages panel is docked to the left side of the document window.

You can place panels anywhere on your workspace, including over the document or on either side of the work area. You may customize panels in any way that makes it easier for you to work. Keep the panel in this location, as you will work with customizing workspaces in the next exercise.

Saving your workspace

Once you have selected the panels that you need, and positioned them in the locations that let you work most efficiently, you can save the location of the panels being used as a workspace.

Once you have saved a workspace, you can quickly access the exact panels displayed and their location by returning to the default setup of that workspace.

1   From the Workspace drop-down menu, located in the Application bar to the left of the Help search text field, choose New Workspace.

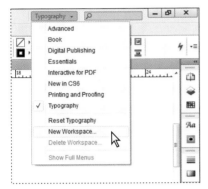

Choose New Workspace to save the panels you are using and their location in the workspace.

2   In the New Workspace window, type **My Workspace** in the Name text field, and then click OK, leaving all the settings at their defaults.

Saving your workspace allows you to easily restore the panel positions.

You've now saved the locations of your panels.

3   From the Workspace switcher drop-down menu, choose Typography. Then click on the Workspace switcher drop-down menu again and choose Reset Typography. Note how the panels revert to their default locations.

4   From the Workspace switcher drop-down menu, choose My Workspace. Alternatively, choose Window > Workspace > My Workspace. All the panels are restored to their location that was part of the workspace you saved earlier in this project.

You can create and save multiple workspaces. Workspaces are not document-specific, and you can use them in any document. Before proceeding to the next section, reset your workspace to the default Typography workspace using the Workspace switcher drop-down menu. This allows the panels to match the descriptions used in the remainder of this lesson. If necessary, you can also choose Reset Typography from the Workspace switcher drop-down menu to reset the workspace to its default appearance.

Working with the Control panel

The Control panel appears across the top of the workspace. The panel is contextual, so the content of the panel changes depending on what tool you are using and what object you have selected.

1 Choose the Selection tool (↖) in the Tools panel. The Control panel changes based upon the tool being used and the items selected in the layout.

2 Using the Selection tool, click the headline, *Fending off the winter blues*, positioned at the top of the page. The Control panel now displays information about this text frame.

3 Double-click the same headline. When you double-click the text frame, the Selection tool switches to the Text tool. The Control panel now displays information relating to the text.

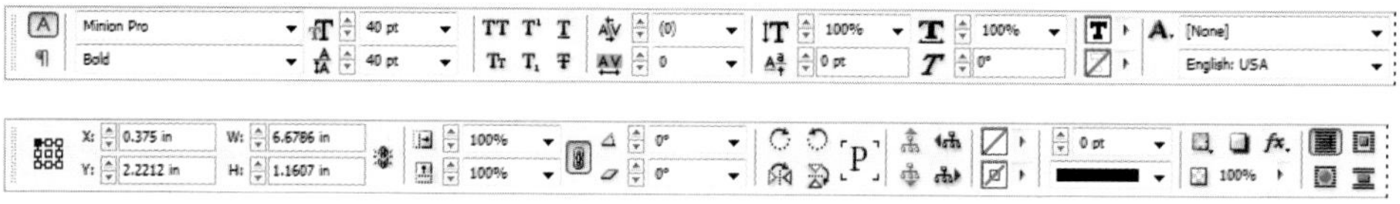

The Control panel displays information about objects in your layout. The information displayed changes based upon the tool used for selection and the object selected. The icons displayed in the Control panel on your computer may differ slightly based on the resolution of your computer's display.

Navigating through an InDesign document

In this exercise, you'll continue working with the id01_done.indd file, which is the completed newsletter that you opened at the beginning of the lesson. You'll explore the tools used to navigate to different pages in an InDesign document, and how to change the document's magnification to see more or fewer details in the document layout.

Using the Pages panel

The Pages panel provides a quick overview of the contents of each page in an InDesign document. You can use it to navigate between document pages, rearrange pages, and also add or remove pages. You can also use it to create transitions between pages that are distributed as electronic documents, and create page variations such as portrait and landscape variations for use on a tablet.

1   Press the Pages button (⊞) in the dock at the right of the workspace to display the Pages panel. The bottom-left corner of the Pages panel indicates that there are four pages displayed in three spreads within this document.

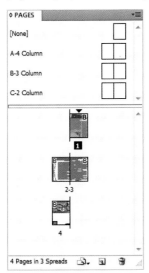

You can use the Pages panel to add and delete pages as well as navigate between pages within your InDesign documents.

2   Double-click page 2 in the Pages panel to display page 2 of the document. The left page of the inside spread, which is page 2, appears in the document window.

3 Double-click page 4 in the Pages panel to display page 4 of your document.

If you are unable to see all the pages displayed in the Pages panel, you can make the panel larger by clicking and dragging on the bottom-right corner of the panel. You can also scroll through the pages in the Pages panel by using the scroll bar along the right side of the panel or the scroll wheel on your mouse.

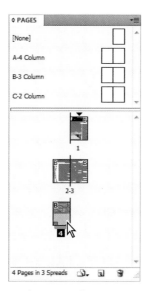

Use the Pages panel to navigate to the different pages in your document.

Changing the magnification of your document

You may want to get a closer look at parts of your document to align objects, check the spacing of type, or position of items in your layout. InDesign makes it easy to change the magnification so you can zoom-in on parts of your document, or zoom out to get a birds-eye view of your layout.

1 In the Pages panel, double-click on the page 1 icon to display the first page of the document.

2 Select the Zoom tool (🔍). Using the Zoom tool, click and hold in the upper-left corner of the Spinnews logo at the top of the page, and then drag down to the lower-right corner of the logo. Release the mouse once you have reached the lower-right corner of the logo. The area you have selected with the Zoom tool is magnified.

You may find that you enlarged the document either too much or not enough. To fine-tune the magnification, click with the Zoom tool to increase the magnification incrementally. Or, if you zoomed in too close, decrease the magnification by pressing and holding the Alt (Windows) or Option (Mac OS) key while clicking with the Zoom tool.

Click and drag to increase the magnification of a specific area.

You can also increase or decrease the magnification of the document by using the keyboard shortcut Ctrl+plus sign (Windows) or Command+plus sign (Mac OS) to zoom in on a document, or Ctrl+minus sign (Windows) or Command+minus sign (Mac OS) to zoom out. If you have an object selected or your cursor is inserted within a text frame when using these key commands, the page will center on the selected object or cursor when changing the magnification.

3   Select the Hand tool (✋) from the Tools panel, and then click and hold down on the page in the document window. The page magnification changes and a red frame appears, indicating which portion of the document will be visible when you finish scrolling.

4   Use the Hand tool to arrange the page so that the logo is in the center of your document window. The Hand tool is used to move pages within the document window, allowing you to focus on specific areas of the layout.

5   Press and hold the page in the document window. Position the red frame so the entire border of the image is visible, and then release the mouse. The zoom returns to its original level, focused on the part of the page you identified using the Hand tool.

You can access the Hand tool temporarily by pressing and holding the spacebar on your keyboard when using any tool except the Type tool. When the spacebar is pressed, the cursor changes to the Hand tool. If you have the Type tool selected, press and hold the Alt (Windows) or Option (Mac OS) key to temporarily access the Hand tool.

6   To view the entire document, choose View > Fit Page in Window or press Ctrl+0 (Windows) or Command+0 (Mac OS). The currently selected page is displayed inside the document window.

7   Choose File > Close to close the document. If asked to save, choose No (Windows) or Don't Save (Mac OS). You've completed your tour of the InDesign workspace, and will move into a tour of working with type.

Working with type

You have significant control over the appearance, formatting, and placement of type, and you can save formatting attributes to easily reapply them to other text so you can work efficiently while maintaining a consistent appearance across your documents. In this section, you'll add the finishing touches to a document, completing the layout and applying formatting to text.

Entering and formatting type

When you add text to an InDesign layout, you will almost always place it inside a frame. Frames are containers that hold text, but they can also hold graphics or may even be used to hold nothing but a color, such as a shape in a design or a background color. In this exercise, you'll be working with text frames.

1   Choose File > Open a File. In the Open dialog box, navigate to the id01lessons folder and select the id01.indd file. Click Open. You will use this project file for the remainder of the lesson.

2   It's a good idea to save a working copy of your document. To do this, choose File > Save As. In the Save As dialog box, navigate to the id01lessons folder. In the Name text field, type **id01_work.indd**, and then press Save. This allows you to work without altering the original file.

3   If necessary, press the Pages button (⊞) in the docking area along the right side of the workspace. The Pages panel opens. In the Pages panel, double-click page 1 to center this page in the workspace.

4 In the Tools panel, click to select the Type tool (T). You will use the Type tool to create a new text frame. Position your cursor along the left side of the page, where the left margin guide and the first horizontal guide meet. Click and hold down, then drag down and to the right, to the location where the right margin guide and the second horizontal guide meet. Release the mouse button. A new text frame is created, and a cursor blinks in the top-left corner of the new frame you have created.

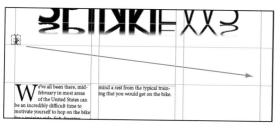

Use the Type tool to create a new text frame. Most text in an InDesign layout is placed within frames.

5 Type **Fending off the winter blues with cross-training** in the text frame you created in the previous step. The text appears in the default font and size. Keep the cursor within this text frame, and keep the Type tool selected.

6 In the panel docking area along the right side of the workspace, click the Paragraph Styles button (◙¶) to open the Paragraph Styles panel. Click to select the Heading style from the list of available styles in the Paragraph Styles panel. The Heading style is applied to the paragraph, which includes all the text within this frame. This saved style includes a variety of formatting attributes including font, style, and size. You'll learn to create your own paragraph styles in Lesson 4, "Working with Styles."

Paragraph styles make it easy to save and reapply multiple formatting attributes to text.

7   The top line of the sentence is much longer than the bottom line. To balance the
    lines, click the panel menu button (⦁≣) in the top-right corner of the Control panel and
    choose Balance Ragged Lines from the submenu. InDesign automatically balances the
    lines within the frame.

The headline before using the Balance Ragged Lines command.

Placing and formatting type

You can add text to an InDesign document by typing text onto the InDesign page, or by
importing the text from an external file, such as a Microsoft Word document or an Excel
spreadsheet. You can import most major text file formats into an InDesign layout.

1   If you've closed the Page panel, press the Pages button (⌗) in the panel dock to open
    the Pages panel. Double-click page 2 in the Pages panel. If the Pages panel is covering
    your work area, click the double-arrows in the upper-right corner of the panel to
    reduce it to a button, or reposition it so you can see the document page.

2   Continuing to use the Type tool (T), click inside the empty text frame that covers the
    center and right columns, under the headline *Caring for Those Wheels*. The cursor is
    inserted into the frame. Next you will import text into your layout that was created
    using word processing software such as Microsoft Word, and saved as a plain .txt file.

*You can import a variety of file types into your InDesign layouts. While this example uses a text
file, the format could be a native Microsoft Word or even Microsoft Excel file, along with many
other file formats.*

3   Choose File > Place. The Place dialog box opens. In the Place dialog box, make
    certain that Show Import Options is *not* selected and that Replace Selected Item is
    selected. These options are explained in more detail in Lesson 3, "Working with Text
    and Type."

    Navigate to the id01lessons folder provided with this book then locate and open the
    Links folder within the id01lessons folder. Choose the file Wheels.txt; then click
    Open. The text from this file is placed inside your text frame where you had placed
    the cursor. The text is formatted using InDesign's Basic Paragraph style. Next you will
    apply a paragraph style to format the text you imported.

4   Place the cursor at the start of the story. Click the Paragraph Styles button to display the Paragraph Styles panel. Click the paragraph style Body, and the first paragraph is formatted using the Body style. Paragraph styles apply formatting to the paragraph where the cursor is located. You will now apply formatting to multiple paragraphs by selecting them and repeating this process.

5   Use the keyboard shortcut Ctrl+A (Windows) or Command+A (Mac OS) to select all the type within the current frame. From the Paragraph Styles panel, choose Body. All the selected paragraphs are now formatted using the Body style.

6   Choose Edit > Deselect All to deselect the type.

Flowing type

Stories often continue from one page or column to another. You will set up links between text frames so the story flows into multiple columns.

1   In the lower-left corner of the document window, click the page number drop-down menu, then select page 3 to navigate to this page. You can also use this menu to navigate to different pages in your document.

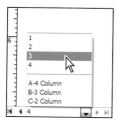

Use the page drop-down menu to navigate between pages.

2   Using the Type tool (T), click inside the first frame on the left side of the page, underneath the headline Race Calendar.

3   Choose File > Place. In the Place dialog box, navigate to the Links folder within the id01lessons folder. Confirm that Show Import Options is not selected, and then click to select the file Calendar.txt and click Open to place this text file into the frame in your InDesign layout.

4   Click to choose the Selection tool (⬧) in the Tools panel. Click to select the text frame where you imported the text if it isn't still selected from the previous step. You can tell the frame is selected by small, square handles that appear on the corners of the frame and at the center of each side of the frame.

Notice the red plus sign located in the lower-right corner of the text frame. This indicates that there is more text in the story than fits within this text frame. You will link this text to another frame so it continues in another location.

The newly placed text on the page doesn't fit into the text frame. InDesign labels this as overset text, displaying a red plus symbol to identify it.

5 Using the Selection tool click once on the red plus sign in the lower-right corner of the text frame. After you click the red plus sign, the cursor changes, indicating that you are about to link the text so it continues in a new location. Some of the text to be linked is displayed in the cursor. You will use the cursor to indicate where the story continues.

6 Move the cursor to the center of the middle column. Notice that the cursor changes to also show a linked chain. Click to link the first and second frames together. The overset text from the first frame continues into the second frame. Because this story contains more text than fits into these two frames, a red plus symbol now appears at the bottom of the second column. Next you will link the second frame to the third frame, continuing the story.

Linking text from one frame to another.

7 Click the red plus sign on the lower-right corner of the second frame, then click inside the frame located along the right side of the page. The frames in the second and third columns are now linked together. As text runs out of space in the second column, it will continue into the frame in the third column.

8 Choose File > Save to save your work.

You have worked with some essential skills for linking text, and will work with these skills further in InDesign Lesson 3, "Working with Text and Type."

Using styles

Earlier in this lesson, you formatted text by applying a paragraph style. You can use styles to easily and consistently format paragraphs, individual words or letters, as well as entire text frames and tables. Here you will apply styles to both paragraphs and individual characters. You'll get a more detailed look at creating and using styles in Lesson 4, "Working with Styles".

Applying paragraph styles

Paragraph styles are applied to all the text between two paragraph returns. Whether several sentences or an individual word, InDesign applies styles to the text between two paragraph returns that were entered by using the Enter (Windows) or Return (Mac OS) key on the keyboard when the text was entered, even if the paragraph consists of only a single word.

1 Select the Type tool (T) from the Tools panel, then on the left side of page 3, click anywhere inside the word *January* located in the first line of the frame on the left side of the page.

2 In the Paragraph Styles panel, choose Calendar Month to apply the correct formatting to the word *January*. Repeat the process to format the words *February*, and then *March* to format these words using the same paragraph style. Because these words have a keyboard return before and after them, they are considered to be a paragraph for the purpose of applying styles.

3 Using the Type tool, click and drag to select the text located between the *January* and *February* headings, then click the Calendar Event style in the Paragraph Styles panel. Repeat this process to select all the text between *February* and *March*, and also all the March events, applying the Calendar Event style to this text.

Format the text using the Calendar Event style
from the Paragraph Styles panel.

Notice that the Calendar Event style applies several attributes to the events in a single click, styling the date bold, the name red, and the web address in italic. The Calendar Event style includes several styles that are grouped together into what InDesign refers to as a *nested style*. A nested style applies several formatting attributes to text within a paragraph in a sequence you can define. You will learn more about nested styles in InDesign Lesson 4, "Working with Styles."

Applying character styles

You can also apply styles to individual words or characters within a group of type, formatting only the type you want to change. For example, you can apply common formatting attributes such as bold and italic. Character styles are the foundation for the nested styles that you applied to the event listings in the previous step. Here you will apply a character style to individual words.

1   Double-click on page 2 in the Pages panel to display page 2 within the workspace.

2   Using the Zoom tool (🔍), increase the magnification so you can easily see the first paragraph, which starts with the text *Your wheels*.

3   Select the Type tool (T) from the Tools panel and select the word *wheels* at the top of the first paragraph. You can select the word by clicking and dragging using your mouse or by double-clicking the word.

When using the Type tool, double-clicking on a word selects the word, triple-clicking selects the line, and quadruple-clicking (that's four clicks!) selects the paragraph.

4   Click the Character Styles button (A) in the dock on the right side of the workspace to open the Character Styles panel. Choose Italic from the Character Styles panel to apply the Italic style to the selected word.

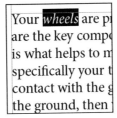

A Character style applies only to selected text.

Apply styles across a story using Find/Change

You've seen how you can use Character Styles to easily apply formatting changes to selected text. In the text you are working in, you will change every instance of the word *wheels* to be italicized, combining character styles with InDesign's ability to find and then change text formatting.

1   Using the Type tool (T), right-click (Windows) or Control+click (Mac OS) anywhere within the text frame on page 2 of the document. Choose Find/Change from the contextual menu that appears—it's near the top of the many choices available in the Contextual menu. The Find/Change window opens.

Contextual menus offer a quick way to access commands that apply to the part of the document in which you are working. The commands change based upon the location of the cursor, the tool you are using, and the object selected. In the previous step, the contextual menu options relate to text because the text tool is selected and the cursor is within a text frame.

2   In the Find/Change window, click in the Text tab and type **wheels** in the Find what text field, then choose Story from the Search drop-down menu. This tells InDesign to search all the text within the current story to locate the word *wheels*. A story is defined as all the columns and text frames that are linked together.

3   In the Change Format section at the bottom of the window, click the Specify Attributes to Change button (⚙). The Change Format Settings window opens.

Be careful to not select the Specify Attributes to Find button, which is an identical button located above the Specify Attributes to Change button.

Click the Specify attributes to change button to modify text attributes in specific words or phrases.

4 In the Change Format Settings dialog box, choose Italic from the Character Style menu and click OK. This changes the format of all text that is found, applying the Italic style to any text InDesign finds within the story.

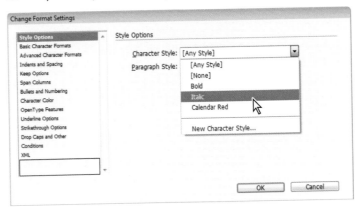

Choose Italic from the Character Style drop-down menu.

5 Click the Change All button. A window appears indicating that five instances of wheels have been found and formatted using the style attributes you specified. Press OK, then Press Done to close the Find/Change dialog box.

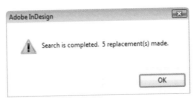

InDesign notifies you of replacements it makes using the Find/Change option.

Applying object styles

You can use Object styles to apply formatting to entire objects rather than individual pieces of text or paragraphs. For example, you can use object styles to format entire text frames and picture frames. You can use object styles to quickly and consistently apply borders to objects, or effects such as a drop shadow. Object styles can combine character and paragraph styles so you can apply multiple formatting attributes to a frame and the contents of the frame in a single step. While doing this, you'll also practice importing text and repositioning objects in a page layout.

Here you'll place some text into a text frame and then apply an object style to the frame so that the entire frame is formatted in a single click.

1   In the Pages panel, double-click page 1. Once the page is displayed, you may need to decrease the magnification to see the full page depending upon the size of your monitor and screen resolution. If you can't see the full page, change the display magnification by choosing a smaller percentage from the Zoom level drop-down menu located to the right of the Help menu in the Application bar.

2   If you can't see the text frame located to the right side of the page in the pasteboard area, choose the Hand tool (✋) from the Tools panel, then click and drag from the right to the left until this text frame is visible.

3   Select the Type tool (T) from the Tools panel, and then click to insert the cursor inside the text frame on the pasteboard. Next you will import some type that was created using a word processor such as Microsoft Word.

4   Choose File > Place to import a text file into this frame. In the Place dialog box, navigate to the Links folder within the id01lessons folder and select the file Sidebar.txt. Confirm that Show Import Options is not selected, and then press Open.

5   Choose the Selection tool (▶) from the Tools panel and confirm that the text frame on which you have been working remains selected. If necessary, click the frame to select it.

You can switch from the Type tool to the Selection tool and select the current text frame in a single step by pressing the Escape key on your keyboard when editing text within a frame.

6   Choose Window > Styles > Object Styles to open the Object Styles panel. In the Object Styles panel, choose Sidebar from the list to apply these attributes to the selected frame. The entire frame, including the text, is formatted.

You can use Object styles to apply background colors, effects, and multiple text styles to a frame in a single click. This makes applying formatting, and keeping your document design consistent as easy as a single click.

Object styles format entire objects, including text within objects.

7   Using the Selection tool (▶), click the middle of the frame and drag it to the column on the right side of the first page, aligning the right edge and bottom edge of the frame with the right and bottom margin guides.

Working with graphics

Graphics are an integral part of page design, and InDesign puts you in control of cropping, sizing, borders, and effects controlling the appearance of images in your layout. You can place a wide variety of graphic types into your layouts, including PDF, TIFF, JPEG, and EPS. You can also place native Creative Suite files such as Photoshop (.psd), Illustrator (.ai), and even other InDesign (.indd) documents into your InDesign layout as graphics.

Placing graphics

Like text, graphics are also placed inside a frame when you import them into your layout. You can create the frame first, and then import the text or you can create the frame at the same time you import the image, depending upon how you prefer to design your documents.

1   Double-click page 4 in the Pages panel to display page 4 of the document, then choose Edit > Deselect All so that no objects are selected. If Deselect All is not available in the Edit menu, then no objects are selected.

2   Click the Layers button in the panel docking area along the right side of the workspace to display the Layers panel, and then click the Graphics layer to make it active. Selecting this layer before placing a new image into the layout causes the image to be placed on this layer. You can put content on any layer, and create layers to help organize content in your InDesign documents.

Use layers to organize content in your InDesign documents.

3   Choose File > Place. In the Place dialog box, navigate to the Links folder within the id01lessons folder and select the file cyclist.psd; then click Open. Because no frame has been selected, InDesign changes the cursor to represent that an image is ready to be placed in the document.

4   Move the cursor to the upper-left corner of the workspace where the red bleed guides intersect, outside of the page area. Click once to place the image at its full size.

5   If the upper-left corner of the image is not correctly positioned at the intersection of the bleed guides, use the Selection tool (k) to click and drag the image to the correct position. Next you will resize the image to cover the top half of the layout and extend (bleed) off the edges of the layout.

6   To scale the image and also the frame in which it is contained, press and hold Shift+Ctrl (Windows) or Shift+Command (Mac OS). While continuing to hold down these keys on your keyboard, use your mouse to click and hold the handle located in the lower-right corner of the picture frame, dragging it down and to the right until the image extends off the page. Align the right edge with the bleed guide lines located just outside the page area. Using the keyboard commands while scaling the image caused both the frame and image to scale proportionately.

Scaling the image and the frame proportionately.

Depending upon the resolution of the original image, it is possible to scale the image too much and cause the image to become pixelated or bitmapped. If this occurs, the image will appear unclear when printed or converted to PDF. Most images can be scaled up to 20% without affecting their quality, but it is best to test the image in its final intended format by printing or creating a digital document such as PDF, depending upon your final destination. For more information about image quality and resolution, see the Adobe Photoshop CS6 Digital Classroom *book, which is available in print or digital format.*

7   Next you will crop the image by reducing the height of the frame, keeping the image the same size, but reducing which parts of it will be visible. Locate the center handle along the bottom edge of the picture frame. Click and drag up on this handle until the bottom edge of the frame snaps to the guide located horizontally along the middle of the page. The image remains the same size, but the bottom is cropped and will not print or display when converted to a digital document.

Moving the handles of a frame using the Selection tool changes the size of the frame and adjusts how much of the image is displayed. If you move the handles while holding the Shift+Ctrl (Windows) or Shift+Command (Mac OS) modifier keys on the keyboard, you can scale the image and content together.

Positioning graphics within a frame

You may need to crop or scale images that are placed in your layout. Here you will explore tools that help you position and scale of graphics in your documents.

1   Navigate to page 1 by using the page drop-down menu located in the lower-left corner of the document window, or by double-clicking Page 1 in the Pages panel.

2   To focus on the graphics, you'll hide the Text layer. In the panel docking area along the right side of the workspace, click the Layers button to open the Layers panel, and then click the Visibility icon (👁) to hide the contents of the text layer.

3   In the Tools panel, choose the Selection tool (▶), then click to select the graphic frame located in the bottom-left corner of page 1. The frame spans the left and center columns. Because the graphic frame is empty, an X is displayed inside the frame.

4   Choose File > Place. In the Place dialog box, navigate to the Links folder within the id01lessons folder and select the snowshoe.psd image. Confirm that Show Import Options is not selected, then click Open. The image is placed inside the selected frame at its original size – 100 percent, and is larger than the frame. Next you will resize the image so it fits within the frame.

5   Position your cursor over the center of the snowshoe image but do not click. A semi-transparent circle appears in the center of the photo. This is the Content Indicator. Click the Content Indicator to select the photo within the frame. The edges of the image are displayed with a light-blue border, showing the size of the graphic. The color of the border varies when you use multiple layers in your documents. You'll now reposition the document so you can see the entire size of the image.

The Content Indicator makes it easy to adjust a graphic within a frame without having to choose a different tool to do so.

6   If you can see the complete border of the image, you can skip to step 7. Otherwise, press and hold the spacebar on your keyboard to temporarily access the Hand tool (🖑). Click and hold on the document. The page magnification changes and a red frame appears when using the Hand tool. Reposition the red frame so the entire border of the image is visible, and then release the mouse. The zoom returns to its original level, focused on the portion of the page you identified. Release the spacebar. If necessary, use the magnification levels located at the top of the menu bar, to the right of the Help menu, to reduce the magnification in order to see the entire bounds of the graphic.

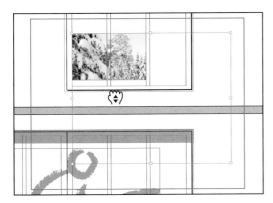

Press and hold the spacebar on your keyboard to access the
Hand tool for repositioning documents.

7   With the content of the frame, the snowshoe image, still selected, press and hold the Shift key on your keyboard. Click the handle in the bottom–right corner of the image and drag the handle up and to the left, reducing the size of the image until its width is slightly larger than the width of the frame, then release the mouse button. Here you scaled the content of the image without modifying the frame. Pressing the Shift key maintained the proportions of the image while it was scaled.

8   Move the cursor to the middle of the picture frame and notice that the cursor changes to a hand. While the cursor is a Hand icon ( ), click and drag to reposition the graphic within the frame so that the person in the light blue jacket is located along the right side of the picture frame.

Clicking the Content Indicator selects the graphic inside the frame. The Hand icon indicates you can reposition the graphic. While the icon is identical to the Hand tool, it is used only to reposition graphics within a frame, while the Hand tool is accessed from the Tools panel and is used for adjusting the display within the document window.

The cropped image should appear similar to this figure.

9   To edit the frame instead of the content of the frame, double-click anywhere on the graphic. The frame becomes selected again.

10   Using your keyboard, press Ctrl+0 (Windows) or Command+0 (Mac OS) to fit page 1 within the document window.

11   If the Layers panel isn't already open, click the Layers button, then click the Visibility icon ( ) in the Text layer so that objects on this layer are once again displayed.

12   Choose File > Save to save your work. Keep the document open for the next part of this lesson.

Applying text wrap

You can control the position of text relative to graphics and other objects. In some cases, you may want text to be placed on top of an image, while in other cases, you may want text to wrap around the shape of an image or object. You'll continue to work on the first page of the brochure, applying text wrap to an image.

1 Using the Selection tool (⭑), click to select the snowshoe image at the bottom of the page. Click between the two columns of text, but be careful to not click the Content Indicator circle at the center of the image, as you will be manipulating the frame attributes in this exercise, and not working with the content. Next you'll enable text wrap on the image to force the text away from the image.

If you have trouble selecting the image, press the Ctrl (Windows) or Command (Mac OS) key and then click again on the image to select it. This enables you to select an object beneath another object in a layout. In this case, the image is positioned below the text frames, so the key command makes it easier to select.

2 Choose Window > Text Wrap to open the Text Wrap panel.

3 Click the Wrap Around Bounding Box button (▣) at the top of the Text Wrap panel to apply the text wrap to the selected image. The text wrap forces the text to flow into the second column, making all the text visible.

The Wrap Around Bounding Box button in the Text Wrap panel wraps the text around the shape of an object.

4 To get a better understanding of how the text wrap is being applied to the text surrounding the graphic frame, use the Selection tool to move the snowshoe image up or down on page 1. As you move the image, see how the text moves around the frame. When you're finished, move the image back to its original location.

5 Click the two arrows pointing to the right in the upper-right corner of the Text Wrap panel to close it. You will work more with Text Wrap in InDesign Lesson 5, "Working with Graphics."

Understanding layers

Layers help you organize your layout. By positioning related objects together on the same layer, you can turn items off and on for viewing, working on your layout, and even for printing. Layers can even be used to create different versions of projects.

Here you will place text and graphics on separate layers making it easier to proofread text.

1 Using the Pages panel, double-click Page 2 to navigate to this page, then choose View > Fit Spread in Window to display both pages 2 and 3 together. Two adjoining pages in a layout are referred to as a Spread.

2 Click the Layers button () in the panel docking area to open the Layers panel.

Use the Layers panel to organize objects in your layout.

 If you have closed a panel instead of placing it in the docking area, you can access it from the Window menu. For example, you can choose Window > Pages to open the Pages panel. The list of available panels is also determined by the current workspace. To access all panels, choose the Advanced workspace from the Workspace switcher located at the top-right corner of the Application bar.

3 In the Layers panel there are three layers: Text, Graphics, and Background Content. Click the Visibility icon (👁) next to the Text layer. Any content on the Text layer is hidden. Click the Visibility icon again to show the contents of the Text layer.

4 Click to turn the visibility of the Graphics and Background Content layers on and off to see the items that are located on each of these layers.

InDesign layers are document-wide. When you create a layer, it is available on every page in the document, including the master pages. When you hide or show a layer, all pages in the document are affected by this change.

5 If necessary, open the Pages panel by clicking the Pages Panel icon (⊞) or choose Window > Pages. In the Pages panel, double-click page 1 to navigate to this page.

6   Using the Selection tool (⬉), click to select the frame containing the snowshoe image at the bottom of the page. If you have trouble selecting it, click the Visibility icon (👁) for the Text layer to temporarily hide the text frames. After selecting the image frame, click the Visibility icon for the Text layer to display the text. In the Layers panel, notice the red square (◼) located to the right of the Graphics layer. This indicates that the currently selected object is located on the Graphics layer.

7   If the Layers panel is not visible, click the Layers panel icon (❤) or choose Window > Layers. In the Layers panel, click and drag the red square to the Background Content layer. The object is moved to this layer, and the edge of the frame containing the snowshoe graphic is now green, the color of the Background Content layer.

Moving an object between layers.

8   Click the Visibility icon of the Background Content layer to hide the contents of the layer, confirming that the snowshoe image is on this layer. Click the Visibility icon again to make the layer visible.

9   Click the square immediately to the left of the Background Content layer to lock this layer. Locking the layer prevents you or others from modifying any contents on a layer.

Locking a layer prevents any changes to objects on the layer.

10   Choose the Selection tool and click the snowshoe picture on page 1. You cannot currently select it because the layer is locked.

11 Unlock the layer by clicking on the Padlock icon (🔒) immediately to the left of the Background Content layer. Locking a layer prevents all items on that layer from being selected. You can use this to organize your layout as you construct your documents. For example, you can create a layer that contains all the guides for your document and lock it so the guides are not accidentally selected, and you can easily show and hide guides that are all placed on a single layer.

If you accidentally select the wrong object, choose Edit > Deselect All, or if you accidentally move an object, choose Edit > Undo to return it to the original location.

Applying effects

You can use InDesign to apply special effects to images or objects in your layout, including adding drop shadows to frames, soft feathered edges to pictures, or adjusting the transparency or opacity of objects and images – all without modifying the original object. Here you will discover how to apply effects to objects.

1 In the Pages panel, double-click page 2 or use the page drop-down menu in the lower-left corner of the workspace to navigate to page 2 of the newsletter.

2 Using the Selection tool (▸), select the blue border in the upper-left corner of the page. The border spans pages 2 and 3.

3 Click the Effects button (*fx*) in the panel docking area or choose Windows > Effects to open the Effects panel.

4 In the Effects panel, confirm that Object is highlighted. Click the Add an Object Effect to the Selected Target button (*fx*) at the bottom of the panel and choose Bevel and Emboss from the menu. The Bevel and Emboss dialog box opens. Click the Preview check box in the lower-left corner of the dialog box to preview the effect before you apply it.

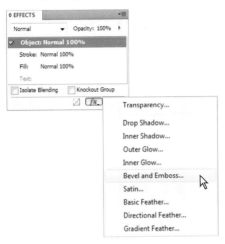

The Effects button at the bottom of the Effects panel allows you to choose effects to apply to selected objects.

5 In the Effects dialog box, leave the settings at their defaults and press OK.

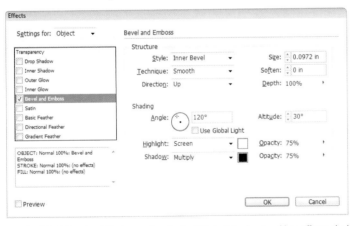

Use the default Bevel and Emboss settings in the Effects dialog box to add an effect to the blue border.

6 Click the Screen Mode button (▣▾) in the Application bar at the top of the workspace and switch to the Preview viewing mode. Use the Preview viewing mode to see the final project without any non-printing elements such as guides and frame edges. You can also press the keyboard shortcut **W** to switch between viewing modes, or use the Screen Mode controls located at the bottom of the tools panel.

7   Choose File > Save, and then choose File > Close to close the file.

Congratulations! You have completed a tour of InDesign CS6, discovering essential skills and concepts for creating layouts using InDesign CS6.

Resources for additional help

While you are on your way to becoming a skilled InDesign user you may still need to get assistance with certain capabilities and features. We've created a comprehensive index at the back of this book which helps you find information about specific topics, or if you are using an eBook version, try the search capabilities to locate specific topics. There are also a number of other ways to get help when using InDesign, as you will discover in this section.

DigitalClassroom.com

The Digital Classroom authors provide updates and respond to inquiries regarding the book content at the DigitalClassroom.com website. By registering your book at *www.DigitalClassroomBooks.com/CS6/InDesign* you will receive updated information regarding any changes in the software, and any reported issues that affect your work with the *Adobe InDesign CS6 Digital Classroom*. Register your book at *www.DigitalClassroomBooks.com/CS6/InDesign* to receive these free benefits.

In-product help

InDesign includes help documentation directly within the application. Choose Help > InDesign Help, and InDesign launches the Adobe Help Viewer, which you can use to search by topic. You can also access help quickly by typing a search query in the help search field, indicated by a magnifying glass ($\wp$) in the Application bar at the top of the workspace.

Online help

You can also find documentation for InDesign online. The online help tends to be more current, as it is updated regularly. The documentation that shipped with the software and is part of the help menu may be out-of-date, as it is often written months before the software is in its final format The online help also gives you the opportunity to add comments to topics that you view, and even receive an e-mail when someone else adds a comment to the topic. You can also download many of the help files in PDF format for printing or easy searching. Find the online help at *adobe.com*.

Forums

Adobe on-line forums are an excellent resource for finding solutions to questions you have about InDesign or how InDesign integrates with other applications. Adobe forums are contributed to by a community of beginning, intermediate, and advanced users who may be looking for the same answer as you, or who have already discovered solutions and answers to questions and are willing to share their solutions with other users. You can access the InDesign Forums page at *http://forums.adobe.com/community/indesign*.

Conferences, seminars, and training

The authors of this book regularly speak at conferences and seminars, and are available to deliver instructor-led professional development training sessions. You can learn more about the authors' professional development training offerings at *www.agitraining.com*.

Self study

Place some of your own graphics into the newsletter that you just created, and then practice cropping and repositioning the graphics within their frames. Move objects to other layers and create your own layer to further refine the organization of the file.

Review

Questions

1 What does a red plus sign in the lower-right corner of a text frame indicate?

2 How do you reposition an image inside of a frame?

3 How can you ensure that if you reposition the panels in InDesign to your liking, you can always bring them back to that state?

4 If you cannot see panels that you need to use, how can you locate and display them in your workspace?

Answers

1 There is more text in the frame than can be displayed within the current frame. This is called overset text. You can fix this by linking the text to another frame, editing the text so that it fits within the existing frame, or enlarging the size of the frame.

2 Clicking the semi-transparent circle known as the Content Indicator located in the center of an image. You can also use the Direct Selection tool to manipulate an image inside a frame.

3 Save a custom workspace by choosing Window > Workspace > New Workspace.

4 When the workspace is changed, the list of available panels also changes. Use the Advanced workspace to view all the panels. All panels can also be found under the Window menu. Simply choose the panel you want to use from the list, and it displays.

Lesson 2

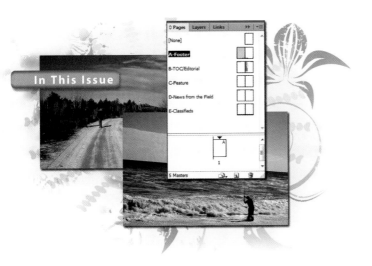

In This Issue

What you'll learn in this lesson:

- Creating and saving custom page sizes

- Creating page guides

- Adding sections

- Using automatic page numbering

- Creating master pages and applying them to document pages

Building Documents with Master Pages

Master pages serve as the foundation for InDesign documents that are more than a few pages in length. You can use master pages to maintain consistency throughout your document and work more efficiently. If you plan to create only short documents, such as one-pages sales sheets or two-page flyers, you may want to skip over this lesson and go to Lesson 3, "Working with Text and Type."

Starting up

Before starting, make sure that your tools and panels are consistent by resetting your preferences. See "Resetting the InDesign workspace and preferences" in the Starting up section of this book.

You will work with several files from the id02lessons folder in this lesson. Make sure that you have copied the id02lessons folder onto your hard drive from the included DVD. See "Loading lesson files" in the Starting up section of this book. This lesson may be easier to follow if the id02lessons folder is on your desktop.

See Lesson 2 in action!

Use the accompanying video to gain a better understanding of how to use some of the features shown in this lesson. The video tutorial for this lesson can be found on the supplied DVD.

The project

In this lesson, you will create a magazine. You will use master pages to create layout templates for each section in the magazine, including running headers, which run across the top of the page, and running footers, which run across the bottom of the page. Master pages give the publication a consistent look and feel.

This lesson provides a foundation in creating InDesign documents, and is focused on a print-layout example.

Planning your document

Before you start creating a print document using InDesign, you need some important information: the final size of the document after it is finished, also known as the *trim size*; how the pages will be held together, also known as the *binding*; and whether the document has images or graphics that extend to the edge of the document—this is known as *bleed*. Once you have this information, you can create the templates for your document pages. Digital documents have different considerations, such as the screen size and resolution.

When you create simple designs or small documents for one-time use you can work directly on the document pages, and not create master pages. Master pages are more suitable for longer documents or documents that use a repeating design on several pages.

Creating custom page sizes

For this lesson, you will create the print version of a custom-sized magazine with colors that extend to the edge of the page. You'll start by creating a new document, and saving the custom size as a preset, which you can use to create subsequent issues of the magazine.

Creating a new custom-sized document

This document will be measured using inches, so you'll start by setting your units of measurement to inches, and then you'll create the custom document size.

1   With no documents open, choose Edit > Preferences > Units & Increments (Windows), or InDesign > Preferences > Units & Increments (Mac OS). When the Preferences dialog box appears, choose Inches from the Vertical and Horizontal drop-down menus in the Ruler Units section. Press OK.

Changing the unit of measurement when no documents are open causes InDesign to use these settings for all new documents you create.

When working in a document, you can switch the unit of measurement for that document by right-clicking (Windows) or Control+clicking (Mac OS) on the vertical or horizontal ruler.

2   Choose File > New > Document, or press Ctrl+N (Windows) or Command+N (Mac OS), to open the New Document dialog box, which is the first step in creating a new InDesign document.

3   In the New Document dialog box, confirm that the Facing Pages check box is selected and that Print is chosen from the Intent drop-down menu. In the Page Size section, type **8.125** in for the Width and **10.625** in for the Height.

Setting the size of the new document.

4   In the Margins section, make sure that the Make all settings the same button (⊛) is not selected. Type **.5** in the Top, Inside, and Outside margin text fields, and **.75** in the Bottom text field.

5   If the Bleed and Slug section is not visible, click the More Options button on the upper-right side of the dialog box. In the Bleed and Slug section, make sure that the Make all settings the same button (🔗) is not selected, and then type **.125** in the Bleed Top, Bottom, and Outside margin text fields and **0** for the inside value. Because this is a magazine, it won't bleed into the spine of the page, where the pages are bound together. Keep the Slug value set at 0.

Bleed area is located outside the edges of a document. By printing an image or color outside the page edge, imperfections in the trimming process go unnoticed.
Slug is additional area beyond the bleed where production notes such as a job number or printing date can be placed and then trimmed off before final delivery of the document.

6   Click the Save Presets button in the upper-right corner of the New Document dialog box. This saves the custom settings you just entered.

Type **Newsletter** in the Save Preset As text field, then press OK. In the New Document dialog box, the Newsletter preset is listed in the preset drop-down menu. This preset is available the next time you need to create a document with similar specifications.

Press OK to leave the New Document dialog box and create your new document using the settings in the New Document dialog box. A new, untitled document is created with the specifications you entered.

7   Choose File > Save As. In the Save As dialog box, navigate to the id02lessons folder and type **id02_work.indd** in the File name text field. Press Save.

It's a good idea to save your work often, even though InDesign includes an automatic recovery feature which helps recover the document if your computer crashes, or InDesign quits unexpectedly.

You formatted some items with styles in Lesson 1, "InDesign CS6 Essential Skills." Here you will also work with styles, but you will import them from another InDesign document. In Lesson 4, "Working with Styles," you will discover how to create and define new styles.

8   Choose Window > Workspace > [Advanced] or choose Advanced from the Workspace drop-down menu in the Application bar at the top of the InDesign interface. Next choose Window > Workspace > Reset Advanced so that all the panels for this workspace are displayed.

9   Click the Paragraph Styles button (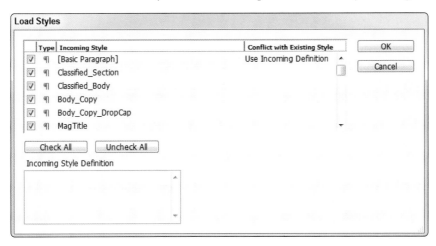) in the panel docking area in the right side of the workspace to open the Paragraph Styles panel. From the Paragraph Styles panel menu (≣) in the upper-right corner, choose Load All Text Styles. The Open a File dialog box appears. In the Open a File dialog box, navigate to the id02lessons folder and select the file named id02styles.indd. Click Open. The Load Styles dialog box appears.

Loading styles lets you import and use styles created in another document.

10 In the Load Styles dialog box, click the Check All button and then click OK. All the paragraph and character styles from this publication are imported into your document.

11 Choose File > Save to save your work. Keep this file open for the next part of the lesson.

Creating and formatting master pages

Master pages serve as a template upon which all document pages are created. They provide the framework for the design of all pages in your document. Different master pages may be created for various sections of your publication, such as a magazine or a catalog. By creating master pages for each section, you can maintain a consistent appearance for all pages in these sections.

The document you are creating for this lesson currently contains one document page and one master page. You will add more document pages and more master pages. You will add master pages for the various sections of the magazine. Each of these sections has a different layout, with a different number of columns, margins, and headers. By creating the master pages before working on the document, you can quickly create pages with a consistent design.

1   Press the Pages button (▤) in the panel docking area, or press the keyboard shortcut Ctrl+F12 (Windows) or Command+F12 (Mac OS), to open the Pages panel. Double-click the A-Master label in the top portion of the Pages panel.

The A-Master page is displayed and centered within your workspace. Keep the A-Master page selected in the Pages panel.

Double-clicking a page label in the Pages panel centers the page in the workspace.

2 In the Pages panel, press the panel menu button (·≡) and select Master Options for A-Master. Alternatively, you can hold down the Alt (Windows) or Option (Mac OS) key and click once on the A-Master text (not the Page icon) in the Pages panel. The Master Options dialog box appears. Next you will rename this master page to reflect the role of this master page in the layout.

3 In the Name text field of the Master Options dialog box, type **Footer**. Leave all other settings unchanged, and press OK. This changes the name from A-Master to A-Footer. You will now add a footer that runs across the bottom of this master page, and then apply this master page to document pages.

Change the name of a master page using the Master Options dialog box.

Formatting master pages

For this publication, the A-Footer page will also serve as the foundation for the other master pages. Although master pages can be used independently of one another, for this publication all items appearing on A-Footer will also appear on all other master pages. This allows you to quickly create a consistent footer across every page. The other master pages will have unique header information identifying each section of the magazine.

Adding automatic page numbers

You can have InDesign automatically apply page numbers, and using master pages makes it easy to have them applied in the same location on every page.

1   In the Pages panel, double-click the Left Page icon for the A-Footer master page. This fits the left side of your A-Footer master page in the window. Before you add a page number, you'll create a guide to help you place it in the ideal location on your page.

2   Using the Selection tool (), position the cursor onto the horizontal ruler running across the top of the page. Ctrl+click (Windows) or Command+click (Mac OS) and drag down from the ruler to create a horizontal ruler guide. Continue dragging until the ruler guide is positioned at 10.25 inches. You can determine the location of the guide in the Control panel, and by using the live transformation values that appear as you drag the guide. The position updates as you drag the guide.

   Pressing and holding the Ctrl or Command key while dragging causes the guide to go across the entire spread, rather than only one page.

If the page rulers aren't visible, choose View > Show Rulers or press Ctrl+R (Windows) or Command+R (Mac OS).

3   Select the Type tool (T) from the Tools panel. Position the Type tool so the intersecting horizontal and vertical lines near the bottom of the tool are positioned at the bottom-left corner of the page margin guides, where the left margin guide and the bottom margin guide meet. This is just above the ruler guide you created in the previous step. Click and drag down and to the right, creating a text frame that extends from the bottom margin guide down to the guide you created in the previous step and to the right to the 1 inch position. You can see the position of the frame being created in the Control panel and in the horizontal ruler located at the top of the page.

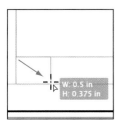

Creating a frame on the master page
for the automatic page number.

4   Choose Type > Insert Special Character > Markers > Current Page Number to automatically have InDesign enter the page number on all pages to which this master page is applied. If you prefer to use keyboard commands, you can press Shift+Alt+Ctrl+N (Windows) or Shift+Option+Command+N (Mac OS) to have an automatic page number inserted. The letter A is inserted into the text frame and acts as a placeholder for the actual page number. The placeholder displays the master page letter when viewed on a master page, and the actual page number when viewed on a document page.

The Insert Special Characters menu can also be accessed by right-clicking (Windows) or Control+clicking (Mac OS) when the cursor is within a text frame.

5   Using the Type tool, select the letter A that you inserted into the text frame so you can customize the appearance of the page number. In the Character Formatting Controls portion of the Control panel, choose Myriad Pro and Bold from the font and style drop-down menus, and choose 12pt from the font size drop-down menu. Continuing to work in the Control panel, click the Paragraph Formatting Controls button (¶) and then click the Align away from Spine button (≡). This aligns the text to the opposite edge of the binding of the publication.

6   Choose Object > Text Frame Options or press Ctrl+B (Windows) or Command+B (Mac OS). The Text Frame Options dialog box appears. In the General tab, locate the Vertical Justification section and choose Bottom from the Align drop-down menu. Click OK. The baseline of the text aligns to the bottom of the text frame.

Now you will place a copy of the automatic page number on the opposite page.

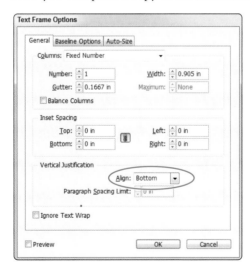
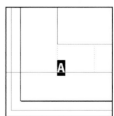

Using the Text Frame Options dialog box to vertically justify text.

7   Choose the Selection tool and make certain the text frame containing the footer is selected. Choose Edit > Copy to copy the frame.

8   Double-click on the right-hand page of the A-Footer master in the Pages panel. Choose Edit > Paste to place the copied text frame into the right-hand page.

9   Use the Selection tool to reposition the text frame so that the top of the frame is aligned to the bottom margin, and the right edge of the frame aligns to the right margin.

Notice that the page number automatically changes to align to the right side of the text frame because you selected the Align away from Spine option.

Using text variables

You use text variables to insert dynamic text that changes contextually. InDesign includes several pre-defined text variables including Chapter Number, File Name, Output Date, and Running Header. You can also edit any of these variables, or create new variables. This makes it easy to consistently apply text across a document, and easily update the text in one place and have all other occurrences of the text updated in a single step.

Defining new text variables

You will create variable text for your magazine title and page footers.

1   Choose Type > Text Variables > Define. The Text Variables dialog box appears.

2   Select Running Header from the Text Variables section of the dialog box and click the New button on the right side of the dialog box. The New Text Variable dialog box appears.

Creating a new text variable.

3 In the New Text Variable dialog box, type **Magazine Title** in the Name text field. Leave the Type text field as Running Header (Paragraph Style). From the Style drop-down menu, choose the MagTitle paragraph style. In the Options section, select the Change Case check box, then select the Title Case radio button below it. Press OK.

A new Magazine Title variable appears in the Text Variables dialog box.

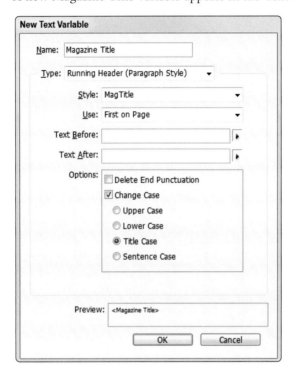

Defining the settings for text variables.

4 Repeat steps 1 and 2 to create another Running Header text variable. Name this text variable **Magazine Issue** and select the MagIssue paragraph style from the Style drop-down menu. All the other settings should match the settings used in step 3. Press OK and note that the variables for Magazine Title and Magazine Issue are now available in the Text Variables dialog box. Press Done to save these new variables, which you will use in the next part of this lesson.

Creating page footers

In the previous steps, you created a Running Header text variable. Even though it is called a Running Header variable, it can be used anywhere on the page. Now you will use these variables to create the footers.

1 In the Pages panel, double-click the left page icon of the A-Footer master page.

2 Select the Type tool (T) from the Tools panel. Position the cursor at the bottom-right corner of the page, where the bottom and right margin guides meet. Click and drag down and to the left until the bottom of the frame you are creating reaches the bottom ruler guide and the left edge of the frame is approximately at the center of the page. A guide appears once the cursor has reached the center of the page.

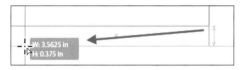

Creating a text frame for the magazine title.

3 In the Control panel click the Character Formatting Controls button (A) and set the font to Minion Pro Italic, the size to 12 pt, and the leading (₍A₎) to Auto. Press the Paragraph Formatting Controls button (¶) and press the Align toward Spine button (≡).

4 Choose Type > Text Variables > Insert Variable > Magazine Title. The variable text <magazine Title> is placed into the frame. Press the spacebar to separate this variable from the next variable that you will enter.

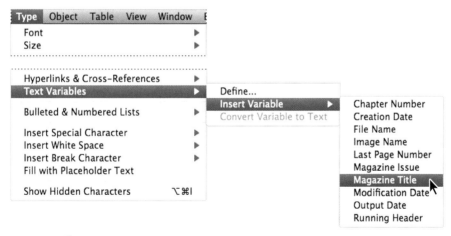

Inserting variable text.

5 In the Control panel, click the Character Formatting Controls button and change the font to Minion Pro Regular. Choose Type > Text Variables > Insert Variable > Magazine Issue. The variable text <magazine Issue> is placed into the frame.

6 Choose the Selection tool (🖈) from the Tools panel and make sure the text frame that you drew in Step 2 is selected. Choose Object > Text Frame Options. In the Text Frame Options dialog box, select Bottom from the Align drop-down menu located in the Vertical Justification section in the General Tab. This causes the text to align to the bottom of the text frame. Press OK. You will now duplicate this box, placing a copy of it on the adjacent page.

7 Continuing to use the Selection tool, press and hold the Alt key (Windows) or Option key (Mac OS). While holding this key, click and drag the box you created to the page on the right side of the layout. The box is duplicated. Pressing and holding the Alt or Option key duplicates objects as you move them.

As you are dragging an object such as the text frame in step 7, you can also add the Shift key while dragging. This constrains the movement of the object horizontally, ensuring that the original and duplicate objects are aligned. The Shift key can also be used to constrain objects movement vertically as well, maintaining the left-right position on the page.

8 Position the duplicate frame so that the left edge aligns with the left margin guide, and the bottom of the duplicate frame remains aligned to the ruler guide you created.

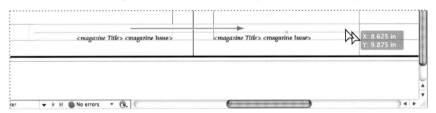

Position the duplicate text frame along the ruler guide, aligning the left edge with the left margin guide.

9 Double-click in the duplicated text frame to switch to the Type tool and place the cursor in the text frame. Press Ctrl+A (Windows) or Command+A (Mac OS) to select the type, and then press the Delete key.

10 Continuing to work in the same text frame, type **DigitalClassroom.com**.

11 Choose File > Save to save your work.

Basing master pages on other master pages

You can create additional master pages, and these pages can use the same formatting and layout that you've already created for the A-Footer master page. In the next exercise, you'll import master pages that have already been created in another document. You'll then apply the A-Footer master page to these master pages to create a consistent layout and appearance.

To create your own master pages, choose the New Master command from the Pages panel menu (⁃≣).

1   If it isn't already open, open the Pages panel by pressing the Pages button (⊞) in the dock. In the Pages panel, press the panel menu button (⁃≣) and choose Master Pages > Load Master Pages. The Open a File dialog box appears.

2   In the Open a File dialog box, navigate to the id02lessons folder and select the file called id02styles.indd. Press Open. Four new master pages are added to your document and are displayed in the Master Pages section of the Pages panel. If necessary, click and drag downward on the horizontal line separating the master pages from the document pages in the Pages panel. These master pages correspond to the various sections of the magazine. Next, you'll apply the A-Footer master page you created earlier to these new master pages so that they have a consistent appearance.

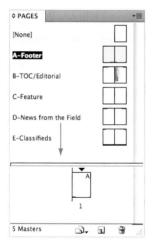

Click and drag downward on the line separating the master pages from the document pages to display the newly added master pages.

3   Double-click on the name B-TOC/Editorial master page in the Pages panel. By clicking the name instead of the icon, the entire spread is displayed.

4   In the Pages panel menu, choose Master Options for B-TOC/Editorial. You can also access the Master Options by holding down the Alt (Windows) or Option (Mac OS) key while clicking on the name of the master page. The Master Options dialog box is displayed.

5   In the Master Options dialog box, click the Based on Master drop-down menu and choose A-Footer, then press OK.

Notice that the B-TOC/Editorial master page now includes the footer you created. In the Pages panel, the page icons for B-TOC/Editorial display the letter A, indicating that these master pages are based on the master page A you created.

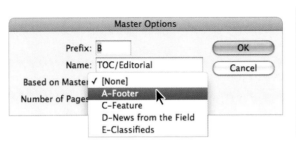
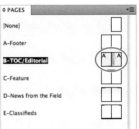

Base the page on the A-Footer master page.   *The A indicates that this master page is linked to master page A.*

6   In the Pages panel, click and drag the name A-Footer onto the name C-Feature in the master page section. This applies the formatting found on Master Page A to the destination page. By dragging the pages using their name, all pages in the spread are affected.

7   Drag and drop the A-Footer master page on top of master pages: master page D and E.

Overriding master page items

When you apply a Master page to another page, the items on the master page are locked and cannot be accidentally modified on the page to which they have been applied.

In the next exercise, you'll unlock some of the master page items that have been applied to another page and then selectively delete items from the master page that may not be needed on certain document pages.

1   In the Pages panel, double-click the left side of the B-TOC/Editorial master page. Notice that the text frames' edges surrounding the footer that you created appear as dotted lines. This indicates that these items are part of a master page that has been applied to this page, and that they are locked and cannot be edited.

2   Choose the Selection tool (⬉) from the Tools panel. Place the cursor anywhere over the footer and click. Notice that it is not selected because it was applied from a master page, and remains locked for editing as long as it remains attached to a master page. To modify this frame, you will indicate to InDesign that the object should be made available for editing. This process is known as overriding a master page item.

3   Continuing to use the Selection tool, press the Shift+Ctrl keys (Windows) or Shift+Command keys (Mac OS) and click the text frames containing the page number and footer. Using these keys you can select master page items and make them available for editing. Press Delete to remove these frames from this page.

4 Choose File > Save to save your work.

When you use Shift+Control+click (Windows) or Shift+Command+click (Mac OS) to select and change a master page item, the changed item is referred to as a local override. The master page remains applied to the page, and only the items you select and modify are considered to have a local override to their appearance. To override all master page items on a page, select a page in the Pages panel and choose Override All Master Page Items from the Pages panel menu (◂▤).

Adding placeholder frames to master pages

Creating text and image frames on master pages makes it easier to develop a consistent layout, and you can quickly add content to the placeholder frames. When you create image frames on a master page, you can use frame-fitting options to control how images are sized after they are placed into the frames.

1 Select the Type tool (T) from the Tools panel and create a text frame on the left side of the B-TOC/Editorial master page, which contains the headline *In This Issue*. The position and dimensions of the text frame you create are not important, as you will define these in the next step.

2 Choose the Selection tool (▸) from the Tools panel and make sure the text frame you created in the previous step is still selected. In the Control panel, set the reference point (▦) to top-left and type **2.95 in** for X and **1.4 in** for Y to set the location of the frame. Then type **4.625 in** for W and **3.6 in** for H to set the width and height of the frame.

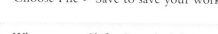

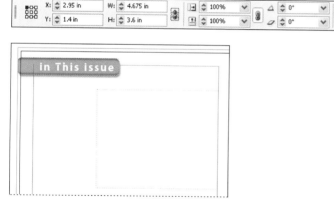

Use the Control panel to set the exact location of the text frame.

3 Now you'll add a number of image frames on the left side of the page. Select the Rectangle Frame tool (⊠) from the Tools panel and draw a small rectangle to the left of the text frame you created in the previous step. You will also use the Control panel to set the exact position and dimensions for this frame.

4 Choose the Selection tool from the Tools panel and make sure the frame you created in the last step is selected. In the Control panel, make sure the reference point (⌗) is set to top-left and type the following values to set the dimensions and position: X: **-.125 in** Y: **1.4 in** W: **2.4 in** H: **1.625 in**.

The image frame you created is aligned to the top of the text frame, and bleeds off the left side of the page. Next you will define how images placed in this frame will be sized. This is not required for frames, although it saves time when creating a design template or master page that may be used for many jobs or publications.

5 Continuing to use the Selection tool, make certain the image frame you created in step three is still selected. If necessary, click to select it. Choose Object > Fitting > Frame Fitting Options. In the Frame Fitting Options dialog box, choose Fill Frame Proportionally from the Fitting drop-down menu, located in the Content Fitting section. Press OK. This will cause any image placed into this frame to be scaled so that it fully fits within the frame.

You'll now duplicate the empty frame, using a process known as Step and Repeat.

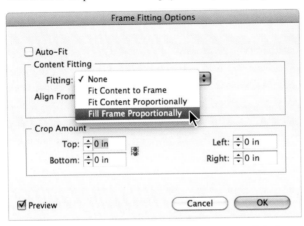

Choose Fill Frame Proportionally in the Frame Fitting Options dialog box to control how images placed in this frame will be sized.

6 With the image frame still selected, choose Edit > Step and Repeat. Step and Repeat makes it easy for you to duplicate an object several times, placing each duplicate copy in a specific location.

7 In the Step and Repeat dialog box, type **3** in the Repeat Count text field, type **2.0625"** in the Vertical Offset text field, and type **0** in the Horizontal Offset text field. Press OK. This creates three copies of the frame, and spaces them 2.0625 inches apart from each other.

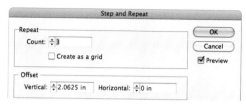

Create three duplicates of the text frame using Step and Repeat.

8 Choose File > Save to save your document, and keep it open for the next part of the lesson.

Locking Master Items and setting text wrap

In the first lesson, you discovered how to wrap text around an object on a document page. Here you will wrap text around a shape on a master page.

1 In the Pages panel double-click the right page icon of the B-TOC/Editorial master page. Using the Selection tool (✦), select the oval shape on the left side of the page and right-click (Windows) or Control+click (Mac OS) on the shape. Be certain to select the oval shape and not the text frame that sits on top of the oval. In the contextual menu, turn off the Allow Master Item Overrides option so that it does not display a check mark. This prohibits designers from making changes to this master page object once it is part of a document page.

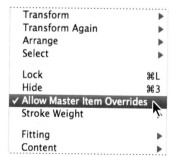

The Allow Master Item Overrides option is enabled by default. When disabled, master items cannot be changed on a document page.

2 Choose Window > Text Wrap. This opens the Text Wrap panel. From the panel, select the Wrap around object shape option (▣) and set the Top Offset to **.25** inches, causing any text that is placed adjacent to this frame to wrap around the oval, placing ¼-inch distance between the text and the oval.

 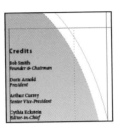

Use the Text Wrap panel to push text away from a frame or object.

Here the text wraps above the image, offset by ¼ inch.

When the Wrap around object shape option is chosen for this object, all the offset fields are grayed-out except for the top value. This is because this object has an irregular shape. The top value will be used to specify the wrap on all sides. For rectangular or square objects, the value can be adjusted on all four sides independently.

3 Close the Text Wrap panel.

Adding layout pages

Now that you have created and formatted all the master pages, you can start to lay out the document pages of the magazine. You'll start by adding pages to the document.

1 Double-click on page 1 in the Pages panel and choose Layout > Pages > Add Page, or use the keyboard shortcut Shift+Control+P (Windows) or Shift+Command+P (Mac OS), to add a page to the document. The Pages panel now displays two page icons, as the new page is added to the end of the document.

Next you'll insert the pages that will contain the Table of Contents and editorial content.

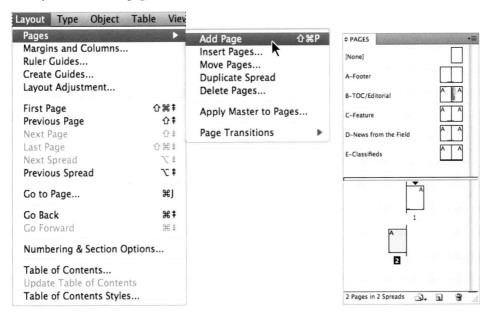

Adding a page to the document using the Layout menu.

2   In the Pages panel, Alt+click (Windows) or Option+click (Mac OS) on the Create new page button (⬚) at the bottom of the Pages panel to open the Insert Pages dialog box.

3   In the Insert Pages dialog box, type **2** in the Pages field, and from the Insert drop-down menu select After Page and type **1** to have two pages added after page 1. Select B-TOC/Editorial from the Master drop-down menu, then press OK.

This causes two pages to be added after page 1, and the new pages use the B-TOC/Editorial master page.

Adding multiple pages to the document. The new pages are based on a specific master page.

Two pages are inserted between pages 1 and 2, and the B-TOC/Editorial master page is applied to the new pages. This magazine has 12 pages. Because the pages will belong to different sections of the magazine, different master pages will be applied to them. Here you will add the pages to the document, and later in the exercise you will discover how to apply master pages to the document pages.

4   At the bottom of the Pages panel, Alt+click (Windows) or Option+click (Mac OS) the Create new page button (⬚). The Insert Pages dialog box appears.

5   In the Insert Pages dialog box, type **9** in the Pages text field. Select After Page from the Insert drop-down menu, and type **4** in the text field. Choose None from the Master drop-down menu, then press OK.

This inserts nine blank pages into your file after page 4. You now have 13 pages in the document. Because the document is only 12 pages, you'll practice deleting a page.

6   Double-click the icon representing Page 4 in the Pages panel. This highlights the icon in the Pages panel and displays this document page.

7   Click the Delete selected pages button (🗑) at the bottom of the Pages panel. This deletes page 4 and leaves you with the 12 pages you need for this issue.

8   Choose File > Save to save your document. Keep it open for the next exercise.

Primary text frames

When creating a master page you can specify a primary text frame. A primary text frame is useful if you have one frame containing the majority of the text on a page, and the master page applied to that document page is subject to change.

If a different master page is applied to a document page that uses a primary text frame, the text automatically flows from the old primary text frame into the new primary text frame. Additionally, primary text frames can be worked with on a document page more easily, as they are automatically overridden and do not require any additional adjustments before using them in your layout.

You can designate a text frame on any master page as a primary text frame by clicking to select the frame and then clicking the primary text frame symbol located near the top of the left edge of a text frame. There is only one master text frame per master page.

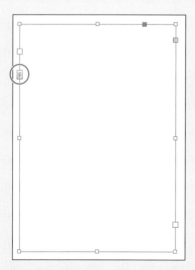
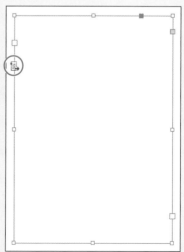

A master text frame before being converted to a primary text frame (left) and after being converted to a primary text frame (right). Designate a primary text frame on a master page to more easily adjust text layout when a new master page is applied to a document page.

Setting numbering and section options

Now that you have the pages needed for the magazine you can define the numbering and sections. The first page of the document is sensibly considered to be page 1 as the page numbers are automatically applied to the document. In this magazine, the first page will be the cover and the back side of the cover will contain the table of contents. The third page of the publication is where the page numbering will start. You will change the page numbering using the numbering and section options.

1   In the Pages panel, double-click the triangle (▼) located above the first page icon. This is the section start icon, and double-clicking it opens the Numbering & Section Options dialog box.

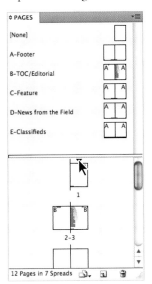

Double-click the section start icon in the Pages panel.

2   In the Numbering & Section Options dialog box, select I, II, III, IV from the Style drop-down menu, located in the Page Numbering section, then press OK.

This change adjusts the document's numbering to uppercase Roman numerals. You will now create a new section on the third page, so that page 1 will be located at the start of the new section.

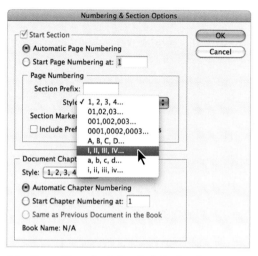

Select Roman Numeral style from the Styles drop-down menu.

3 In the Pages panel, double-click page III to select it. Press the panel menu button (·≡) in the Pages panel and select Numbering & Section Options. Select the Start Page Numbering at radio button and type **1** in the text field. In the Page Numbering section, select 1, 2, 3, 4 from the Style drop-down menu and press OK.

This starts a new section on the third page of the document. The new section starts using the page number 1.

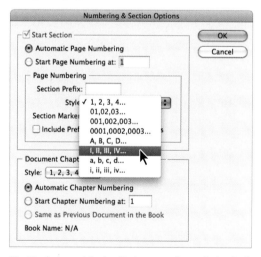

Use Numbering and Section Options to set the numbering for the new section of the magazine.

Placing formatted text

Next you will add some content to the editorial page, importing text from a Microsoft Word document that includes pre-formatted text styles. You'll then complete the editorial page by adding a picture of the editor.

1 In the Pages panel, double-click the third page of the document. This is the page you set to page 1 in the previous exercise.

2 Select the Type tool (T) from the Tools panel and draw a small text frame on the right side of the page. The exact size and location isn't important; you'll use the Control panel to specify these values.

3 Choose the Selection tool (↖) from the Tools panel—or you can press the Escape key on your keyboard to switch to the Selection tool—and make sure the text frame is selected. In the Control panel at the top of the workspace, make sure the reference point is set to top-left. Type **11"** in the X text field and **3"** in the Y text field. Also type **4.75"** in the W text field and **6.875"** in the H text field.

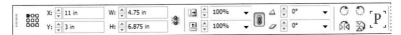

Use the Control panel to define the size and position of the text frame after you create it.

4 With the text frame still selected, choose File > Place At the bottom of the Place dialog box, make sure *Show Import Options* and *Replace Selected Item* are both selected. Navigate to the id02lessons folder and select the file Editorial.doc, then click Open. The Microsoft Word Import Options dialog box appears.

5 In the Microsoft Word Import Options dialog box, make sure the Preserve Styles and Formatting from Text and Tables radio button is selected. Confirm that Import Styles Automatically is selected, and that Use InDesign Style Definition is selected for both Paragraph Style Conflicts and Character Style Conflicts. Leave all other settings unchanged, and then press OK.

The Word document is placed into the selected text frame and text styles from the Word document are automatically converted to the InDesign paragraph styles because the styles in each application have been identically named.

Use the Import Options to adjust styles created in Microsoft Word when importing a Microsoft Word document into an InDesign layout.

When importing text from Microsoft Word, you can have headlines, titles, body copy, and other formatting defined in the Microsoft Word document carried over into the InDesign layout. By choosing the Use InDesign Styles option in the Import Options dialog box, you can have identically named styles in a Microsoft Word document mapped to an InDesign style of the same name. You can use this to have editors and writers identify which styles should be applied to text before it is brought into a layout.

6   Because the editor's picture is likely to remain the same in every issue of the magazine, it makes sense to place this photo on the master page. In the Pages panel, double-click the right-hand page of the B-TOC/Editorial master page. Choose File > Place. In the Place dialog box, navigate to the id02lessons folder and select the file editor.jpg. Uncheck *Show Import Options* and also uncheck *Replace Selected Item*. Click Open to import this image. The cursor changes to a loaded cursor, indicating that InDesign is ready to place an image into your layout.

7   Move the loaded cursor to the top-right portion of the page, below the From the Editor text. Click once to place the photo.

8   Choose the Selection tool from the Tools panel, then click and drag the photo until the right side of the frame snaps to the right margin guide. If necessary, you can use the arrow keys to nudge the photo into place.

Place the editor's photo on the master page, then position it beneath the From the Editor text.

9   Choose File > Save to save your work.

Creating the classified page

Goods for sale and professional services are often advertised on a classified advertising page located in the back of a magazine. Because most of the space is sold to smaller merchants, these layouts typically involve narrow columns to pack as many small ads as possible into the space. In this case, a four-column layout with an appropriate header has already been created for you. You will apply the master page and then import the text for the classified advertisements.

1   In the Pages panel, double-click page 9. Press the Pages panel menu button (⋅≣), and choose Apply Master to Pages. The Apply Master dialog box appears.

2   From the Apply Master drop-down menu, choose the master page E-Classifieds. Confirm that the page to which this will be applied is listed as page 9. If necessary, type **9** in this field. Click OK. The header, footer, and four-column layout of the E-Classifieds master page are applied to page 9.

Use the Apply Master option to apply a master page to page 9 of the document.

3   Choose File > Place to import the text into the page. At the bottom of the Place dialog box, check *Show Import Options*, and leave *Replace Selected Item* unchecked. Navigate to the id02lessons folder and select the file Classifieds.rtf. Click Open.

4 In the RTF Import Options dialog box, make sure the *Preserve Styles and Formatting from Text and Tables* radio button is selected. Leave all the other settings at their defaults and click OK.

InDesign remembers the last settings used in the Import Options dialog box. Settings you make will impact similar files you import until you change the import options.

5 On page 9, move the cursor anywhere within the first column.

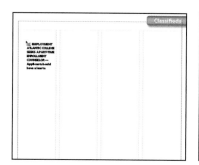

Press and hold the Shift key to automatically flow the text across the different columns as it is placed in the document.

Here the text flowed into a single frame containing multiple columns. If there are column guides on the page but no text frame, you can have InDesign automatically create frames within the column guides by pressing the Shift key while clicking to place the text onto the page.

6 Choose File > Save to save your work.

In this lesson, you have imported Microsoft Word files and Rich Text Format files. You can use InDesign to create layouts using most common file formats for text and graphics. The Import Options dialog box changes to reflect the type of file being imported.

Adding images and text to the master frames

Earlier in this lesson, you added frames to a master page. Now that this master page has been applied to document pages, you will add content to these frames on the document pages.

1 In the Pages panel, double-click page II, which will contain the table of contents. The image and text frames you added earlier have dotted borders, indicating that these frames are located on a master page.

2 Choose File > Place. In the Place dialog box uncheck *Show Import Options* and *Replace Selected Item* so these items are not selected. If necessary, navigate to the id02lessons folder and locate the TOC images folder. Double-click to open the folder and select the file photo1.jpg. Click Open to select this file. The cursor changes to reflect that an image is ready to be placed into the layout.

3 Move the cursor over the top image frame located on the left side of the page, and click, placing the image inside the frame. The image is automatically resized using the fitting options you specified when creating the frame on the master page.

When images and text are placed into frames that were created on master pages, the frames become document page items, and can be selected or modified, although they retain the properties from the master page. These objects are considered to have a local override applied to them, and will update if changes are made to their original master page objects.

4 Choose File > Place and click on the image photo2.jpg, and Shift+click on photo4.jpg to select all three images at the same time. Click Open. The cursor icon contains the number (3), indicating that there are three images to place in the document.

5 Click the second frame from the top, placing the next photo. Continue clicking the empty frames, placing the remaining photos.

If the photos in your loaded cursor don't appear in the order that you'd like, pressing the up- or down-arrow keys on your keyboard cycles through the images that you have selected to place into your layout.

Now you'll finish the TOC/Editorial spread by adding the Table of Contents to the text frame on the right side of page II.

6   Choose File > Place. In the Place dialog box, navigate to the id02lessons folder. Select the TOC.rtf file. Make sure that *Show Import Options* and *Replace Selected Item* are still unchecked. Click Open.

Primary Text Frame

When applying a new master page layout to a document page that has an existing layout, you may end up duplicating the existing text and its frame along with any frames in the new master page that has been applied to the existing document page. To avoid this, you may want to specify a primary text frame on a master page.

To establish a primary text frame, click the primary text frame icon in the upper-left corner of the text frame or right–click (Windows) or Control+click (Mac OS) on a master page text frame and select "Primary Text Frame" from the contextual menu. Only one story on a master page can be specified as primary text frame.

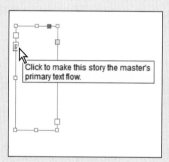

Specifying that a text frame on a master page contains the primary text flow.

7   Move your cursor over the text box on the right side of page II, to the right of the four images, and click to place the text into the layout.

Just like the Editorial and Classified sections, the TOC.rtf file is pre-formatted using paragraph styles. In the next section of this exercise, you'll apply the remaining master pages and see how InDesign updates the content in the footer of each page.

The completed Table of Contents page.

Applying master pages to multiple pages

Next you'll complete your work on this magazine by assigning master pages to the remaining pages in the magazine. The editorial content for this publication may not be complete, but you'll get the design ready for the final text to be placed as soon as it is completed.

1   In the Pages panel, press the panel menu button (⋅≡) and choose Apply Master to Pages. In the Apply Master dialog box, choose C-Feature from the Apply Master drop-down menu. In the To Pages text field, type **2–4** so that master page C-Feature is applied to pages 2–4. Be sure to add the hyphen (-) between the 2 and 4. Click OK. The master page is applied to the pages.

2   Click the Pages panel menu button again and choose Apply Master to Pages. In the Apply Master dialog box, choose D-News from the Field from the Apply Master drop-down menu and type **5–8** in the To Pages text field. Click OK to apply master page D to pages 5–8.

In the main document window, scroll through the document pages. The text variables inserted in the footer have been automatically populated with the magazine title and issue. The master pages and text variables provide a convenient way to save time and maintain consistency throughout your design.

3   Choose File > Save to save your work. After reviewing your document, choose File > Close to close the document.

Congratulations! You have finished this lesson.

Self study

Create a newsletter for your friends or family. Include a number of sections such as a page with profiles of people, stories relating to events or travels, favorite quotes, top ten lists, and photo galleries. Think about which of these sections share common elements, and design master pages to create a consistent design across these sections. Use headers, footers, guides, text frames, and picture frames on your master pages. If you find yourself repeating steps on multiple pages, consider how you can use features like master pages and text variables to streamline your design process.

Review

Questions

1   Do automatic page numbers always start with page 1?

2   If you want to modify content on a page that is linked to a master page, how do you select this locked content?

3   How can you access styles created in other InDesign documents?

Answers

1   No, you can start page numbering with any page number using the Numbering and Sections dialog box to specify where automatic page numbers start and end.

2   Using the Selection tool (🖈), Shift+Control+click (Windows) or Shift+Command+ click (Mac OS) on content that is linked to a master page to break the link.

3   Use the Load Styles command found in the panel menu of the Paragraph or Character Styles panels, to import styles created in other documents.

What you'll learn in this lesson:

- Importing text

- Adding text to your layouts

- Formatting text

- Using the Story editor

- Spell-checking and customizing the dictionary

- Applying styles to text

Working with Text and Type

This lesson covers the essential capabilities for importing, formatting, and flowing text using InDesign CS6.

Starting up

Before starting, make sure that your tools and panels are consistent by resetting your preferences. See "Resetting the InDesign workspace and preferences" in the Starting up section of this book.

You will work with several files from the id03lessons folder in this lesson. Make sure that you have copied the id03lessons folder onto your hard drive from the included DVD. See "Loading lesson files" in the Starting up section of this book for details. This lesson may be easier to follow if the id03lessons folder is on your desktop.

See Lesson 3 in action!

Use the accompanying video to gain a better understanding of how to use some of the features shown in this lesson. The video tutorial for this lesson can be found on the supplied DVD.

The project

In this lesson you will use add text into your layout and import type created using a word processing program such as Microsoft Word. You will also use InDesign's text controls to control text formatting as you create a layout for a fictitious magazine, *Tech*.

To view the finished project before starting, choose File > Open, navigate to the id03lessons folder, select id0301_done.indd, and then click Open. Choose View > Fit Page in Window or press Ctrl+0 (Windows) or Command+0 (Mac OS). After reviewing the layout, you can keep the lesson open for reference, or close it by choosing File > Close. You'll use InDesign's Typography workspace for this lesson. From the Workplace Switcher menu, choose Typography.

Adding text to your document

Text in an InDesign layout is typically contained within a text frame. You can create text frames using the Type tool or use any of the other frame or shape tools to create an object that can easily be converted to a text frame. You can also add text into your layout that was created using other programs, such as Microsoft Word.

Creating a frame is usually the starting point for adding text to a layout. You'll start by using the most efficient way to define a new text frame: clicking and dragging with the Type tool.

Creating a text frame

You will start by creating a new text frame and then enter text into the frame.

1   Choose File > Open. In the Open dialog box, navigate to the id03lessons folder, select the file id0301.indd, and then click Open. You'll start by working on the first page of this document. If necessary, double-click the page 1 icon in the Pages panel to navigate to this page.

   The lower-left section of page 1 has a listing of the stories featured in this issue. You will create a text frame above this box and add text to it.

If necessary, use the Pages panel to navigate to the first page.

2 Choose the Type tool (T) from the Tools panel. Position the cursor on the left edge of the page so it is at the margin guide, approximately one-half inch above the list of stories. Use your mouse to click and drag diagonally down and to the right to create a new text frame. Release the mouse when it is positioned just above the existing text frame that contains the list of stories. The new frame should be placed above the existing frame and the left and right edges should be similarly positioned to the corresponding edges of the existing frame

*Click and drag with the Type tool
to create a new frame.*

3 Type **Inside this issue:** into the text frame.

If you need to reposition the text frame, choose the Selection tool (▶) from the Tools panel, then click and drag the frame to move it. You can also use the frame handles to adjust the size of the frame. When using the Selection tool, you can switch to the Type tool (T) by double-clicking on a text frame.

4 Choose File > Save As. In the Save As dialog box, navigate to the id03lessons folder and type **id0301_work.indd** in the Name text field. Click Save to save the file.

Creating multiple frames

When drawing a text frame, pressing the right-arrow key one time will divide the text frame being created into two linked text frames. Pressing the arrow key a second time will create a third linked frame, which you can continue until you have the desired number of frames. Similarly, pressing the up-arrow key divides the text frames vertically into separate frames. You can divide a frame both vertically and horizontally to create a grid of text frames. This can also be used when creating image frames or other shapes.

Changing character attributes

You can use the Control panel located at the top of the workspace to adjust text formatting. The Character Formatting Controls button (A), and, below that, the Paragraph Formatting Controls button (¶) are located at the left side of the Control panel, and you can use them to switch between controls that affect either paragraphs or characters.

Additional character and paragraph formatting options are available through dedicated panels for formatting type. You can access these other options by choosing Type > Character, or Type > Paragraph.

Changing font and type styles

You can make adjustments to text formatting using the Control panel which you'll explore in this exercise.

1   Make sure you have the Type tool (T) selected, then click and drag the text *Inside this issue:* to highlight it so that it is selected.

The Character Formatting Controls.

In the Control panel at the top of the workspace, make sure the Character Formatting Controls icon (A) is selected.

You will change the font by typing the font name to access it more quickly.

Previewing fonts in the Control Panel

When you click the arrow to the right of the font name, the drop-down menu lists all the fonts that InDesign is able to access. InDesign has a *WYSIWYG* (what you see is what you get) font menu, which shows the word *SAMPLE* displayed in the different fonts. Pick any font you'd like, just to see the font change.

The WYSIWYG font menu.

2   In the Font drop-down menu in the Control panel, click and drag to select (highlight) the font name and type **Adobe Garamond Pro**. As soon as Adobe Garamond Pro is displayed, press Enter (Windows) or Return (Mac OS) to select this font and the text is formatted appropriately.

You will now change the type style to bold.

To see how text in your document will appear when using a certain font, first select the text to be changed, then click to place the cursor in the Font drop-down menu in the Control panel. With the text in the document still selected, use the up- and down-arrows on your keyboard to apply different fonts to the text.

3   With the text still selected, locate the Font Style drop-down menu, under the menu where you changed the font in the previous step. Choose Bold from the Font Style drop-down menu. Your type now appears as bold Adobe Garamond Pro. Keep the text selected.

Use this drop-down menu to set the style of the font, such as bold, italic, or black. InDesign only makes available font styles that are installed on your computer. For example, if you have Arial, but you don't have Arial Bold, you can choose Arial, but the Bold option will not be available. This avoids possible problems when printing, but is different from many other software programs which allow you to apply styles such as italic or bold to any font.

Changing the type style to bold.

Adjusting size

You can increase or decrease text size from the Control panel. Here you will increase the size of the selected text.

1   In the Control panel, use the mouse to click and select the font size (T) and replace it by typing **20** and then pressing Enter (Windows) or Return (Mac OS). The font size increases to 20 points. You can also choose from pre-defined sizes in the drop-down menu, but entering a specific value can be faster if you know the exact size you want. Similarly, if the size you want to use isn't part of the predefined sizes, you'll need to enter the value by typing it into the Control panel.

2   Choose File > Save to save your work.

Adjusting line spacing

The space between lines of text is known as *leading*. Before computers were used to set type, original letter presses used bars of lead to separate the lines of type, and so the term leading remains, even though it now only requires the click of the mouse instead of inserting a piece of metal between the lines of type. Leading is measured from the bottom of one line (the "baseline") to the bottom of the line above it.

Here you will continue to work on the cover, adjusting the leading for the list of stories located below the text you formatted in the previous exercise.

1   Using the Type tool (T), click to insert the cursor in the text frame containing the list of stories in this issue. To select all the text in the frame click five times, or choose Edit > Select All.

2   In the Control panel, set the Leading (⅍) to 16 by selecting the existing value and typing **16**. Press Enter (Windows) or Return (Mac OS) to set the leading. This sets the space from the bottom of one line to the bottom of the next at 16 points. Keep the text selected as you will continue formatting it in the next part of this exercise.

As with the text size, if you want to use one of the pre-set choices, you can select them from the drop-down menu.

Changing the leading.

Leading controls in InDesign are applied to individual lines of text. To apply line spacing to an entire paragraph, select all the text in the paragraph before adjusting the leading, or incorporate the leading value in a paragraph style, which you will learn about in the next lesson, "Working with Styles."

Adjusting character spacing: kerning and tracking

Just like you can adjust the space vertically between lines of type, you can also adjust the space between either a specific pair of characters or between a range of characters. Adjusting the space between two characters is kerning, while adjusting the space between a range of characters is tracking.

1   Click to place the cursor in the Tracking value (ᴀᴠ) portion of the Control panel, then type **10** and then press Enter (Windows) or Return (Mac OS) to increase the tracking.

Tracking is measured using a fraction of an em space. A full em space is the width of the letter M of a particular font in a particular size—simply put, an em space varies depending upon the size and font you are using. In this case, the value 10 represents 10/1000ths of an em space.

Changing the tracking.

Next you will use the word *Tech* in the lower-left corner of the page to serve as a logo for the start of the High Tech Corner section. You will kern the letters closer together, and then use baseline shift to further adjust some of the letters to create a visual effect with the type.

2   Using the Type tool (T), click between the e and the c in the word *Tech* in the same block of text where you are currently working. Click to select the kerning value (A͞V) which is currently set to 0 and type **–120**, being certain to include the minus symbol to indicate a negative value. Press Enter (Windows) or Return (Mac OS) to set the kerning.

Changing the kerning.

Using a baseline shift

The baseline is the horizontal line upon which the bottom part of characters rests. Some characters, like lowercase q or p fall below the baseline, but most characters sit upon the baseline. You can use baseline shift to change the vertical position of individual characters. This is useful for trademark and copyright symbols along with fractions and footnotes or endnotes. Here you will use baseline shift to style the text to gain an understanding of how to access these capabilities using InDesign.

1   Select the letters e and c of the word *Tech* and change their size to 10 using the Font Size drop-down menu in the Control panel.

2   Select only the letter *e* and in the Baseline Shift value (A a͟ₜ) in the Control panel type **6 pt**, and then press Enter (Windows) or Return (Mac OS). The e is shifted upward, 6 points off the baseline.

Apply the baseline shift to the letter.

3   Choose File > Save to save your work.

Changing paragraph attributes

The text formatting you applied earlier in this lesson impacted only the text you had selected. In this part of the lesson, you will work with attributes that are applied to an entire paragraph, including text alignment, spacing, and tabs. Because these attributes apply to an entire paragraph, you do not need to select any text. Simply placing your cursor within a paragraph to be formatted is all that is needed to apply paragraph attributes. The adjustments you will be making are found in the paragraph controls section of the Control panel.

Horizontally aligning text

For most Western languages, text reads from left-to-right, and aligns to the left side of a text frame. You can change the alignment of text so that text aligns to the right side of the frame, is centered, or aligns along both sides of the frame (justified), or have InDesign adjust the alignment depending upon whether the text is on the left or right side of a publication.

1   Press the Pages button (⬚) to open the Pages panel. Double-click page 2 to navigate to it, which also centers this page in the workspace.

2   On page 2, click anywhere in the line of text that reads *Average Cell Phone Usage*. You don't need to highlight the line of text; simply place the cursor in this line.

3   In the Control panel, click the Paragraph Formatting Controls button (¶) to access the paragraph portion of the Control panel.

The paragraph formatting controls.

4   Press the Align Center button (≡) to align the text to the center of the text frame. The text is now centered. Keep the cursor in this text.

Changing the spacing before and after paragraphs

Adding space before or after paragraphs makes each paragraph stand out, and creates a clear transition between ideas and sections. A common mistake is to apply additional returns between paragraphs. Applying additional returns quickly adds space, but the space cannot be easily refined, or made to be consistent between all paragraphs in a single step. Using the space before and space after option provides more control over spacing between paragraphs than simply inserting an additional return.

In this section, you will adjust the spacing between the headline and the list of city names. You will start by placing some extra space after the text *Average Cell Phone Usage*.

1   Using the Type tool (T), click anywhere within the line of text that reads *Average Cell Phone Usage*.

2   In the Control panel, locate the Space After text field (.≡), type **.0625**, and then press Enter (Windows) or Return (Mac OS).

3   Choose File > Save to save your work.

Using tabs

Tabs, or tab stops, are used to align text and insert space between words or numbers. Tabs are inserted into text by pressing the Tab key on the keyboard, and you can then use InDesign to specify exactly where the tab stops should be positioned. A common use of tabs is in a restaurant menu, where menu items are positioned on the left side of the menu, and prices are aligned along the right side of the menu, with a series of periods, or dot leaders, separating the menu items from the prices. Similarly, a Table of Contents at the start of a book such as this one uses tabs to align page numbers and separate the content from the these page numbers. In this exercise, you will use tabs to separate the city name from the average hours of cell phone usage.

1   Using the Type tool (T), select all the text in the Average Cell Phone Usage text frame by clicking in the text frame and choosing Edit > Select All or by clicking five times with your mouse in the text frame.

2   Choose Type > Show Hidden Characters to see the tab, represented by a (>>). You can see that when the text was entered, a tab was placed between the city name and the hours. Choose Type > Hide Hidden Characters to hide these non-printing characters from view. Next you will specify where the tabs should be positioned using the Tabs panel.

3   Choose Type > Tabs to open the Tabs panel. The Tabs panel appears aligned to the top of the selected text frame.

If the Tabs panel is not aligned to the top of the text frame, use the Zoom tool (⊕) to reduce the magnification so that the top of the text frame is fully visible within the workspace. After reducing the magnification, select the Type tool (T), click within the text frame, and select all the text within the frame. In the right-hand corner of the Tabs panel, click the Position Panel above Text Frame button (⌂). You can also use this if you move the Tabs panel or adjust the page magnification. The Position Panel above Text Frame button positions the Tabs panel over the text frame as long as the entire width of the text frame is visible within the workspace.

Understanding the Tabs panel

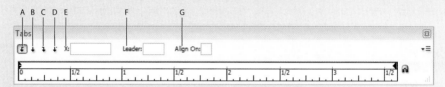

*A. Left-Justified Tab. **B**. Center-Justified Tab. **C**. Right-Justified Tab.*
*D. Align to Decimal (or Other Specified Character) Tab. **E**. X text field.*
*F. Leader text field. **F**. Align On text field.*

InDesign provides four options for aligning tabs. Located at the top-left of the Tabs panel, front left to right, are the Left-Justified Tab (⌄), Center-Justified Tab (⌄), Right-Justified Tab (⌄), and Align to Decimal (or Other Specified Character) Tab (⌄) buttons.

Next to the tab buttons is the X text field which identifies the numerical location of the tab in the layout. The Leader text field specifies any characters used between tab stops, such as a period placing leader dots between tabbed items in a Table of Contents or a list of menu items. The Align On field specifies if a tab aligns on special characters, such as a decimal point to align currency values or a colon to align time values. You can also insert and move tabs visually rather than using the numerical values. To create a tab visually, click directly above the ruler to insert the tab stop, or click and drag an existing tab stop to reposition it. The triangles on the left and right sides of the Tabs panel ruler control the left, right, and first-line indents for the paragraph where the cursor is located.

4 In the Tabs panel, press the Right-Justified Tab button (⬦), then click in the space above the ruler toward the right edge of the tab area. In the selected text, the time values now align to the right of the frame at the location where you placed the tab.

5 Confirm that the tab stop you entered in the previous step is selected. You can see the tab stop positioned above the ruler. Highlight the X value in the Tabs panel and type **3.3611** to specify the exact location for this tab stop. Press Enter (Windows) or Return (Mac OS) to set this as the new location for this tab stop. The text that corresponds to this tab stop is repositioned to the new location.

6 With the tab stop still selected in the ruler, type a period (.) into the Leader text field in the Tabs panel, then press Enter (Windows) or Return (Mac OS). A series of periods now connects the cities with the time values.

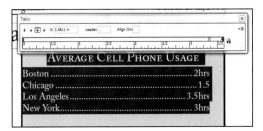

Add leader dots to the listing.

7   Close the Tabs panel, and then choose File > Save to save your work.

Other ways to organize data: Lists and Tables

While this example used tabs to organize the data, there are several other options. You can place data in tables. You can also use bulleted or numbered lists which can be accessed from the Paragraph controls option of the Control panel. After applying bullets or numbers to a list, choose the Bullets (≣) and Numbering (≣) command from the Control panel menu to specify the bullet characters to use, any text that should be placed after the bullet, any indent that should occur, and any character style to use on the bulleted text.

*Another way to organize lists
of data is using bullets and
numbering.*

Creating hanging indents

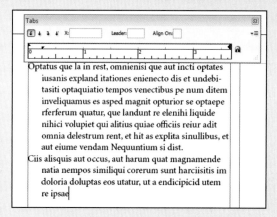

*An example of a hanging indent, where the first line is aligned to
the left of all other text within a paragraph.*

A hanging indent is created when the first line of the paragraph starts at the left margin, but the second and subsequent lines are indented. This is called hanging indentation because the first line hangs out over the rest of the paragraph. To make a hanging indent, make your First line indent a negative value, and the Left indent a positive value.

Adding rules above or below paragraphs

Rules are horizontal lines placed above or below a paragraph. You can use rules to separate paragraphs or call attention to headlines. Rules move with the text to which they are attached, making them different from a line you might draw separately and place on the page. You will add a rule below the words *Average Cell Phone Usage*.

1 Using the Type tool (T), click anywhere inside the text *Average Cell Phone Usage*.

2 Press the panel menu button (▾≡) located at the far-right side of the Control panel, and choose Paragraph Rules from the drop-down menu.

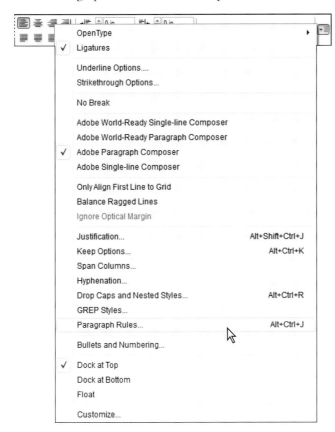

Choose Paragraph Rules from the panel drop-down menu in the Control panel.

3 In the Paragraph Rules dialog box, choose Rule Below from the drop-down menu and select the *Rule On* check box to enable the rule. Select the *Preview* check box in the lower-left corner of the dialog box to see the rule applied. Keep the dialog box open.

The line appears and is automatically aligned relative to the baseline of the text. Next you will examine the offset value, allowing you to move the rule vertically.

4 In the Offset text field, make sure the offset value is set to 0.0625. This shifts the line below the baseline. If the offset is set to 0 it aligns to the baseline, so by giving it a positive offset value, the rules is moved down below the baseline for the headline. A negative value would shift the rule upward.

5 Confirm that Text is chosen from the Width drop-down menu so that the line appears only beneath the selected text. Click OK.

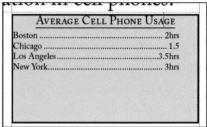

The Paragraph Rules dialog box with the correct settings.

Changing text color

Changing the color of text can make it more visually appealing or stand-out from the text around it. When changing text color, you can adjust either the fill or stroke of the text.

1 Using the Type tool (T), select the words *Average Cell Phone Usage*. Clicking three times with your mouse selects the entire line. Choose Type > Show Hidden Characters to make certain that the paragraph return at the end of the line is also selected. After verifying this, choose Type > Hide Hidden Characters or press Ctrl+Alt+I (Windows) or Command+Options+I (Mac OS).

2 Press the Swatches button (🔠) in the panel docking area to open the Swatches panel. You can also access the Swatches panel by choosing Window > Color > Swatches.

3   In the top-left corner of the Swatches panel, make certain the Fill icon (**T**) is displayed in the foreground. If not, click to select it so that color adjustments affect the fill of the selected object.

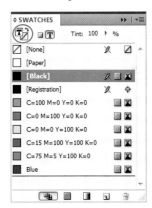

The Fill and Stroke controls in the Swatches panel. Make certain the fill option is selected.

4   With the words *Average Cell Phone Usage* still selected, locate the color Blue in the Swatches panel, and then click to select it. The color of the text is changed. The color of rule below the text is also changed because the rule was specified to be the same color as the text. If the rule color does not change with the text color, make sure that the return at the end of the line was also selected as described in step 1.

Select the blue swatch in the Swatches panel.

5   Choose File > Save to save your work.

Creating drop caps

Drop caps, or initial caps, help to draw a reader's attention to the start of a story. You will create a drop cap for the beginning of a story on the second page of the magazine.

1   Using the Type tool (T), click anywhere in the first paragraph of the story on page 2. You do not need to highlight the text.

2   In the Paragraph Formatting Controls area of the Control panel (¶), locate the Drop Cap Number of Lines text field (⬛) and change the value to **3**. Press Enter (Windows) or Return (Mac OS) to commit the change, causing the first character to become the size of three lines of type.

3   Press the panel menu button (▾≣) located at the far right side of the Control panel and choose Drop Caps and Nested Styles.

4   In the Drop Caps and Nested Styles dialog box, select the *Preview* check box on the right side to view the changes as they are made. Select the *Align Left Edge* check box to align the left edge of the letter I to the edge of the text box, then click OK.

The drop cap's left edge is aligned to the edge of the text box.

Finding and changing text

Finding and changing text automatically can be a big time-saver. You might discover that a product name needs to be changed across an entire document, or that a website address needs to be located and made italic in every location it is used. In both cases, InDesign's Find/Change feature helps to automate the process.

Finding and changing text and text attributes

In this exercise you will make the text *Tech Magazine* bold across the top of each page.

In Lesson 2, "Building Documents with Master Pages," you discovered that a master page could be used to format and adjust an object that is placed in a consistent location across a document. Here we elected to not use a master page, which makes the Find/Change feature especially useful.

1   Choose the Zoom tool (Q) from the Tools panel and increase the magnification on the top of page 2 so that the words *Tech Magazine* are clearly visible. After the words are visible, switch to the Type tool (T).

If you are working with the Type tool and want to temporarily switch to the Zoom tool, press and hold Ctrl+spacebar (Windows) or Command+space bar (Mac OS) to temporarily activate the Zoom tool while working with the Type tool.

2   Choose Edit > Find/Change to open the Find/Change dialog box. In the Find/ Change dialog box, type **Tech Magazine** in the Find what text field. Next you'll identify the changes to make to this text.

3   In the Change Format text field at the bottom of the Find/Change dialog box, press the Specify Attributes to Change button (A). The Change Format Settings dialog box appears.

4   On the left side of the dialog box, choose Basic Character Formats. Select Bold from the Font Style drop-down menu, and then click OK. This changes text that meets the Find criteria to bold.

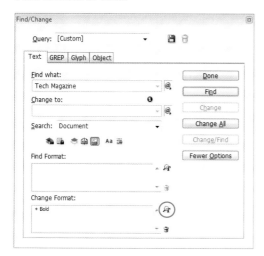

Using Find/Change to find specific text and change its formatting.

You can also search for text based upon style attributes. For example, you can have InDesign locate all text that uses a certain font, style, or color, and have it changed to another font, style, or color. This is accomplished by using the Specify Attributes to Find button in the Find Format section of the Find/Change dialog box. The Find what: and Change to: sections can be left blank when locating or changing only the text formatting.

5   In the Find/Change dialog box, make sure the Search drop-down menu is set to Document so that the entire document is searched. In this example you want to search the entire document, but in other cases you can use this to limit the area being searched.

6   Click Change All. A dialog box appears, indicating that the search is complete and that four replacements were made.

7   Click OK to accept the changes, then click the Done button. All four instances of the words *Tech Magazine* are now bold. If desired, you can scroll or use the Pages panel to navigate to the other pages to confirm the changes.

8   Choose File > Save to save your work.

Finding and changing text using GREP

InDesign offers another powerful option to find and change text and objects in your layout. GREP, or Global Regular Expression Print, makes it possible to search for patterns across your layout and change, organize, or format the text or object.

In this exercise, you'll use GREP to standardize the formatting of phone numbers that appear on the last page of the document.

1   In the Pages panel, double-click page 6 to center the page in the workspace and make it the active page. When the page is displayed, use the Zoom tool to increase the magnification of the Information box in the lower-right corner of the page.

This box lists companies and their phone numbers so that customers can contact them. Notice that the phone numbers have been entered in a variety of formats and are inconsistent. You'll use GREP to make the formatting more consistent.

2   Select the Type tool (T) and select the entries that contain phone numbers. There are a total of five lines to select.

3 Choose Edit > Find/Change to open the Find/Change dialog box, and click the GREP tab to make it active. Confirm that Search area is set to Selection rather than searching the entire document.

4 For this exercise, you'll use a built-in GREP search that is included with InDesign. From the Query drop-down menu, choose Phone Number Conversion (dot format). The Find what and Change to fields are automatically populated.

Choosing a predefined GREP search from the Query drop-down menu.

5 Click the Change All button. A window is displayed, indicating that five replacements have been made. Click OK and notice that all the phone numbers in the information box have been standardized. You can also use GREP to change other items in the text.

6 With the Find/Change dialog box still open, click in the Change to text field and make these changes:

- add parentheses around the $1 text
- replace the period after the number 1 with a space
- replace the remaining period with a hyphen.

The text in the Change to field should read: **($1) $2–$3**. Click the Change All button. A window appears indicating that five replacements have been made. Click OK, then click Done.

The GREP expression used in the Find/Change dialog box and the text after applying the GREP search.

GREP explained

In the GREP exercises that you performed in this lesson, you may have noticed the characters in the Find what and Change to fields. These characters tell InDesign what pattern to detect and how to change the text. In the Find what section of the Find/Change window, the string of characters starts with the following:

$$\backslash(?(\backslash d\backslash d\backslash d)\backslash)?[-.]$$

The beginning part of this text string \(is used to search for a specific character when using GREP. The backslash is an escape character and it forces GREP to search for the character immediately following it. In this case the \(is searching for an open parenthesis.

The question mark ? that follows the open parenthesis indicates that the parenthesis may or may not be there. If it exists, GREP acknowledges it and will adjust it based upon your instructions. If the search doesn't turn-up the character being searched for, then GREP ignores it. This is like telling InDesign "You may or may not find a left parenthesis."

The next section (\d\d\d) is looking for three numeric digits in a row. These three digits are wrapped in parentheses so that they can be protected when the change is performed.

The next three characters \)? are similar to the start of the search, except in this case GREP is looking for a closing parenthesis that may or may not be there instead of the opening parenthesis that was searched for at the start.

Finally, [-.] looks for a hyphen, a period, or a space. Any one will be acceptable. The remainder of the expression is just a repeated variation on the first section.

Now in the Change to field is $1.$2.$3. Each $ followed by a number is a variable. $1 is capturing whatever was found in the first section of text that was surrounded by parentheses—in this case (\d\d\d). So whatever numbers GREP found as those first three digits, it will retain in the change expression, keeping the found numbers and the changed numbers the same. Any characters can be placed between the groups of $1, $2, and $3 as these represent the parts of the phone number. The default option places a period between these groups.

Checking and correcting spelling

Checking spelling is an important part of creating a professional-looking document, and InDesign has several options to help you prevent and correct spelling mistakes and simple typographical errors.

The Dynamic Spelling and Autocorrect options alert you to misspelled words and can automatically change them for you. In this exercise, you will take a closer look at the ability to find and change words across an entire document or group of documents.

Checking spelling

InDesign can help you locate misspelled words, repeated words, uncapitalized words, and uncapitalized sentences.

1   In the Pages panel, double-click page 2 to center the page in the workspace.

2   Select the Type tool (T) from the Tools panel, and then click anywhere in the headline at the top of page 2 that reads *What is the next inovation in cell phones?*.

The word *innovation* is intentionally misspelled to help you gain an understanding of InDesign's the spell-checking capabilities.

3   Choose Edit > Spelling > Check Spelling. The Check Spelling dialog box appears.

4   Select Story from the Search drop-down menu at the bottom of the dialog box so that only this text frame is searched. A story is the InDesign term for a text frame and any other text frames that are linked to it. The Check Spelling dialog box is displayed.

5   *Inovation* is displayed at the top of the Check Spelling dialog box under the Not in Dictionary category. The correctly spelled innovation appears in the Suggested Corrections field. Select the correct spelling, innovation, and then click Change.

Checking and correcting spelling.

Because InDesign has completed spell-checking the story, the Start and Done buttons are both available. The Start button would recheck the story, while Done closes the Check Spelling dialog box.

6   Click Done.

Adding words to the dictionary

You can add words to the dictionary so they are not listed as incorrectly spelled, such as proper names, or business-specific terms that should be ignored when checking spelling.

1 Using the Type tool (T), insert the cursor at the very beginning of the first paragraph at the top of page 2.

2 Choose Edit > Spelling > Check Spelling.

In the Not in Dictionary section, *Blippa* appears. This is the name of a new product that appears throughout this document.

3 Click Add to place *Blippa* in the user dictionary, and then click Done.

Adding a word to the dictionary.

You can add or remove words from your user dictionary by choosing Edit > Spelling > User Dictionary. You can add or remove individual words, or use the Import option to import a list of words to add to the dictionary.

4   Choose File > Save to save your work.

Creating a centralized user dictionary

You can create a central user dictionary to share with colleagues so that all workers in your office or team don't need to create their own dictionary.

To create and share a dictionary, choose Edit > Preferences > Dictionary (Windows), or InDesign > Preferences > Dictionary (Mac OS). Click the New User Dictionary button (⊒). When the New User Dictionary dialog box appears, name the new dictionary. The location and name of the new dictionary file appear listed under the Language drop-down menu.

After adding your commonly used words to the new dictionary, access the new dictionary file on another user's InDesign program using the Add User Dictionary button (⊕) in their Preferences > Dictionary dialog box and specifying the location of the user dictionary file that you created.

Checking spelling as you type

InDesign's Dynamic Spelling can help you avoid spelling errors by checking spelling as you type. Words not found in the InDesign dictionaries are marked with a red underline in your layout. If you use word processing applications such as Microsoft Word, this will look familiar to you.

1   Press the Pages button (⊞) in the dock to open the Pages panel. Locate page 3 and double-click the page 3 icon to center the page in the workspace.

2   Using the Type tool (T), click inside the text frame containing the headline *When is the best time to update equpment?*

3 Choose Edit > Spelling > Dynamic Spelling to activate the Dynamic Spelling feature. A red line appears under the word *equpment*. This may take a moment to occur, as InDesign will review the entire document once Dynamic Spelling is enabled.

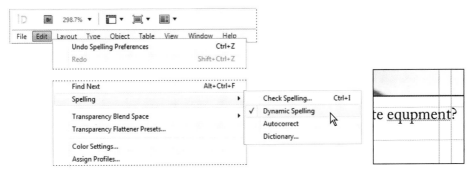

Accessing Dynamic Spelling through the Edit menu.   *Dynamic Spelling turned on.*

4 Right-click (Windows) or Control+click (Mac OS) the word *equpment*. A list of suggested corrections appears in the contextual menu. Choose the word *equipment* from the list, and the misspelled word is corrected.

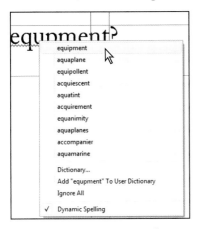

Replacing a word using Dynamic Spelling.

5 Disable Dynamic Spelling by choosing Edit > Spelling > Dynamic Spelling.

Automatically correcting spelling

You can use the Autocorrect feature to correct commonly misspelled words and typographical errors as you type. For example, if you type **hte** when you intend to type **the**, you can have InDesign automatically correct this error as you enter text while typing. You will now enable Autocorrect and add a word to the list of those that are automatically corrected.

1   Using the Pages panel, navigate to page 2 by double-clicking the page 2 icon.

2   Choose Edit > Preferences > Autocorrect (Windows), or InDesign > Preferences > Autocorrect (Mac OS).

3   When the Preferences dialog box appears, select the *Enable Autocorrect* check box, if it is not already selected.

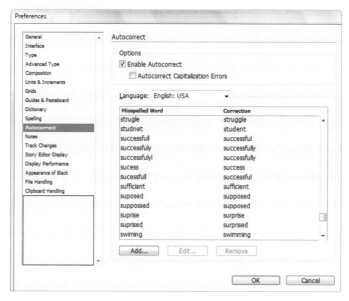

The Autocorrect Preferences dialog box.

4   Click the Add button at the bottom of the dialog box to add your own word to be automatically corrected.

5   In the Add to Autocorrect List dialog box, type **useage** in the Misspelled Word text field, and **usage** in the Correction text field.

This provides InDesign with the incorrect spelling that should be changed and the correct spelling that should be used instead.

Entering a word into Autocorrect.

6   Click OK, then click OK again to close the Preferences dialog box.

7 In the *Average Cell Phone Usage* text frame on page 2, highlight the word Usage and delete it from the text frame. You will now retype this word, intentionally spelling it incorrectly.

8 Type **Useage**, and then press the spacebar. The Autocorrect feature corrects the misspelled word. Press the Backspace (Windows) or Delete (Mac OS) key to remove the extra space.

Editing text using the Story Editor

Sometimes it is easier to view the text separately from the layout. Instead of following text across multiple text frames, or across different pages, it can be easier to edit text in one window. You can use the Story Editor to more easily work with text in one window, even if it is linked across multiple pages or text frames.

The Story Editor also displays text that does not fit into existing frames, known as overset text. Overset text is indicated by a red plus sign that appears at the bottom-right corner of a frame when there is more text than fits into the frame.

1 In the Pages panel, double-click on page 5 to center the page in the workspace. Using the Type tool (T), click anywhere inside the text frame on page 5 containing the story.

2 Choose Edit > Edit in Story Editor to open the Story Editor window and view the entire story across several pages.

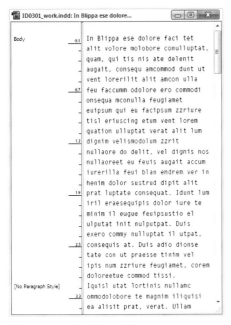

Viewing text using the Story Editor.

3   Use the scroll bar on the right side of the window to navigate to the bottom of the story and see any overset text that does not fit into the text frame.

The Story Editor identifies overset text, which does not fit in the current text frames.

4   Highlight the overset text and delete it, then close the Story Editor.

While the overset text was simply deleted in this example, there are several other ways in which overset text is typically addressed. Making edits to the existing story can create room for the text to fit into the existing text frames. Creating additional space by adding new text frames or enlarging the existing frames can also eliminate overset text. Similarly, linking the text to a new frame can give the overset text a page onto which it can be displayed. You can also reduce the size of the text, decrease the leading, or adjust the tracking so that more text fits in the same area.

5   Notice that the red plus sign at the end of the text frame has disappeared, indicating that there is no longer any overset text.

6   Choose File > Save to save your work.

Using Track Changes

If you collaborate with other users, you may find Track Changes useful for displaying changes that have been made to the text in your documents. You can use it to view changes and also approve or reject changes made by others.

1   If, necessary, click the Pages panel button to display it, and double-click the page 3 icon. Zoom in on the text frame below the photo.

2   Choose Window > Editorial > Track Changes to display the Track Changes panel.

Use the Track Changes panel to see edits made to text in your documents.

3 Select the Type tool (T), and click anywhere within the text frame on page 3.

4 Click on the Enable Track Changes in Current Story button (◉). This enables the Track Changes feature for the current story only.

You can enable all stories at once by choosing the option from the Track Changes panel menu (◦≡).

5 Highlight the word *ultimate* and change it to **best**. Also, highlight the word *update* and change it to **replace**.

Although Track Changes is enabled, the current view shows the revised text and doesn't provide any indication that the text has been modified. To see the original and updated text, you will switch from the layout view to the Story Editor.

6 Choose Edit > Edit in Story Editor to display the Story Editor. Note that all the text changes made within this story are highlighted.

Changes highlighted in the Story Editor.

7 Click at the very beginning of the text in the Story Editor and then click the Next Change button (➜) in the Track Changes panel to highlight the first change displayed in the current story. The word *best* is highlighted.

8 Click the Accept Change button (✔) to accept the insertion of the word *best* into the final text of the story.

9 Click the Next Change button again to highlight the next change, which is the deletion of the word *ultimate*.

10 This time, press and hold the Alt key (Windows) or Option key (Mac OS) when accepting the change. The next change is automatically highlighted in the Story Editor. The word *replace* is highlighted.

11 To change this word to its original state press and hold the Alt key (Windows) or Option key (Mac OS) and then click the Reject Change button (✘) to reject the change and automatically highlight the next change.

12 Finally, click the Reject Change button to reject the deletion of the word *update*.

After accepting or rejecting changes in the Story Editor, the changes are displayed in layout view. Any changes made to the text in your document appear in the layout view, whether the changes have been accepted or not. The Track Changes feature allows you to monitor the changes and revert to the original text, but the text revisions are displayed immediately in the layout view.

13 Close the Story Editor window and the Track Changes panel. View the final text as it appears in your document layout.

Drag-and-drop text editing

When editing text, it can be faster to use your mouse to move text instead of using menu commands to cut, copy, and paste it. Here you will use drag-and-drop text editing to highlight words or characters, and then drag them to a different location. You can use this option in both the Story Editor and in layout view, although you need to enable this option in layout view, as it is turned off by default.

1 Choose Edit > Preferences > Type (Windows), or InDesign > Preferences > Type (Mac OS).

2 When the Type Preferences dialog box appears, in the Drag and Drop Text Editing section, select the *Enable in layout view* check box, then click OK.

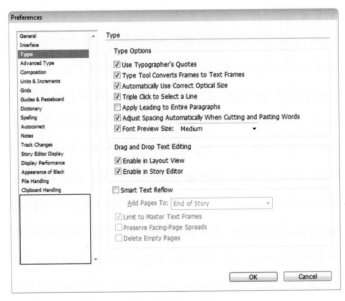

Enabling Drag and Drop text editing in the layout view.

3 Navigate to the headline on page 5. Click and drag to select the words *cell phone*, without the *s*, in the headline. With the text selected, click and drag the highlighted words so that they are placed before the word *innovation*. Release the mouse to relocate these words.

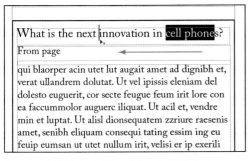

Once text is highlighted, click and drag the highlighted text to a new location to reposition it.

4 Delete the word *in* and also the letter *s*. Also add a space after *phone*, if necessary. The question mark now follows the word *innovation*.

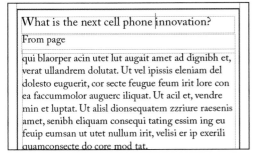

The final text after editing.

5 Choose File > Save to save your work.

Special characters and glyphs

You can use the Glyphs panel in InDesign to see all the characters, known as *glyphs*, within every font. This makes it easy for you to easily access symbols such as those used for dollars, cents, bullets, copyrights, and registered trademark, without needing to remember the appropriate keystrokes. You will use the Glyphs panel to add a trademark symbol to the words *Tech Magazine*, and you will then use the Find/Change feature to add the symbol to all instances of the name throughout the layout.

1 Choose the Zoom tool (🔍) from the Tools panel and increase the magnification so you can clearly see the words *Tech Magazine* in the top text frame on page 5.

2 Choose the Type tool (T) from the Tools panel and click after the word *Magazine* to insert the cursor.

3 Choose Type > Glyphs to open the Glyphs panel. From the Show drop-down menu, choose Symbols and scroll down until you see the trademark glyph (™).

4 In the Glyphs panel, double-click the trademark symbol to place it after the word *Magazine*.

Insert the trademark glyph from the Glyphs panel into the text.

The symbol after it is placed into the layout.

5 Using the Type tool, highlight the word Magazine along with the trademark glyph you just inserted.

6 Choose Edit > Copy to copy these characters.

7 Choose Edit > Find/Change to open the Find/Change dialog box. Click on the Text tab to make it active.

8 In the Find what: text field, type **Magazine**.

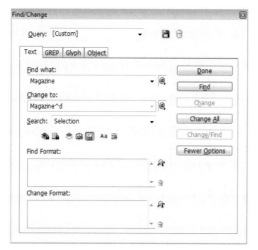

Find the word Magazine, and change it to include the trademark symbol.

9 Click inside the Change to text field and choose Edit > Paste. The notation for the symbol is pasted.

10 Click the Clear Specified Attributes icon (🗑) to the right of the Change Format section to remove these attributes.

This is necessary because the Bold attribute remained from a previous use of the Find/Change dialog box.

11 Make sure that Document is chosen from the Search drop-down menu and click Change All. A dialog box appears, indicating that the search is complete and that five changes have been made. Click OK.

12 Click Done. All instances of the words *Tech Magazine* now include a trademark symbol.

13 Delete the extra trademark symbol from the Tech Magazine text on page 5, and then choose File > Save to save your work.

Using the Glyphs panel and glyph sets

You can use the Glyphs panel to create a set of commonly used glyphs, making it easy to access the special characters and symbols you use most frequently.

1 In the Glyphs panel, press the panel menu button (▾≡), and then choose New Glyph Set. In the New Glyph Set dialog box, type **Adobe Caslon Pro** in the Name text field. Leave the Insert Order drop-down menu at its default, and then click OK.

Creating a new glyph set.

2 In the Glyphs panel, select the trademark symbol, if it is not already selected. Click the panel menu button and choose Add to Glyph Set; then choose Adobe Caslon Pro from the menu that appears.

3   In the Glyphs panel, click the Show drop-down menu, and choose Adobe Caslon Pro from the top of the list. You can add as many glyphs as you need to this glyph set. You can add different glyphs from various fonts to a set. You may prefer to add only glyphs from one font to each glyph set so that you are certain that you are inserting the correct version of a glyph whenever you use the glyph set.

Use a custom glyph set to easily access commonly used symbols and characters.

4   Close the Glyphs panel.

Text frame options

Use text frame formatting options to control the vertical alignment of type, the distance text is inset from the edge of the frame, and the number of columns inside a text frame. Some of these options are accessible only within the Text Frame Option dialog box, while others are also accessible in the Control panel. In this exercise, you will change some of the text frame options for a text frame on page 2.

Adjusting text inset

Inside the *Average Cell Phone Usage* text frame, the text touches the side of the text frame. You will adjust the position of the text relative to the frame on the outside edge of the frame.

1   In the Pages panel, double-click the page 2 icon to center the page on the workspace.

2   Using the Type tool (T), click inside the *Average Cell Phone Usage* text frame on page 2.

3   Choose Object > Text Frame Options to access the Text Frame Options dialog box.

The keyboard shortcut to open the Text Frame Options dialog box is Ctrl+B (Windows) or Command+B (Mac OS).

4   When the Text Frame Options dialog box appears, make sure the Make all settings the same button (⦿) in the Inset Spacing section is selected.

5   In the Top text field, highlight the current value, and then type **.125**. Press the Tab key, and the cursor moves to the next text field. Click to select the *Preview* check box, and notice the text is pushed in from the edge of the frame by .125 inches.

6   Click OK. The text has moved and is no longer touching the sides of the frame.

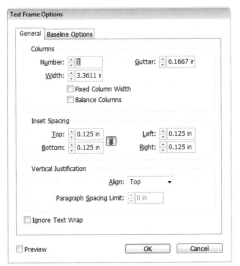

Setting a text inset.

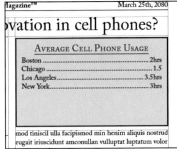

The text inset from the edge of the text frame.

Vertically aligning text

You can align text inside a frame both horizontally and vertically. With vertical alignment, you determine whether text aligns with the top, bottom, or center of a frame. You can also justify the type so that multiple lines of type are evenly distributed between the top and bottom of a text frame.

1   With the Selection tool (⬂) active, click to select the text frame containing the text *Average Cell Phone Usage*.

2   Choose Object > Text frame options. In the Vertical Justification section, choose Justify from the Align drop-down menu.

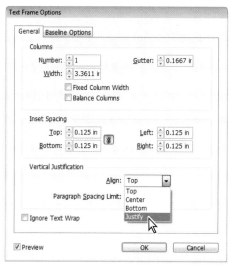

Use text frame options to set the text to be vertically justified.

You can also access the Text Frame Options dialog box by pressing and holding the Alt (Windows) or Option (Mac OS) key and double-clicking the text frame. Or use the keyboard shortcut Ctrl+B (Windows) or Command+B (Mac OS).

3   Click OK. Notice that the text now snaps to the top and bottom of the frame, although the text inset remains.

4   Choose File > Save to save your work.

Automatic sizing of text frames

You can also specify that InDesign increases the width or height of columns as you enter additional text. Do this in the text frame options by selecting the text frame and choosing Object > Text Frame Options and specifying whether you want the text frame to grow in height, width, or both as additional text is added to the frame.

Importing text

There are three ways to flow text into an InDesign document: You can flow text manually, and link the text boxes yourself. You can also flow text semi-automatically, and you can automatically flow text into your InDesign document so that new frames and pages are created for you.

Flowing text manually

In this first exercise, you will manually flow text and practice threading text between frames.

1   In the Pages panel, locate and navigate to page 3 by double-clicking the page 3 icon, then choose Edit > Deselect All to make certain nothing is selected.

2   Choose File > Place. In the Place dialog box, navigate to the id03lessons folder, select the id0301.doc file, make sure *Show Import Options* is checked, and click Open. The Microsoft Word Import Options dialog box appears because this text file was created using Microsoft Word.

3   In the Microsoft Word Import Options dialog box, confirm that the *Remove Styles and Formatting from Text and Tables* option is selected, and directly under this option, that *Preserve Local Overrides* is not checked. Click OK to close the dialog box.

This keeps styles used in the Microsoft Word document from being accidentally imported into your InDesign layout.

If you accidentally flow text into your previously selected frame, choose Edit > Undo.

4   A preview of the file you are importing is displayed inside the cursor. The cursor previews the first few sentences of text being imported. Click just below the headline text frame and the imported text from the Microsoft Word document fills the column.

Flowing text into a column.

You can also create text frames at the time you import by clicking and dragging with the loaded cursor. The size of the frame is determined by how large or small a frame you draw. You can also create multiple frames in a single step by pressing the up-arrow on the keyboard to create additional frames stacked vertically, or press the right-arrow on the keyboard to split the frames horizontally. After pressing the up- or right-arrow you can press the other to split the frames again at the time you are creating them, or press the left- or down-arrow to reduce the number of frames.

You have successfully placed a story in the first column, but there is more type than fits into this frame. You can tell this because a red plus sign appears in the bottom-right corner of the text frame indicating that there is overset text. In the next exercise, you will thread the text from this frame to another frame, creating a link where the story will continue.

Threading text between frames

You can flow text between columns, pages, and between different text frames. At the top-left corner of a text frame is the In Port, which indicates if text flows into the frame from another location. At the bottom-right corner is the Out Port which indicates if text flows to another frame or if there is more text than fits within the frame. You will use the Out Port to thread it to another frame.

Anatomy of a text frame

A. In port. B. Handles for resizing text frame. C. Out port.

The arrow within the In Port or Out Port indicates that text flows from another frame. With a text frame selected, choose View > Show Text Threads to display links connected to the selected frame. The arrow shows that text continues in another frame or from another frame, depending upon the port. The Out Port may also display a red plus sign (+), indicating that there is overset text that does not fit in the frame, or it may be empty, indicating that all text fits within this frame.

1   Choose the Selection tool (⬈) from the Tools panel.

2   Click the red plus sign in the bottom-right corner of the text frame. This is the Out Port, and the red plus sign indicates that there is overset text that does not fit in this frame. After clicking the Out Port, the cursor is ready to link to another text frame so that the story can continue in a different location in the document.

The Out Port showing overset text.

3   Move the cursor under the headline to the top-left side of the second column. Click and drag from the top-left side of the column down to the bottom-right side of the column. The two text frames are now linked because you created the second text frame after clicking the out port in the first text frame.

4   If the links between the text frames are not showing, choose View > Extras > Show Text Threads. InDesign displays the link between the two frames. Choose View > Extras > Hide Text Threads to stop displaying the linked frames. Linked frames are visible when one of the frames in the link is selected.

5   Choose File > Save to save your work.

Using semi-autoflow to link several text frames

Clicking the out port for each individual text frame may work on smaller documents, but it is not efficient for longer documents. Fortunately you can place text into one frame, then move to the next frame to continue linking without clicking the out port. This allows you to link multiple text frames without needing to click the Out Port of each frame. To achieve this, press and hold the Alt (Windows) or Option (Mac OS) key when importing text into the first frame, or after linking text from a text frame, as you will see in the following exercise.

1   In the Pages panel, double-click the page 4 icon to center the page in the workspace.

2   Choose the Selection tool (⬈) from the Tools panel and click anywhere in the pasteboard to make sure that there is nothing selected, or choose Edit > Deselect All.

3   Choose File > Place. In the Place dialog box, navigate to the id03lessons folder and select the id0302.doc file. Deselect the *Show Import Options* check box, and then click Open.

4   With the loaded cursor ready to place text, press and hold the Alt (Windows) or Option (Mac OS) key on your keyboard, and then click in the first column, just below the headline. Release the Alt or Option key.

The text flows into the first column and the cursor is automatically loaded so you can link the first column to another frame without clicking the Out Port.

5 In the second column, click and drag to draw a new frame below the image of the Data Center Server. The text flows into the new frame.

You can also have InDesign automatically add columns and pages as needed by pressing and holding the Shift key while clicking with a loaded cursor that is ready to flow text into your layout. When you automatically flow text, InDesign creates new frames based on where you click inside the margin guides. InDesign automatically generates enough frames to flow all the text based on the column guides defined for each page.

Linking to an existing text frame

If you have an existing frame that you want to link text into, first click the Out Port in the frame containing the overset text. Then move the cursor over the existing text frame and click anywhere within the frame.

Linking the text to a new frame.

Changing the number of columns in a text frame

You can change the size and shape of a text frame at any time. In this exercise, you will make a new text frame, and then resize it.

1 Choose the Selection tool (▶). Click to select the frame you created in the previous exercise, located on the right side of the page below the image. Press the Delete key to delete only this frame. The first column displays the symbol for overset text.

2 Continuing to use the Selection tool, click to select the text frame in the first column. Move the cursor to the right side of the frame and locate the white dot located at the halfway point of the right side of the frame. The white dot is a handle. Click, hold, and drag the handle to the right. As you drag the handle, the column expands so that it overlaps the picture and extends to the right side of the page.

Release the mouse when the text spans the entire width of the page. You will divide this single text frame into two columns.

3 Choose the Type tool (T) from the Tools panel. In the Paragraph Formatting Options section of the Control panel, type **2** for the number of columns (▥), then press Enter (Windows) or Return (Mac OS).

4 Continuing to work in the Paragraph Formatting Options section of the Control panel, type **.167 in** in the gutter field (▦), which sets the distance between the columns. Press Enter/Return.

*Setting the number of columns
and gutter distance.*

The text does not flow over the image because the image has text wrap applied to it, causing the text to flow around the image. See Lesson 5, "Working with Graphics," for more on text wrap.

5 Choose File > Save to save your work.

Flexible columns

You can have InDesign determine the number of columns that are needed in a text frame rather than specifying an exact number of columns, and InDesign can even determine the width of the columns. Do this by selecting a text frame and then choosing Object > Text Frame Options. In the Text Frame Options dialog box, choose one of the following options from the Columns drop-down menu to have InDesign automatically determine the number of columns to fit into a text frame:

Fixed Width causes InDesign to generate as many columns as fit into the text frame, with all text frames maintaining a specified width.

Flexible Width causes InDesign to create columns that fit between the minimum and maximum size you specify for the columns. If the text frame becomes larger, the columns will be made larger until they reach their maximum size—at which point a new column will be added.

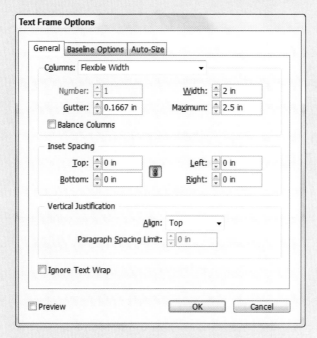

Specifying flexible column width using the Text Frame Options controls.

Spanning and splitting columns

You can specify that text in a layout span across columns that are part of a text frame. You could use for a headline, or you could also split a text column into additional columns. You can control spanning or splitting of columns in the Paragraph controls portion of the control panel.

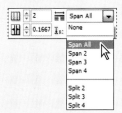

Text can span across columns or be split into additional columns.

Baseline grid

If you create documents with multiple columns, you can use the baseline grid to align the text across the different columns. In this part of the lesson, you will display the baseline grid, change the grid settings, and align the text to the baseline grid.

Viewing and changing the baseline grid

1   To view the baseline grid, choose View > Grids & Guides > Show Baseline Grid.

The baseline grid guides may not be visible when viewing the document at a magnification less than 100 percent. If the baseline grid is not displaying after selecting the Show Baseline Grid command, increase the magnification at which you are viewing the document.

The baseline grid displays horizontal lines across the page at increments you can define. You can specify that text aligns to the grid lines.

If you plan to have text align to the baseline grid, the grid should be spaced at least at the value as used for leading for the body copy. Defining the leading values for text was discussed earlier in this lesson. In this exercise, you will adjust the spacing for the document's baseline grid.

2   Select the Type tool (T) from the Tools panel and click in the body text in either of the columns on page 4.

3 In the Control panel, press the Character Formatting Controls button (A); notice that the Leading (⫯A̧) is set to 14.4 pt. You will use this this value for the baseline grid, which is controlled using the Baseline Grid Preferences.

4 Choose Edit > Preferences > Grids (Windows), or InDesign > Preferences > Grids (Mac OS). In the Baseline Grid section of the Grids Preferences dialog box, type **14.4 pt** in the Increment Every text field. Click OK to close the Preferences dialog box.

Although this step establishes the value for the grid, you have not yet specified that the text needs to align to the grid. In the next part of this exercise, you will align the text to the baseline grid.

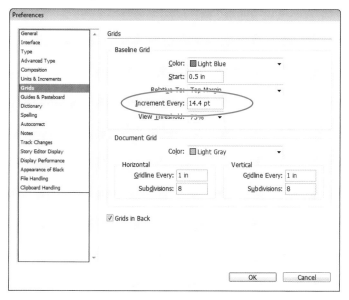

Specifying the spacing for the baseline grid.

5 Making certain that the cursor is still in the body text, choose Edit > Select All, then press the Paragraph Formatting Controls button (¶) in the Control panel.

6 In the Control panel, press the Align to Baseline Grid button (≣). The selected text in both columns aligns to the baseline grid. Aligning to the baseline grid is defined on a paragraph-by-paragraph basis, which is why the different paragraphs needed to be selected before specifying the text should align to the grid.

7 Choose View > Grids & Guides > Hide Baseline Grid, and then choose File > Save to save your work.

Adding story jumps

If you create documents with text that flows from one page to another, you will want to direct the reader to the location where a story continues. Rather than manually entering the page number where each story continues, InDesign makes it easy to automatically tell your readers where stories continue.

You will use a page marker on page 2 of this document, helping readers to see that a story continues on page 5. We've created text frames for you to enter the marker that will specify where the text continues. In this exercise, you will enter in the marker that automatically reflects where text continues and see how InDesign displays the linked page information.

1   In the Pages panel, navigate to page 2 by double-clicking the page 2 icon.

2   Select the Type tool (T) from the Tools panel and place the cursor in the text frame located in the lower-right corner of page 2, directly after the words "Please see page".

3   Press the spacebar once to put a space between the word "page" and the marker you will insert to specify where the story continues.

4   Choose Type > Insert Special Character > Markers > Next Page Number. This marker displays the number 5. For the page marker to function, the text frame containing the marker needs to be touching a text frame that flows to another text frame on a different page. Now you will add the page marker on page 5, specifying where the story originates.

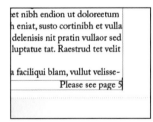

The text frame with the Next Page marker.

5   In the lower-left corner of the workspace, click the page drop-down menu to navigate to page 5. You can use this method or use the Pages panel if you prefer to navigate to page 5 in the layout.

6   Using the Type tool, place the cursor after the words *From page*.

7   Press the spacebar to put a space between the words and the marker.

8   Choose Type > Insert Special Character > Markers > Previous Page Number. The number 2 appears because the text in the adjacent frame is linked from page 2.

9   Choose File > Save to save your work.

Linked stories and collected content

You can take the text in one part of an InDesign document and link it to another part of the same document or to a different document altogether. This can be useful if you are using InDesign to create multiple versions of a document, such as a brochure and a data sheet that both describe the same item. Similarly, you can create one layout for print and another for a digital version of a document. To link a story in an InDesign document, follow these steps:

1   Using the Type tool, place the cursor anywhere within a text frame that contains text. Make sure the document has been saved.

2   Choose Edit > Place and Link. You can also use the Content Collector tool (📑), located in the Tools panel, to gather linked content.

3   Move the cursor to the page where you want the text to be repeated and click. This can be in the same document or in a different InDesign document. If you used the Content Collector tool to gather the content to be linked, then use the Content Placer tool (📑) to place the content into the same or a different InDesign document.

If you make changes to the original text or object that has been collected, the linked frames indicate that the original has changed by displaying a yellow triangle in the upper-left corner of the frame. Double-click this triangle or use the Links panel to display the most recent version of the file. While this example illustrates text being used, other objects such as images can be collected and linked across various InDesign layouts.

Using styles to format text

Styles save time when you're working with text that shares the same look and feel across a document. If you decide that your body text should be a different size or font, styles let you make the change in one location, avoiding the need to make changes on every page. Additionally, styles make it easy to keep a consistent design, as you can use styles to apply multiple text attributes in a single click. A more complete discussion of styles occurs in the next lesson, Lesson 4, "Working with Styles."

Creating a headline and applying a style

In this exercise, you will create a style and apply it to a headline.

1   In the Pages panel, double-click the page 2 icon.

2   Select the Type tool (T) from the Tools panel.

3   Select the text in the headline *What is the next innovation in cell phones?*

4   Choose Type > Paragraph Styles or click the Paragraph Styles button in the panel docking area. The Paragraph Styles panel opens.

---

5   Press the panel menu button (⁃≣) in the upper corner of the Paragraph Styles panel and choose New Paragraph Style. In the Style Name text field, type **Headline**, and then click OK.

The new style contains the text attributes from where the cursor was located when you created the new style, including font, style, color, and spacing.

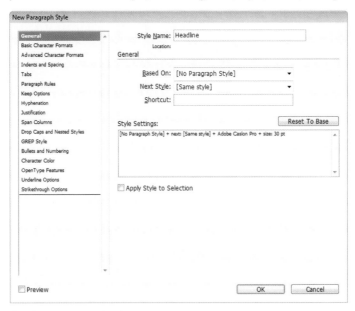

Creating a new paragraph style.

6   Select the Headline style in the Paragraph Styles panel to apply the style to the text. The appearance of the text does not change, but the text is now attached to the style. If the style is updated, the appearance of this headline will also update.

When you create a new style, you can also have InDesign apply it to the current selection. In the General section of the New Paragraph Style dialog box, select the Apply Style to Selection check box.

7   On page 3, click to place the cursor in the headline *When is the best time to update equipment?* In the Paragraph Styles panel, select the Headline style to apply it. The headline is formatted with the paragraph style you created.

Importing styles from other documents

You can import styles from one InDesign document to another, making it possible to share formatting across various documents. In this exercise, you will import a Drop Cap style from another document and use the style in this document.

1 In the Paragraph Styles panel, press the panel menu button (▾≡) and choose Load Paragraph Styles. You will locate a file from which to import a style.

2 In the Open a File dialog box, navigate to the id03lessons folder and select the id0301_done.indd file. Click Open. The Load Styles dialog box appears.

3 In the Load Styles dialog box, click the Uncheck All button to deselect all the styles, because you will only import one specific style. Select the *Drop Cap* check box to select only this one style.

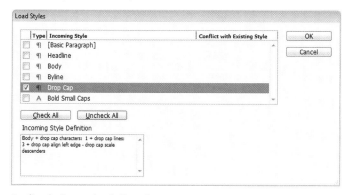

Loading the Paragraph style Drop Cap.

4 Click OK. Drop Cap is now added to the styles in the Paragraph Styles panel in your document. In the next exercise, you will update an existing style, and then apply the Drop Cap style.

Redefining styles

You will now update the Body paragraph style to contain a new attribute, which will align the text to the baseline grid you specified earlier in this lesson.

1 Navigate or scroll to view page 2.

2 Choose the Type tool (T) and click in the text frame containing the story on page 2; then choose Edit > Select All.

3 Select the Body style in the Paragraph Styles panel to apply this style to all the selected paragraphs.

4 If a plus sign appears next to the style name, press and hold the Alt (Windows) or Option (Mac OS) key and select the style name again. This removes any formatting changes that have been made since the style was applied.

Changes made to text after a style has been applied are known as overrides. If you edit a style attribute outside the Paragraph Styles panel, the style is manually overridden, and a plus sign displays next to the style name in the styles panel. If you place your cursor over the style in the Paragraph Styles panel without clicking, and pause, a tooltip appears. The tooltip identifies which attribute is causing the override.

Applying the Body style.

5 In the Paragraph Formatting Controls section of the Control panel, click the Align to Baseline Grid button (☰).

6 In the Paragraph Styles panel notice that a plus sign (+) is displayed next to the style name. This plus sign indicates that the style was changed after it was applied to this text. You changed the text by aligning it to the baseline grid—something that was not part of the original style definition. Next you will change the style so it includes this change as part of the definition of this style, and all text using this style will include this modification.

7 In the Paragraph Styles panel, click the panel menu or right-click (Windows) Control+click (Mac OS) on the style name, and choose Redefine Style. All the text styled with the Body style now aligns to the baseline grid.

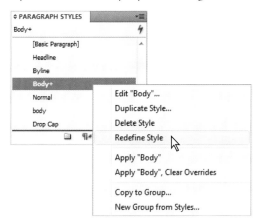

Redefining the Body style.

8 Click anywhere in the first paragraph of the story. In the Paragraph Styles panel, click to select the Drop Cap style. The first paragraph is now formatted with the Drop Cap style, and the rest of the story is formatted using the Body style.

9 Choose File > Save to save your work.

Placing text on a path

Text placed on a path can follow a line or shape, such as the outline of a circle or an arc.

1 In the Pages panel, double-click page 4 and navigate to the logo at the top of the page. If necessary, increase the magnification to zoom-in on the logo containing a green arrow using the Zoom tool (🔍).

2 Notice that there is an oval surrounding the word *Tech* in this logo. The logo should read *High Tech Corner.* You will place the word *High* on the oval.

3 Click and hold the Type tool (T) in the Tools panel until the hidden tools are revealed, then choose the Type on a Path tool (꙰).

4   Move your cursor over the top center of the oval until you see a plus sign appear next to the cursor, and then click once.

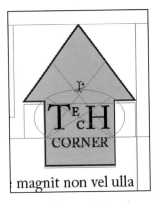

*The cursor changes to indicate that you
are able to place text on the path.*

5   Type **HIGH**, and then highlight the text using the Type on a Path tool by clicking and dragging or double-clicking to select the word.

6   In the Paragraph Formatting Controls section of the Control panel, press the Align Center button (☰). You will adjust the exact position of the text in the next steps, as the text may be positioned upside-down or along the bottom of the circle.

7   Choose the Selection tool (➤) from the Tools panel. Notice that there are two vertical handles that appear directly to the left of where you clicked on the path. These are handles and they mark the starting and ending points for the text on the path.

8   Select the left-most vertical handle that appears along the path and drag it clockwise, stopping when the line is centered between the top and bottom half on the right side of the oval—where the 3 o'clock location would be on a clock. If the text moves so that it is placed inside the oval as you are moving the handle, choose Edit > Undo and repeat the process, carefully following the oval as you drag clockwise. Be careful to not click the boxes when you move the handles, as these boxes are the In and Out Ports, which are used for flowing text into and out of the path.

9   Take the handle that marks the starting point of the text and drag it counterclockwise, positioning it so it is centered along the left half of the oval—where the 9 o'clock location would be on a clock.

Because you had already centered the text, aligning the start and end points of the text to the opposite sides of the circle lets you know that the text is centered correctly.

The new start and end points of the text.

10 Choose File > Save to save your work.

To center text on a path you can also click the bottom of the circle using the Type on a Path tool (↙). This causes text to start and end at the bottom of the shape and you can quickly center the text by simply setting the paragraph alignment to align center.

Importing text from Microsoft Word

You've already seen that you can import text from Microsoft Word documents into your InDesign layouts. When importing text from Microsoft Word, InDesign uses the *Remove Styles and Formatting from Text and Tables* option to automatically eliminate styles applied to the text using Microsoft Word. You can also have the styles imported or even converted to styles you've set-up in your InDesign layout, as you'll discover in this exercise.

1 Navigate to page 6 in the document.

2 Choose File > Place. In the Place dialog box, navigate to the id03lessons folder and select the id0302.doc file. Select the *Show Import Options* check box, which is located toward the bottom of the Place dialog box, and then click Open. The Microsoft Word Import Options dialog box opens.

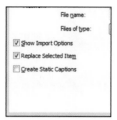

The Show Import Options and Replace Selected Item check box.

 To open the Import Options dialog box automatically when opening a file, hold down the Shift key while you click Open.

3   In the Microsoft Word Import Options dialog box, select the *Preserve Styles and Formatting from Text and Tables* radio button. This maintains styles and other text formatting in the imported file. Also select the *Customize Style Import* radio button.

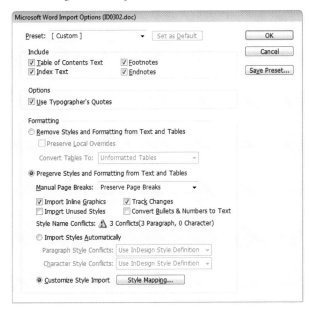

The Microsoft Word Import Options dialog box.

About Microsoft Word import options

Any Table of Contents text, index text, footnotes, and endnotes can be brought from a Microsoft Word document into an InDesign layout. By default, the *Use Typographer's Quotes* option is checked, which changes all quotes to typographer's (curly) quotes. This means that every inch- and foot-mark quote will be converted as well.

If the *Remove Styles and Formatting from Text and Tables* radio button is selected, all text will be imported and formatted using the default Paragraph style, which is usually the Basic Paragraph style. If you want to keep all the character attributes that were applied in Microsoft Word, select the *Preserve Local Overrides* check box.

If you select the *Preserve Styles and Formatting from Text and Tables* radio button, the styles created in Word are imported into your document, and the text adopts the imported styles, trying to mimic the styles from Word. However, if you create a template in Word that contains styles with the same names as the styles in your InDesign document, there will be paragraph style conflicts upon importing, and the imported text will use InDesign's style definition by default. This means that, regardless of how text looked in Word, once imported into InDesign, the text is formatted with InDesign's styles. This only occurs if the Microsoft Word document and the InDesign document have styles with identical names.

4 Click the Style Mapping button at the bottom of the dialog box, next to the *Customize Style Import* radio button. The Style Mapping dialog box appears.

Microsoft Word Import Options shows that the Normal, Body and Byline styles from the Word document have mapped to the InDesign styles with the same names. Identically named styles are automatically mapped so that they use the InDesign style when you use Style Mapping at the time you import the Microsoft Word document into your InDesign layout.

5 The dialog box shows that the Microsoft Word style *Normal* is mapped to a style in this InDesign document. Next to Normal, select the New Paragraph Style and choose Basic Paragraph style from the drop-down menu. This causes the text in the Word document that uses the style Normal to be formatted using the Basic Paragraph style once it is imported into InDesign.

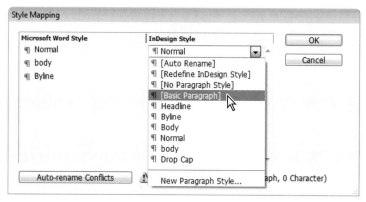

Mapping styles.

6 Click OK to close the Style Mapping dialog box. Click OK again to accept the Microsoft Word Import Options. The cursor is loaded with text that is ready to be placed with already-applied paragraph styles.

7 Click in the left column on page 6 to place the text from the Microsoft Word document into the InDesign layout.

Missing fonts

Fonts, like graphics, are not embedded within an InDesign document. If you receive an InDesign document from a colleague, you may need the fonts that they used when creating the document if you don't have them installed on your computer. In this exercise, you will import text from a Microsoft Word document that uses a font that you may not have installed on your computer, and you will discover how to address errors that are displayed when fonts are not available.

By default, InDesign highlights missing fonts in pink within a layout to alert you to the fact that the font being displayed is not the same as what was used when the text was originally formatted.

Finding and fixing missing fonts

1 In the Pages panel, navigate to page 5 by double-clicking the page 5 icon.

2 Select the Type tool (T) in the Tools panel.

3 Click inside the empty text frame at the top of page 5.

4 Choose File > Place. In the Place dialog box, navigate to the id03lessons folder and select the id0303.doc file. Select the *Show Import Options* check box if it is not selected, and then click Open.

5 Confirm the *Preserve Styles and Formatting from Text and Tables* radio button is selected. Click OK.

The Missing Font dialog box appears if you do not have the font Futura Bold already installed on your computer.

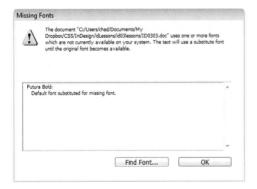

The Missing Font dialog box.

6   Click the Find Font button. The Find Font dialog box opens. Highlight the font
Futura Bold by clicking on it in the Fonts in Document section. Notice the Warning
icon (⚠) next to the font name. This indicates that the font is missing.

7   In the Replace With section at the bottom of the dialog box, highlight the text in the
Font Family text field and type **Adobe Caslon Pro**. You are going to replace Futura
Bold with Adobe Caslon Pro Regular. If you do not have Adobe Caslon Pro Regular,
you may use another font that is available on your computer.

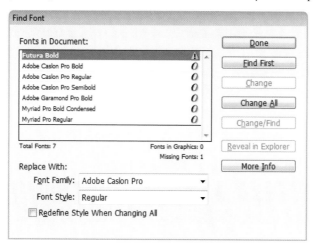

Replacing a font.

8   Click Change All. To see the missing font replaced, click Done.

9   Choose File > Save to save your work, and then choose File > Close.

Congratulations! You have completed the lesson.

Self study

1 Starting on page 1, navigate through the document and apply styles to all text, including body, byline, drop cap, and headline.

2 Change the color of the body text and redefine the style.

3 Turn on Show Text Threads and use the Selection tool (⬉) to select the linked text frames on page 5, create a new page at the end of the document and drag the frames to the new page. Return to page 2 and see if the story jump automatically updates.

4 Make a new headline box on page 7 and type in a fictitious headline. Format the headline using the headline style as a starting point. You may need to adjust the size depending on how many words you enter.

Review

Questions

1 If you have a font that doesn't have the style of italic, can you make it italic?

2 Can you flow text into an existing frame?

3 Can you divide one text frame into multiple columns?

4 How can you add Previous and Next page markers?

5 What is the best way to see changes that have been made to text in a given story?

Answers

1 No, you cannot create a false italic style using InDesign. You need the actual font with the italic style to make this change, which is also true for other styles, including bold or outline. One exception to this is the ability to apply a skew or false italic using the Skew button (*T*) in the Character formatting panel. Although this is possible, it's typically not recommended because it is not a true italic font.

2 Yes, you can flow text into existing frames, including frames that already contain text.

3 Yes, you can have many columns in a single frame. You make column adjustments in the Control panel or by choosing Object > Text Frame Options.

4 Choose Type > Insert Special Characters > Markers or use the context menus when entering the text.

5 Enable Track Changes for a story by choosing Window > Editorial > Track Changes and view the changes made in the Story Editor.

Lesson 4

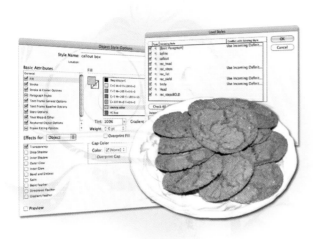

What you'll learn in this lesson:

- Creating and applying paragraph, character, and object styles
- Using nested styles
- Updating and editing styles
- Importing styles from other InDesign documents
- Quickly applying styles
- Organizing styles into groups

Working with Styles

Styles make it easy to create consistent designs across text and objects. Styles also help you simplify adjustments to the formatting of text and objects. By using styles, you can update text or objects across an entire document in a single step.

Starting up

Before starting, make sure that your tools and panels are consistent by resetting your preferences. See "Resetting the InDesign workspace and preferences" in the Starting up section of this book.

In this lesson, you will work with several files from the id04lessons folder in this lesson. Make sure that you have copied the id04lessons folder onto your hard drive from the included DVD. See "Loading lesson files" in the Starting up section of this book. This lesson may be easier to follow if the id04lessons folder is on your desktop.

See Lesson 4 in action!

Use the accompanying video to gain a better understanding of how to use some of the features shown in this lesson. The video tutorial for this lesson can be found on the supplied DVD.

The project

You will use paragraph, character, and object styles to enhance the appearance of a two-page recipe layout and gain an understanding of how Styles make the design process more efficient.

Creating styles saves a significant amount of time and effort as you design and format your document. If you need to make changes to text or objects, styles make it a quick and easy process to update 10 or 10,000 objects that share similar formatting attributes. The initial set-up may take a few minutes when using styles, yet the time savings in the long-run are significant.

In this lesson you will also discover how to import styles from other documents, re-using the design work from these other documents, and keeping a consistent identity across multiple files. You will also learn how to organize your styles using style sets, keeping them organized, and you'll also find tips for quickly and efficiently applying styles to documents.

Style types

There are several types of styles you can use when designing your documents, including paragraph, character, object, GREP, table, and cell styles. Each type of style applies to different page elements. These styles speed up the process of formatting and changing the appearance of text and page elements, and are especially helpful when working with longer documents. You'll work with these types of styles when using InDesign:

- **Paragraph styles** define text attributes that affect an entire paragraph of text, including line spacing (leading), indents, and alignment. Paragraph styles may also include character attributes such as font family and size that apply to an entire paragraph. Paragraph styles are commonly used for headlines and body copy.

- **Character styles** contain character formatting attributes, such as font family, size, and color. These attributes are only applied to a specified range of text. Character styles are commonly used for single words or numbers that must be formatted differently within a paragraph, such as a proper name, technical terms, or numbers used in a list.

- **Object styles** apply to page elements such as boxes and lines. For example, sidebars containing text or image frames can be made to look consistent across a layout using object styles.

- **GREP styles** are used to format specific content within a paragraph. For example, using a GREP style, you can find a text pattern such as a phone number, and format it so the area code or country code is a different color.

- **Table and Cell styles** apply formatting to portions of a table. This lesson is focused primarily on using paragraph, character, and object styles, and table styles are covered in detail in the *Adobe InDesign CS6 Digital Classroom* book.

In this lesson, you will create customized style definitions and share the styles between different InDesign documents, defining the formatting one time, and reusing the formatting across multiple InDesign files. You will also explore how to create default styles that are available within all new documents you create.

Paragraph styles

Paragraph styles generally include attributes for both characters and paragraphs. When applying a paragraph style, all text within the paragraph is formatted in a single click, specifying the font, size, alignment, spacing, and other text attributes. InDesign identifies a paragraph by locating paragraph returns entered using your keyboard, and even a single word on a line by itself can be considered a paragraph. In this lesson, you'll start by defining a style, and then applying it to text.

Defining paragraph styles

When building styles, it is useful to see what the style will look like when it is applied. You can format a paragraph to your liking, and then use the formatting you've defined as the foundation to create a style that can be reused. You'll start by building a paragraph style for the body text used in a cookie recipe.

1   Choose File > Open. In the Open dialog box, navigate to the id04lessons folder and select the id0401.indd file. Click Open. A two-page spread from a cookbook opens, displaying pages 72 and 73. The pages displayed are listed in the lower-left corner of your document window and also in the Pages panel.

2   Choose Advanced from the workspace switcher drop-down menu, or choose Window > Workspace > Advanced, then choose Window > Workspace > Reset Advanced to reset the InDesign panels to their default positions for the Advanced workspace. This ensures that your panels are in position, making them easier to locate during this lesson.

3   Choose File > Save As. In the Save As dialog box, navigate to the id04lessons folder and type **id0401_work.indd** in the Name text field. Click Save to save a working copy of this lesson file so you do not overwrite the original lesson.

4   Click the Paragraph Styles button (⬛) in the dock on the right side of the workspace to open the Paragraph Styles panel. The styles that have been created and used in this document are listed. This document contains four styles: basic paragraph, callout large, and two recipe-specific styles: rec_steps and rec_yield.

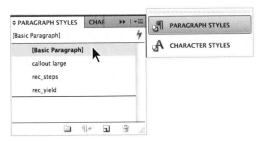

The Paragraph Styles panel lists styles that are available for formatting paragraphs.

5   Select the Type tool (T) from the Tools panel. Position the cursor over the first paragraph of text located in the middle column on the left-hand page. The paragraph starts with the text, *The smell of fresh baked cookies...* Click four times to select the entire paragraph.

6   Press the Character Formatting Controls button (**A**) in the top-left corner of the Control panel located at the top of the workspace, to display the character options. Choose Minion Pro from the Font drop-down menu, and, if necessary, choose Regular from the Font Style drop-down menu. Set the size to 10 pt from the Font Size (T) drop-down menu.

Setting the character formatting options in the Control panel.

7   Press the Paragraph Formatting Controls button (**¶**) in the Control panel to display the paragraph formatting options, and type **0.2** in the First Line Left Indent (˙⊟) text field. Press Enter (Windows) or Return (Mac OS) to indent the paragraph by 0.2 inches.

In the paragraph formatting options section, type 0.2 in the First Line Left Indent text field.

8   With the paragraph still selected, press the panel menu button (˙≡) in the upper-right corner of the Paragraph Styles panel and choose New Paragraph Style. The New Paragraph Style dialog box appears.

Use the Paragraph Styles panel menu to create a new style.

9   In the New Paragraph Style dialog box, type **body** in the Style Name text field, then click to select the *Apply Style to Selection* check box so that the text you've formatted will be connected to the new paragraph style, and then click OK to establish the name of the new style. The body style is added to the list of styles in the Paragraph Styles panel, and uses the formatting you created as the foundation for the style.

Choosing the *Apply Style to Selection* option also linked the selected text to the new style, and if the style is updated, the selected text will reflect any changes to the formatting.

10   Save the file by choosing File > Save.

Applying paragraph styles

You can now apply the new paragraph style to paragraphs in this document. You can apply the style to individual paragraphs, or multiple paragraphs. Here you will apply the formatting to all the paragraphs in this text frame.

1   With the cursor still within the recipe, click once in the second paragraph. Do not select the text, simply placing the cursor in the paragraph is all that is needed.

2   In the Paragraph Styles panel, select the body style to apply the style to the second paragraph. The style applies to the entire paragraph where the cursor is located, even though the text is not selected.

3   With the cursor still within the recipe, choose Edit > Select All, or use the keyboard shortcut Ctrl+A (Windows) or Command+A (Mac OS), to select all the text in the frame.

4   In the Paragraph Styles panel, select the body style to apply the style to all selected text. The entire recipe now uses the same character and paragraph formatting as the initial paragraph you formatted.

The smell of fresh baked cookies wafting through the house is always a welcome greeting, but when you catch a whiff of my mother's recipe for molasses gingersnaps, you will find yourself quick-stepping towards the kitchen.

Niatue tet autat. Raessi bla feu facidunt am, conullam, quamet aut lamcommy nostis nim zzriuscilis num et adionse ndiat. Niam in ercipit nonsequi tem iusciliquisl utpat, con et nullutp atiscipit am, si endre feu facipisl dolenis alit prate commod magnim iustiscidui tatum ipisl iriureet, quisi.

Oborperci bla alis aliquatie modo od magnim do od moleniam nulla commodiat, si blandre magna adigna feuisi.

Format all the text within the text frame with the body style.

To format an individual paragraph, use the Type tool to click within the paragraph to be formatted, then click the style to be applied in the Paragraph styles panel. When applying formatting to a single paragraph, you only need to insert the cursor within the paragraph to be formatted, and do not need to select the entire paragraph.

Character styles

Building character styles is similar to the process you used for creating paragraph styles in the previous exercise. You'll start by formatting text, and then you'll define the character style based upon the attributes of the text you have formatted. Character styles affect only character attributes, such as font and size. Character styles are typically used for words that need special treatment, such as bold, italics, or a unique font, and character styles only apply to text that you have selected.

Defining character styles

On the right page of the document you will make the text bold at the start of each step. You'll format the first step, and then define a style to apply to the others.

1 On page 73 of the recipe layout, use the Type tool (T) to double-click and highlight the word *Create* located under the Yield section.

2 Press the Character Format Controls button (A) in the Control panel, and then choose Bold from the Font Style drop-down menu. Keep the text selected.

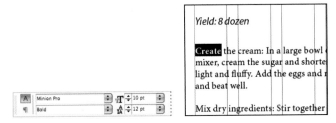

Use the character portion of the Control panel to set the type style.

3 Press the Character Styles button (A) in the dock on the right side of the workspace to open the Character Styles panel.

4 With the bold text still highlighted on the page, press the panel menu button (·≡) in the upper-right corner of the Character Styles panel, and choose New Character Style.

5   In the New Character Style dialog box, type **Bold** in the Style name text field. Note that the only attribute being defined by this style in the Style Settings section is "bold." This is because the Bold attribute is the only difference from the paragraph style that is also applied to this text. This style can be applied to any text using any font to apply the bold style of that font family. Click OK to create a new style. The new style name appears in the Character Styles panel.

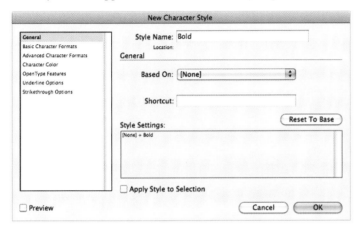

Bold is the only attribute being defined in the character style because that is the only attribute that is different from the paragraph style that is applied to the text.

6   Choose File > Save to save your work.

Applying character styles

Applying character styles is also similar to applying paragraph styles. You will highlight the text you want to format, and then click the style name to apply the style.

1   Continuing to work on the right-side of the layout, highlight the text *Create the cream* under the Yield section.

2   In the Character Styles panel select the style Bold, applying the new style to the selected text.

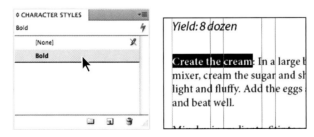

Applying the character style.

3 Highlight the phrase *Mix dry ingredients* and apply the Bold style by selecting it in the Character Styles panel.

When both character and a paragraph styles are applied to the same text, the attributes defined in the character style take precedence over the attributes defined in the paragraph style. In this exercise, the Bold attribute of the character style is applied even though the rec_steps paragraph style is applied and uses the Regular attribute.

Using nested styles

Nested styles combine character styles with paragraph styles, so you can apply both character and paragraph styles in a single step. For example, you can use a nested style to make the first word of a paragraph bold and blue, while the rest of the paragraph is regular and black.

In this exercise, you will create a nested style by modifying one of the existing paragraph styles so it also includes a character style for the initial portion of the paragraph.

1 Using the Type tool (T), click in the bottom paragraph on the right page, which starts with the text, *Bake in oven*. If you closed the Paragraph Styles panel, click the Paragraph Styles button to open it, or choose Type > Paragraph Styles.

2 In the Paragraph Styles panel, double-click the rec_steps style to open the Paragraph Style Options dialog box for this style.

3 Select the *Drop Caps and Nested Styles* option along the left side of the Paragraph Style Options dialog box, then click the New Nested Style button. A new nested style is added to the nested style section of this dialog box.

4 In the Nested Styles section's drop-down menu, choose Bold to select the character style you created in the previous exercise. Keep the dialog box open, and next you will specify the characters to which the Bold style will be applied.

5 Click to select *Words* located to the right of the *Through 1* option. Change *Words* to : by pressing the Colon key (:) on your keyboard.

The Bold style will apply to all text up to, and including, the colon (:). You can define where nested styles stop, or string together multiple nested styles to create different formatting for the start of a paragraph or line of text.

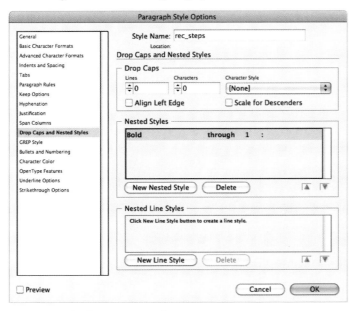

Creating a nested style to automate text formatting.

If you do not replace Words with a colon, only the first word of the recipe step will have the character style applied to it.

6 Click the *Preview* check box in the lower-left corner of the dialog box to view the changes in your document. If necessary, reposition the dialog box to view your page.

7 Click OK to close the Paragraph style options dialog box.

If the formatting isn't being applied as expected, select all four paragraphs under the Yield: 8 dozen heading and in the Character Styles panel choose none to remove any existing character styles. If character styles have been manually applied to the text, it prevents nested styles from being able to format the text.

8 Choose File > Save to save your work. Keep the file open for the next part of the lesson.

Updating styles

You have applied multiple attributes to text in a single click using styles. Next you will see how Styles save time when changing or updating formatting, making it easier to keep your text consistent across your documents. You will update all text associated with a style by modifying the style definition. Here you will change the size of the recipe steps. By making a single update, all text using the rec_steps style will be updated. Although you are working with two pages in this example, the same time-saving technique works just as easily on documents with 10 or 100 pages.

1   Continuing to use the Type tool (T), click in the bottom paragraph on the right page, which starts with the text, *Bake in oven.*

2   In the Paragraph Styles panel, the rec_steps paragraph style is highlighted, indicating that the style is applied to this paragraph. Double-click the style to open the Paragraph Style Options dialog box.

3   Click to select Basic Character Formats on the left side of the Paragraph Style Options dialog box.

4   Choose 11 points from the Size drop-down menu, and then choose Auto from the Leading drop-down menu to change the vertical line spacing.

5   Select the *Character Color* option along the left side of the dialog box, and then choose *cookie color* from the list of available colors.

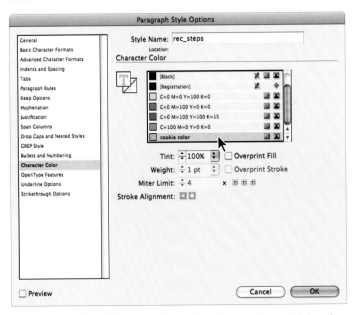

Changing Paragraph Style Options attributes updates all paragraphs to which the style has been applied.

6   If necessary, click the *Preview* check box in the lower-left corner to see the changes in the document as you make them.

7   Click OK to commit the changes and close the dialog box. All text formatted with the rec_steps style has been updated.

The updated text after the paragraph style is changed.

Loading styles from another InDesign document

After you create a style, you can use it in other InDesign documents. This lets you reuse your styles and formatting in other files, keeping their appearance consistent, and saving time because you do not need to recreate similar styles. The Paragraph Styles and Character Styles panel menus both include an option to load styles from other documents. Here you will import previously created styles used in another recipe.

1   With the document open, choose Load All Text Styles from the Paragraph Styles panel menu (⁻☰). The Open a File dialog box appears.

If you only want to use paragraph or character styles from another document, you can choose to load only these styles by selecting either Load Paragraph Styles or Load Character Styles from the respective panel menus. For this example, you are importing all styles created in another document.

2   In the Open a File dialog box, choose the file id0402.indd from the id04lessons folder. This is the document from which you'll import the styles. Click Open, and the Load Styles dialog box appears.

To see the entire contents of the Load Styles dialog box, you may need to click and drag the lower-right corner of the dialog box until all the styles available for importing are visible.

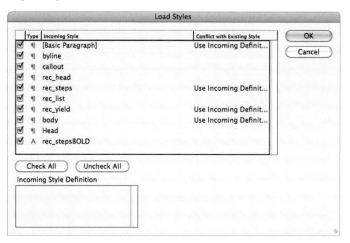

The Load Styles dialog box appears after selecting a document from which you want to import styles. Use the Load Styles dialog box to select the styles you want to import into your document.

If you want to import styles that use the same name as existing styles in your document, the Load Styles dialog box lets you choose how to handle the conflicting names. The "Use Incoming Definition" option causes the imported style definition to be used, replacing the definition used in your current document. The "Auto-Rename" option causes the imported style to be renamed, allowing you to use both the existing and imported styles. Click the words "Use Incoming Definition" to see the drop-down list, where you can change it to the "Auto-Rename" option. The Incoming Style Definition boxes below each style's name displays the highlighted style's definition for easy comparison.

3 Click the Uncheck All button, deselecting all styles in the Load Styles dialog box, then click to select the rec_head, rec_list, and Head styles by clicking the check box to the left of the name of each style.

You can import all the styles in a document or choose to only import selected styles. Only the styles you selected will be imported into your document.

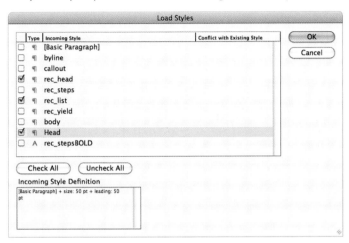

Check the styles you want to import into your document.

4 Click OK to close the Load Styles dialog box. The Paragraph Styles panel now includes the imported styles rec_head, rec_list, and Head, which can be used in this document.

5 Choose File > Save to save your work.

Quick Apply

Using Quick Apply allows you to rapidly apply styles without needing to locate them in one of the styles panels. You'll use a key command and type the first few letters of a style's name, applying the style.

1 In the Pages panel, double-click the left side of the document spread, page 72.

2 Using the Type tool (T), click to place the cursor in the text frame located at the top of the left page, in the text *Molasses Won't Slow Eating These Gingersnaps.*

3 Press Ctrl+Enter (Windows) or Command+Return (Mac OS). The Quick Apply window opens.

You can also use the Quick Apply button (⚡) located in the upper-right corner of the Paragraph Styles, Character Styles, or Control panels.

4 Using your keyboard, type **hea** in the window's search field. The Head style appears at the top of the list. Press the Enter (Windows) or Return (Mac OS) key on your keyboard to apply the style to the text. The Quick Apply window closes.

Because paragraph styles format an entire paragraph, you don't need to select or highlight the text to apply the paragraph style.

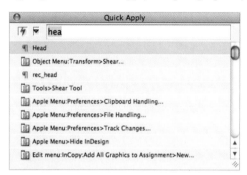

The Quick Apply window makes applying styles faster and easier.

5 In the Pages panel, double-click the right side of the document spread, page 73.

6 Using the Type tool, click to place the cursor in the text frame located at the top-right corner of the page, in the line of text that reads *Cookie Color.*

7 Click the Quick Apply button in the Control panel and type **rec** in the text field. Three styles starting with rec appear in the list. If necessary, use the arrow keys on your keyboard to navigate to and highlight the rec_head style if it isn't already highlighted, then press Enter (Windows) or Return (Mac OS) to apply the style.

You can also use Quick Apply to access menu commands and panel options even if you have forgotten the location where the command is accessed—you only need to know the name of the command you want to access.

8 Continuing to work in the text frame in the upper-right corner of the layout, click to place the cursor in the paragraph below *Cookie Color*. Click the Quick Apply button along the right side of the Control panel, or use the keyboard command Ctrl+Enter (Windows) or Command+Return (Mac OS), and type the letters **ca** in the text field. Select the callout large style, and then press Enter (Windows) or Return (Mac OS) to apply the callout large style to the text.

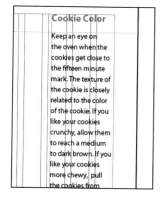

Applying the callout large style to the text.

9 Choose File > Save to save your work.

Organizing styles into groups

If you create documents that contain a large number of styles, you can organize them into groups to make them easier to manage and locate. Here you will organize the recipe's styles into a group.

1 Choose Edit > Deselect All to make sure nothing in the document is selected.

If the Deselect option is disabled, you have nothing selected and can proceed to the next step. You can also make certain nothing is selected by using the Selection tool (⬉) and clicking on an empty area of the pasteboard, outside the document page area.

2 In the Paragraph Styles panel, click the rec_steps style to select it. Press and hold the Ctrl key (Windows) or Command key (Mac OS) and select the remainder of the rec paragraph styles.

You may need to expand the panel to see all the styles. You can expand the panel by clicking and dragging the lower-right corner of the panel.

3 Press the Paragraph Styles panel menu button (⁃≣). Choose New Group From Styles to create a new group from the selected styles. The New Style Group dialog box appears.

4   In the New Style Group dialog box, type **recipe** in the Name text field, then click OK. The group folder now appears open in the Paragraph Styles panel.

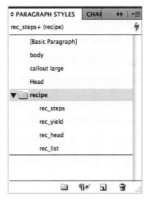

All recipe styles are now grouped within the recipe folder.

 You can also create style groups without first selecting styles, and then manually drag styles into the group. You can also create subgroups, which are groups within groups.

5   Click the arrow to the left of the Folder icon (▣) in the recipe style group listing to hide the styles in the group, and then click it again to display the styles.

6   Choose File > Save to save your work.

Object styles

You'll now work on the overall layout of the document and use object styles. Object styles can be applied to frames, lines, and other graphic elements. Object styles apply to an entire frame, not just text, and can include attributes such as background color, borders, and effects such as drop shadows. Object styles that are applied to a text frame can also include paragraph styles.

Creating object styles

In this exercise, you'll format the frame surrounding the Cookie Color text on the right side of the layout, and then use this formatting as the foundation for an object style.

1   Choose the Selection tool (▸) from the Tools panel, and then click to select the Cookie Color frame in the upper-right corner of the layout.

2   Choose Object > Text Frame Options. Confirm the Make all settings the same button (⧉), located to the right of the Top and Bottom text fields, is selected. This applies the same value to all the text fields. In the Text Frame Options dialog box, type **0.125 in** for the Top Inset Spacing and press the Tab key on your keyboard. Keep this dialog box open for the next step in this exercise.

3   In the Vertical Justification section of the Text Frame Options dialog box, choose Center from the Align drop-down menu, centering the text vertically within the frame. Click OK to apply the formatting.

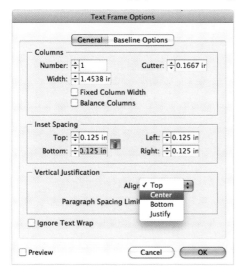

Use the Text Frame Options dialog box to apply attributes to a selected text frame.

4   Click the Object Styles button (⧉) in the dock on the right side of the workspace or choose Window > Object Styles to open the Object Styles panel.

If necessary, click and drag the bottom-right corner of the Object Styles panel to display more available styles.

5   With the Cookie Color frame still selected, click the Object Styles panel menu button (⧉) and choose New Object Style. The New Object Style dialog box opens.

6 In the New Object Style dialog box, type **callout box** in the Style Name text field and click the *Apply Style to Selection* check box. Click OK to create the new object style, and then choose File > Save to save your work. Keep the file open.

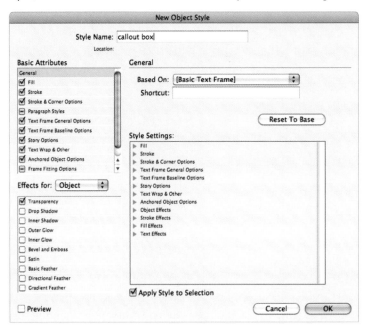

Name your new object style in the New Object Styles dialog box.

Applying an object style

Applying an object style is similar to applying text styles: start by selecting the object to be formatted, then choose the style to be applied to the object. In this exercise, you will apply the callout box style to another frame in the layout.

1 In the Pages panel, double-click the left side of the document spread, page 72.

2 Using the Selection tool (⬆), select the frame that contains the headline that starts with the text Light Color in the bottom-left corner of the layout.

3 Apply the callout box style to the frame by clicking the style in the Object Styles panel.

Applying the object style to the text frame containing the headline and byline formats the frame and its contents in one click.

4 Choose File > Save, or press Ctrl+S (Windows) or Command+S (Mac OS), to save your work.

Changing an object style

When you change an object style's definition, you update all elements to which the style is applied. In the following steps, you will update the object style by changing the background color of the frames.

1 With the headline and byline frames still selected, in the Object Styles panel double-click the callout box style to open the Object Style Options dialog box.

2 In the Basic Attributes section click to select the *Fill* option. The available color swatches are displayed.

3   Click to choose the swatch named cookie color to add it to the callout box object style. You may need to scroll through the list of color swatches to see this color.

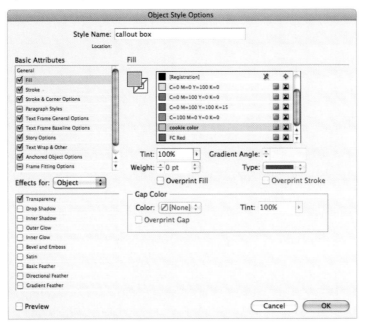

Modifying the object style definition to add a fill color.

4   Click OK. Both frames now reflect the changes to the background color.

Finishing up

As a review, you'll import some additional styles and review the process of applying them to your document.

1   With the id0401_work.indd document open, choose Load All Text Styles from the Paragraph Styles panel menu. The Open a File dialog box appears.

2   In the Open a File dialog box, choose the file id0402.indd from the id04lessons folder. Click Open, and the Load Styles dialog box appears.

3   In the Load Styles dialog box, select only the styles named callout and byline to import these into your document. Click OK to close the dialog box and import the styles.

4   Choose the Type tool (T) from the Tools panel, and then click to place the cursor within the words *by Larry Happy* located at the bottom of the left page, and then click the byline style to apply it to this text.

5   In the Pages panel, double-click the right side of the document spread, page 73.

6   Click and drag to select the ingredients, selecting from sugar through cinnamon. In the Paragraph Styles panel, click to apply the rec_list paragraph style to the ingredients.

7   Click to place the cursor within the words *Molasses Gingersnaps* located above the ingredients, and then click the rec_head style in the Paragraph Styles panel to apply the style to this text.

8   Choose File > Save to save your work.

GREP Styles

In the previous lesson, "Working with Text and Type" you discovered that GREP provides powerful options for finding and changing text. GREP styles use the same expressions to change formatting of specific text. In the following exercise, you'll modify an existing style so that certain numbers are formatted in bold, making them easier to read.

1   In the Pages panel, double-click the right page in the Spread, page 73, to center this page in the document window.

2   Click within any of the bottom four paragraphs in the Molasses Gingersnaps recipe.

3   In the Paragraph Styles panel, right-click the rec_steps paragraph style and choose Edit "rec_steps". The Paragraph Style Options dialog box is displayed.

4   Click on the GREP Style category on the left side of the dialog box, and then click the New Grep Style button. A new entry is created in the GREP Style section of the dialog box. Options for applying a style to specific text are then listed in the dialog box.

5   Next to Apply Style, click [None] and choose New Character Style from the drop-down menu. Name the Style **Myriad Bold**, and then click to select the Basic Character Formats section and set the Font Family to Myriad Pro and the Font Style to Bold. Click OK. The new character style you created now displays next to Apply Style, indicating this style will be applied to text specified using GREP. Keep the Paragraph Style Options dialog box open.

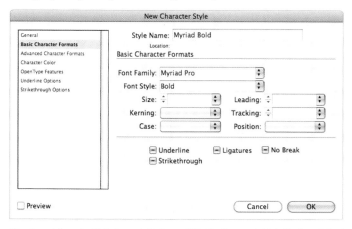

Creating a Character Style dynamically from within the Paragraph Style Options dialog box.

6 Click the area to the right of To Text and delete any content that is there. Click on the @ symbol to the right and choose Wildcards > Any Digit. This will search for any digit, or number, within the text that has the rec_steps Paragraph Style applied to it. Click the @ symbol again and choose Repeat > One or More Times. This GREP expression looks for any digit that occurs one or more times in a row within the rec_steps styled text. Click OK.

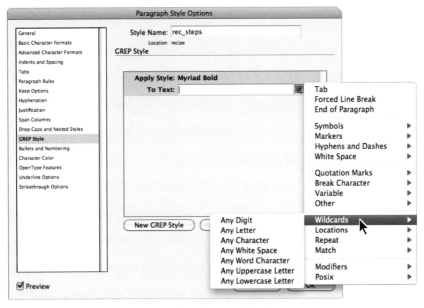

Building a GREP expression in the Paragraph Style options dialog box.

Note that any numeric character that appears within the recipe steps is now bold and uses the font Myriad Pro to make it easier to identify key areas in the steps of the recipe that need special attention.

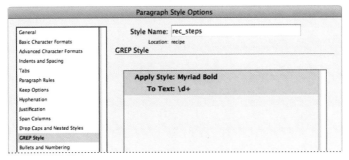

This GREP Style formats any numerical digit that exists within this Paragraph Style, applying Myriad Pro Bold to the number.

7 Choose File > Save to save your work, and then choose File > Close.

Congratulations! You have finished the lesson.

Self study

To practice creating styles, create your own layout using your favorite family recipes. Import the styles from this lesson and apply them to the text and frames in your own recipes. Import the object styles as well.

Review

Questions

1 What is the difference between character and paragraph styles?

2 What is a nested style and why is it used?

3 What is the keyboard shortcut to access the Quick Apply option?

4 If there are multiple styles in a document and scrolling becomes tedious, how can you organize the styles?

Answers

1 Paragraph styles apply to all text between paragraph returns, while character styles apply only to selected text. Character styles do not include paragraph attributes such as indenting, alignment, or tabs.

2 A nested style is a paragraph style that also includes one or more character styles, that formats specific areas of a paragraph style. Nested styles allow you to combine multiple formatting steps into a single click.

3 You can apply the Quick Apply option by pressing Ctrl+Enter (Windows) or Command+Return (Mac OS).

4 You can use style groups to organize your styles. They allow you to group together styles and determine which styles are displayed or hidden.

What you'll learn in this lesson:

- Adding graphics to your layout

- Managing links to imported files

- Updating and relinking modified or missing graphics

- Using graphics with clipping paths and alpha channels

Working with Graphics

Graphics add depth and style to your documents. You can use InDesign's powerful controls to place, position, and enhance graphics using most common file formats, as well as integrate images from Adobe Illustrator and Photoshop.

Starting up

Before starting, make sure that your tools and panels are consistent by resetting your preferences. See "Resetting the InDesign workspace and preferences" in the Starting up section of this book.

You will work with several files from the id05lessons folder in this lesson. Make sure that you have copied the id05lessons folder onto your hard drive from the included DVD. See "Loading lesson files" in the Starting up section of this book. This lesson may be easier to follow if the id05lessons folder is on your desktop.

See Lesson 5 in action!

Use the accompanying video to gain a better understanding of how to use some of the features shown in this lesson. The video tutorial for this lesson can be found on the supplied DVD.

The project

In this lesson, you will work on a fictional travel magazine called *SoJournal*, adding graphics to the layout using different techniques. You will learn how to resize graphics, precisely change positioning, set display quality, and wrap text around graphics. You will also learn how to manage graphics that have been updated, replaced, or are missing.

Understanding how InDesign handles graphics

When you place a graphic into an InDesign layout, the graphic file remains a separate file. Imported images or illustrations are not embedded into the InDesign document, so both the separate graphic files and the InDesign document are necessary for printing, archiving, or sharing your document with collaborators who might need to otherwise manipulate the original files. InDesign keeps track of graphic files used in your InDesign documents using the Links panel, as image files are considered to be linked. This is different from text files that are imported from programs like Microsoft Word or Excel. Text files are placed into the InDesign layout, and the original file is no longer needed to manipulate the text. For every rule there are exceptions, and graphic files can be embedded within an InDesign layout—although this is generally not advisable because it increases the size of the InDesign document and limits the ability to share a graphic for use in other media, such as on the Web or as part of an interactive campaign.

You'll start this lesson by opening a document where images have been imported, but InDesign can no longer locate the image files. You will help InDesign locate the missing files.

Locating missing images

If an image is renamed or moved from its original location after you import it into an InDesign file, InDesign loses the link to the image. Likewise, if you copy an InDesign document to a different computer, and don't transfer the images, InDesign will alert you that linked files are missing.

You'll use the Links panel and a new feature in InDesign CS6 called the Link badge to reconnect the InDesign layout with a missing image. In the Links panel, and in the Link badge indicator located in the upper-left corner of a graphics frame, missing links display a Red Warning icon (☉) next to their names, and links that have been modified or edited since they were originally placed in the layout, display a Yellow Warning Icon (⚠), indicating that the original image was modified. In this exercise, you will fix a link that was broken because the associated files were moved, and also fix a link to a graphic in the layout that was modified or changed.

1　Choose File > Open. In the Open dialog box, navigate to the id05lessons folder and select id0501.indd. Click Open. As the file opens, InDesign displays a message informing you that the document contains links to missing or modified files.

2　Click the Don't Update Links button to open the document without updating the links.

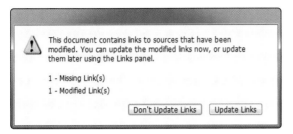

When opening a file with missing or modified links, you can choose Update Links to help reconnect the linked image files with the InDesign layout.

Depending on which workspace you have active, the Links panel will display in the middle of your screen or on the right side of the screen in the panel dock. Notice the citytravel.psd file displays a Red Warning icon—indicating that the link is missing—while the id0507.psd file displays the Yellow Warning symbol—indicating that the link has been modified or changed since it was placed into the layout. In the next part of the lesson, you will work with the Links panel to discover how to update image files that are missing or modified.

When using the Update Links option, any other broken links located in the folder are also updated when you update the first linked item. For example, if an entire folder containing images is relocated, you can update the link to all the missing items using the Update Links option, eliminating the need to update multiple broken links individually. You can also use the Relink to folder command from the Links panel menu.

3　Choose File > Save As. In the Save As dialog box, navigate to the id05lessons folder and type **id0501_work.indd** in the File name text field. Click Save and keep the file open.

Working with the Links panel and the Link badge

When you import an image into your layout, InDesign doesn't copy the complete image into your document file. Instead, it saves a reference, or a link, to the location of the original graphic file so it can access the image when necessary. This process lets you import many files into your layout without significantly increasing the file size of the document. For example, you can create a catalog with hundreds of images, but the InDesign document remains a small file with many linked images.

Because graphic files are generally linked, and not embedded within the InDesign file, you need to know how to manage linked graphic files. The Links panel and the Link badge let you manage these links, find files in the document, find missing files, and update graphics in the document when changes are made to the image file. In this exercise, you will fix two links to previously imported images that have been moved and are missing or modified.

1 If the Links panel isn't open, choose Window > Links to display it or click the Links button (%) in the panel docking area on the right side of the workspace.

2 Click once on citytravel.psd, and then click the Go To Link button (↱▯) at the bottom of the Links panel.

InDesign navigates to the selected image that accompanies the City Travel article. Note that in addition to the Missing Link icon (❷) appearing in the Links panel, there's a Link badge in the upper-left corner of the graphic frame that indicates that the link is missing.

The Go To Link button displays
a selected link within the layout.

3 With the citytravel.psd link still selected in the Links panel, click the Relink button (⊜⊜) at the bottom of the Links panel. In the Locate dialog box that appears, navigate to the links folder in the id05lessons folder and select the citytravel.psd file. Click Open.

Notice that the warning symbol indicating that the link was missing is now gone because you've reconnected the link to InDesign.

4 Select the id0507.psd link in the Links panel and click the Go To Link button ( ) at the bottom of the Links panel. InDesign navigates to the location of the modified image in the document.

One of the new features in InDesign CS6 is the addition of a Link badge that appears in the upper-left corner of a linked frame. Notice that the link that you just navigated to contains the Modified Link icon ( ) in the upper-left corner of the frame.

The Link badge is a real-time display of the link status of an image within a frame.

5 If you hover your cursor over the Link badge, you'll see a tooltip that gives you instructions for using the Link badge. Click the Link badge once with your cursor and notice that the link updates immediately. Press Alt+click (Windows) or Option+click (Mac OS) on the Link badge to open the Links panel with the link selected.

The Links panel now displays the list of links without any warning icons. You've updated both a missing link and a modified link.

6 Choose File > Save, or press Ctrl+S (Windows) or Command+S (Mac OS), to save your work. Keep the file open for the next part of the lesson.

When you click the Relink button (⬌) in the Links panel, the Relink All Instances check box appears at the bottom of the Links dialog box. Click this check box, and all instances of the image throughout the document are relinked.

Understanding the Links Panel

The Links panel displays all imported objects, the color space they use, and where they are used within the file.

A. Show/Hide Link Information. B. Number of Links Selected.
C. Relink. D. Go to Link. E. Update Link. F. Edit Original.

Customizing the Links panel

You can choose to have the Links panel display additional information regarding the links used in your layout.

1 From the Links panel menu, choose Panel Options.

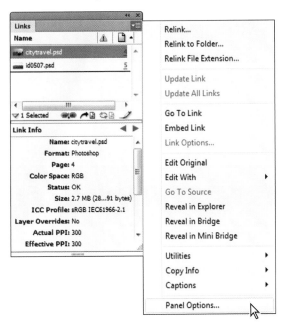

Use the Panel Options command to customize the display of the Links panel.

2 In the Panel Options dialog box, click to select the *Size* and *Color Space* options in the Show Column located in the center of the dialog box. These options determine which information is displayed in a column within the Links panel.

3 Click OK to close the Panel Options window. The additional information is now displayed within the Links panel.

4 To view the additional information, click the tab at the top of the Links panel, and drag it away from the panel docking area. Click in the lower-right corner of the Links panel and then drag to the right, expanding the width of the panel. To expand the panel without removing it from the panel dock, position your cursor on the left side of the expanded panel, and then drag to open up the panel.

5 Click the heading of each of the items displayed in the Links panel, including Name, Page, Size, and Color Space. As you click each item, the links sort by the selected criteria.

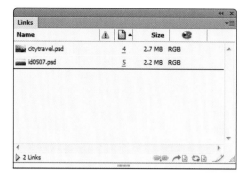

You can customize the information displayed in the Links panel and sort the display by clicking the column titles.

6 Click the Links panel tab and drag the panel over the Pages panel in the dock. When a blue border appears around the edge of the Pages panel, release the mouse to dock the Links panel with the Pages panel.

Adding graphics to your layout

You can add graphics that are created using a number of different programs or use a variety of graphic file types, such as JPEG, EPS, PSD, TIFF, AI, and many others. InDesign lets you import native Photoshop, PDF, and Illustrator files into your layouts. You can also import other InDesign documents (.indd format) into your layouts. In all, InDesign supports more than a dozen graphic file formats.

The most common way to add graphics to your InDesign layouts is to use the Place command, located under the File menu. In this exercise, you'll use the Place command to add an image to the front page of your travel magazine.

You can also import movies and audio in QuickTime, .avi, .wav, .aif, and .swf formats, as well as .au sound clips, into InDesign. These can be exported to the PDF and SWF file formats.

1   Use the pages drop-down menu in the lower-left corner of the page to navigate to page 1 of the file id0501_work.indd, and then choose View > Fit Page in Window. This page displays the magazine title *SoJournal* at the top of the page.

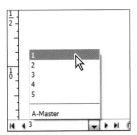

Use the page drop-down menu to navigate to page 1.

2   To make certain that nothing is selected, choose Edit > Deselect All. If the Deselect All option is unavailable, nothing is currently selected; proceed to the next step.

3   Choose File > Place and navigate to the id05lessons folder. Select the id0501.psd file to import this image. In the Place dialog box, make sure the *Show Import Options* check box is unchecked, and then click Open to import the image.

The Place dialog box.

4 The cursor displays a thumbnail of the image you are importing. Position the thumbnail image in the upper-left corner of the red bleed guides, positioned outside the edge of the page, and then click to place the image. InDesign imports the image at its original size.

If you accidentally clicked in a different spot on the page and need to reposition the image, use the Selection tool (↖) to drag the image until it snaps to the upper-left corner of the red bleed guides.

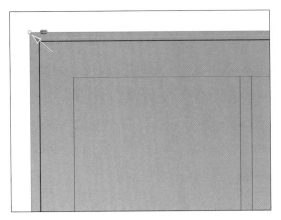

Place the image in the upper-left corner of page 1 so it extends above and to the left of the edge of the page.

5 Scroll down to the bottom of page 1. Notice that the image frame extends beyond the edge of the bleed guides. You will resize the graphic frame to fit within these guides.

6 Position the Selection tool over the lower-right corner of the image frame. When the pointer becomes a diagonal arrow (↘), click and drag the corner of the frame to reduce the size of the frame. Stop when it snaps to the lower-right corner of the bleed guide. The arrowheads turn white when they are positioned over the corner of the bleed guides.

Using the Selection tool to resize the image.

7 Adjust the image by clicking on the Content Indicator in the middle of the image with the Selection tool. This targets the photo itself and your cursor changes to a Hand icon (🖑). Click and drag to reposition the image and change how it is cropped by the frame.

Adjusting the position of an image within a frame using the Content Grabber.

The Content Grabber provides an easier and more efficient method of adjusting an image within its frame. You can still adjust an image with the tried-and-true method of using the Direct Selection tool (▹) to click on an image and adjust its position within a frame.

8 With the cover image still selected, choose Object > Arrange > Send Backward. The cover image moves behind the magazine title.

9 Choose File > Save to save your work. Keep the file open for the next part of the lesson.

Fitting options

You can use several options to get images to fit correctly to the frames on your page, including the following:

Object > Fitting > Fill Frame Proportionally causes the smallest size to become larger or smaller to fit within the frame, eliminating any additional space around the edge of the frame.

Object > Fitting > Fit Content Proportionally resizes the image to fit inside the frame, maintaining the original image proportions. If the proportions of the box do not match the proportions of the image, extra space will display around one or more of the frame edges.

Object > Fitting > Fit Frame to Content causes the frame to snap to the edges of the image. The frame either reduces or enlarges to fit the exact size of the image.

Be careful when using **Fit Content to Frame**, because it distorts the image to fit the frame. The proportional options are generally a better choice for most images.

Object > Fitting > Center Content centers the graphic or image within the graphic frame.

These options are also available from the context menu, either by right-clicking (Windows) or Control+clicking (Mac OS) with the mouse.

Fitting an image within an existing frame

You will now explore options for controlling where graphics are placed within your layout and how the graphics fit within their respective frames.

1 Navigate to page 2 using the page drop-down menu in the lower-left corner of the document window.

Page 2 includes four graphic frames for pictures to accompany the paragraphs about Athens, Austin, Chicago, and Honolulu.

2 If necessary, choose the Selection tool (⬉) from the Tools panel and click the empty picture frame accompanying the Athens story at the top of the page. Handles appear around the edge of the frame, indicating the frame is selected.

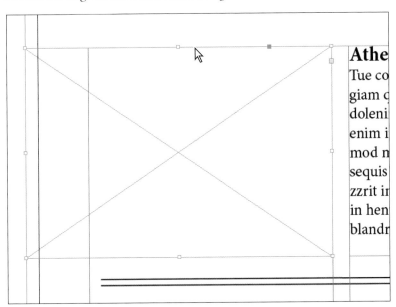

Select the empty frame to make it active.

3 Choose File > Place to import an image into the selected frame. In the Place dialog box, confirm that *Replace Selected Item* is selected. Navigate to the id05lessons folder, select the id0502.psd image, and click Open. The image appears in the selected frame, but only a part of the image is visible. You will reposition the graphic within the frame in the next part of this exercise.

Importing an image into the selected frame.

4 Choose the Direct Selection tool (⟩) from the Tools panel and position the cursor over the image. The cursor changes to a Hand icon (☝). Click and drag the image inside the frame until the image is relatively centered in the frame.

While dragging the image, a light-brown bounding box appears around the edge of the image that is outside the cropping area, and InDesign also displays any part of the image that is cropped by the frame. This "live" screen drawing is an improved feature in InDesign that allows you to see the entire image as you drag it, "ghosting" the image where it is being cropped by the frame.

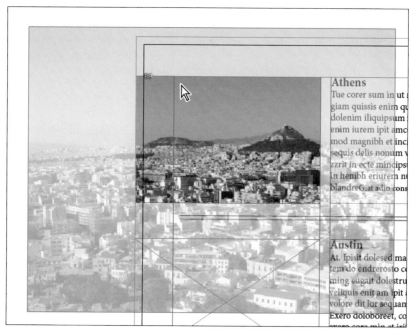

When clicking and dragging an image with the Direct Selection tool, InDesign displays the complete size, even any part outside of the frame.

5 Right-click (Windows) or Control+click (Mac OS) the graphic and choose Fitting > Center Content. The image is centered within the frame.

6 Using the Selection tool, right-click (Windows) or Control+click (Mac OS) the graphic, and choose Fitting > Fill Frame Proportionally.

These fitting options provide different ways to reposition the image. After using the Fill Frame Proportionally option, you may want to manually refine the image position using the Direct Selection tool or the Content Grabber.

Auto Fitting

You can use the Frame Fitting Options to choose settings and create default options for whenever you place graphics inside existing empty frames. In this part of the exercise, you will create default fitting options for frames.

1   Choose Edit > Deselect All, or press Shift+Ctrl+A (Windows) or Shift+Command+A (Mac OS), to make sure nothing in your document is selected.

2   Using the Selection tool (▸), Shift+click the three remaining empty frames on page 2 of the layout.

3   Choose Object > Fitting > Frame Fitting Options.

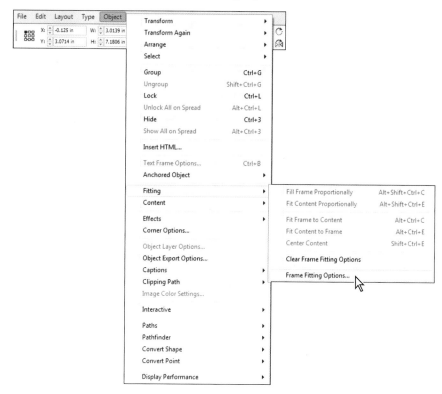

Choose Frame Fitting Options to set the defaults for placing graphics in frames.

4 Choose Fill Frame Proportionally from the Fitting drop-down menu and click the center box on the Align From icon (⠿); then click OK. Graphics placed into these frames will fill each frame proportionally and center them automatically.

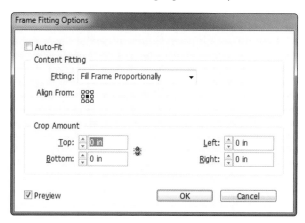

Set the default frame fitting option to Fill Frame Proportionally.

5 Choose Edit > Deselect All, or press Shift+Ctrl+A (Windows) or Shift+Command+A (Mac OS) to make sure nothing in your document is selected. Choose File > Save.

Using Adobe Bridge to import graphics

Adobe Bridge is a separate application that ships with InDesign. It provides a way to manage and view your digital assets, including images and InDesign documents. You can use Bridge to get previews of your documents, and view information about files before you even open them. Bridge works like a specialized version of your operating system for managing and arranging the files you import into an InDesign layout, and files you have created using InDesign.

In this section, you will import an image into the document by dragging it from the Bridge window directly into the InDesign document.

1 With id0501_work.indd still open, choose File > Browse in Bridge, or click the Go to Bridge button (Br) in the Application Bar to launch Adobe Bridge.

2 When Adobe Bridge opens, click the Favorites tab in the upper-left corner to bring it forward, and then click once on the Desktop listing, or click the location where you placed the files for this lesson.

3   In the Content tab at the center of the Bridge window, locate the id05lessons folder and double-click to open the folder.

Open the lessons folder using Adobe Bridge.

4   In the upper-right corner of the Bridge window, click the Switch to Compact Mode button (⊟). This results in a smaller version of Bridge that allows you to work simultaneously with Bridge and your InDesign document.

5   Position the compact Bridge window so you can see the empty frame next to the second city description, Austin, located on page 2 of the InDesign document.

Adobe Bridge in compact mode lets you work directly with another program while Bridge remains visible.

6   Using the Bridge window, locate the Photoshop image id0503.psd, an image of the Austin Capitol building. Click and hold, then drag the image into the empty Austin frame on page 2 of the InDesign document. When your cursor is positioned inside the frame, release the mouse. The photo is placed into the frame.

7   Click the Switch to Full Mode button (⌨) to maximize the Bridge window. Then, minimize Bridge by clicking the minimize button (use same as before) in the upper-right corner of the Bridge window (Windows) or by clicking the yellow button (◉) in the upper-right corner of the Bridge window (Mac OS). Click anywhere within the InDesign document window to make it active; then choose File > Save.

Placing multiple graphics using Mini Bridge

With InDesign, you can place multiple graphics into your InDesign layouts in a single step using the Mini Bridge panel. Mini Bridge offers features found in the Adobe Bridge application, but is built into Adobe InDesign as a panel. This alleviates the need to view images on your computer using a completely separate application. In this section, you will place two graphics in the remaining frames on page 2 of the layout.

1   If necessary, choose Edit > Deselect All so that nothing is selected, and then choose Window > Mini Bridge.

2   In the Mini Bridge panel, click the Launch Bridge button if the full Adobe Bridge application is no longer running. Mini Bridge still relies on the full Adobe Bridge application.

3   Click the drop-down menu in the upper-left corner of the Mini Bridge and choose Favorites. Click Desktop or select the folder where you placed the files for this lesson.

4   In the Navigation Pod area of the Mini Bridge panel, navigate to the id05lessons folder by double-clicking on the folders to open them.

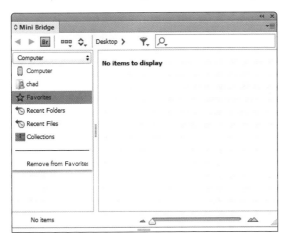

You can navigate the file structure of your computer in the Mini Bridge to locate images that you want to work with.

5   In the Mini Bridge panel, Ctrl+click (Windows) or Command+click (Mac OS) to select both the id0504.psd and id0505.psd images; then click and drag either of the selected images anywhere in the InDesign document. The cursor changes to a Paintbrush icon (🖌) and displays the number 2 in parentheses, along with a thumbnail of the first image. Click inside the empty frame to the left of the Chicago entry to place the first graphic. The paintbrush's number disappears, and a thumbnail of the Honolulu image appears.

6 Position your cursor over the remaining empty frame and click to place id0505.psd in the frame.

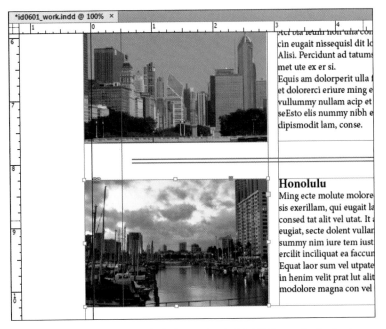

You can place multiple graphics in multiple frames using the Mini Bridge panel or by choosing File > Place.

When you have multiple images loaded in the place cursor, you can use the arrow keys on the keyboard to cycle through the various images. As you press the arrow keys, the preview of the image to be placed changes, letting you choose which image will be placed. Press the Esc key to remove an image from the list of images that are being placed.

Contact Sheet place

You can have InDesign create multiple frames and place images into a grid, known as a contact sheet. After choosing multiple images to place, click and drag to define the area for the grid. As you drag, use the left- and right-arrow keys to add or reduce the number of columns in the grid, and use the up- and down-arrow keys to add or reduce the number of rows in the grid.

7   Close the Mini Bridge panel and choose File > Save to save your work. Keep the file open for the next part of the lesson.

Adjusting the display quality of images

InDesign typically provides a low-resolution preview of placed graphics. The higher-resolution information is not displayed, as the high-quality information is often unnecessary for layout, and displaying many high-quality images can slow the performance of InDesign.

You may need to view the high-quality images, and you can choose to display high-quality image data for specific images, or for all images.

To change the display quality of an individual image, right-click (Windows) or Control+click (Mac OS) and choose Display Performance. Choose Fast Display to display a gray box instead of the image preview. Choose Typical to display a medium resolution for the image and choose High Quality display to show the high-resolution image information—the same data you would see in programs like Photoshop or Illustrator.

To change the display performance for all images in a document, choose View > Display Performance and select the desired quality level to use for the document.

Using object styles for images

In Lesson 4, "Working with Styles," you applied object styles to frames. You can also apply object styles to frames that contain images, quickly giving them a consistent, finished appearance. In this exercise, you'll create and apply an object style that adds a black stroke and applies rounded corners to all the frames on page 2.

1   Zoom in on the first image, the picture of Athens, on page 2 of the layout. Press Shift+Ctrl+A (Windows) or Shift+Command+A (Mac OS) to deselect all items on the page.

2   Click the Stroke button (◼) in the Control panel and drag and drop it onto the frame edge of the picture of Athens to apply the default stroke to the frame. Your cursor will change to indicate that you are applying the stroke to the frame (➤).

3 Click the frame to make it active. In the panel dock on the right side of the workspace, click the Stroke button (≡) to expand the Stroke panel. In the Stroke panel, click the Align Stroke to Inside button (▯) to set the stroke to align to the inside of the frame, and make sure that the stroke weight is set to 1 point.

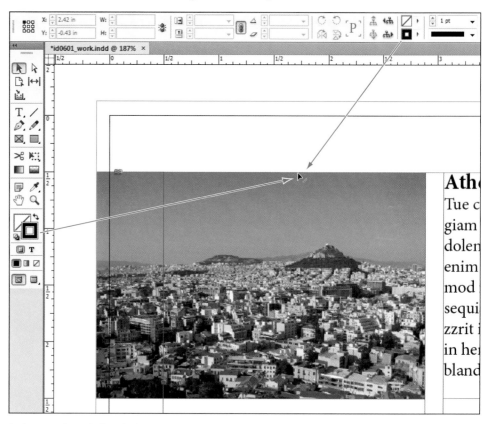

Applying a stroke to the frame by dragging and dropping the Stroke icon onto the frame edge.

4 Click on the Stroke button in the panel dock to collapse it back into a button.

5 Click on the yellow square in the upper-right corner of the Athens photo frame to enable Live Corner Effects edit mode. Diamonds appear in each corner of the frame, indicating that the Live Corner Effects have been enabled.

6 Hold down the Shift+Alt (Windows) or Shift+Option (Mac OS) keys and drag the diamond in the upper-right corner of the frame to the left to change the radius of that corner only. Drag to about .25 inches by monitoring the smart guide for that corner. Repeat this step for the diamond in the lower-right corner of the frame. You can also precisely adjust each corner by choosing Object > Corner Options and changing the values using the Corner Options dialog box.

Drag the diamond in the corner of the frame to adjust the Live Corner Effects.

You will now use the formatting of this initial frame to create an object style, and then apply it to the other frames.

7 In the dock, click the Object Styles button (◙). If the button is not visible, choose Window > Styles > Object Styles to open the Object Styles panel.

8 With the Athens image on page 2 still selected, Alt+click (Windows) or Option+click (Mac OS) on the Create New Style button (◄) at the bottom of the Object Styles panel to create a new object style.

Pressing the Alt/Option key when creating a new style causes the New Style dialog box to open, making it easy to confirm the settings and name the style. If you do not press the Alt/Option key, the new style is created and given a generic name.

Alt/Option+click the Create New Style button.

9   In the New Object Style dialog box, click the *Apply Style to Selection* check box to link the new style to the selected object.

10   Make sure the check box for Frame Fitting Options is selected (it is located along the left side of the dialog box in the Basic Attributes section). Next, click the words Frame Fitting Options to highlight it and display the Frame Fitting Options.

11   From the Fitting drop-down menu, choose Fill Frame Proportionally, and then click on the center box of the Align From icon (⬚) if not already selected.

12   In the Style Name text field, enter the name **Image Frame** to name the style, and then click OK. InDesign saves the attributes of the selected object as a new style and applies them to the selected frame.

13   Shift+click to select the remaining three images on page 2 that have not yet been formatted.

14   In the Object Styles panel, click the Image Frame style, applying it to all four images simultaneously.

To better view the 1-point strokes and rounded corners on the four image frames, you may need to press Ctrl+(plus sign) (Windows) or Command+(plus sign) (Mac OS) to zoom in. This shortcut brings you progressively closer to the page. After you view the final result, choose View > Fit Page in Window or press Ctrl+0 (Windows) or Command+0 (Mac OS) to bring you back to a broad view of your file.

15   Choose Edit > Deselect All to deselect the images, and then choose File > Save. Keep the document open.

Wrapping text around images

To force text away from graphics, and cause the text to wrap around the shape of the graphic, you can use text wrap to determine how far text should be pushed away from an object.

Wrapping text around the bounding box

When you place a graphic on a page, you might want the text to wrap around the frame that contains the graphic.

1　With the Selection tool (⬧), select the image of Athens on page 2. Click, hold, and drag it to the right so the upper-left corner of the image fits into the corner where the top and left margins intersect. Part of the image overlaps the text because the image frame is positioned above the text frame at the half-inch mark.

2　Move the remaining three photos to the right so that the left edge of the frame is aligned with the left margin of the page. Holding down the Shift key while moving these frames will constrain their movement horizontally.

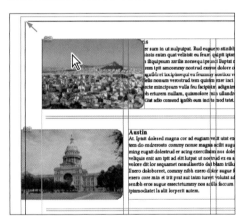

Move the image to the intersection of the top and left margins.

3　Make sure that the first image of Athens is currently selected.

4　Choose Window > Text Wrap. The Text Wrap panel opens.

5   Click the Wrap Around Bounding Box button (⊡), which causes the text to wrap around the edge of the frame.

Wrapping text around the image frame.

6   In the middle of the panel are the offset values, which determine how closely the text wraps around the image. Confirm that the Make All Settings the Same button (⊛) in the middle of the offset values is selected. Click the up-arrow, next to any one of the offset options, twice to set the offset to 0.125 inches. The text is positioned at least .125 inches away from the image frame.

7   Click the Object Styles button to display the Object Styles panel. Notice that the Object Style Image Frame that was applied to this image in the previous exercise contains a plus sign next to it. This indicates that a change has been made to the selected object beyond what the Object Style defines. If you don't see this, verify that you have the frame selected with your Selection tool (▶). Right-click the Image Frame object style and choose Redefine Style. This applies the changes made to the object to the Object style, and the remaining three images on the page update to reflect the updated Object style and now have the text wrap applied as well.

8   Choose File > Save to save your work. Keep the file open for the next exercise.

Using graphics with clipping paths and alpha channels

Some images contain clipping paths or alpha channels. Clipping paths and alpha channels can be used to hide information in an image, typically the background, enabling users to wrap text around part of the image. Clipping paths are stored in the Paths panel in Photoshop, and alpha channels are saved selections stored in the Channels panel in Photoshop.

The formats that utilize paths and channels include .psd, .eps, and .tif. These formats can hide parts of the image that are outside the path or channel when they are used in an InDesign layout. You will add a graphic to your layout that contains a clipping path from Photoshop, and then use the text wrap option to wrap text around the object's shape. You will place the next image in the Transportation article on page 3 of the InDesign document.

1   Click the Pages button in the dock to open the Pages panel. Double-click on the page 3 icon, and page 3 centers in the workspace.

2   Choose Edit > Deselect All to make sure nothing is selected; then choose File > Place, and navigate to the id05lessons folder. Click once to select the image id0509.psd, and click to select the *Show Import Options* check box at the bottom of the Place dialog box. Click Open. The Image Import Options dialog box appears.

3   In the Image Import Options dialog box, click the Image tab. If necessary, click the *Apply Photoshop Clipping Path* check box so that it is checked, and confirm that Alpha Channel is set to None. Click OK to import the image.

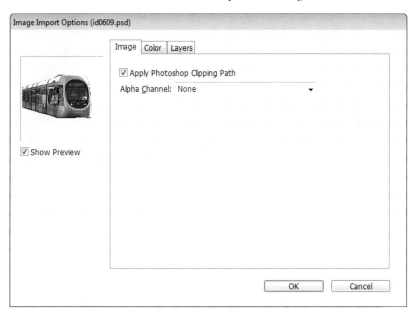

Choosing the import options when placing an image with a clipping path.

4 Position the paintbrush-and-thumbnail cursor (🖌) at the top of the left column in the Transportation article, and then click to place the graphic. The train image, without a background, appears over the text. By selecting the Apply Photoshop Clipping Path option, you set the image to appear without its background.

When placing the image, be certain the cursor does not display the paintbrush inside parentheses, as this indicates the image will be placed into an existing frame on the page. If you unintentionally place the image into a frame, choose Edit > Undo and repeat the process.

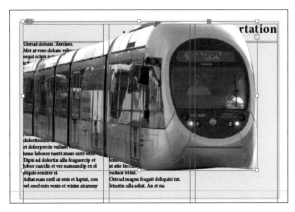

When Apply Photoshop Clipping Path is enabled, images display only the information inside a clipping path that was created in Photoshop.

5 With the image still selected, click the lower-left reference point locator (⊞) in the Control panel.

Set the train image's lower-left corner as the reference point.

6 In the Control panel, make sure that the Constrain Proportions for Scaling button (●) is selected. This constrains the proportions to keep them equal when the image is scaled.

7 Choose 50% from the Scale X percentage drop-down menu (⊞). The resulting image is a smaller train positioned in the lower-left corner of the Transportation article.

8 Choose Window > Text Wrap to open the Text Wrap panel, if it is not already open. Click the Wrap Around Object Shape button (⊞) to wrap the text around the shape of the image, and then change the offset amount to **0.1875** inches, then press Enter (Windows) or Return (Mac OS).

The text now wraps around the clipping path that was created using Photoshop.

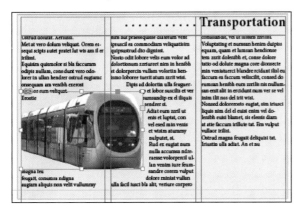

Wrap text around the object shape.

9 Choose File > Save to save your work. Keep the file open for the next part of the lesson.

Removing an image background using InDesign

You don't have to use Photoshop to remove the background from an image. You can use InDesign to create and apply a clipping path to an image. Clipping paths added to images using InDesign impact only the image in the InDesign document, and are not saved back into the original image file.

1 Choose Edit > Deselect All, to make sure nothing is selected. This keeps you from accidentally editing items in your layout. You will place a new image in the Discoveries article on page 3.

2 Choose File > Place. In the Place dialog box, navigate to the id05lessons folder. Select the id0510.psd image. At the bottom of the dialog box, make sure the Show Import Options check box is selected, and then click Open.

3 In the resulting Image Import Options dialog box, choose the Image tab. Notice that the Clipping Path options are not available. This is because no clipping path exists for this image. You will use InDesign to remove the background from the image. Click OK to place the image into your layout.

4 Position the paintbrush-and-thumbnail cursor (🖌) anywhere in the *Discoveries* article on page 3 and then click to place the image. Using the Selection tool (▶), position the image in the center of the text. Keep the image selected for the next step in the exercise.

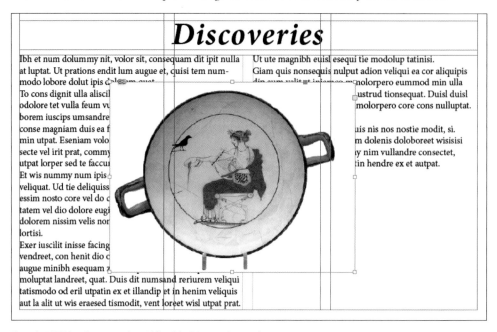

Place the id0510.psd image in the middle of the Discoveries *article.*

5 Choose Object > Clipping Path > Options. Select Detect Edges from the Type drop-down menu, leave the other settings at their defaults, and then click OK. You have removed the background by using the Detect Edges option to create a clipping path.

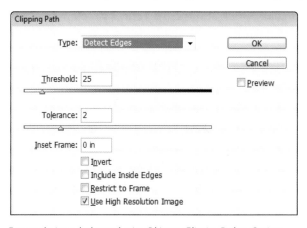

Remove the image background using Object > Clipping Path > Options.

6 Choose Edit > Deselect all or press or Shift+Ctrl+A (Windows) or Shift+Command+A (Mac OS) to deselct all objects on your page. If the Text Wrap panel is not visible, choose Window > Text Wrap. In the Text Wrap panel, click the Wrap around object shape button (▣) to wrap the text around the image. You can enter a higher value to push the text away from the object shape, or set it at a lower value, causing the text to follow the contour of the object more closely.

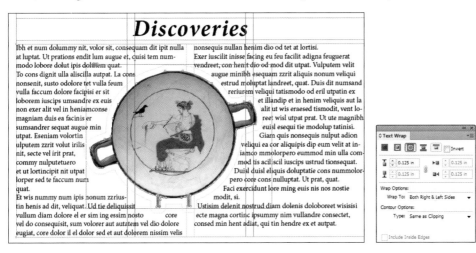

Wrap text around the object's shape.

7 Choose File > Save to save your work.

Using anchored objects

Anchored objects, sometimes called inline objects, allow a graphic to follow text that relates to the image. For example, if you are creating a dictionary and have an image associated with an entry, you want the image to move with the definition. If the text moves, the image should move with the text.

Anchoring an object attaches it to the associated text. When the text moves, the object moves with the text. In this exercise, you will explore how to create anchored objects using the skills you have already learned to place images and text.

1 Use the page drop-down menu in the lower-left corner of the document window to navigate to page 4.

2 Using the Selection tool (▸), click to select the City Art text frame on page 4. Press Ctrl+(plus sign) (Windows) or Command+(plus sign) (Mac OS) twice to zoom in on the selected frame.

3 Choose File > Place. At the bottom of the Place dialog box, click to uncheck the *Show Import Options* check box. Navigate to the id05lessons folder, select id0513.psd, make sure the Replace Selected Item check box is selected, and then click Open. Position your cursor in the upper-right corner of the City Art text frame, and click to place the image at that location. Use your Selection tool to reposition the image, if necessary.

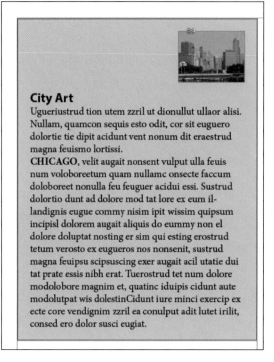

Place the image at the location where you want it to appear.

4 Using the Selection tool, click the image to select it. Notice a blue box located in the upper-right corner of the image. This blue box allows you to anchor the image to a specific location within text. Click the blue box and drag to the beginning of the word Chicago within the text.

Notice that an anchor now appears in the upper-right corner of the image frame indicating that it is anchored to the text. To see the exact location where the image is anchored, choose View > Extras > Show Text Threads.

Drag the blue box from the image to a location in the text to easily create an anchored object.

5 Switch to the Type tool (T), click to position the text cursor at the end of the paragraph in the line above the word Chicago, and then press Enter (Windows) or Return (Mac OS) one time. The text moves down, and the graphic moves with the text.

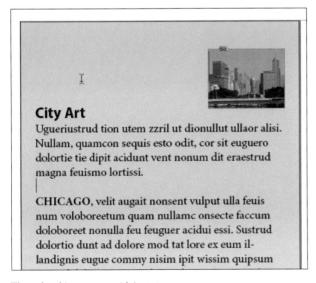

The anchored image moves with its text.

InDesign has made the process of creating anchored objects quite easy, and allows for great flexibility when designing layouts where images need to be anchored to a specific location in a text frame.

6   Press Ctrl+Z (Windows) or Command+Z (Mac OS) to undo the paragraph return, bringing the image back to its original position.

7   To gain greater control of the positioning of the anchored image, switch to the Selection tool and then click once on the anchored image to select it. Choose Object > Anchored Object > Options. The Anchored Object Options dialog box appears.

8   In the Anchored Object Options dialog box, click to select the *Preview* check box in the lower-left corner. Choose Custom from the Position drop-down menu, and click the *Relative to Spine* check box. This causes the image position to remain consistent to the spine of the document if pages are added or deleted, and the page on which it is placed reflows.

Notice that the image remains linked to the text. If the text position changes, the image will continue to flow with the text. Leave all the other settings at their defaults, and then click OK to close the dialog box.

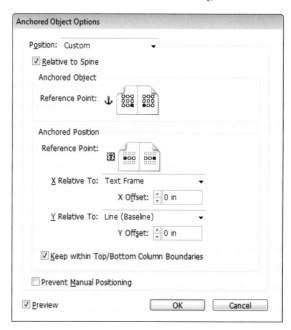

Set the anchored image to Custom and Relative to Spine to place the image outside the text frame.

9 To test the spine-sensitive options, choose View > Fit Spread In Window. Use the Selection tool to select the City Art frame. Drag the frame to the empty column on the right side of the City Music box on Page 5. Notice that the graphic automatically adjusts its position within the City Art box relative to the spread's spine. Likewise, if the text flowed from a left page to a right page, the anchored object would reposition itself automatically.

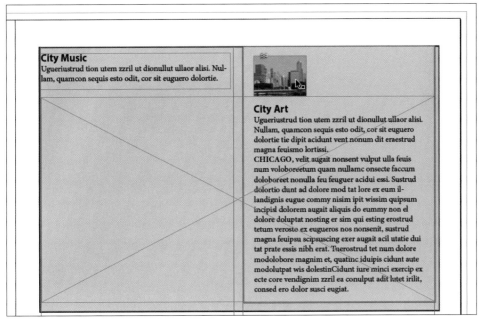

When you reposition the City Art frame to Page 5, the graphic adjusts its position relative to the spine.

10 Press Ctrl+Z (Windows) or Command+Z (Mac OS) to undo the repositioning of the text frame, or drag the City Art frame back to its original position.

11 Save the file by choosing File > Save. Keep the file open for the next part of the lesson.

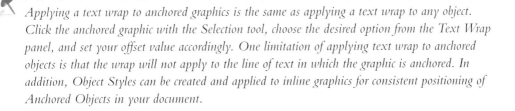

Applying a text wrap to anchored graphics is the same as applying a text wrap to any object. Click the anchored graphic with the Selection tool, choose the desired option from the Text Wrap panel, and set your offset value accordingly. One limitation of applying text wrap to anchored objects is that the wrap will not apply to the line of text in which the graphic is anchored. In addition, Object Styles can be created and applied to inline graphics for consistent positioning of Anchored Objects in your document.

Advanced importing

You can import more advanced graphics into your layouts, including Photoshop files that use layers, and InDesign documents, without converting them to any other file type. Even if you don't work extensively with Photoshop, you can still follow along with these steps.

Importing layered Photoshop files

In this exercise, you'll work with an imported Photoshop file that uses a group of layers that have been organized using a layer comp. Layer comps are a snapshot of the current state of the Photoshop Layers panel. Within Photoshop, you can change the visibility, position, and appearance of the layers to create different versions of a file. When you create a layer comp, it saves these settings by remembering the state of each layer at the time the layer comp was saved. You can use layer comps to create multiple compositions from a single Photoshop file.

When you import a .psd document into InDesign and select the *Show Import Options* check box, you can choose which layer comp to use from the Photoshop file within the InDesign document.

When you use layered Photoshop files in your InDesign layouts, you can change the visibility of the layers directly within InDesign. You do not need to go back to Photoshop to create or save different versions of an image. In this exercise, you will display different versions of an image by changing the visibility of the Photoshop layers and layer comps.

1 With the Zoom tool (🔍), click and drag to draw a box around the empty frame under the Sculpture article on page 4 of the InDesign document. This increases the magnification of the page, making the frame more clearly visible.

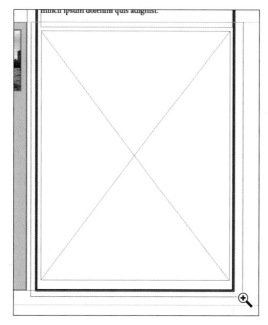

Use the Zoom tool to increase the magnification of the empty frame.

2 With the Selection tool (↖), click to select the empty frame under the Sculpture article. Choose File > Place, and at the bottom of the Place dialog box, click to select both the *Replace Selected Item* check box and the *Show Import Options* check box so that both options are enabled. Navigate to the id05lessons folder, select id0511.psd, and then click Open. The Image Import Options dialog box opens.

3 In the resulting Image Import Options dialog box, click the Layers tab to bring the layers options forward. Notice that several layers are listed in the Show Layers section. Make sure the *Show Preview* check box is selected, and then click the box next to the hsbGray layer to display that layer's option. The appearance of the image changes when you display the hsbGray layer.

4 Choose 3w/hsbGray from the Layer Comp drop-down menu to display a number of layer visibility changes that were defined by this layer comp when the image was edited in Photoshop.

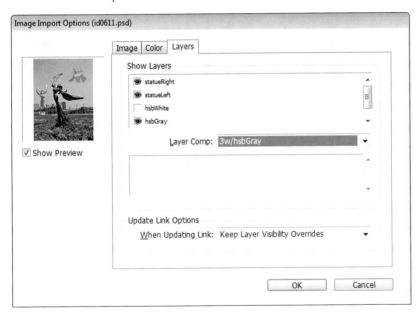

Use the layer comp visibility options to change the visibility of layers in placed Photoshop files.

5 Click OK. The image imports into the InDesign layout and displays the layers from the Photoshop image that you selected in the Image Import Options dialog box.

Now you'll explore how to change layer visibility of images after they've been placed in a layout.

6   If necessary, click the image with the Selection tool. With the image selected, choose Object > Object Layer Options. Choose Last Document State from the Layer Comp drop-down menu to return the image to its original settings, and then click OK.

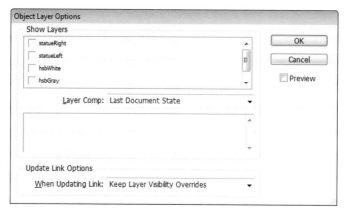

Return the image to its original state using Object Layer Options.

7   Continuing to use the Selection tool, right-click (Windows) or Control+click (Mac OS) the image, and from the contextual menu, choose Fitting > Fill Frame Proportionally so the image fits nicely inside the frame.

8   Choose File > Save to save your work.

Importing InDesign layouts as graphics

Along with traditional image formats, you can also import other InDesign layouts into your document, placing them as graphics. You may have an ad or a flyer that was created in InDesign that you want to use in another InDesign layout. By importing an InDesign file as a graphic, you can make changes to the imported file and the modifications are automatically updated in your layout. In this exercise, you will import a CD booklet design, created using InDesign, into the layout.

1   Open the Pages panel from the dock on the right side of the workspace and, in the panel, double-click on page 5 to navigate to this page; then choose View > Fit Page in Window. Use the Selection tool (▸) to select the frame beneath the City Music headline.

2   Choose File > Place or press the keyboard shortcut, Ctrl+D (Windows) or Command+D (Mac OS). At the bottom of the Place dialog box, make sure that both the *Replace Selected Item* and the *Show Import Options* check boxes are checked, navigate to the id05lessons folder, and select the id0514.indd file. Click Open. The Place InDesign Document dialog box appears.

3 In the Place InDesign Document dialog box, click the General tab to bring it forward, and make sure the Crop to drop-down menu is set to Page bounding box, this determines how much of the page is displayed. The other two crop options for bleed and slug would be used if you wanted those additional layout options to be visible. Leave the Layers tab options unchanged, and then click OK.

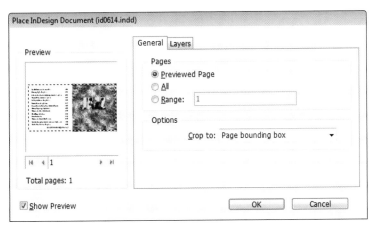

Set the Crop options to Page bounding box when importing the InDesign document into your layout.

When you import InDesign files that have links, you need to have those links available for the new layout as well. In order to print or export the layout properly, those links need to be available at that time.

4 The CD booklet design fills the frame. Because it doesn't fit entirely in the frame, right-click (Windows) or Control+click (Mac OS), and from the contextual menu, choose Fitting > Fit Content Proportionally.

5 Choose File > Save.

At the very bottom of the Tools panel, click and hold the Normal button (🖫) if the Tools panel is in single-column mode to reveal more viewing options, and then choose Preview. If the Tools panel is in double-column mode, click the Preview button (🗐) directly. Scroll through your completed layout. When you're finished, choose File > Close to close the document.

Congratulations! You've finished Lesson 5, "Working with Graphics."

Self study

For a different text wrap option, try placing id0509.psd in a block of text and, using the Text Wrap panel, select the Wrap around Object Shape button and choose Alpha Channel from the Contour Options drop-down menu. Make sure to go to the Object menu and choose Clipping Path > Options. Change the Type field to Alpha Channel, and set Alpha to trainOpenWindow.

Use Adobe Bridge or Mini Bridge to add more images to your document. Once you get used to this workflow, you will find that it can speed up the design process.

Create additional anchored images in the text frames of your document. Explore the offset options to change the positioning of anchored objects.

Customize the display of the Links panel, and change the sorting order of the links. Then use the Links panel to collect the links used in the document by using the Utilities > Copy Links To option in the Links panel menu.

Review

Questions

1   How can you have InDesign automatically fit images to frames or frames to images?

2   To flow text around the shape of a clipping path, which panel can you use?

3   How do you reposition a graphic inside its frame?

4   Which graphic format supports the visibility of layer comps?

5   Once a layered graphic is placed in an InDesign document, how do you change the layer visibility?

Answers

1   You can do this by using the Object > Fitting command.

2   You can use the Text Wrap panel.

3   You can reposition the graphic by using the new Content Grabber or by using the Direct Selection tool (⟨).

4   The Photoshop .psd file format supports the visibility of layer comps.

5   With the graphic selected, choose Object > Object Layer Options, or right-click (Windows) or Control+click (Mac OS), and choose Object Layer Options from the contextual menu.

What you'll learn in this lesson:

- Creating and importing tables
- Pasting text into a table
- Editing tables and table options
- Formatting cells, rows and text
- Defining a header cell
- Using graphics in tables
- Creating cell and table styles to format tables

Creating and Using Tables

Tables are an effective way to convey large amounts of data in an organized manner. Whether you import a table from Microsoft Word or Excel, or build a new one using InDesign, you can use many powerful methods for designing impressive, professional-looking tables. After designing a table, you can save all the attributes as a style and quickly apply those attributes to another table with just one click using table styles.

Starting up

Before starting, make sure that your tools and panels are consistent by resetting your preferences. See "Resetting the InDesign workspace and preferences" in the Starting up section of this book.

You will work with several files from the id06lessons folder in this lesson. Make sure that you have copied the id06lessons folder onto your hard drive from the Digital Classroom DVD. See "Loading lesson files" in the Starting up section of this book. This lesson may be easier to follow if the id06lessons folder is on your desktop.

See Lesson 6 in action!

Use the accompanying video to gain a better understanding of how to use some of the features shown in this lesson. The video tutorial for this lesson can be found on the supplied DVD.

The project

In this lesson, you will add tables to a brochure for Bella's Bakery. The first page of the brochure is complete, but the second page needs tables to list the products for sale. To preview the results you'll be working toward, navigate to the id06lessons folder and open id0601_done.indd. Once you've looked over the layout, you can close the file by choosing File > Close, or keep it open for reference as you work.

CAKES			PIES			COOKIES		
CHERRY CHEESECAKE		Cheesecake is quite possibly the best food in the world. Our cheesecake, topped with fresh cherries is delicious. $15	APPLE PIE		Just like Grandma's apple pie, our signature apple pie is full of only the freshest apples, picked at the height of the season. $12	CHOCOLATE CHIP		Tons of chocolate morsels in each cookie, and a soft out-of-the-oven texture make this our number one seller. $24
CHOCOLATE CAKE		Our Chocolate Cake is so dark and rich it is nearly sinful. $20	PUMPKIN PIE		It doesn't have to be fall to enjoy this classic pie. It has that real pumpkin taste you've come to expect. $11	OATMEAL RAISIN		You can almost smell them cooking! Packed with raisins, these cookies are scrumptious $19
BUNDT CAKE		Our Bunt Cake is simply heatlelble. With tons of our signature icing. $20	PECAN PIE		This is our gooiest pie we have ever offered. One slice and you'll know what we're talking about. $14	DAINTY AMARETTI		Crisp and crunchy on the outside and soft inside with the sweet taste of amaretto. $17
POUND CAKE		Whether you enjoy a slice of this cake plain or with whipped cream, it is truly scrumptious. $20	CHERRY PIE		Packed with only the freshest cherries, harvested at local farms, this is one treat you don't want to miss. $14	PEANUT BUTTER COOKIES		These cookies are soft and chewy, with that peanut butter taste you have grown to love. $15
STRAWBERRY ICE CAKE		This cake features fresh strawberries, with both chocolate and strawberry icing and topped with caramel balls. $24	BLUEBERRY PIE		Over 3,000 blueberries in just one pie! This is a sweet pie, with just a hint of tartness. $12	CRANBERRY SHORTBREAD COOKIES		Shortbread cookies Ingredients have gone far beyond the original recipe of butter, sugar and flour $16
CHOCOLATE CHEESECAKE		The Chocolate cheesecake has huge chunks of rich milk chocolate cooked right into the cake! $23	LEMON MERINGUE PIE		If you prefer more lemon taste in your pie, this is your Lemon Meringue! It's delicious from start to finish. $11	SPICED OATMEAL CRANBERRY		This recipe for spiced oatmeal cranberry cookies is thick and chewy, just the way oatmeal cookies should be! $20
CHOCOLATE TOFFEE CHERRY CAKE		This cake is a real mouthful. It's a chocolate-cherry flavored cake covered with vanilla icing and toffee bits. $24	APPLE BLACKBERRY PIE		This pie mixes the best of both worlds, with the sweetness of the apples, and the tartness of the blueberries. It's a must-try! $15	DARK CHOCOLATE CHIP		These cookies are a chocolate lovers dream. Chocolate cookies filled with huge chunks of real milk chocolate. $19

This is what the final layout should look like.

Creating a table

You can create a table using one of three methods: from scratch by typing in your data, by copying and pasting information from another table, or by converting tabbed text into a table. In this section, you'll start with creating a table from scratch, and then explore the other two options as well. Tables exist inside text frames, so to create a table you must first make a text frame. To select or modify a table, you must use the Type tool.

Creating new tables

The Bella's Bakery brochure needs multiple tables. For this first one, you'll use the Insert Table control to design your own tables.

1 Within InDesign, choose Window > Mini Bridge to display the Mini Bridge panel. Click the Launch Bridge button, navigate to the id06lessons folder, and open the file id0601.indd. The file opens in InDesign.

2 Click the Pages button (⊞) in the dock on the right side of the workspace to open the Pages panel. Page 2 should be highlighted in blue to indicate that it's the active page. If it's not highlighted, double-click page 2 in the Pages panel to make it the active page.

3 Choose View > Fit Page in Window or press Ctrl+0 (Windows) or Command+0 (Mac OS) to that you can see all of page 2 of your document.

4 Activate the Type tool (T) from the Tools panel, then click and drag to create a new text frame starting in the upper-left corner of the layout's middle column to the lower-right corner of the same column.

5 Choose Table > Insert Table.

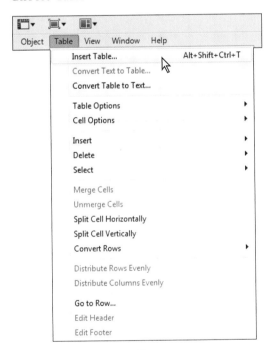

Choose Insert Table from the Table menu.

6   In the Insert Table dialog box that appears, type **7** for the Body Rows, and **4** for the Columns.

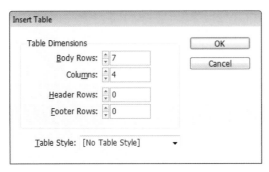

The Insert Table dialog box with the correct settings.

7   Click OK to close the dialog box and insert the table. A table with four columns and seven rows appears in the second column's text frame.

The resulting table has four columns and seven rows.

Copying and pasting table information

You now have a table with no data. You could type the information into the table, but InDesign offers an easier way: cutting and pasting data from another table. InDesign CS6 provides great flexibility when copying information by allowing you to copy data from a Microsoft Excel or Word table and paste those entries into a selected table in InDesign. Using the Clipboard Handling section of the InDesign Preferences, you can specify whether the text pasted from another application retains its original formatting or not. If you check *Text Only*, the information appears as unformatted text, which you can then flow into a selected table. If *All Information* is selected, the pasted text appears as the table looked in Word or Excel, and InDesign imports the styles from those programs. You must select the destination table's cells prior to pasting.

Because you may or may not have Word or Excel, for this exercise you will practice copying and pasting just between InDesign tables.

1   With the id0601.indd file still open, choose Window > Layers, or click the Layers button (◈) in the dock to reveal the Layers panel. If you can't find the panel under the Window menu, choose Window > Workspace > Advanced.

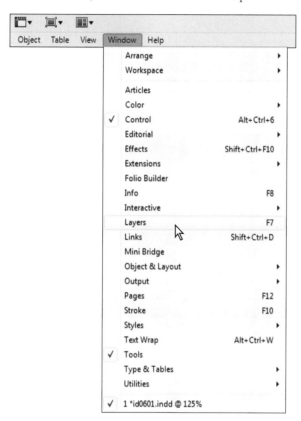

Open the Layers panel.

2 Within the Layers panel, click to select the Pies layer. To the left of the Pies listing, click in the left-hand box to reveal the visibility icon (👁), which makes the layer's contents visible. The layer's contents appear on the pasteboard to the right of the page.

Click the gray square to reveal the layer's contents.

3 Select the Hand tool (🖑) from the Tools panel. Click the page with the Hand tool, and drag left to reveal the pasteboard on the right side of the page. Next to the pie images is a table with information on the bakery's pies. Use the Hand tool to position this area so that you can see both the table and the pie images.

4 Select the Type tool (T) from the Tools panel. You edit a table by selecting either the table or its cells with the Type tool, as they reside in text frames.

5   Hover over the top-left corner of the pies table until you see an arrow that points diagonally toward the lower-right corner. Click to select the entire table.

Click when the arrow in the upper-left corner is displayed to select the entire table.

When hovering over a table, the cursor image indicates which parts of the table you can select. The diagonal arrow means you can select the whole table. An arrow pointing to the right indicates that clicking selects a row. Click when the arrow points straight down, and you select a single column. You can also click and drag across the top or left side of the table to select a range of columns or rows, respectively.

6   Choose Edit > Copy to copy the selected table to the clipboard.

7   On page 2, you need to select the table you created in the previous exercise, which is the destination table. Double-click the Hand tool to fit the page to the window. Select the whole table by moving the Type tool over the top-left corner of the table, and clicking when you see the diagonal arrow.

8   Choose Edit > Paste to paste the information from the existing pies table into your new table. You have successfully moved table information from an existing table to another new table.

9   Choose File > Save As. In the Save As dialog box, navigate to the id06lessons folder and type **id0601_work.indd** in the File name text field. Click Save.

Converting text to a table and a table to text

If you prefer, you can bypass the step of creating a table grid, and simply paste data from an existing table into a text frame in your document. The information appears as tab-delimited text, which you can then convert into a table using the Table menu's Convert Text to Table command. You can also perform this process in the opposite direction using Convert Table to Text. When you choose this command, InDesign removes the table lines and inserts the separators you specify at the end of each row and column.

To demonstrate both commands, you will convert the table you just created to text and then convert the text back to a table.

1 With the table on page 2 still selected, choose Table > Convert Table to Text.

2 In the Convert Table to Text dialog box, Tab should be set as the Column Separator and Paragraph should be set as the Row Separator.

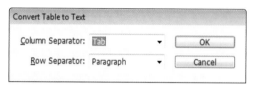

Specify your item separators in the Convert Table to Text dialog box.

3 Click OK. InDesign inserts tabs between each column entry, and paragraph returns after each row, removing all table lines.

Apple Pie» » Just like Grandma's apple pie, our signature apple pie is full of only the freshest apples, picked at the height of the season.$12¶
Pumpkin Pie » » It doesn't have to be fall to enjoy this classic pie. It has that real pumpkin taste you've come to expect. » $11¶
Pecan Pie» » This is our gooiest pie we have ever offered. One slice and you'll know what we're talking about. » $14¶
Cherry Pie» » Packed with only the freshest cherries, harvested at local farms, this is one treat you don't want to miss. » $14¶
Blueberry Pie » » Over 3,000 blueberries in just one pie! This is a sweet pie, with just a hint of tartness. » $12¶
Lemon Merengue Pie» » If you prefer more lemon taste in your pie, this is your Lemon Merengue! It's delicious from start to finish. » $11¶
Apple Blackberry Pie» » This pie mixes the best of both worlds, with the sweetness of the apples, and the tartness of the blueberries. It's a must-try! » $15#

The table is now tab-delimited text.

You will now take this mess of text and turn it back into a table.

4 With the Type tool (T), click inside the text frame, and then choose Edit > Select All, or press Ctrl+A (Windows) or Command+A (Mac OS), to highlight all the text.

5 Choose Table > Convert Text to Table. In the resulting Convert Text to Table dialog box, keep the default separator settings and click OK to display the selected text as a table again.

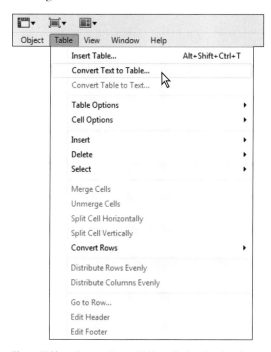

Choose Table > Convert Text to Table to display the selected text as a table.

6 Press Shift+Ctrl+A (Windows) or Shift+Command+A (Mac OS) to deselect everything in the document. Choose File > Save to save your work.

Importing a table

For some projects, you may need to incorporate an existing table created in Microsoft Word or Excel into your layout. Instead of simply pasting a table into the document, the better approach is to use the Place command, which gives you more control over formatting. When you place a Word or Excel document, you can edit the resulting table in InDesign using its Microsoft Word Import options to control the formatting.

1 With id0601_work.indd still open, activate the Type tool (T) and choose File > Place to insert the Microsoft Word document with a table into page 2 of your InDesign file.

2 Click to turn on the *Show Import Options* checkbox at the bottom-left of the Place dialog box. Navigate to the id06lessons folder, select id0601.docx, and click Open. InDesign supports the latest XML-based open format from Word and Excel.

3 The Microsoft Word Import Options dialog box appears. Click the *Remove Styles and Formatting from Text and Tables* radio button, located in the Formatting section of the dialog box, to strip the incoming document of all Word formatting and replace it with the InDesign Basic Paragraph style. This is a good idea if you don't want any of the styles, colors, or other formatting from Word in your InDesign document. Later in this lesson, you will format the text and save the results as your own styles.

For more on importing text, see Lesson 3, "Working with Text and Type."

Strip the Word document of its formatting to avoid any inconsistencies once it's in InDesign.

4 Click OK in the Microsoft Word Import Options dialog box. It closes, and to the right of the cursor is a miniature preview of the text.

5 In the left-hand column on page 2, click and drag from the top-left margin to the bottom-right corner to designate the area in which to place the table. You can also just click in the upper-left corner of the margin area to flow the text into the first column. If you see a red overflow box at the bottom-right corner of the text frame, which indicates that there is more placed text than the column can hold, don't worry: you'll fix the proportions of the frame soon.

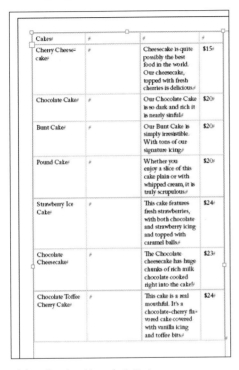

Click to place the table on the InDesign page.

6 Choose File > Save to save your work.

Editing tables and table options

InDesign CS6 has all the same table tools you've come to rely on to make your table presentations visually pleasing. In this series of exercises, you will concentrate on ways to adjust the entire Word table you imported. First you'll change the height of the top row, and then you will explore Table Options to change the border row strokes, column strokes, and fill of the table.

Changing row height

If your rows are too short to hold your entries, you can easily expand them.

1 With the Type tool (T) selected, click inside the table you imported in the left-hand column.

2 Hover between the top row, which holds the word *Cakes*, and the row below it, which contains *Cherry Cheesecake* in its left-most cell. When the cursor is directly over the row separator, it becomes a double arrow.

Cakes			
Cherry Cheese-cake		Cheesecake is quite possibly the best food in the world. Our cheesecake, topped with fresh cherries is delicious	$15
Chocolate Cake		Our Chocolate Cake is so dark and rich it is nearly sinful	$20
Bunt Cake		Our Bunt Cake is simply irresistible. With tons of our signature icing	$20
Pound Cake		Whether you enjoy a slice of this cake plain or with whipped cream, it is truly scrupulous	$20
Strawberry Ice Cake		This cake features fresh strawberries, with both chocolate and strawberry icing and topped with caramel balls	$24
Chocolate Cheesecake		The Chocolate cheesecake has huge chunks of rich milk chocolate cooked right into the cake	$23
Chocolate Toffee Cherry Cake		This cake is a real mouthful. It's a chocolate-cherry fla-vored cake covered with vanilla icing and toffee bits	$24

The cursor changes to a double arrow when it is directly over a row separator.

3 Click the row separator with the double-arrow cursor, and drag it to resize the top row. Drag up or down enough so that the height of the row is at a desired size.

To change just the size of a row or column without affecting the entire table, hold the Shift key as you drag. You can do this for all rows and columns except the right-most row and bottom-most column, where holding the Shift key alters all the rows at the same time.

Editing the border

Now you will change the size of the table border.

1 With the Type tool still active, click once inside the cell holding the Cakes heading, and then choose Table > Table Options > Table Setup. The Table Options dialog box opens.

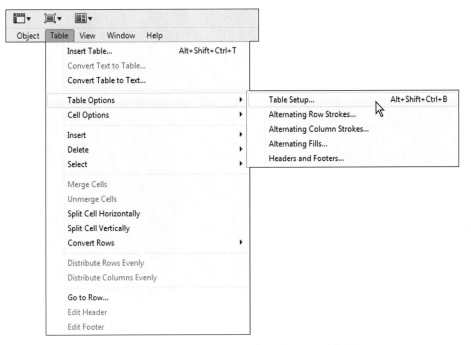

Choose Table Options > Table Setup in the Table menu to open the Table Options dialog box.

2   In the Table Options dialog box, type **3** in the Weight text field in the Table Border section. Check the *Preview* checkbox in the bottom-left corner of the dialog box to see the change take effect. Your bottom row may disappear. If not, keep the dialog box open and jump down to the next section. If it does disappear, click OK; then, with the Type tool selected (T), click the divider between the first and second rows, drag it up to resize the top row again, and then choose Table > Table Options > Table Setup. The Table Options dialog box opens again.

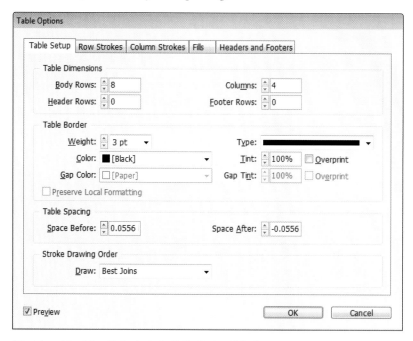

Adjust the weight of the table border in the Table Options dialog box.

Formatting rows and columns

In the previous section, you have changed the border size, and now you will change the color and size of the row and column separators.

1   With the table still selected, and the Table Options dialog box still open, click on the Row Strokes tab at the top of the dialog box.

2   From the Alternating Pattern drop-down menu, choose Every Other Row. This setting allows you to control the appearance of the rows. The options on the left side of the Alternating section are for the first row, and the options on the right side are for the next row. It repeats this pattern throughout the table's rows.

3   In the Alternating section, beneath the First text field, type **3** in the Weight text field, and choose Dark Blue from the Color drop-down menu. These settings affect the first row and every alternating row beneath it.

4 Type **3** in the Weight text field beneath the Next text field, and choose Light Blue from the Color drop-down menu. This setting affects the second row and every second row beneath that.

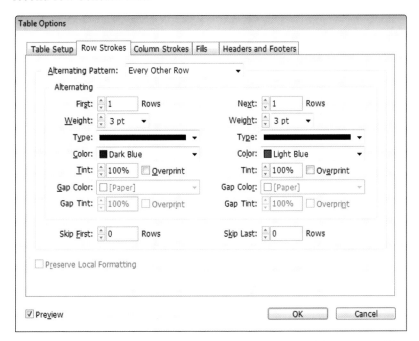

The Row Strokes category in the Table Options dialog box allows you to control the appearance of the row strokes in a table, including alternating strokes.

5 Click the Column Strokes tab in the Table Options dialog box.

6 Choose Every Other Column from the Alternating Pattern drop-down menu.

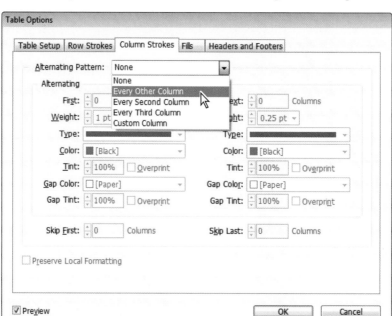

The Alternating Pattern drop-down menu.

7 In the Alternating section, beneath the First text field, type **3** in the Weight field, and choose Dark Blue from the Color drop-down menu. These settings affect the first column and every alternating column after it.

8   Beneath the Next text field, type **3** in the Weight field, and choose Light Blue from
the Color drop-down menu. Click OK to apply the changes. Choose the Selection
tool. Then press **W** on your keyboard to toggle into Preview mode to see how the
table will appear when printed. Press **W** again to return to Normal view.

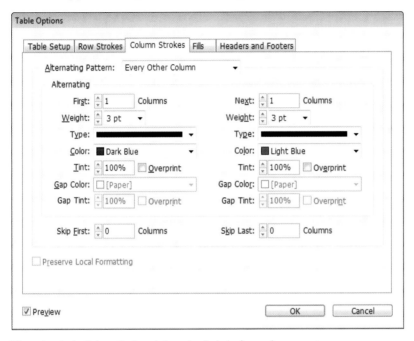

The settings in the Column Strokes tab determine the look of your column separators.

Using fills

To put the finishing touch on your table, you will fill it with color.

1   Select the Type tool (T) and click inside any cell; then choose Table > Select > Table.
Choose Table > Table Options > Alternating Fills. This opens the Fills section of the
Table Options dialog box.

2   Choose Every Other Row from the Alternating Pattern drop-down menu.

3   In the Alternating section, beneath the First text field, choose Light Chocolate from
the Color drop-down menu and type **20** in the Tint Percentage text field.

4   In the color section beneath the Next text field, choose Light Blue from the Color drop-down menu and type **20** for Tint Percentage. With *Preview* checked, you should see the changes happen instantaneously.

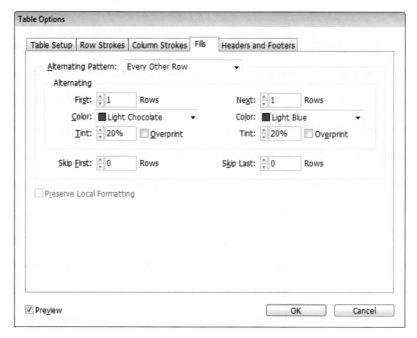

Set the fill color and tint percentage in the Fill section of the Table Options dialog box.

5 Click OK to apply all your fill colors. Press the Esc key to deselect the table. Note that when a table is highlighted, the colors applied to the table appear to be the inverse of their actual color. You need to deselect the table in order to view the actual colors.

Cakes			
Cherry Cheese-cake		Cheesecake is quite possibly the best food in the world. Our cheesecake, topped with fresh cherries is delicious.	$15
Chocolate Cake		Our Chocolate Cake is so dark and rich it is nearly sinful.	$20
Bunt Cake		Our Bunt Cake is simply irresistible. With tons of our signature icing.	$20
Pound Cake		Whether you enjoy a slice of this cake plain or with whipped cream, it is truly scrupulous.	$20
Strawberry Ice Cake		This cake features fresh strawberries, with both chocolate and strawberry icing and topped with caramel balls.	$24
Chocolate Cheesecake		The Chocolate cheesecake has huge chunks of rich milk chocolate cooked right into the cake!	$23
Chocolate Toffee Cherry Cake		This cake is a real mouthful. It's a	$24

The table now reflects all the Table Options changes.

6 Choose File > Save to save your work.

Formatting cells and text

Unlike the Table Options settings that apply to the whole table, your cell styles and Cell Options settings can be different for each cell in the table. You can select and format one cell at a time, an entire row, an entire column, or any other group of cells. You will now format the table on a cell-by-cell basis. You will start by resetting the cell style of all the cells in the table, and then you'll change the vertical alignment of type within all cells. Finally, you will make four paragraph styles, one each for the table's header, name, description, and price sections. In later exercises, you'll use these paragraph styles to create cell styles that will speed the rest of the table's formatting, and ultimately you'll use the cell styles to create a table style with which you'll format the entire Pies table.

Resetting the cell styles within a table

Soon you will make both cell and table styles so that you can quickly apply all the attributes of a table and also the cells within a table using a single click of the mouse. But as we start this lesson, this table has mixed cell styles, which means that some of the settings from Microsoft Word have remained with the table. You'll start by clearing the additional formatting.

1 With the Type tool (T) selected, hover over the top-left corner of the cakes frame until you see a diagonal arrow, then click to select the Cakes table.

2 Choose Window > Styles > Cell Styles to open the Cell Styles panel. Notice the plus sign next to None in the panel's list of styles. This means that the selected table contains *overrides*, which are Word styles left over from the original document.

Manage the styles used in your table cells from the Cell Styles panel.

3 Hover your cursor over the plus sign to prompt a small yellow box listing all the items on your page that are formatted using settings not defined in the None style. Alt+click (Windows) or Option+click (Mac OS) the word *None* to clear the overrides. This ensures that the cells are not using any additional formatting.

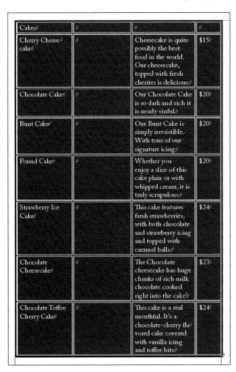

Clear the overrides to ensure consistent formatting of the table cells. Alt+click (Windows) or Option+click (Mac OS) to remove any style overrides from the selected cells.

4 Choose File > Save.

Text alignment and inset within a cell

Some cell formatting options are similar to the Text frame options you worked with in previous lessons. For example, you can use the same alignment options within a cell—top, center, bottom, and justified—as you can in a text box. You also have the same text inset settings that control how far from the edge of a cell text is inset. You will now change these settings for the whole table. You can also change these options one cell at a time, for a range of cells, or for all the cells at once. For the Bella's Bakery table, you will change the alignment and inset settings for all the cells at once.

1 Make sure the whole table is selected, and then choose Table > Cell Options > Text to open the Cell Options dialog box.

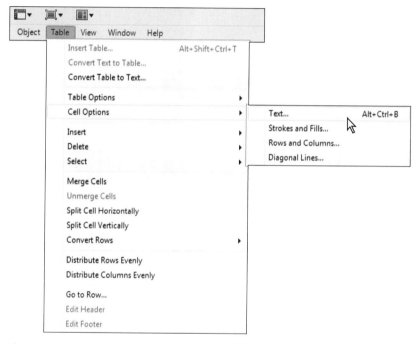

After you select the table, choose Cell Options > Text from the Table menu.

2 In the Cell Insets section of the Cell Options dialog box, type **0.0625** in the Top text field. Press the Tab key to apply the settings to all the insets. If this does not insert 0.0625 automatically in the Bottom, Left, and Right fields, type **0.0625** again and click the Make All Settings the Same button (⬤) to the immediate right of the top and bottom inset values.

3 In the Vertical Justification section, choose Align Center from the Align drop-down menu.

4 Click the *Preview* checkbox to see your changes. The text in each cell is centered and inset from each edge. Click OK to apply the settings.

Set the text alignment and inset in the Cell Options dialog box.

Formatting text within a cell and saving paragraph styles

You can also format the text color and font size in your cells. You can then save these settings as a paragraph style for reuse later; applying styles to cells is as easy as applying them to text frames. In this exercise, you'll create several paragraph styles from your cell formatting. In the next section, you'll apply these styles to other cells and see how much time you can save by using styles.

1 With the Type tool (T), click inside the first cell of the second row, and then choose Edit > Select All to highlight the cell's contents (the words *Cherry Cheesecake*).

2 Type **10** in the Font Size field in the character formatting section of the Control panel, and then click the Small Caps button (Tr) to apply small caps.

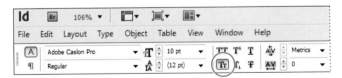

Set the font size and toggle on Small Caps in the Control panel.

3 Open the Swatches panel. Select the Dark Chocolate swatch to make the text dark brown. Make sure your text fill icon is in the foreground.

Select Dark Chocolate from the Swatches panel.

4 Press Shift+Ctrl+C (Windows) or Shift+Command+C (Mac OS) to center the type in its box.

5 Choose Type > Paragraph Styles to open the Paragraph Styles panel. Click the panel menu button (•≡) in the Paragraph Styles panel and choose New Paragraph Style from the contextual menu.

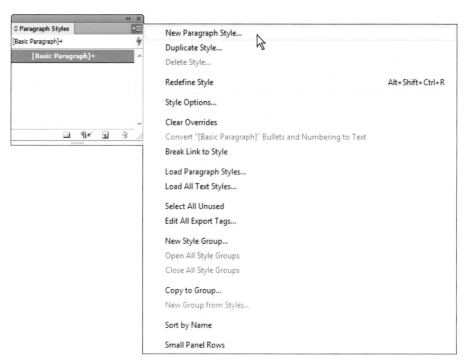

Create a new paragraph style in the Paragraph Styles panel.

6   In the resulting New Paragraph Style dialog box, type **Name** in the Style Name text field, click the *Apply Style to Selection* checkbox, then click OK to create a new style based upon the attributes from the selected text. You'll use the Name style to format the names of all the baked goods listed for Bella's Bakery.

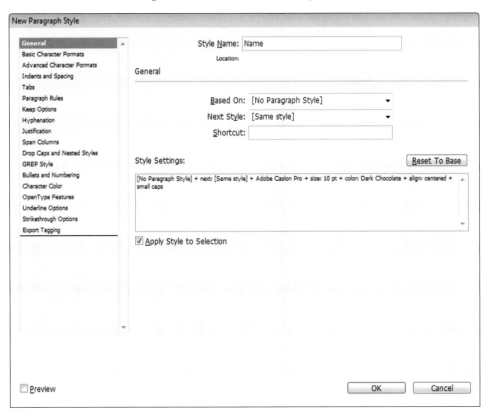

Name your style in the New Paragraph Style dialog box.

Making a style does not automatically apply that style. By checking Apply Style to Selection *in the New Paragraph Style dialog box, InDesign applies the newly created style to the selected text, linking the selected text to the style. If the style is updated, the text that was selected when the style was created will also be updated.*

7   Select the Name listing in the Paragraph Styles panel. If a plus sign appears next to it, Alt+click (Windows) or Option+click (Mac OS) it to clear all overrides.

The Paragraph Styles panel automatically lists your new style.

You will now make a paragraph style for the cake's descriptions.

8   Repeat steps 1 to 6, using the text in the third-from-left cell in the second row, the paragraph that starts with the sentence, *Cheesecake is quite possibly the best food in the world*. Set the font size to 8 points if it isn't already, and leave Small Caps toggled off. Set the paragraph alignment to center and name this new style **Description**.

You will now make a paragraph style for the price listings.

9   With the Type tool, click inside the last cell on the right in the second row (the one containing *$15*). Choose Edit > Select All, and repeat steps 3 to 6, naming the new style **Price**.

10 Select the Price listing in the Paragraph Styles panel to apply the style to the selected cell. If necessary, clear all overrides.

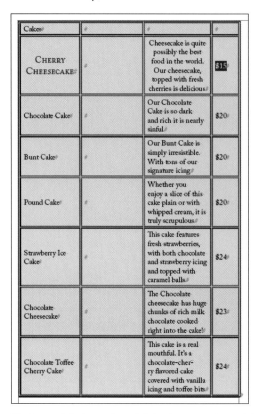

The Paragraph Styles panel now includes three new styles, and the Cakes table is taking shape.

11 Choose File > Save to save your work.

Formatting text in tables by column

You can easily apply paragraph styles to groups of cells, such as a column. The process involves selecting the group and then applying a paragraph style. You will now select the first column of the table and apply one of the paragraph styles created in the last exercise.

1   With the Type tool selected (T), click in the Cherry Cheesecake cell (second row, first cell), and drag down until all the cells below it in the column are highlighted.

2   Click on the paragraph style Name in the Paragraph Styles panel to apply it to all the selected cells.

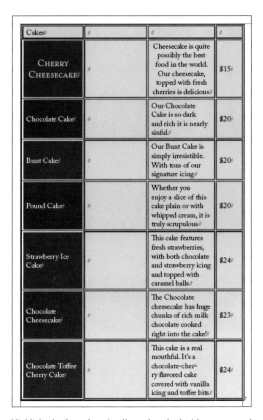

Highlight the first column's cells, and apply the Name paragraph style.

3 Now click in the second cell of the third column (*Cheesecake is quite possibly…*), drag to select all the cells below it, and select Description in the Paragraph Styles panel to apply the Description style.

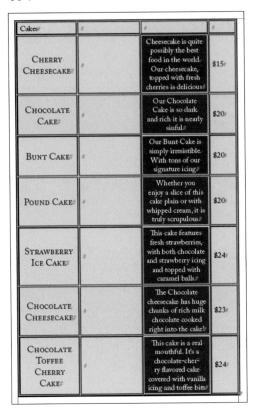

Select the third column, and apply the Description style.

4 Click the *$15* cell, drag down until all the price column's cells are highlighted, and select the Price style in the Paragraph Styles panel.

Working with tables in Story Editor

InDesign CS6 lets you view tables in the Story Editor. You can use the Story Editor to make sure you have applied the correct paragraph styles to the selected columns.

1　Click anywhere inside the table with the Type tool (T).

2　Choose Edit > Edit in Story Editor. The Story Editor opens up and allows you to view the table away from the page, while you can still see which styles are applied to each row and column. Each row is displayed in blue text in the Story Editor and each entry within each row represents a column or cell within that row.

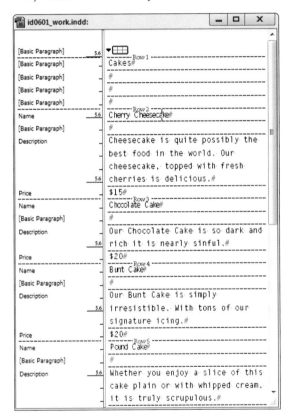

The Story Editor in InDesign CS6 displays tables and identifies styles applied to them.

Make sure that the correct styles are applied. You can make edits directly in the Story Editor and the changes are immediately applied to the layout. Close the Story Editor by clicking the "X" in the top-right corner (Windows), or the red circle in the top-left corner (Mac OS).

Merging cells

You can merge multiple cells in the same row or column into a single cell. To demonstrate, you will merge the top four cells (the first row) of the example table so that the top row (with the word *Cakes* in it) looks more like a title. In the next section, you'll format it to stand out even more.

1 Select the cells in the first row by hovering your cursor over the left edge of the box until you see an arrow pointing to the right. Click to select the entire row.

2 Choose Table > Merge Cells or click the Merge Cells button (⊠) in the Control panel to make the top four cells into a single cell.

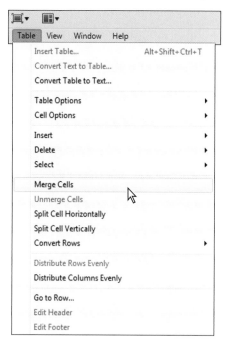

Merge the top four cells into one cell for the Cakes *header.*

Defining a header cell

For a large table that spans multiple columns, frames, or pages, you can designate header or footer rows in order to repeat identifying information at the top or bottom of each portion of the divided table. If your table spans over several pages, headers are vital to orienting readers with the table's data. For instance, if the number of cakes sold by Bella's Bakery increased enough to require two columns in its brochure, the next linked frame would automatically contain a header row. This saves you the time of inserting the header on each subsequent page.

Because it treats header cells as special cases, InDesign enables you to color and format them independently, without changing the features of the rest of the table. You can take advantage of this to help the headers stand out from the body of your table. Your header will be instantly identifiable when repeated in a multi-page, -column, or –frame layout, and your readers will be able to more easily decipher the information in the table. In this exercise, you will convert the Cakes cell into a header cell, apply unique formatting, and create a new paragraph style from it. Then you'll create a header for the Pies table.

If you just click in a cell or even highlight its contents, InDesign thinks you want to color the text. Either click with the right-pointing arrow or press the Esc key to select an entire cell.

1   Making sure the top row is still selected, choose Table > Convert Rows > To Header to make the top cell a header cell. Click once inside the cell with the Type tool (T), and notice how the color drops out of the cell. It's a header cell now, so InDesign strips the normal cell formatting. You'll now add some header-specific formatting.

2   The cell's fill should automatically change to None because it is now separate from the rest of the table. Select the cell in the first row by hovering your cursor over the left edge of the box until you see an arrow pointing to the right. Click to select the entire row. In the Swatches panel, make sure the Fill icon ( ) is in the foreground and click the Paper swatch to color the topmost cell.

Paper is opaque and represents the background on which the document will print. By contrast, the None option is transparent and displays any objects beneath it.

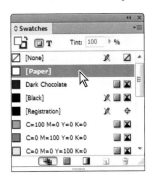

Choose Paper for the fill in the Swatches panel.

3   With the Type tool (T), click anywhere in the header cell to activate the cell, and then double-click on the word *Cakes* to select only the text.

Now you will stylize the type and make a paragraph style.

4 Center the type in the cell by pressing Shift+Ctrl+C (Windows) or Shift+Command+C (Mac OS). In the Control panel, click on the Small Caps button (Tʀ) to convert the title to a mix of large and small caps, and type **24** in the Font Size text field. Press Enter (Windows) or Return (Mac OS) to increase the size of the text.

If the type disappears from the cell, the type is too large for the cell to contain it. Hover over the bottom of the header cell until you see the double-arrow cursor, and then click and drag down. Make sure you don't lose any of the table at the bottom because of overflow.

5 Choose Type > Character to reveal the Character panel. Type **100** in the Tracking text field and press Enter (Windows) or Return (Mac OS). You can use either the Character panel or the Control panel to control character formatting.

Change the tracking in the Character panel.

6 Click the Swatches button (▦) in the dock to open the Swatches panel. Bring Fill to the foreground and click Light Blue to choose it for the fill color. Click the Stroke icon to bring it to the foreground, then choose Black to add a black stroke around the text.

7 With the formatting finished, you can now save it as a paragraph style. Choose Window > Styles > Paragraph Styles to reveal the Paragraph Styles panel. Alt+click (Windows) or Option+click (Mac OS) the Create New Style button (≝) to open the New Paragraph Style dialog box. Type **Header** in the Style Name text field, and click OK.

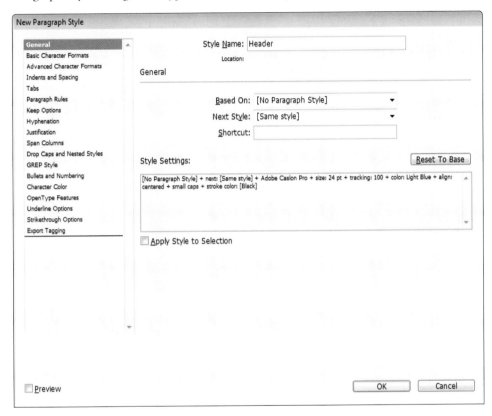

Create a new header style based on the formatting settings you've chosen.

8 In the Paragraph Styles panel's list, click Header to apply the style to the selected text.

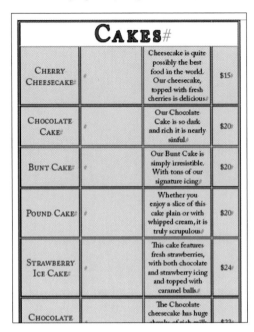

The title Cakes *stands out from the rest of the table thanks to its Header style.*

9 The Pies table in the second column on page 2 needs a header as well. Click anywhere in the table with the Type tool.

10 Choose Table > Table Options > Headers and Footers to open the Table Options dialog box.

11 In the Table Dimensions section, type **1** in the Header Rows text field. Click OK to create a header row.

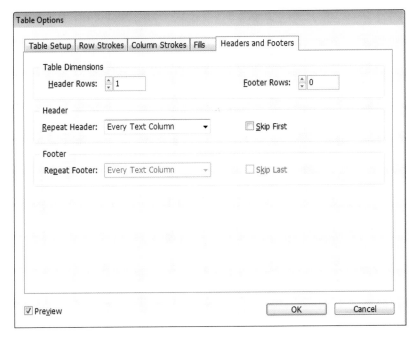

Create a header row for the Pies table.

12 Select the header row in the Pies table, and then choose Table > Merge Cells to convert the row to a single title cell.

13 Click inside the header row with the Type tool, then type **Pies**.

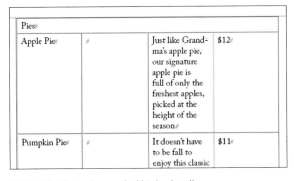

Add the title Pies *to the second table's header cell.*

14 Choose File > Save to save your work.

Setting column and row dimensions

At this point, you've adjusted the contents of rows and columns, but you haven't modified the row height or column width directly. By default, row height is determined by the height of the current font. Tables imported from Microsoft Word or Excel, however, can retain their original, exact row heights. If neither of these options fits your layout, InDesign enables you to change row height and column width in the Cell Options dialog box. Here you can specify whether you want a fixed row height that does not change when you add to or delete from the row, or, if you prefer, a variable height. For a fixed height, choose Exactly from the Row Height drop-down menu, and then specify the height you need. Choose At Least to specify a minimum row height; with this setting, rows increase in height as you add text or increase the font size, but will not be smaller than the minimum you set. Try out these cell options on the Cakes and Pies tables.

Setting a fixed row height

For the Cakes and Pies tables, a fixed row height works best. In the steps that follow, you'll adjust the size of the cells and also change their Row height to be an exact value. Then you will do the same for the Pies table.

1 Using the Type tool (T), click in the Cakes header cell, and then press the Esc key to select the cell.

2 Choose Table > Cell Options > Rows and Columns to open the Cell Options dialog box. In the Row Height section, choose Exactly from the drop-down menu. Type **0.5** in the Row Height text field, and then click OK. The height of the header row changes.

Set the row height to exactly 0.5 in the Cell Options dialog box.

3   Click and drag from the Cherry Cheesecake cell in the top-left corner to the *$24* cell in the bottom-right corner to select the rest of the table.

4   Choose Table > Cell Options > Rows and Columns. Choose Exactly from the Row Height drop-down menu, type **1.0625** in the Row Height field, and click OK.

5   Now you need to set the row height for the Pies table. Click and drag from the Apple Pie cell in the top-left corner to the *$15* cell in the bottom-right corner to select the rest of the table.

If the table is overset, use the Selection tool ( ) to extend the boundaries of the text frame down below the page. Setting row height fits the table into the column.

6   Choose Table > Cell Options > Rows and Columns to open the Cell Options dialog box. If it is not already selected, choose Exactly from the Row Height drop-down menu. Type **1.0625** in the Row Height text field, and then click OK.

7   Using the Type tool, click in the Pies header cell, and then press the Esc key to select the cell.

8   Choose Table > Cell Options > Rows and Columns. In the resulting Cell Options dialog box, choose Exactly from the Row Height drop-down menu and type **0.5** in the Row Height field. Click OK.

Pies			
Apple Pie	#	Just like Grandma's apple pie, our signature apple pie is full of only the freshest apples, picked at the	$12
Pumpkin Pie	#	It doesn't have to be fall to enjoy this classic pie. It has that real pumpkin taste you've come to expect.	$11

The Pies table now has a header row height of 0.5 and a body row height of 1.0625.

9   Choose File > Save to save your work.

Setting column width

You will now fix the column width for the Pies table.

1   Activate the Type tool (T), and then click inside the $12 cell, to the right of, or after, the text. Press Shift+down-arrow to select the current cell, and then press Shift+down-arrow six more times to select the whole column.

2   Choose Window > Type & Tables > Table to open the Table panel, and make similar changes as you did using the Cell Options dialog box. Type **0.4215** in the Column Width text field and press Enter (Windows) or Return (Mac OS).

Enter the desired width in the Column Width text field of the Table panel.

3   Click inside the cell in the top-right part of the table containing the paragraph that starts with *Just like Grandma's*. Press the escape key once to select the cell, then press Shift+down-arrow several times to select the entire column.

4   In the Table panel, type **1.0438** in the Column Width text field, and press Enter (Windows) or Return (Mac OS).

Use the Table panel to adjust the column width for the column containing the pies' descriptions.

5   Click inside the topmost empty cell (the second from the left), and then press Shift+down-arrow seven times to select the whole column.

6   Type **0.9715** in the Column Width text field in the Table panel, and press Enter (Windows) or Return (Mac OS).

7   Click the Apple Pie cell, and then press Shift+down-arrow seven times to select the whole column.

8   Return to the Table panel and type **0.9382** in the Column Width text field. Press Enter (Windows) or Return (Mac OS). All row and column formatting is now complete for the Pies table.

9   Choose File > Save to save your file.

Using graphics in tables

Images can spice up any table and, perhaps, help sell a few more of Bella's pies and cakes. InDesign offers three ways to insert graphics into tables: select a cell with the Type tool and choose File > Place, or select the graphic with the Selection tool, cut or copy it, and then paste it into the table with the Type tool, or use the blue anchored object indicator located in the upper-right of a frame to drag and drop into position. When you add a graphic that is larger than the cell, the cell height increases to contain the graphic; the width of the cell doesn't change, but the image may extend beyond the right side of the cell. If you place a graphic in a cell of a row set to a fixed height and that image is taller than the row height, InDesign marks the cell as overset and adds a red circle, instead of the image, to the cell. You then need to correct either the height of the table row or the size of the image so the image appears in the cell.

Placing graphics in cells

In this exercise, you'll add images to the Bella's Bakery tables. To expedite the process, the document's pasteboard contains appropriately sized graphics that are ready to place. Instead of using the Selection tool to select them, changing to the Type tool, and then back to the Selection tool, you'll use a much more efficient shortcut to manage this task.

1   With the Selection tool (↖), click the cherry cheesecake picture in the top-left area of the pasteboard to select it. If you are still in Preview mode, you can't see your pasteboard. Press **W** on the keyboard to exit or enter Preview mode.

Choose the cherry cheesecake image on the pasteboard to the left of the document.

2   Choose Edit > Cut, or use the keyboard shortcut Ctrl+X (Windows) or Command+X (Mac OS) to cut the image to the clipboard. You will put all the graphics into the empty table cells in exactly the order they already appear on the pasteboard.

3   In the Cakes table, double-click the second-from-left cell in the second row. Double-clicking any cell that can contain text automatically turns the Selection tool into the Type tool (T).

4   Press Ctrl+V (Windows) or Command+V (Mac OS) to paste the picture into the selected cell.

5   Move back over the pasteboard, and then press and hold Ctrl (Windows) or Command (Mac OS) to change the Type tool to the Selection tool, and click the picture of the chocolate cake.

6   Press Ctrl+X (Windows) or Command+X (Mac OS) to cut the picture.

7 Click the second cell of the third row, and then press Ctrl+V (Windows) or Command+V (Mac OS) to paste the picture into the cell.

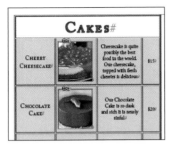

Cut and paste the cheesecake and cake images into the Cakes table.

When you paste a figure into a table cell, you're creating an inline graphic or graphic that behaves as a piece of text. InDesign CS6 offers an efficient way to create inline graphics with drag and drop ease.

8 With the Selection tool, click the third graphic on the pasteboard and hover your cursor over the blue box located in the upper-right corner of the frame. Press and hold the Shift key on your keyboard, click the blue box, and drag it to the second cell in the Bundt Cake row. The graphic is immediately added to that location.

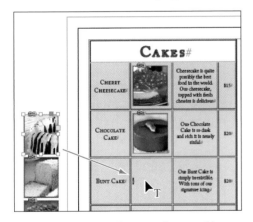

Shift+drag the blue box in the upper-right corner of the graphics frame to the empty cell in the table.

9 Repeat step 8 for the remaining cake pictures, and then repeat them again to paste the pie graphics from the right side of the pasteboard into the Pies table to fit in their respective rows, or use the copy/paste method.

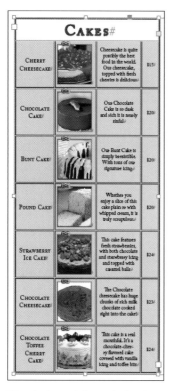

Using the drag-and-drop method to place graphics in table cells lets you format the tables quickly.

It is possible to make a photo fit entirely within a table cell; however, there are a few things to account for. Every cell has a text inset applied by default. To ensure that a photo fits within the cell, remove the cell inset so the photo can extend to the cell border. In addition, if you have any strokes applied to a cell, you need to reduce the size of the graphics frame by the value of those stroke values.

Cell styles and table styles

With InDesign CS6, you can use cell styles to format cells, and table styles to format tables, in the same way you use paragraph and character styles to format text. Beyond that, you can nest cell styles into a table style in the same way that you can nest character styles into paragraph styles. Cell styles contain such information as paragraph styles, cell insets, strokes, and fills, which means that you can apply all these attributes to a cell or range of cells with one click. When you make a cell style, however, it does not automatically include all the selected cell's formatting. From a collection of cell styles, you can build table styles. Table styles contain cell styles as well as Table Options settings, including table borders and row and column strokes. As with all InDesign styles, when you update a table or cell style, all elements to which the style is applied update automatically. These Table styles give you the ability to format an entire table with one click and implement changes throughout a document's tables.

By default, each new document contains a Basic Table style with basic table formatting. However, you can customize Table styles to apply to the tables you create. In addition, each document contains a default cell style called None, which is a quick way to remove all cell attributes, as you discovered in the "Resetting the cell styles within a table" section. You cannot modify the None style.

When you use cell styles in a table style, you can specify which cell styles are applied to different sections of the table: header and footer rows, left and right columns, and body rows.

Cell styles

Because you have already formatted the table and cells and also created paragraph styles, you can now reap the rewards of setting up a table using the correct process. With all these elements in place, you can now easily create cell styles. In this exercise, you'll create four cell styles—Header, Name, Description, and Price—that contain the paragraph styles you made earlier.

1   Using the Type tool (T), click inside the Cherry Cheesecake cell, and then press Ctrl+/ (Windows) or Command+/ (Mac OS) to select it.

2   Choose Window > Styles > Cell Styles, to open the Cell Styles panel.

3 Choose New Cell Style from the Cell Styles panel menu (⋅≡).

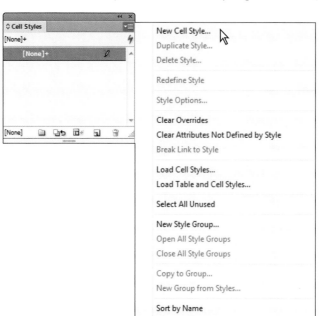

Choose New Cell Style from the Cell Styles panel menu.

4 In the New Cell Style dialog box that opens, type **Name** in the Style Name text field. Note that because the cell was selected when creating a new style, all the attributes of the cell have been incorporated into the cell style definition. Choose Name from the Paragraph Style drop-down menu, and click OK to create the Name cell style. You have now created a cell style that contains a paragraph style.

You will apply the style in the next exercise.

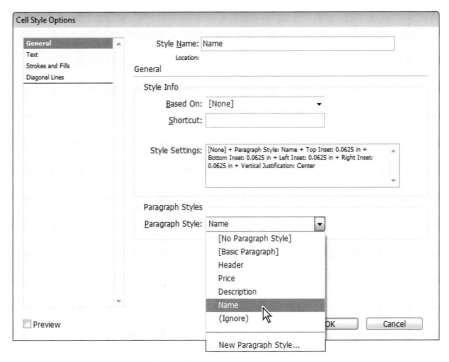

Choose Name from the Paragraph Style drop-down menu.

5   Click the Cakes header cell using the Type tool, and then press the Esc key to select it.

6   Choose New Cell Style from the Cell Styles panel menu, type **Header** in the Style Name field, choose Header from the Paragraph Styles drop-down menu, and click OK to create the Header cell style.

7   Click the first description cell (*Cheesecake is quite possibly the best...*), and then press the Esc key to select it.

8   Repeat step 6, naming the new cell style **Description** and choosing Description for the associated paragraph style.

9   Click the *$15* cell, and then press the Esc key to select it.

10 Repeat step 6, naming the final cell style **Price** and choosing Price for the associated paragraph style.

Applying cell styles

You can apply cell styles to cells with the usual point-and-click ease. Try it out by applying the styles you just created to the Cakes table.

1   Click inside the Cakes header cell using the Type tool (T), and then press the Esc key to select it.

2   Click the Header style in the Cell Styles panel to apply that style to the selected cell.

Click a name in the Cell Styles panel's list to apply a cell style to a selected cell.

3   Click at the end of the Cherry Cheesecake text, press Shift+down-arrow to select its cell, and then press Shift+down arrow six more times to select the rest of the column.

4   Click the Name style in the Cell Styles panel's list to apply that style to the selected cells.

5   Click in the first description cell (*Cheesecake is quite possibly the best...*) and drag down and to the left to select all the images and descriptions.

6 Click Description in the Cell Styles panel to apply the style. This centers the images in the cells for you as well.

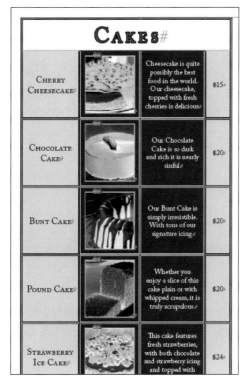

Click and drag to select both the images and descriptions, and then apply the style.

7 Click in the *$15* cell, and then drag down to select it and the rest of the price cells. You can also press Shift+down arrow seven times to select the remaining cells.

8 Click Price in the Cell Styles panel to apply the final style.

Creating table styles

Compared to setting up the initial attributes, making a table style from a group of cell styles is fast and easy. All you have to do is choose which cell styles you want to use and tell InDesign which style to use where. The action takes place in the New Table Style dialog box. Here you can specify which cell styles are applied to different sections of the table: header and footer rows, left and right columns, and body rows.

In this exercise, you'll compile the cell styles from your Cakes table into a table style for use on the Pies table.

1 Using the Type tool (T), select the entire Cakes table by clicking in the top-left corner of the table frame when you see a diagonal arrow.

2   If necessary, choose Window > Styles > Table Styles to open the Table Styles panel.

From the Table Styles panel, you can create and apply table styles.

3   Alt+click (Windows) or Option+click (Mac OS) the Create New Style button located at the bottom of the Table Styles panel. The New Table Style dialog box opens. Notice the Cell Styles section, which contains five drop-down menus. This is where you match the cell style to the location where it should be applied. Header and Body Rows are self-explanatory. The Left and Right Column menus, however, let you specify unique styles for the cells, so that you could have unique formatting for each.

4   In the New Table Style dialog box, type **Bella's Bakery** in the Style Name text field.

5   In the Cell Styles section, choose Header from the Header Rows drop-down menu.

6   Choose Description from the Body Rows drop-down menu, choose Name from the Left Column drop-down menu, and choose Price from the Right Column drop-down menu. Click OK.

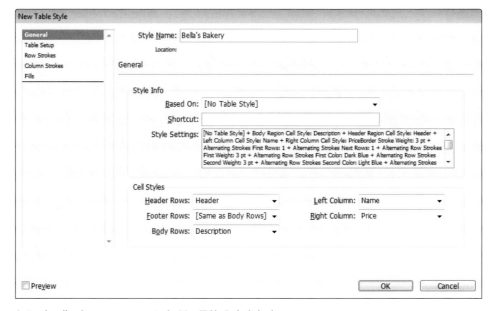

Assign the cell styles you want to use in the New Table Style dialog box.

7 With the table still selected, choose the Bella's Bakery style to apply it. Open the Cell Styles panel and click None to remove any manually applied Cell Styles as the Table Style is now doing all the work. Choose File > Save.

Applying table styles

Here's where all that hard work pays off: you can format an entire table with one click. In this exercise, you'll style the Pies table and a new Cookies table.

1 Select the entire Pies table using the Type tool (T) by clicking in the top-left corner of the table's frame when you see the diagonal arrow.

2 Choose Bella's Bakery from the Table Styles panel to apply the style. If there are any plus signs to the right of the table style name, Alt+click (Windows) or Option+click (Mac OS) to clear the overrides. You may need to hold the Shift key and adjust the vertical size of the table with the Type tool. Now you can try it again.

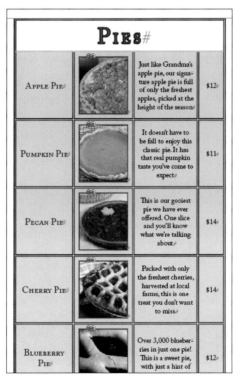

Choosing Bella's Bakery from the Table Styles panel formats the entire Pies table with one click.

3 Click the Layers button (◆) in the panel dock to open the Layers panel, and then click on the left-hand gray box next to the Cookies layer (the visibility button). A table listing different types of cookies appears in the right-hand column of the document.

4 Select the entire Cookies table by clicking with the Type tool in the top-left corner of the table frame when you see a diagonal arrow.

5   From the Table Styles panel, choose Bella's Bakery from the list to apply the style to the Cookies table. You may need to adjust the height of the cells in the Cookies table so that they match the other tables.

6   Click the left-hand gray box next to the Background layer (the visibility button) in the Layers panel. This shows you the intended background color that has been set to the bleed.

7   Choose Edit > Deselect All so that nothing in the layout is selected, and then press the **W** key on your keyboard to preview the finished layout. If necessary, choose Edit > Fit Spread in Window to view the project. Press **W** again when you are done previewing the project.

8   Select File > Save and you're done!

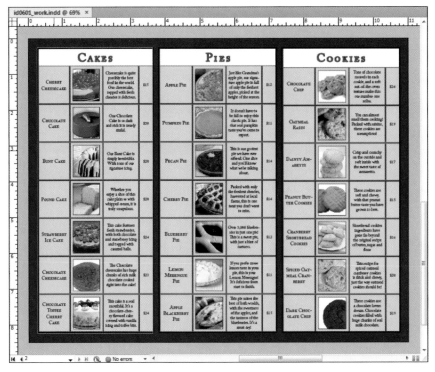

Take a look at the finished Bella's Bakery brochure.

Self study

Save another copy of your document as id0602_work.indd.

1 Because all three of your tables are designed with styles, you can make universal changes. Try changing the paragraph style Description, changing the font, and turning hyphenation off; click the Preview button to see all three tables change as you choose different options.

2 Select a cell and give the cell a stroke; then redefine the style in the drop-down menu of the Cell Styles panel to see the global change.

3 Change all the fonts and colors in the first table. Make new paragraph styles, and apply them. Change the attributes of the four sections of cells you used. Make a new set of cell styles, apply them to the first table, and then create a table style from that table. Apply your new table style to the other two tables.

Review

Questions

1 What are four ways to select a cell?

2 Can paragraph styles be included in cell styles?

3 In which five sections of a table style can you apply cell styles?

4 If you needed to remove all formatting to reduce a table down to its basic appearance, how would you make these changes?

5 If a plus sign (+) appears next to your table style name, it indicates that some change has occurred and there are overrides to some of the cells, tables, or text within the table. How do you clear these overrides?

Answers

1 Click and drag until the whole cell is highlighted; press Ctrl+/ (Windows) or Command+/ (Mac OS); click in a cell and press Shift+down arrow; press the Esc key.

2 Yes, but they are not chosen by default; you must select them in the Cell Style drop-down menu.

3 You can apply cell styles in a table style in these sections: header rows, footer rows, left columns, right columns, and body rows.

4 In the Table Styles panel, click on Basic Table.

5 Alt+click (Windows) or Option+click (Mac OS) the style name to clear overrides.

Lesson 7

What you'll learn in this lesson:

- Applying colors to fills and strokes
- Using and saving spot colors
- Updating and editing colors
- Creating and applying gradients

Using Color in Your Documents

Using color for text, frames, and paths is a basic task in InDesign. The more ways you know how to apply, change, and control color, the faster you can work. Color choices are not limited to picking from the small selection that appears in the Swatches panel. You can create your own colors, gradients, and tints, as well as choose from a number of swatch libraries, such as Pantone colors, that are supplied for you within InDesign.

Starting up

Before starting, make sure that your tools and panels are consistent by resetting your preferences. See "Resetting the InDesign workspace and preferences" in the Starting up section of this book.

You will work with several files from the id07lessons folder in this lesson. Make sure that you have copied the id07lessons folder onto your hard drive from the Digital Classroom DVD. See "Loading lesson files" in the Starting up section of this book. This lesson may be easier to follow if the id07lessons folder is on your desktop.

See Lesson 7 in action!

Use the accompanying video to gain a better understanding of how to use some of the features shown in this lesson. The video tutorial for this lesson can be found on the supplied DVD.

The project

To explore InDesign's color controls, you will add color to a fictional ad for FiFi's Face Cream. You'll use multiple types of colors, as well as tints and gradients, in the course of this lesson. If you want to see what the finished project will look like, open id0701_done. indd from the id07lessons folder now.

The finished project.

Applying colors to frames and text

There are several ways to assign color to an object with InDesign. You can assign color through the Tools panel, the Swatches panel, the Color panel, and the Color Picker. You can also assign color using the Eyedropper tool. No matter which method you choose, you must perform the same three steps: select the text or object that you want to color, specify which part of the object you want to color, and then choose the color to apply.

Applying color to text

Applying color is a quick, straightforward process. To practice, you will color the text in the FiFi's Face Cream ad.

1   Choose File > Open. Navigate to the id07lessons folder, select the file id0701.indd, and then click Open.

2   Choose File > Save As. In the Save As dialog box, navigate to the id07lessons folder and type **id0701_work.indd** in the Name text field. Click Save.

3   Select the Type tool (T) from the Tools panel and click inside the frame containing the text, *It leaves your skin feeling noticeably clean and absolutely radiant.*

4   Choose Edit > Select All to select all the text inside the frame.

5   Select Window > Swatches or click the Swatches button (▦) in the dock on the right side of the workspace to open the Swatches panel.

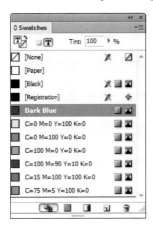

Color the object from the Swatches panel.

The first thing to consider is whether you want to color the border (stroke) or the inside (fill) of the selected text. In the upper-left corner of the Swatches panel are two icons overlapping one another. The icon with the outlined T and the red diagonal line running through it is the Stroke icon (⬚). The icon with the solid black T inside it is the Fill icon (**T**). In order to apply color, you must click the appropriate icon to bring it forward and make it active. In this case, you want to fill the text with the color Dark Blue. If necessary, bring the Fill icon forward.

You can also press the X key on your keyboard to toggle between Fill and Stroke in the Swatches panel, as long as you don't have the Type tool activated.

To quickly reset the default colors, click the icon in the lower-left area (⬛) near the Fill/Stroke box in the Tools panel. The default color for objects is no fill (None) with a black stroke; a black fill with no stroke (None) is the default color for text.

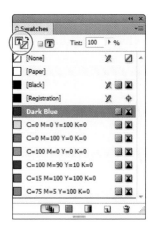

Choose the fill and stroke colors in the Swatches panel by bringing their respective icons forward.

6   In the Swatches panel make sure the Fill icon is forward, then click on the Dark Blue option. The text turns blue. Choose Edit > Deselect All to view the change.

Applying color to frames

Next you will color the border, or stroke, of the frame around the text. Follow the same three basic steps that you went through to apply color to the text: Select the frame, specify fill or stroke, and choose the color.

1   Activate the Selection tool (▶) in the Tools panel, and click on the frame that begins *It leaves your skin...*. Notice that the Stroke and Fill icons no longer have a *T* (for Type), but now appear as a solid square for the Fill, and an outlined square for the Stroke. Make sure the text frame is selected.

2   Click the Stroke icon (▣) in the Swatches panel to bring it forward.

3 Select Dark Blue in the Swatches panel to apply the color to the frame. Note that depending on your current zoom level, it may not look like the color of the stroke is changing. For a more accurate view, zoom in on the frame prior applying the new color.

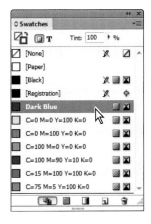

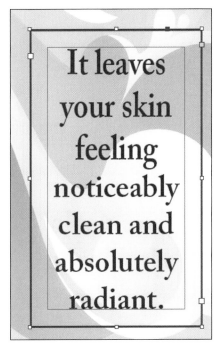

Choose Dark Blue in the Swatches panel to color the text frame's stroke.

Applying Live Corner Effects

InDesign provides a new feature called Live Corner Effects that enables you to adjust the radius and style of the corners of a frame visually without the need to open a separate dialog box. To give the frame a little more style, you will round its edges.

1 With the Selection tool (▸) active, click on the text frame on the right side of the ad to select the frame.

2 You'll notice a yellow square in the upper-right corner of the frame. This square is the Live Corner Effects indicator. Click on the yellow square to enable Live Corner Effects, and you'll notice that a yellow diamond appears in each corner of the text frame, indicating that Live Corner Effects has been enabled.

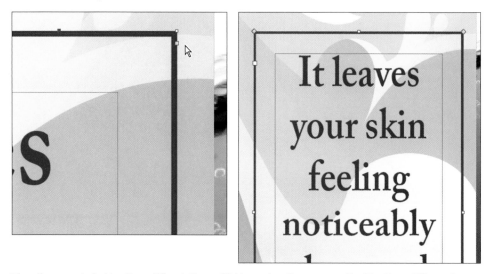

The yellow square is the Live Corner Effects indicator. Clicking on the yellow square enables Live Corner Effects and displays yellow diamonds in each corner of the frame.

3 Click on any of the yellow diamonds and drag toward the center of the frame to increase the corner radius for all corners of the frame. The further you drag, the higher the radius value will be. Drag until the smart guides display about .15 inches. Click anywhere in your document to deselect the frame.

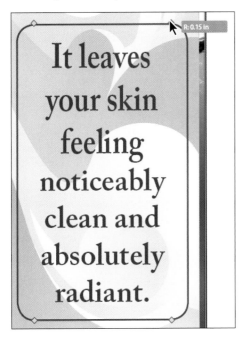

Clicking on a yellow diamond and dragging toward the center of the frame adjusts the corner radius of the frame.

4 Choose File > Save.

Corner shape options

Although the rounded corner effect is the default when using the Live Corner Effects feature, it's not the only choice available. With a frame selected, you can quickly choose a different corner effect by clicking on the corner shape drop-down menu in the Control panel and choosing from a variety of shapes, including Fancy, Bevel, Inset, Inverse Rounded, and Rounded.

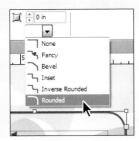

The corner shape drop-down menu.

Creating and saving a new swatch

You can create your own custom color swatches, or use those supplied by InDesign. When you create a color or gradient, InDesign automatically shows it in the Fill/Stroke box in the Tools panel, and also displays it in the Swatches panel and Color panel. Because InDesign also automatically applies the new color to whatever you have selected, you need to be very careful to select only the items you want colored before you begin. In the next exercises, you will create, name, and apply two new colors.

The Swatches panel can contain spot colors, process colors, mixed inks (combinations of multiple spot and process colors), RGB or Lab colors, gradients, or tints. This exercise concentrates on CMYK colors, Cyan, Magenta, Yellow, and Black, but you'll learn more about the specialized color options in later sections.

1   To make sure nothing on the pasteboard is selected, press Shift+Ctrl+A (Windows) or Shift+Command+A (Mac OS).

If you activate any of the InDesign drawing tools, such as the Rectangle tool, or any of the tools hidden beneath it—Line tool, Pen tool, Pencil tool, or the Type tool—and choose a color swatch, the default color is set for these tools, and every time the tool is used, it will be preset to this color. If you choose a color with one of these tools active and no objects selected, you will establish the new default color for this group of tools.

2   If necessary, click the Swatches button (▦) in the dock to open the Swatches panel. From the Swatches panel menu (•≡), choose New Color Swatch.

3   In the resulting New Color Swatch dialog box, uncheck the *Name with Color Value* checkbox so you can name this color swatch as you create it. Type **Green** in the Swatch Name text field.

4 Increase the Cyan percentage to 80 percent by moving the slider bar to the right of Cyan or typing **80** into the % text field. Using the sliders or typing the percentages, set Magenta to **10** percent, Yellow to **100** percent, and Black to **0** percent. These percentage tints of the process inks combine to create the new color.

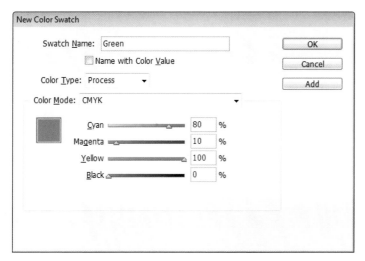

To create a new color, adjust the percentages in the New Color Swatch dialog box, and then click OK.

5 Click OK to create the new color. Green now appears at the very bottom of the Swatches panel. When you make a new color swatch, it always appears at the bottom of the list of swatches. You can change the order of the swatches by simply clicking and dragging them within the Swatches panel.

6 In the Swatches panel, click and drag the Green swatch upward so it is positioned just below Dark Blue, and then release it. You should see a black line indicating where the swatch will appear before you drop it. You may want to expand the size of the Swatches panel to minimize scrolling within the panel.

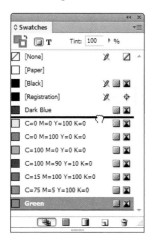

Click and drag to rearrange swatches in the Swatches panel.

7 Choose File > Save to save your work.

Applying strokes to text

In the next exercise, you will fill text with the new color, as well as create a contrasting color for the text's stroke. You'll also get your first look at the Stroke panel, which gives you control over the weight and appearance of an element's stroke or border.

1 With the Selection tool (▶) active, double-click the frame containing the words *Face Cream* in the lower-left corner of the document. This automatically converts the Selection tool to the Type tool (T). Alternately, you can also choose the Type tool and click inside the frame. Press Ctrl+A (Windows) or Command+A (Mac OS) to select all the text in the frame.

2 In the Swatches panel, click the Fill icon (**T**) to bring it forward, and click the Green swatch you made in the previous exercise. *Face Cream* is now green.

Turn the Face Cream *text green.*

You will now make a new color for the stroke.

3   Click the Stroke indicator icon (⬚) to bring it forward. From the Swatches panel menu (▾≡), choose New Color Swatch.

Bring the Stroke icon forward, and then choose New Color Swatch from the panel menu.

4   In the resulting New Color Swatch dialog box, uncheck the *Name with Color Value* checkbox, and type **Light Blue** in the Swatch Name text field.

5 Change the Cyan to 32 percent by moving its slider bar or typing **32** in the % text field. Using the sliders or typing in the percentages, set Magenta to **6** percent, Yellow to **3** percent, and Black to **0** percent.

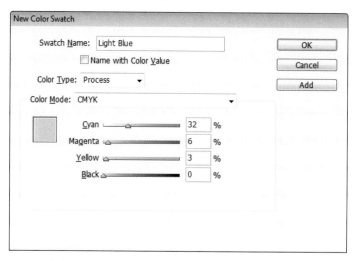

Create a light-blue color by adjusting the CMYK percentages.

6 Click OK. InDesign automatically applies Light Blue to the stroke of the text. The stroke doesn't quite stand out enough, however. In the next steps, you'll use the Stroke panel to increase the stroke's width.

Don't forget to reorganize the swatches for the best workflow. For example, because Green and Light Blue will be used in combination for text in the ad, click and drag the Light Blue swatch just below Green in the Swatches panel. A black line indicates where the swatch will appear before you drop it. Rearranging swatches into logical groups for your project is a good practice to follow.

7 With the text still selected, click the Stroke button (≣) in the panel dock to open the Stroke panel.

8   Type **1.5** in the panel's Weight text field and press Enter (Windows) or Return (Mac OS) to increase the selected stroke's size.

Apply a stroke to the Face Cream *text and increase its size with the Stroke panel.*

9   Select File > Save to save your work.

Creating a tint reduction

A tint, sometimes called a screen, is a lighter shade of a color. Tinting is a great way to use colors at different intensities. Just as you can with regular colors, you can (and should) save tints in the Swatches panel to make editing tints fast and easy. Because colors and their tints maintain their relationship in the Swatches panel, a change to the original color swatch also updates any tints of that swatch that have been made. In this exercise, you will create a tint to use in the ad.

1   Using the Selection tool (⬤), click the frame that contains the word *FiFi's*. Use the Selection tool to select the frame as an object because it is no longer type. It was converted to outlines and is now a path, and is therefore no longer editable as text.

2   Click the Swatches button (⊞) in the dock to open the Swatches panel, and make sure the Fill icon is in the foreground. Select the Light Blue swatch to apply the color to the fill.

3 At the top of the Swatches panel, click the right-facing arrow to expose the Tint slider. Drag the slider to the left to reduce the fill's tint from 100 percent to 60 percent. Click the right-facing arrow again to accept the new value. The change is reflected in the selected object. Now that you have made the tint, you can save the modified version of the Light Blue swatch in the Swatches panel.

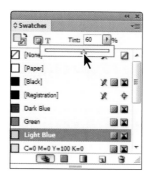

The Tint slider changes the tint percentage for the selected swatch.

4 In the Swatches panel, click and drag the Fill icon from the top of the Swatches panel into the list of swatches, and drop it below the Light Blue color swatch to add the tint Light Blue at 60 percent to the list.

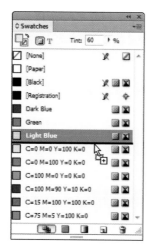 

Creating a tint swatch (left) and the logo after applying the color tint (right).

5 Select File > Save to save your work.

Making a dashed stroke

You've practiced applying, coloring, and widening a basic stroke, but InDesign offers many more ways to customize strokes. To demonstrate, you will make a custom dash around the border of the FiFi's ad.

1 Using the Selection tool (✹), select the black frame running around the edge of the ad.

2 In the Swatches panel, click the Stroke indicator icon (❑) to bring it forward.

3 Open the Stroke panel by clicking the Stroke button (≣) in the panel dock. Use the up-arrow to the left of the Weight text field to increase the stroke thickness to 4 points. Notice that the frame, which was aligned to the size of the page, is now bigger than the page. This is because the default alignment of a stroke is centered on the frame. In this case, half the width of the stroke (two points) is now inside the frame and half the width of the stroke (two points) is outside the frame. You will change this stroke alignment next.

If every time you make a frame, you notice yourself changing the alignment to the inside so that the frame doesn't extend beyond the path, you can make an Object Style with the stroke aligned to the inside. Or, better yet, change the settings right in the Object Styles panel by adjusting the Basic Text Frame and the Basic Graphics Frame options.

4 In the Stroke panel, click the Align Stroke to Inside button (▣). The border appears to jump inside the frame, because all stroke edges are now aligned to the inside of the frame.

5   Still in the Stroke panel, click the Type drop-down menu to reveal all the various styles of strokes you can make. Choose Dashed. Dash and Gap options appear at the bottom of the Stroke panel. The dash is the stroke segments, and the gap is the space between the dashes.

Choose Dashed for the ad's border.

6   Make sure the first dash text field shows 12 pt. This sets the length of the dash. In the first gap text field, type **3**, which sets the length of the gap between dashes. Type **11** in the third text field to set a second dash length. In the remaining gap and dash text fields, type **2** and **10**, respectively, leaving the final gap field empty. This sequence of dashes and gaps will repeat where this stroke is applied.

Set the dash and gap options in the Stroke panel.

7 Press Enter (Windows) or Return (Mac OS) to apply the settings. You have created a custom dash.

Now you can change the color of both the dash (stroke) and gap.

8 In the Swatches panel, make sure the Stroke icon is forward, and choose Light Blue to apply it to the dash. Be sure to pick the original Light Blue swatch and not the tinted version.

9 In the Stroke panel, choose Dark Blue from the Gap Color drop-down menu.

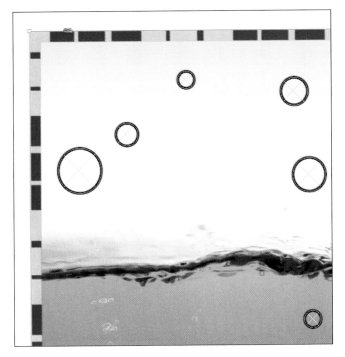

The finished border has light-blue dashes separated by dark-blue gaps.

10 Choose File > Save to save your work.

Creating and saving gradients

A *gradient* is a smooth and gradual transition between two or more colors. When you first apply a gradient, the default is set to two color stops. A *color stop* is one of at least two colors used to create a gradient. You can add as many stops as you want to a gradient, and also control how quickly or slowly the colors fade into each other. You can also change the direction of a gradient, and even choose whether it is a linear gradient, appearing as a straight-line transition, or a radial gradient, which appears in a circular form. In this series of exercises, you will make and save linear and radial gradients, as well as use the Gradient tool to change the direction of the gradient.

Linear gradients

You create gradients in the Gradient panel, and then add colors to the transition by dragging and dropping them as color stops on the gradient bar in the panel. You'll build a gradient next.

1 Using the Selection tool (⬈), click the frame containing the words, *It leaves your skin feeling noticeably clean and absolutely radiant.*

Always select an object before starting the gradient. It's easier to build a gradient when you have something selected because you can preview exactly how the color transitions will look.

2 Toward the bottom of the Tools panel are overlapping Fill and Stroke icons, just as in the Swatches panel. Select the Fill icon to bring it forward.

3 Choose Window > Color > Gradient to display it. From the Type drop-down menu in this panel, choose Linear. The frame now has a white-to-black linear gradient applied by default.

Use the Gradient panel to apply a white-to-black gradient to the frame.

You will now add colors to the gradient. Make sure you can see both the Gradient and Swatches panels, as you will be dragging colors from the Swatches panel into the Gradient panel. Because you can't have two docked panels displayed at the same time, it will be necessary to have one of the panels undocked for this exercise.

4   Click and hold the Light Blue swatch in the Swatches panel. Don't just click or you will simply apply the color to the selected frame. Drag the swatch to the right side of the gradient color bar until the cursor becomes a hand with a plus sign (⊞). The line cursor on the gradient bar disappears, indicating that it will replace the black color stop with the light blue one. Be careful to replace the original color rather than add another color stop next to it. Whether replacing or adding a color stop, the cursor displays a plus sign when you add a color stop to the gradient.

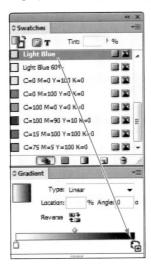

This cursor indicates that you are dragging a color
from the Swatches panel to the Gradient panel.
Drop the color over a color stop to apply it.

5   Release the mouse to drop the color. The gradient bar now has a White color stop on the left and a Light Blue color stop on the right. The frame in the ad should look the same way, with the color fading from white on the left to light blue on the right.

6   Choose File > Save to save your work.

Saving a gradient

You can save gradients in the Swatches panel to apply them later to other objects with a single click. You save a gradient by dragging its preview from the Gradient panel into the Swatches panel. Try it with the White-to-Light Blue gradient.

1 Click and hold the preview of the gradient in the top-left corner of the Gradient panel.

2 Drag the cursor to just below Light Blue 60% in the Swatches panel. A heavy black line appears, showing where the new gradient swatch will appear before you release it. The cursor changes to a white box with a plus sign (🖿) as you drag, indicating that you are about to add a gradient to the Swatches panel.

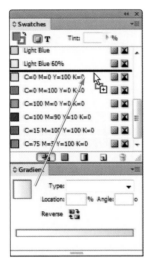

This cursor indicates that you are adding a gradient to the Swatches panel.

3 Release the mouse to drop the gradient into the Swatches panel. InDesign automatically names the gradient New Gradient Swatch. You will now change the name to something more recognizable.

4 Double-click the New Gradient Swatch. The Gradient Options dialog box appears.

5 In the Swatch Name text field, type **Light Blue Linear**, then click OK.

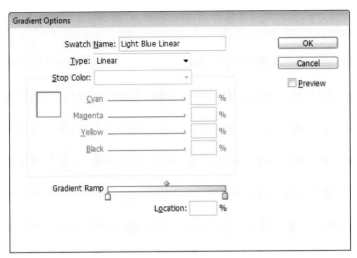

In the Gradient Options dialog box, you can name the gradient.

6 Drag the Gradient panel by its tab over the Swatches panel until a border appears. Release the Gradient panel, placing it into the dock.

7 Choose File > Save to save your work.

Adjusting fill opacity

As a preview of what's to come in Lesson 8, "Using Effects," you will now decrease the opacity of the fill so you can see through the frame. This effects feature lets you control fill, stroke, and text opacity separately.

1 Using the Selection tool (▶), select the text frame that you modified in the previous exercise and choose Window > Effects, or click the Effects button (*fx*) in the dock, to open the Effects panel.

2 Select Fill from the target list inside the Effects panel. Double-click inside the Opacity text field and type **70%**, or click the arrow to the right of the text field and move the slider to 70 percent. Press Enter (Windows) or Return (Mac OS) to apply the settings.

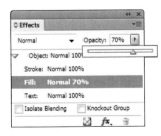

The Effects panel with the proper settings.

3   Choose File > Save. You have just changed the opacity of only the object's fill. You will learn more specifics of this and other effects in Lesson 8, "Using Effects."

Radial gradient

The last gradient you made was a linear gradient, which means it fades from one color to another along straight lines. This is the default in InDesign. You will now explore radial gradients, which are gradients that don't fade color in the form of lines, but as circles. If you wanted to make a sphere that looked like light was hitting the top of it, with the shadow at the bottom, you could use the radial gradient to accomplish this. You will use the radial gradient to make bubbles in this next exercise.

1   Using the Selection tool (⬉), click the far-left circle in the ad.

2   In the Swatches panel, click the Stroke icon (▫) to bring it forward. Select None for the stroke.

3   Bring the Fill icon forward. Select the Light Blue Linear gradient that you saved earlier.

4   If it is not already open, choose Window > Gradient, or click the Gradient button (▦) in the dock, to open the Gradient panel. Here you will change the type of gradient that is applied.

You can also double-click the Gradient Swatch tool in the Tools panel to open the Gradient panel.

5   Choose Radial from the Gradient panel's Type drop-down menu. The circle now has a radial gradient.

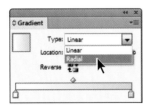

*Choose Radial from the Type
drop-down menu to change from
a linear to a radial gradient.*

6   Choose File > Save to save your work.

Adjusting the direction of a radial gradient

The Gradient Swatch tool in the Tools panel allows you to change the direction of both linear and radial gradients. In this case, the radial gradient appears with white in the middle of the circle and blends from the center outward to the Light Blue color. You will change that now using the Gradient Swatch tool.

1 Select the Gradient Swatch tool (◼) in the Tools panel. You will use this tool to set the span and direction of an applied gradient.

Using the Gradient Swatch tool is a three-step process: Click to set the position of the first color stop. Drag to set the angle and direction of the gradient span. Then release the mouse to set the position of the last color stop. Remember that in order to use this tool, a gradient must already be applied to the fill or stroke.

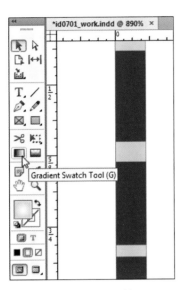

The Gradient Swatch tool enables you to change a gradient's span and angle.

2 Click and drag from the top-left to the bottom-right of the circle to give the sphere the look of a highlight in its top-left part. When you release the mouse, the top-left area appears white, and then fades radially into Light Blue.

Drag with the Gradient Swatch tool in the direction you desire.

3 In the Gradient panel, right-click (Windows) or Control+click (Mac OS) the gradient color swatch and select Add to Swatches to add the radial gradient to the Swatches panel. In the Swatches panel, move the New Gradient Swatch so that it is underneath the Light Blue Linear gradient.

4 Double-click the New Gradient Swatch in the Swatches panel to rename it.

5 In the resulting Gradient Options dialog box, type **Light Blue Radial** in the Swatch Name text field. Click OK.

You may notice that saving a gradient swatch does not save the angle of the gradient. To capture the gradient's angle, you must make the gradient an Object Style.

One-click edits

InDesign makes it easy to share attributes among document elements, so that you can make global changes with minimal effort.

Using the Eyedropper tool to copy frame attributes

When you need to copy attributes from one element to another in a document, choose the Eyedropper tool. It can pick up both type and frame attributes, such as fill and stroke settings, and apply those characteristics to other text or frames. By default, the Eyedropper tool picks up all attributes, but you can choose to transfer only specific settings using the Eyedropper Options dialog box. You will use the Eyedropper tool to quickly copy the attributes from one frame to another.

1 Press Shift+Ctrl+A (Windows) or Shift+Command+A (Mac OS) to make sure nothing is selected.

2 In the Tools panel, select the Eyedropper tool (✐).

3 Click on the circle that you previously filled with the radial gradient. The Eyedropper tool now appears filled; it contains all the formatting attributes of that circle.

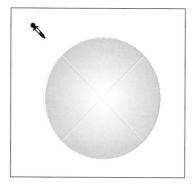

When you click an object with the Eyedropper tool, the tool fills with formatting information.

4 Move the filled eyedropper cursor to the center of the nearest circle and click. The attributes are applied: the gradient fills the circle, and the existing stroke disappears.

5 Click a few more of the circles to apply the gradient attributes, but leave some circles, as they will be used in the next exercise.

6 Choose File > Save to save your work.

Applying colors to multiple objects

Although the Eyedropper tool is quite handy for copying multiple attributes to single objects, sometimes you want to apply changes to multiple objects at once. InDesign makes this simple. When you select a group of objects, you can apply a fill or stroke to all of them with one click. Practice this by adding gradients to the ad's remaining circles.

1 Choose the Selection tool (k) from the Tools panel, and then click a circle that still has a black stroke and no fill.

2 Shift+click every circle that does not have the gradient fill.

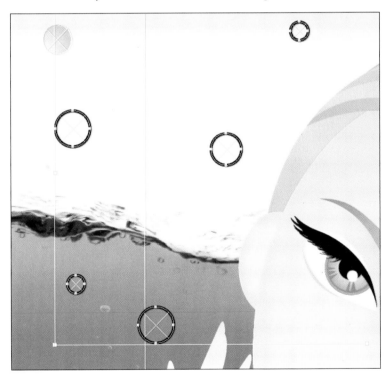

Shift+click to select all the unfilled circles.

3 In the Swatches panel, click the Fill icon to bring it forward, and then click the Light Blue Radial swatch for the fill color.

4 Select the Stroke indicator icon (▫) to bring it forward, and scroll up to select None for the stroke. All the selected circles now have the Light Blue Radial gradient and no stroke.

Apply the Light Blue Radial gradient to the selected circles.

5 Select File > Save.

Updating and editing colors

When you apply a swatch to multiple objects in InDesign, each of those objects is related to that color in the Swatches panel. If you then change the color of the swatch, all instances of the color throughout the document change. This makes it quick and easy to make global color changes. In this exercise, you will change the Light Blue swatch to experiment with a new look for the ad.

1 Press Shift+Ctrl+A (Windows) or Shift+Command+A (Mac OS) to make sure nothing is selected.

2 Double-click the Light Blue swatch in the Swatches panel to open the Swatch Options dialog box.

3 In the Swatch Options dialog box, click the *Preview* checkbox (below the OK and Cancel buttons) so that you can see the changes take effect as you apply them.

4 Drag the Magenta slider to the right so that Magenta appears at 38%. All the Light
Blues you added to the ad now appear more purple.

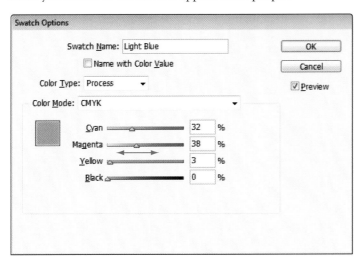

*Increase the Magenta slider to 38% to change all instances of the Light Blue color in the
ad to purple.*

5 Click OK to implement the changes.

6 Choose File > Save As. In the Save As dialog box, navigate to the id07lessons folder,
and then type **id0702_work.indd** in the Name text field. Click Save. You can use
this file later for the Self study section.

Save the purple project to use later.

7 Choose File > Close, and then reopen id0701_work.indd. It should look as it did
before you changed the light blue to purple.

Using and saving spot colors

Spot colors are premixed ink colors that provide very accurate and vibrant color when printed. They are often used to maintain brand identity when printing corporate logos or simply to add visual appeal to a job. Spot colors can produce colors that simply are not possible using process (CMYK) colors. Spot colors require their own printing plates on a printing press, which may increase the cost of a commercial printing job; however, when critical color matching is required, spot colors are second to none.

For the most accurate representation of a spot color, certain things must be considered. First, you should pick the spot color from a color-matching system supported by your commercial printer. Several color-matching libraries ship with InDesign. You must also remember that a color's appearance depends on many variables such as the limits of your printer, and the paper stock it's printed on.

Fortunately, you can manipulate spot colors in InDesign just as you can ordinary CMYK colors. You can create your own spot colors in the Swatches panel, or place an image that contains a spot color to add that color automatically to the panel. You can adjust and apply spot colors in the Swatches panel, using them for fills, strokes, or gradients. In this exercise, you will create a spot color to apply to the ad.

1   Press Shift+Ctrl+A (Windows) or Shift+Command+A (Mac OS) to make sure nothing is selected.

2   In the Swatches panel, click the panel menu button (·≡) and choose New Color Swatch.

3   In the resulting New Color Swatch dialog box, choose Spot from the Color Type drop-down menu.

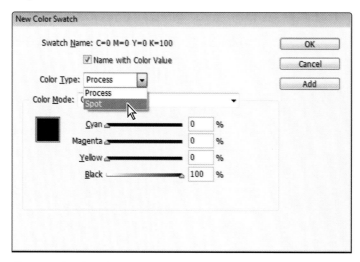

Choose Spot from the Color Type drop-down menu to designate a swatch as a spot color.

4   Choose PANTONE+ Solid Coated from the Color Mode drop-down menu to change it from CMYK. PANTONE+ solid coated and PANTONE+ solid uncoated are the two most common ink color libraries; coated is for a coated or glossy paper, while uncoated is for uncoated paper stock. Now you need to specify which spot color you want to work with.

5   In the Pantone text field, type **662**. This automatically brings you to that Pantone color, a dark blue.

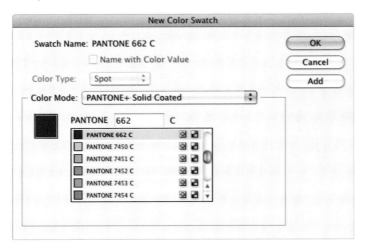

Choose PANTONE+ Solid Coated from the Color Mode drop-down menu, and then enter color **662**.

6   Click OK to close the dialog box and add the swatch named Pantone 662 C to the Swatches panel. The swatch is automatically named.

7   Drag the Pantone 662 C swatch up in the Swatches panel and drop it directly beneath the Light Blue Radial gradient swatch. You will apply the new spot color in the next exercise.

Colorizing a grayscale image

InDesign can colorize any grayscale image you import as long as it does not contain any spot colors or alpha channels. The two raindrops in the ad are grayscale images that had clipping paths applied. This format enables you to change the colors of black and gray into whatever color you would like. You will use the Pantone 662 C color created in the last exercise.

1   To color only the pixels of the image, choose the Direct Selection tool ( ) from the Tools panel. If you try to colorize the image when it is selected with the Selection tool instead, the fill of the whole box will be colored.

2   Select one of the raindrops. A path appears around the edge of the raindrop.

3   In the Swatches panel, make sure the Fill icon is forward. Select the Pantone 662 C swatch to apply the color to the raindrop.

4   Select the other raindrop with the Direct Selection tool ( ).

5 In the Swatches panel, select Pantone 662 C to apply it to the second raindrop.

Apply color to the grayscale raindrops.

You can select the graphic or image of the raindrop without using the Direct Selection tool. Simply use the Selection tool, and double-click on the image of the raindrop to select the content (image) instead of the frame.

6 Choose File > Save to save your work.

Congratulations! You have completed the lesson.

Self study

Open the id0702_work.indd file you saved earlier in the id07lessons folder to practice some additional color variations:

- Try adjusting more colors in the Swatches panel to make universal changes across the ad.

- Create another spot color and recolor the grayscale raindrops again.

- Select the text frame with the linear gradient. Experiment by dragging more colors into the gradient, and use the Gradient Swatch tool to change the gradient's direction.

- Make a new color and put a stroke on the text, *It leaves your skin feeling noticeably clean and absolutely radiant.*

- Design a new radial gradient for the bubbles, and practice coloring some of them individually with the Eyedropper tool.

- Experiment with the Adobe Kuler panel to try different swatch groups and create new color combinations. Access the Kuler panel by choosing Window > Extensions > Kuler, and then create new color themes and add them to the Swatches panel or upload and share them.

Review

Questions

1 How do you change the fill of an object you are trying to color? How do you change the color of the stroke?

2 How do you save a gradient you have already made?

3 If you change a color in the Swatches panel, will it change the color wherever it is applied throughout the document?

4 Can you colorize any grayscale image?

5 True or False: You cannot change the direction of a linear gradient.

Answers

1 With an object selected, in either the Tools panel or the Swatches panel, click the Fill icon to bring it forward, and then click the color desired for the fill. To change the stroke, bring the Stroke icon forward, and then click a color.

2 Drag and drop it from the Gradient panel into the Swatches panel.

3 Yes. That is why the Swatches panel is especially handy for making universal changes to colors throughout your document.

4 Yes, as long as the image does not contain spot or alpha channels.

5 False—the Gradient Swatch tool lets you change the direction of any gradient.

Lesson 8

What you'll learn in this lesson:

- Applying opacity to objects
- Singling out stroke and fill
- Adjusting effects for objects
- Combining object styles with effects
- Exploring blending modes
- Working with imported files that use transparency

Using Effects

You can use Photoshop-like effects directly in your InDesign documents. You can apply effects such as Inner Shadow, Outer and Inner Glow, Bevel and Emboss, and Gradient Feather to objects in InDesign. In this lesson, you will discover how to modify the appearance of images, objects, and text using a sampling of the effects.

Starting up

Before starting, make sure that your tools and panels are consistent by resetting your preferences. See "Resetting the InDesign workspace and preferences" in the Starting up section of this book.

You will work with several files from the id08lessons folder in this lesson. Make sure that you have copied the id08lessons folder onto your hard drive from the Digital Classroom DVD. See "Loading lesson files" in the Starting up section of this book.

This lesson may be easier to follow if the id08lessons folder is on your desktop.

See Lesson 8 in action!

Use the accompanying video to gain a better understanding of how to use some of the features shown in this lesson. The video tutorial for this lesson can be found on the supplied DVD.

The project

In this lesson, you will jazz-up a two-page spread using the Effects panel in InDesign CS6. You can experiment with blending modes, opacity, and other effects without permanently changing the objects, and then you can save effects as an object style so that you can easily apply the effects to other objects. If you want to take a peek at what the finished project should look like, open the id0801_done.indd file located in the id08lessons folder.

The appearance of the final layout after you have completed the lesson.

Creative effects

InDesign's Effects panel offers a way to use Photoshop-like effects in InDesign documents. You can apply feathering and drop shadows, as well as control the opacity and blending modes of objects, text, and photos. Not only can you apply effects, but you can also apply them to either the whole object, or to just the fill, stroke, or text in a frame. Better yet, you can turn those effects on or off nondestructively, without permanently changing the objects.

Applying opacity to objects

Opacity settings make an object or text appear transparent; to varying degrees, you can see through the object to the objects that appear behind it. If the opacity is set to 0 percent, the object is completely invisible. By default, all objects are set to 100 percent, or completely opaque. Some people get confused about the difference between tint and opacity. Tint is a screened (lighter) version of a color and is not transparent, but opaque. Opacity is the way you control the transparency of an object. Adjusting the transparency allows objects below to show through the object that is transparent or semi-transparent.

Using these tools, you can apply many effects to images. For example, placing a red frame over a grayscale image and changing the opacity to 50 percent makes the image appear as if it has been colored. This is a task you might think is more suitable for Photoshop, but InDesign can give you that kind of control. Practice on a few objects now.

1   Choose Window > Mini Bridge to open the Mini Bridge panel. Click the Launch Bridge button and navigate to the id08lessons folder. Double-click the id0801.indd file to open the file and begin the lesson. Dock the Mini Bridge panel in the panel dock for quick access later.

2   Save a work version of this file before making any changes. Choose File > Save As. In the Save As dialog box, navigate to the id08lessons folder, type **id0801_work.indd** in the Name text field, then click Save.

Open the Effects panel by choosing Window > Effects, or by clicking the Effects button (*fx*) in the panel dock, and take a tour of where you'll be working.

The Effects panel has blending modes and opacity controls at the top, and the ability to target an effect to the stroke, fill, or text appears in the bottom portion of the panel. It's time to put these controls to work.

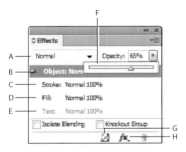

A. Blending mode.
B. Opacity and blend settings applied to the object.
C. Opacity and blend settings applied to the stroke.
D. Opacity and blend settings applied to the fill.
E. Opacity and blend settings applied to the text.
F. Opacity level.
G. Clear all effects and make object opaque.
H. Add an object effect to the selected target.

3 Click the Pages button (⊞) in the panel dock on the right side of the workspace to open the Pages panel. Notice that the two pages are numbered 6 and 7. You will work on page 7 first. Double-click the page 7 icon in the Pages panel to center the page in the workspace.

4 Choose the Selection tool (⬚) from the Tools panel, and select the blue rectangle in the lower-right corner of the page. Hidden underneath this blue frame is an image. You will change the opacity settings of the blue frame to see the image beneath.

5 If the Effects panel is not open, choose Window > Effects, or click the Effects button (*fx*) in the dock to display the Effects panel.

6 The opacity is set to 100 percent. Click on the right-facing triangle to the immediate right of the Opacity text field to access the Opacity slider.

7 Drag the slider to the left to change the opacity to 65 percent. You can now see the image—a pile of vintage vinyl music albums—underneath the blue, but you still have the effect of the blue coloring. Click the triangle again to collapse the slider.

Set the Opacity slider to 65 percent to see the image beneath the blue frame.

8 Click the blue bar at the very bottom of the page using the Selection tool.

9 Highlight 100 percent in the Opacity field of the Effects panel and type **40**. This is yet another way to change the opacity of an object, without using the slider. Press Enter (Windows) or Return (Mac OS) to implement the change in opacity. The bar, with an opacity of 40 percent, is slightly more transparent than the frame, which has an opacity value of 65 percent.

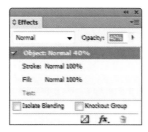

Adjust an object's opacity by entering the number directly in the Opacity text field.

10 Choose File > Save. Keep the file open, as you'll need it for the rest of the lesson.

Apply effects to stroke or fill only

In InDesign, an effect can be applied to an entire object, or to an object's stroke, fill, or text individually.

1   Use the Selection tool (⬉) to select the white box containing a quote in the upper-left corner of page 7.

2   In the Effects panel, click the right-facing triangle next to Opacity to reveal the slider, then drag the slider left to 50 percent. Click the triangle again to commit the change. Notice that both the text and the fill are now fairly transparent. Applying the effect to the entire object in this way makes the text difficult to read, which is something you don't want. The text needs to stand out and remain legible.

Apply the opacity change to both the fill and text.

3   Before you can apply the opacity change to the fill only, you must undo the last step. Either highlight 50 percent in the Opacity text field in the Effects panel and type **100** to return to the previous settings, or press Ctrl+Z (Windows) or Command+Z (Mac OS) to undo the previous action.

4   In the Effects panel, click to target the Fill listing. Selecting the Fill property ensures that the opacity applies only to the fill inside the frame and not to the text.

5 Click to reveal the Opacity slider, and drag it to the left to 50 percent. Commit the change by clicking the triangle again after setting the new value. The fill is transparent, but the text keeps an opacity value of 100 percent.

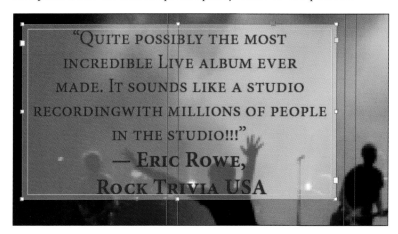

Adjust the opacity of the box's fill only.

Drop shadow

As with opacity, you can apply the drop shadow effect to a whole object or to just the stroke, fill, or text of the object. A drop shadow creates a three-dimensional shadow effect below whatever you have chosen in the document. You can also change such parameters as the drop shadow's color, offset, and blending mode, to name a few. This exercise demonstrates the effect and provides you with your first look inside the Effects dialog box.

1 Click the Pages button (⊕) in the dock on the right side of the workspace to reveal the Pages panel. Double-click the page 6 icon to center the page on screen. Press Ctrl+0 (Windows) or Command+0 (Mac OS) to fit page 6 on your screen.

2 With the Selection tool (▸), click the box containing the words, *Johnny Guitar rocks again!* at the top of the page.

3   In the Effects panel, click the Add an object effect to the selected target button (*fx*) at the bottom of the panel. From the contextual menu that appears, choose Drop Shadow.

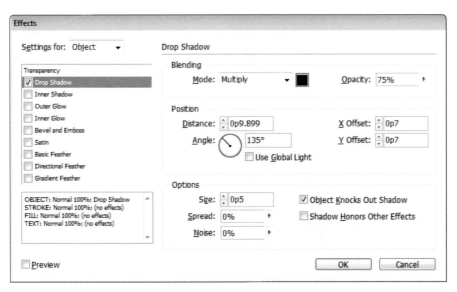

A drop shadow is one of many effects that can be applied in the Effects dialog box.

4   When the Effects dialog box opens, check the *Preview* checkbox in the bottom-left corner. Look at the change: InDesign applies a drop shadow to the frame because it has a fill of paper. If there were no fill color or stroke color, it would have applied a drop shadow to the text. Because InDesign lets you apply an effect to the fill, stroke, or text individually, you will adjust the settings in the Effects dialog box in the next step so that only the text gets the drop shadow.

5   Still in the Effects dialog box, click the *Drop Shadow* checkbox in the list on the left side of the dialog box to turn it off. A drop shadow is no longer applied to the whole object.

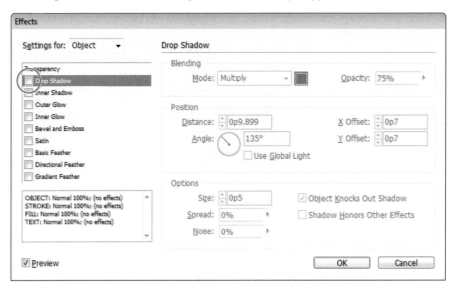

Turn off the drop shadow for the object.

6   In the Settings for drop-down menu at the top of the dialog box, choose Text to affect only text with the effect.

7   Click the *Drop Shadow* checkbox to turn it on and apply the drop shadow to the text only. Click OK to close the dialog box and apply the effect.

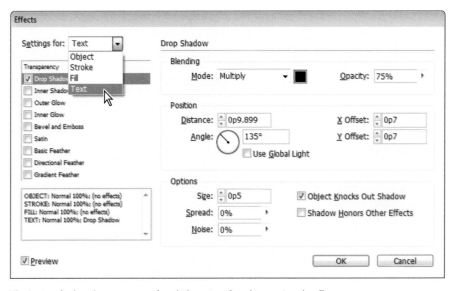

The Settings for drop-down menu specifies which portion of an object receives the effect.

8   Choose File > Save to save your work.

Adjusting effects for objects

All InDesign's effects are nondestructive. In other words, when you implement an effect, you always have the option of turning it on or off, as well as re-editing it. You can, for example, change the Drop Shadow effect you applied to the text in the previous exercise. In this exercise, you will change the position of the drop shadow and add the Use Global Light effect, which makes any lighting effects consistent across the entire document. In other words, all drop shadows and other lighting effects appear as if they have the same light source. When the Use Global Light effect is on and you alter the drop shadow's position, all instances of the effect change. Think of a light shining in a room: if the light source changes position, all the shadows and highlights in the room also change accordingly.

1   Continuing from where you left off in the previous exercise, be sure that the box containing the words *Johnny Guitar rocks again!* is still selected. Double-click the effects symbol (*fx*) next to the Text listing inside the Effects panel, to open the Effects dialog box. Once you apply an effect, this symbol appears in the Effects panel next to the component of the document to which the effect was applied. This instance of the effects symbol appears because of the drop shadow you applied to the text earlier. By double-clicking the symbol, you can edit the effects you applied.

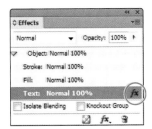

Double-click the fx symbol next to the Text listing in the Effects panel to open the Effects dialog box.

2   In the Position section of the Effects dialog box, click the *Use Global Light* checkbox to turn it on.

3 Type **0p7** (7 points) in the Distance text field. The Distance parameter controls how far from an object the drop shadow appears.

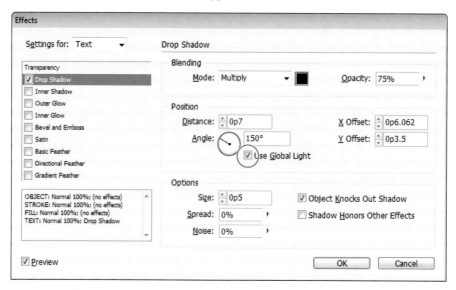

Turn on Use Global Light *and set the drop shadow's Distance parameter in the Effects panel.*

If you are not familiar with working in picas and would rather work in inches, simply right-click (Windows) or Control+click (Mac OS) the ruler and change the unit of measurement. The Distance field should then be set to 0.0972 inches.

4 Click OK to apply the changes and close the Effects dialog box. The Drop Shadow changes from its former position to be consistent with other lighting effects in the document.

Global Light coordinates all transparency effects that use shading, such as Drop Shadow, Inner Shadow, or Bevel and Emboss. Effects that use Global Light will have the light source angle and altitude synchronized across the entire document. Angle represents the direction that the light source is coming from. The Altitude setting, used for Bevel and Emboss, indicates how close the light source is to the object. Change the direction of the light source on any object's effect, and all other effects controlled by Global Light will adjust accordingly. Using Global Light gives the appearance of a common light source shining on the objects, adding consistency and realism to the effects.

5 Choose File > Save to save your work.

Bevel and Emboss

The Bevel and Emboss effect, familiar from Photoshop, gives an object a three-dimensional look. In this exercise, you will apply Bevel and Emboss to one of the stars, and then apply this effect to another star more quickly by dragging and dropping the effect from the Effects panel.

1   Using the Selection tool (⬉), select the leftmost star beneath the *Johnny Guitar rocks again!* article on page 6.

2   Click the Add an object effect to the selected target button (*fx*) at the bottom of the Effects panel. From the resulting contextual menu, choose Bevel and Emboss.

3   When the Effects dialog box appears, leave the settings at their defaults and click OK to apply a Bevel and Emboss lighting effect to the star. Press Ctrl+(plus sign) (Windows) or Command+(plus sign) (Mac OS) to zoom in on the stars and compare the changed star with the others. Now you'll apply the same effect to the second star, taking advantage of the ability to drag-and-drop.

Apply the Bevel and Emboss effect to one of the stars.

4   With the first star still selected, take a look at the Effects panel. To the right of the Objects entry is the same effects symbol (*fx*) that appeared next to the Text entry when you applied the drop shadow. Click and drag the symbol from the Effects panel into the layout and over the second-from-left star. When the cursor, which now looks like a hand with a plus sign over it (⊞), is positioned over the star, release the mouse to apply the Bevel and Emboss effect. Dragging and dropping is an easy way to reapply an effect without having to work within the Effects dialog box. InDesign offers even more ways to apply effects. In the next exercise, you will apply Bevel and Emboss using object styles.

Simply drag and drop the effect to apply Bevel and Emboss to the second star.

5   Choose File > Save.

Object styles with effects

In Lesson 4, "Working with Styles," and Lesson 5, "Working with Graphics," you explored using object styles to record stroke, fill, and paragraph styles. With InDesign, you can also use object styles to record and apply effects. As with other style attributes, a change to an effect is reflected wherever you applied the style. In the next exercise, you will record an object style for the Bevel and Emboss effect and apply it to the rest of the stars.

1   On page 6, select the first star using the Selection tool (⯆).

2   Choose Window > Styles > Object Styles, or click the Object Styles button (▣) in the dock, to open the Object Styles panel. From the Object Styles panel menu (▾≣), choose New Object Style.

3   In the New Object Style dialog box, type **Embossed** in the Style Name text field to name the new style. Although the style automatically inherits all effects applied to the selected object, you can choose which of them you want to save with the style.

Notice the section in the bottom-left corner of the dialog box that details all the effects currently applied to the selected object, in this case Transparency and Bevel and Emboss. Before you save the style, you can turn these on and off individually by clicking the check box next to each attribute. For now, leave them as they are.

4   Make sure the *Apply Style to Selection* check box is selected to automatically apply the new object style to the star. Click OK.

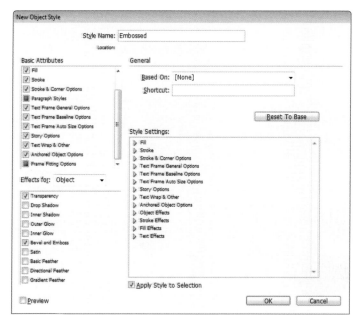

Note the listing of applied effects in the New Object Style dialog box when you create a new object style.

5   Using the Selection tool, Shift-click to select the remaining stars on the right side of page 6. Click the Embossed object style in the Object Styles panel to apply it to all the stars.

Using Find/Change to apply object styles

There are 13 more stars remaining on pages 6 and 7 that need the Embossed object style applied to them. Although the object style will make quick work of this, imagine if you had even more stars that needed the object style applied to them. Fortunately, InDesign provides an efficient method for you to do this.

1 Press Shift+Ctrl+A (Windows) or Shift+Command+A (Mac OS) to make sure that nothing is selected in the document.

2 Choose Edit > Find/Change to open the Find/Change dialog box. Click the Object button at the top of the dialog box.

3 In the Find Object Format section, click the Specify attributes to find button (📎). Click on the Fill category under the Basic Attributes section, and then click on the red swatch (C=15, M=100, Y=100, K=0) under the Fill category to tell InDesign to find objects with a red fill color. Click on the Stroke category under the Basic Attributes section, and then click on the Black swatch under the Stroke category. Click OK.

4 In the Change Object Format section, click on the Specify attributes to change button. Click on the Style Options category under the Basic Attributes section and choose Embossed from the Object Style drop-down menu. Click OK.

You've just told InDesign to search for any object with a red fill and black stroke and then apply the Embossed object style to the objects that it finds.

The Find/Change attributes are defined for the objects you want to find and change.

5   Click the Change All button. A dialog box appears, indicating that 18 objects have been changed. This is because it found the five original stars that had the object style already applied. InDesign simply applies the object style again, which is not a problem since an object style can only be applied to an object once. Click OK, and then click Done.

The object style applied to every star on the page.

Basic Feather

Feathering fades the transparency of an object's border from opaque to invisible over a distance along the edges. Instead of using Photoshop to feather an image's border, you can use InDesign. You can produce some pleasing effects by softening the edge of an image to make it appear as if the image fades into the page. Another feature is Directional Feathering, which allows you to control which side of an image or a colored frame receives the feather. The Basic Feather effect's settings include Corners, which determines how the corners of the feather appear; Noise, which sets how smooth or textured the feather transition appears; and Choke, which controls how much of the feather is opaque or transparent.

In this exercise, you will apply a Basic Feather effect to the image on page 6, and then use the Gradient Feather tool to apply a one-sided feather to the image on page 7.

1   Change the unit of measurement to inches by right-clicking (Windows) or Control+clicking (Mac OS) in the upper-left corner where the ruler guides meet. This will change both the horizontal and vertical measurement units at the same time.

2   In the Pages panel, double-click page 6 to activate it.

3 Use the Selection tool (🡤) to select the image of Tommy Acustomas in the lower-left area of the page.

4 If necessary, choose Window > Effects to open the Effects panel, then click the Add an object effect to the selected target button (*fx*). From the resulting contextual menu, choose Basic Feather.

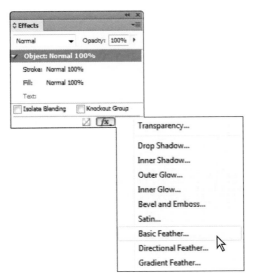

Choose Basic Feather to open the Effects dialog box and apply the Basic Feather effect to the photo.

5 Click the *Preview* checkbox to see what the feather looks like. All edges of the image are diffused and quickly blend into the background.

6 In the Effect dialog box's Options section, click in the Feather Width text field, which currently reads 0.125 in.

7 To change the Feather Width, which is the distance the feather will be applied, press the Up Arrow key on the keyboard twice to increase the amount in the Feather Width text field to 0.25 inch.

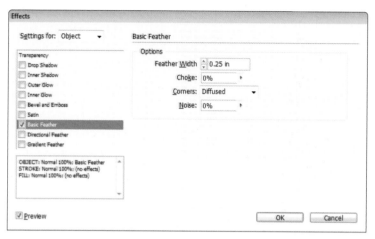

Adjust the Basic Feather settings to tweak the effect.

8 Click OK to close the Effects dialog box and apply the Basic Feather effect. Next, you will apply the same feather settings to the quote box on page 7.

This is how the image looks after Basic Feather is applied.
Notice how the edges of the image appear to fade out.

9 Double-click the Hand tool (✋) in the Tools panel to fit the InDesign spread in the workspace.

10 Make sure you still have the lower-left image on page 6 selected; if not, do so using the Selection tool.

You will now apply the same effect to the quote box on page 7, using a different method.

11 From the Effects panel, drag the effects symbol (*fx*) that appears just to the right of *Object* and drop it over the quote box at the top of page 7. Now the quote box is also feathered; it is very easy to add and share effects this way.

12 Choose File > Save to save your work.

When dragging the fx symbol onto another object, watch for the cursor icon to change (⊞), indicating that the effect will be applied. You may need to aim for the edge of a frame (rather than the center) to get the effect to transfer.

The Gradient Feather tool

The Gradient Feather tool eases the transition of an object's opacity, from fully opaque to fully transparent. In this section, you will use the tool to fade the bottom of the Garage Band image on page 7 to transparency. In the previous exercise, Basic Feather applied the feather to all sides equally. InDesign also has a Directional Feather effect to adjust each feathered edge separately. You can use the Gradient Feather tool to dynamically fade one side of an image to transparency without affecting the other sides. You also have control over the angle at which the gradient effect is applied. By using this tool, you can click and drag as many times as you like, adjusting the gradient feather to whichever angle you want, without a dialog box.

1 Use the Selection tool (▶) to select the Garage Band image at the top of page 7.

2 Select the Gradient Feather tool (▨) from the Tools panel.

3   Click just below the baseline of the phrase *Summer of '88*, drag down so the cursor touches the bottom of the image, and then release the mouse. The bottom of the image fades to transparency. The longer you click and drag, the larger the area to which the fade is applied, and the more dramatic the effect. Try holding Shift as you drag to keep the gradient effect horizontally straight.

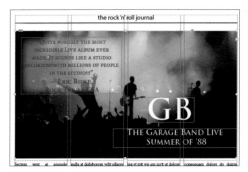

Drag down from the lower-middle area of transparency along the direction you choose.

The Gradient Feather effect fades the image to transparency.

4   Choose File > Save to save your work.

Converting text to a path

Here you'll learn how to modify the text so that instead of filling it with a standard color, you fill it with a photo, producing a cool effect that's fairly simple to implement. You cannot place an image directly into text while it is still editable; you can only place an image into text after it is converted to outlines.

You can use the Type menu's Create Outlines command to convert the original font outline information into a set of compound paths. Compound paths are separate paths combined into a single object. In this exercise, you will convert the letters *GB* on page 7 to compound paths and place a photo inside them.

1   Using the Selection tool (⬥), click the box on page 7 that contains *GB*.

Make sure you did not accidentally select the type with the Type tool; although you can still convert text to outlines this way, it will create an in-line graphic. Although this technique can be useful in some cases, it could make it hard to modify and position the outlined text.

2 Choose Type > Create Outlines to convert the font information to paths.

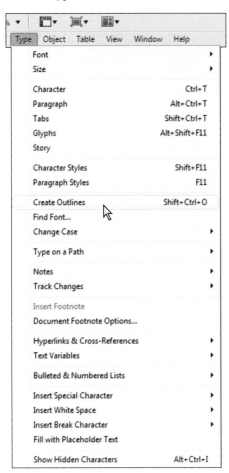

Choose Type > Create Outlines to convert text to paths.

3 Choose the Direct Selection tool (↘) in the Tools panel to view the paths you created. Because these are compound paths, you can now place a picture inside them.

View the new paths around the type.

4 Open the Mini Bridge panel and navigate to the Links folder inside the id08lessons folder, select id0807.psd, right-click (Windows) or Control+click (Mac OS), and choose Place > In InDesign. The photo fills the GB compound paths.

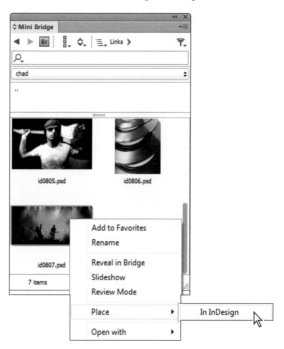

Choose Place > In InDesign to position an image inside the paths.

5   With the Direct Selection tool still selected, click and drag the image to reposition it. You should see the image ghosted where it does not fall inside the path area. The photo you imported is the same as the image over which it appears, only cropped. Drag to fit the photo in the box however you like.

When repositioning an image inside a path, do not click and drag until you see the hand cursor. If you click and drag when it appears as the Direct Selection tool (⬚), you could accidentally select and move a point on the path.

Click and drag an image to see the ghosted portions of the image outside the path area.

6   Choose File > Save to save your work.

Applying blending modes to objects

If you have ever placed a black logo with a white background on a colored page, and then wondered how to get rid of the white background, you'll appreciate blending modes. While there are several ways you can resolve this using InDesign, in this exercise you will discover how to use blending modes to manipulate a logo.

Blending modes affect how color pixels on one level blend with color pixels on the levels and layers below it. The two most commonly used blending modes are Multiply and Screen. You can remember what they do in the following way: Multiply blends out the white; Screen blends out the black. In more detailed terms, Multiply looks at the color information for the items and multiplies the base color by the blend color. The outcome is always a darker color. Screen examines each item's color information and multiplies the inverse of the blend and base colors. The outcome is always a lighter color.

In the next two exercises, you will practice applying Screen and Multiply to examine how blending modes work.

The Screen blending mode

The Screen blending mode is useful for colorizing the black within an image. You will apply a Screen blending mode to the blue box that's part of the record albums image on page 7 to give the records below the box a blue tint.

1   With the Selection tool (✹), click the blue box in the lower-right corner of page 7. This box is the one you altered in the first opacity exercise. Because InDesign effects are editable, you will remove the opacity.

2   Choose Window > Effects or open the Effects panel from the dock, reveal the Opacity slider (click on the right-facing triangle next to the settings), and drag it to 100 percent. Click the triangle again to commit the value. The blue box covering the records image becomes solid blue.

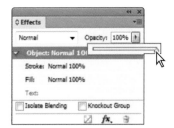

Return the box's opacity to 100 percent in the Effects panel.

3 To the left of the Opacity setting in the Effects panel is the Blending Mode drop-down menu. It is currently set to Normal. Click Normal to reveal the other options, and choose Screen. The color of the blue box is now blending with the image of the records.

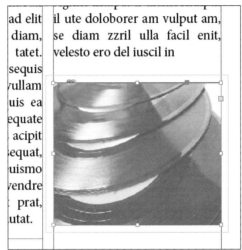

Once you change the blending mode to Screen, the records look blue where they were formerly black.

Remember that the Screen effect drops the black out of an image, so if you put a Screen blending mode on the blue box, the black parts of the image beneath the box appear blue.

The Multiply blending mode

You will now work with an image that has so far been hidden on a layer. You will use the Multiply blending mode to visually remove the logo's white area, while leaving the black areas unchanged.

1 From the Pages panel, double-click page 6 to center it on the page.

2 Click the Layers button (❤) in the dock. There is a hidden layer called Johnny that you will need for this exercise and the next one.

3   Click in the leftmost box to the left of the Johnny layer to make that layer visible. An image of Johnny Guitar appears on page 6. On his T-shirt, in the upper-right corner of the image, is a swirly *J* and *G*—his signature and logo.

When the visibility icon is turned on next to a layer, the layer is visible.

4   Select the signature using the Selection tool (⬥).

5   Open the Effects panel, if necessary, and from the Blending Mode drop-down menu at the top of the panel, choose Multiply. The white box around the logo disappears and the logo appears directly on Johnny's T-shirt.

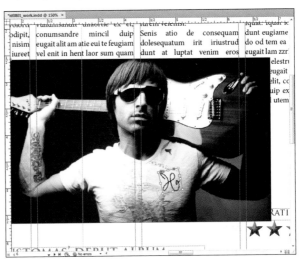

Applying the Multiply effect blends Johnny Guitar's logo with his shirt.

Because Multiply blends away the white, applying it is a handy trick to get rid of only the white in black-and-white images. This blending mode does not work with full-color images that have white around them, because it tries to blend white throughout the image, making it appear transparent or blended into the colors beneath.

As you'll learn in the next section, there are alternative ways to achieve this same effect, such as using a clipping path or alpha channel selection.

6   Choose File > Save to save your work.

Working with imported files that use transparency

If you have worked through the previous lessons in this book, you probably have noticed that incorporating images created or modified in Photoshop into InDesign is a well-established part of a production workflow. In this exercise, you look at the ways that InDesign supports transparency in images edited in Photoshop.

Photoshop has a number of ways to define areas of transparency in an image. While Photoshop is not required for this lesson, there are concepts such as alpha channels, clipping paths, and selections that are worth investigating in Photoshop and that can help you get the most out of this lesson.

The choice of using alpha channels or clipping paths depends on which tools you are more comfortable using and the content of your image. As a rule, paths are cleaner because they are created using vectors, which give you nice, smooth curves, while an alpha channel selection is based on pixels and gives you an edge that is choppier yet more realistic in some cases. For example, if you were removing the background of a product such as a television or soda can, vector paths would be the better choice. However if you are removing the background from a person, especially around their hair, an alpha channel might be the better choice. Know that regardless of which method you choose in the clipping options in InDesign, a vector edge will be created.

In this next exercise, you will place two images with different types of transparency. The first image simply has a transparent background, and the second has an alpha channel and a clipping path that were created in Photoshop. After learning how to control these transparent areas in InDesign, you will examine how transparency interacts with text wrap.

1   Press Shift+Ctrl+A (Windows) or Shift+Command+A (Mac OS) to deselect all objects in the document. In the Layers panel, select Layer 1.

2   Open the Pages panel from the dock and double-click page 7 to select it. You will be placing a photo on this page. Double-click the Zoom tool (🔍), if necessary, to view the page at 100 percent.

3   Use the Mini Bridge to navigate to the Links folder within the id08lessons folder, select the id0802.psd file, then right-click (Windows) or Control+click (Mac OS), and choose Place > In InDesign.

4 The cursor now contains a thumbnail image of the file being placed. In the second column of page 7's Allison Copper story, click in the white space to place the image. Using the Selection tool, click and drag to move the picture into position.

Use the Selection tool to position the image on page 7.

Move the image over some text; notice that it does not have a white background. Instead, the file has a transparent layer. InDesign automatically recognized the .psd file's transparency. Adjust the image position to match the example above.

Applying an alpha channel selection

The photo of the band members (id0802.psd) contains an alpha channel selection that was saved in Photoshop. An alpha channel is a way to save a selection you created in Photoshop so that you can later access it in InDesign for visibility and text wrap options. Alpha channels are stored, along with the color channels of an RGB or CMYK image, to capture a selection or indicate transparency. In this exercise, you will access an alpha channel using the Clipping Paths option. A clipping path is another term for the visibility edge that exists with this type of partially transparent image. Consider the outline of the two band members. This outline represents the clipping path; all areas inside the path are opaque, while all areas outside the path are transparent.

You could use InDesign's Detect Edges feature, which would build a path for you around the two band members based on the transparency or background contrast, but an even more accurate way is to access the saved alpha channel selection that is already made for you.

1 Make sure you still have the band photo selected. If it is not, select the image using the Selection tool (⬈), and then choose Object > Clipping Path > Options.

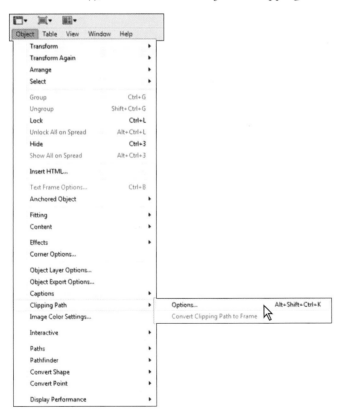

Choose Clipping Path > Options in the Object menu.

2   In the Clipping Path dialog box, choose Alpha Channel from the Type drop-down menu and rockers from the Alpha drop-down menu. Notice that the Alpha setting default is Transparency, based on the transparent pixels of the file. Click to turn on the *Preview* checkbox to see the path you created from the alpha channel. This path is also helpful when applying the text wrap.

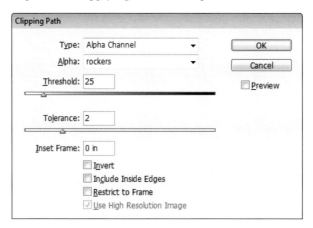

Choose Alpha Channel and rockers in the Clipping Path dialog box.

3   Click OK to accept the path shown in the preview and close the dialog box. Next you will apply a text wrap around the alpha channel selection.

4   Choose Window > Text Wrap to access the Text Wrap panel.

5   In the panel, click on the Wrap around object shape button (▣) to wrap the text around the image's shape rather than its bounding box. In the Text Wrap panel, enter an offset value of **10 pt (.1389 in.)** or experiment with different values, and then close the Text Wrap panel.

Notice that in the Contour Options section of the Text Wrap panel, the default Type setting is Same as Clipping. Although this is useful, it is possible to choose another contour method for the text wrap that is totally separate from what is used for the clipping. This opens up a world of possibilities to you as the designer.

Wrap the text around the object shape.

6   Choose the Selection tool (▸), and then click and drag the image slightly to the left to allow the text to wrap slightly around the guitarist's leg.

7   Choose File > Save to save your work.

Applying a path selection

A path selection is a selection made and saved in Photoshop using the Pen tool. You can access these selections in InDesign the same way you select a .psd file's alpha channel. Pen tool selections are cleaner than alpha channels in InDesign because they are vector paths and InDesign doesn't need to create this path on its own. Alpha channel selections are based on pixels, and InDesign makes the path for you. You will now apply a pre-made path to Johnny Guitar and apply a text wrap again.

1 Open the Pages panel from the dock, and double-click page 6 to bring it into view.

2 Select the image of Johnny Guitar using the Selection tool.

3 Choose Object > Clipping Path > Options.

4 In the Clipping Path dialog box, check the *Preview* checkbox, and then choose Photoshop Path from the Type drop-down menu. *Guitarist* should automatically appear as the Path name.

5 Click OK. Notice how the black around the image disappears based on the saved Photoshop path. Now you can apply the text wrap.

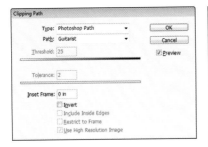

With the path applied, you're ready to wrap text around Johnny.

6   With the image of Johnny still selected, choose Window > Text Wrap to open the Text Wrap panel, and then click the panel's Wrap around object shape button ( ). Again, the text wraps around the object's shape and not its box, just as it did in the previous exercise with alpha channels. Set the offset value to **10 pt (.1389 in.)** or adjust it to a value you find acceptable.

Here is the final design with all the effects applied.

7   Choose File > Save to save your work. Take a look at the *rock 'n' roll journal* spread. You're finished working with imported files and transparency. Close this completed file by choosing File > Close.

Congratulations! You've finished the lesson.

Self study

Here are some projects you can create on your own:

- Apply a drop shadow to Johnny Guitar and choose Use Global Light to coordinate the effects throughout the document. Then adjust the direction of the Drop Shadow effect and watch the headline drop shadow update as well.

- Select the top photo on page 7, and remove the Gradient Feather effect. Try to accomplish the same effect with Directional Feathering.

- Apply more effects to Johnny Guitar, save the result as an object style, and then apply that style to the images of Johnny and Allison Copper. Change the object style so that both images update simultaneously.

- Experiment with blending modes by making a colored frame over Tommy Acustomas; then change the Blending modes and Opacity settings to get different effects.

Review

Questions

1 Can you alter an effect after you've applied it?

2 What is the difference between opacity and tint?

3 If you apply Create Outlines to type, can you still edit the text with the Type tool?

4 Can you feather only one edge of a photograph?

Answers

1 Yes, you can always return to the Effects panel, select the effect again, and double-click the effect to make adjustments.

2 Tint is a screened (lighter) version of a color, and is not transparent. Opacity achieves a similar result; however, it allows objects behind the transparent object to show through.

3 No, if Create Outlines is applied, the text is made into paths and is no longer related to the font information.

4 Yes, with the Directional Feather effect or the Gradient Feather tool, you can control the angle and direction of a feather to include only one of the image's edges.

What you'll learn in this lesson:

- Adding dynamic text variables to your document

- Managing multiple InDesign documents using the Book feature

- Generating a Table of Contents

- Generating an Index

- Generating captions

Advanced Document Features

Although the lessons so far have used single, small documents as examples, InDesign can manage complex, book-length documents, and maintain consistency across multiple files. The software's advanced document features enable you to add dynamic text, cross-reference and index information, and synchronize many files at once.

Starting up

Before starting, make sure that your tools and panels are consistent by resetting your preferences. See "Resetting the InDesign workspace and preferences" in the Starting up section of this book.

You will work with several files from the id09lessons folder in this lesson. Make sure that you have copied the id09lessons folder onto your hard drive from the Digital Classroom DVD. See "Loading lesson files" in the Starting up section of this book. This lesson may be easier to follow if the id09lessons folder is on your desktop.

See Lesson 9 in action!

Use the accompanying video to gain a better understanding of how to use some of the features shown in this lesson. The video tutorial for this lesson can be found on the supplied DVD.

The project

In this lesson, you will work with several chapters of a book to see for yourself the capabilities of InDesign's book feature. You will add chapters to a book file, and update the page number of each page based on its position in the book. Using text variables, you will automate the generation of elements on each page, which can save hours of manual work. You will then synchronize each chapter to give the book a consistent appearance.

Adding text variables

InDesign enables you to add dynamic text called *variables* to your documents. In a general sense, a variable is a way to store information that is not necessarily permanent. In InDesign, a variable is text-based content that dynamically changes when certain criteria are met or specific changes occur in the document. For example, you might want a running footer in the document that contains the title of the chapter. Traditionally, you would type the static text on a master page for the content to appear properly. Inserting a variable provides a more powerful option. In this case, using a variable would automatically update all footer text when the chapter title is modified.

When you place a text variable on a page, you must place it within a text frame, just like normal text. That frame can be in the live, printable area of the documents or in the non-printing portion. In this exercise, you will use text variables in a non-printing area to display the filename and modification date of the documents, which can be helpful in a collaborative environment.

1   In InDesign, choose File > Open. Navigate to the id09lessons folder, choose
     TOC.indd, and click Open. Notice the light blue outline that extends beyond the edge
     of the page on the right side. This area is called the *slug*, and information entered here
     doesn't automatically print on the final page. You will use the slug area to house the
     filename and modification date variables, displaying the name of the file and the date it
     was modified. This is useful when viewing a printout of a document or when viewing
     it onscreen to determine when the most recent edit or modification was made.

About the trim and slug area

A slug is information placed outside of the final print area of the document. The final print
area is known as the trim area, and the space immediately outside of where a document will
be trimmed (cut) is the slug area. The slug may contain the job name, client name, a place
for approval of the job, or colors used in the job. Slugs can be included when printing or
generating PDF files from InDesign. The slug prints only when you choose Include Slug Area
in the Marks and Bleed section of the Print dialog box or the Export Adobe PDF dialog box.

2   Select the Type tool (T) from the Tools panel, and then click and drag to create a text
     frame within the top of the slug area on the page. Be careful to keep the frame within
     the slug's bounds.

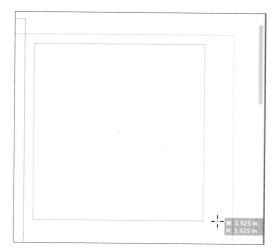

*The slug area can hold information that will not show up in the final
printed project but can appear when printed.*

3   Open the Paragraph Styles panel by choosing Window > Styles > Paragraph Styles or by clicking the Paragraph Styles button () in the dock on the right side of the workspace. Before inserting text or typing into this frame, choose the Variable Text style from the Paragraph Styles panel. This assigns the Variable Text style to text you type in the frame, and gives the text a standard appearance. Make sure the cursor is blinking in the text box before you choose this style.

4   With the cursor inside the text frame, choose Type > Text Variables > Insert Variable > File Name to insert the value of the File Name variable in the slug area's text frame. Because you're working in the file TOC.indd, InDesign inserts *TOC* in the frame. Choose File > Save.

5   Press the Enter key (Windows) or Return key (Mac OS) on your keyboard to move the cursor under the filename text you inserted in the previous step, then choose Type > Text Variables > Insert Variable > Modification Date. InDesign inserts the value of the second variable, Modification Date, beneath TOC in the text frame. The Modification Date's value reflects the time and date of the file's most recent save, and because you saved the document in the last step, the current date and time appear.

Later in the lesson, you will see how the File Name and Modification Date variables can be useful in a production environment. A quick look at the variable text tells which file you're working in and whether the file has been updated recently.

> **TOC**
> **March 21, 2012 10:52 AM**

Text variables can provide dynamic information about the document.

Usually, when text variables are used, you'll want to modify or customize the variable so it appears in the correct way. In the next steps, you'll customize the File Name variable.

6 Choose Type > Text Variables > Define. In the resulting Text Variables dialog box, choose File Name from the list, then click the Edit button. Enable the Include File Extension check box and in the Text Before field, type **Document Name:** (be sure to put a space after the semicolon). This will modify the appearance of the variable anywhere that it occurs in your document. Click OK, and then click Done.

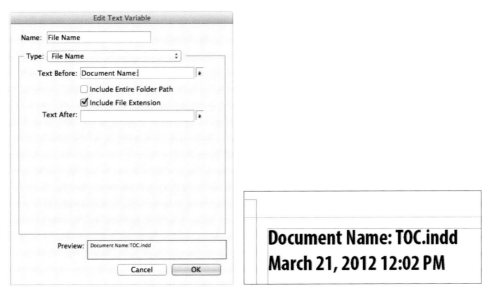

By modifying the text variable, you change how it displays in your document.

Note that the text you previously inserted in the slug area has updated to reflect the change you made in the Text Variables dialog box.

7 Choose File > Save, and then close the document.

Creating a book from multiple files

Any project that contains numerous pages, whether it's a book, magazine, or other long document, can be large and cumbersome. Not only is file size an issue—especially if the project contains a lot of graphics—but the more pages the document contains, the more challenging it is to navigate through the document. InDesign's Book feature offers some help. The Book feature enables you to divide up a project into smaller, more manageable sections or chapters. It also boasts a number of document management capabilities that allow for easy navigation between sections and maintain consistency from one file to the next. You can also have different people work on different files, and use the Book feature to join the files together into one project.

To demonstrate the Book feature, you will work with five files that represent the different chapters of a work in progress. An important task in managing a large job like this is to create a book file.

1   Choose File > New > Book. When the New Book dialog box opens, navigate to the id09lessons folder, type **Book.indb** in the Name text field, then click Save. The Book panel appears and gives you access to the book file of the same name. If the welcome screen is displayed, you may need to close it before accessing the Book panel.

2   Click the Add documents icon (⊕) at the bottom of the Book panel.

3   In the resulting Add Documents dialog box, Press Ctrl (Windows) or Command (Mac OS) to select the TOC.indd, 1_Trees.indd, 2_Flowers.indd, 3_Plants.indd, and Index.indd files located in the id09lessons folder. Click Open.

If you don't have the Times New Roman font loaded on your system, you may receive a warning that the pages will recompose using a substituted font and the resulting page numbers may not be accurate. Click the Don't Show Again checkbox to avoid viewing this dialog box in the future, and then click OK. You will fix the fonts later in this exercise when you synchronize the book. If requested, save the files. InDesign now lists the documents in the Book panel. Although the documents in the Book panel are still separate files, they are now being managed by the Book panel and are now related to each other.

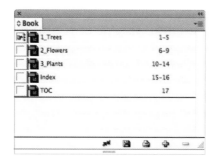

Add the documents from the id09lessons folder to the Book panel.

Defining pagination and document order

When you choose files from the Add Document dialog box, InDesign adds them to the Book panel and adjusts the page numbers within each document so they are sequentially numbered. Unfortunately, this does not always match the logical sequence for your documents. For example, in this book, the TOC and Index files should be first and last, respectively, in the panel. Because InDesign adds files to the Book panel in numerical, then alphabetical order, based on each document's filename, they are currently fourth and fifth in the list. Rearranging the file order is a simple matter of clicking and dragging.

Once a book's pages are in order, you can turn your attention to the pagination within the files. Do you need the book documents to open on left pages, for example? InDesign's Book Page Numbering Options help you tweak the document flow.

In this exercise, you will resolve some typical pagination issues, rearrange files, and explore the Book Page Numbering Options dialog box.

1   Within the Book panel, click and drag the TOC document to the top of the list. A bold divider rule indicates the destination of the selected document. Release the mouse button.

The TOC file is now the first document of the book; the page numbers to the right of the list adjust to accommodate the change.

2   Rearrange the documents within the Book panel. After moving the files, put them back in the following order: TOC, 1_Trees, 2_Flowers, 3_Plants, Index. Notice that when you rearrange the documents, the Book panel updates the page numbering based on the new page order.

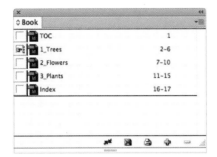

*The documents in the Book panel after arranging
them in the correct order.*

3   Double-click the 2_Flowers file in the Book panel. If any messages appear regarding modified links, click the Update Links button and if a missing font message appears, simply click OK.

The document opens just like it would if you opened it from the Open dialog box. The Book panel performs several automated management tasks, such as pagination, which is only available when you use the Book feature. Look in the Pages panel and notice that the page numbering continues from the previous document in the book file. This book is designed so that each chapter begins with a photo on the left page and the chapter intro on the right page. Currently, the document is not set up that way, but you'll fix that in the following steps. Close the document. If you receive a message asking you to save your documents, click OK to save them.

4 Deselect all files in the Book panel by clicking in the empty area below the panel's list. Click the Book panel menu button (▼≡), and from the resulting menu, choose Book Page Numbering Options.

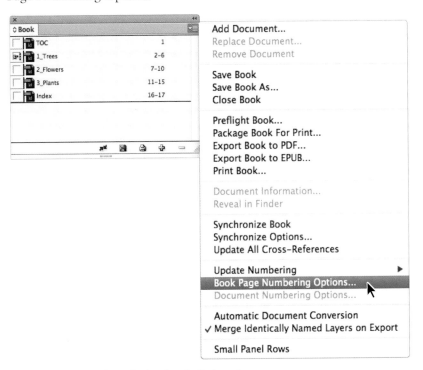

Choose Book Page Numbering Options from the Book panel menu.

5 In the Book Page Numbering Options dialog box that appears, confirm the Continue on next even page option is selected. Also make sure that the Insert Blank Page check box is selected so that InDesign can insert a blank page when necessary.

6   Make sure that the Automatically Update Page & Section Numbers check box is selected. This tells InDesign to update pagination and section numbering automatically when pages are added, removed, or rearranged. For example, if new pages are added to documents at the start of the book, the pages in the following documents will be updated. Click OK. A progress bar may appear while InDesign rearranges and adds pages to the documents as needed. The page numbers in the Book panel adjust to reflect the changes.

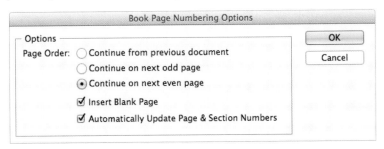

Control pagination within the Book Page Numbering Options dialog box, which is available in the Book panel menu.

7   Scroll down the Book panel and note that the pages are numbered consecutively at this point. The book numbering flows from one chapter to the next.

8   Double-click on the 2_Flowers document to open it, and notice that the document now begins on the left side (the even page). Close the document.

Synchronizing attributes across a book file

When multiple people collaborate on files for a large project, inconsistencies sometimes sneak in, no matter how well coworkers try to keep each other informed. Different colors may be used, styles may be defined differently, and fonts might even vary from one part of a document to another. The Book feature solves these hard-to-trace problems by synchronizing elements to maintain consistency across the documents within the book file. InDesign can synchronize the following items:

- Styles, including character, paragraph, object, table, cell, and TOC styles
- Swatches
- Numbered lists
- Text variables
- Conditional text settings
- Cross-reference formats
- Trap presets
- Master pages

In the design process, it isn't always feasible to start from a template with established master pages and styles, but it definitely helps when using the Book feature in InDesign. You can, however, create a base set of styles, such as body, subhead, and so on, and then synchronize all the related documents to these styles and any other attributes agreed upon later.

The book files in this lesson suffer from their own inconsistencies: The text and look of each document differs, which is the result of multiple designers using fonts unique to their system. This, in turn, creates conflicts in the chapters that need to be resolved. In this exercise, you will fix these discrepancies to establish cross-document consistency in the book.

1   Double-click the 1_Trees listing in the Book panel to open it. Update any modified links, if necessary. Notice the word *Chapter* at the top of page 3. You want the chapter number to appear next to the word for all the interior chapters in the book. To do this, you will use a variable.

2   Click the Pages button (⊡) in the dock to open the Pages panel. Double-click on the right page icon of the A-Chapter Intro master page in the Pages panel. This displays the contents of the right-hand master page for the chapter.

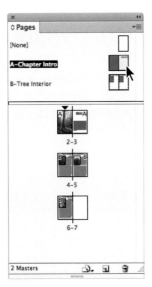

Double-click on the right page icon of the A-Chapter Intro master page.

3   Select the Type tool (T) from the Tools panel, and click to the immediate right of the word *Chapter* on the master page.

4   Type a space, then choose Type > Text Variables > Insert Variable > Chapter Number.

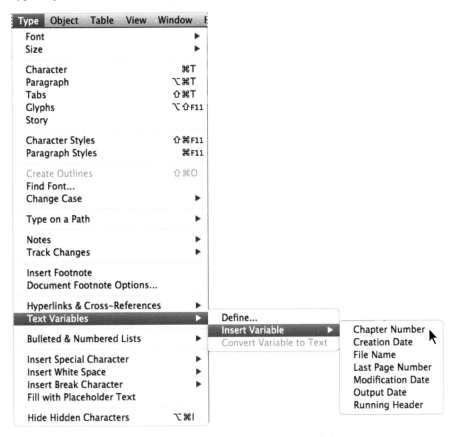

Add a text variable to the master page so that the chapter number will automatically be generated.

The chapter number appears where you insert the variable text.

5   To understand how InDesign knows the chapter number to insert, double-click the triangle above page 2 in the Pages panel to open the Numbering and Section Options dialog box. At the bottom of the dialog box, note that this document is set to Start Chapter Numbering at 1. This is the information that the Text Variable uses to display the proper number. Click OK to close the dialog box. Choose File > Save and then choose File > Close to close the document.

6 Now you're ready to synchronize attributes across multiple chapters. If necessary, click in the column to the left of the 1_Trees document name in the Book panel. This column selects the style source of your book. The style source is the document to which all other documents in the book synchronize.

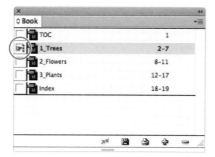

The style source icon indicates the document to which all other documents synchronize.

7 Before you synchronize documents, you must specify the synchronize options. From the Book panel menu (•≡), choose Synchronize Options. In the resulting Synchronize Options dialog box, you can specify which styles or elements to synchronize. For this project, make sure all options are selected. Click OK.

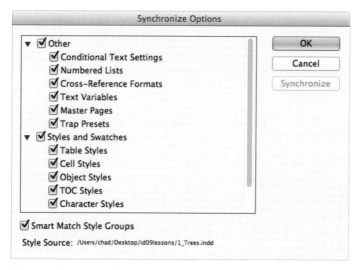

Choose synchronize options for the book.

8 In the Book panel, click 1_Trees, and then Shift+click 3_Plants to select all three of the interior chapters. You won't use Select All, because you don't want to synchronize the TOC or index.

9 Click the Synchronize styles and swatches using the Style Source icon (⇄) at the bottom of the Book panel to initiate the synchronization of the selected chapters.

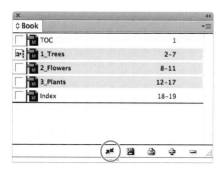

Select the documents and click the Synchronize styles and swatches with the style source icon to begin synchronization.

You may receive messages during synchronization that indicate some text has become overset or non–overset. Overset means that the text no longer fits into the text frame that contains it. Accept these messages by clicking OK. When finished, InDesign displays a message to convey that synchronization completed successfully and that some documents may have changed. InDesign changes the styles, master pages, and so on, in the selected documents to match those of the style source document. Here synchronization changed the definition of the paragraph styles to match the style source.

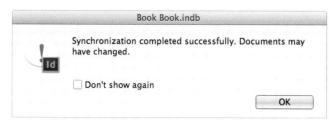

Successful synchronization.

10 Click OK to accept the synchronization. To confirm the changes, click, then double-click to open the 2_Flowers document. If necessary, update any links. The chapter introductory pages now feature the appropriate chapter number because you included master pages in the synchronization options. The body text matches that of the style source document and the Times New Roman font no longer exists in any of the documents. Similar changes were applied to the 3_Plants file.

To add the finishing touches, you'll change the names of the chapters to reflect the actual name of each chapter, as each file had originally started from the same template file.

11 Go to page 9 of the 2_Flowers document and, using the Selection tool, press Shift+Ctrl (Windows) or Shift+Command (Mac OS) while you click the green title bar at the top of the page. This overrides the item from the master page so you can edit it. For information on master pages, refer to Lesson 2, "Building Documents with Master Pages."

12 Select the Type tool (T), highlight the word *Trees* in the green title bar, and type **Flowers**.

13 Choose File > Save to save your changes, and then choose File > Close to close the 2_Flowers file.

14 Double-click 3_Plants in the Book panel, choose to Update Links if necessary, then double-click on page 13 in the Pages panel, and repeat the process of using Shift+Ctrl (Windows) or Shift+Command (Mac OS) on the green title bar on the title page, changing the word *Trees* to *Plants*. Choose File > Save and then close the file.

15 Double-click to open 1_Trees, and Shift+Ctrl+click (Windows) or Shift+Command+click (Mac OS) on the green title bar at the top of the page to detach it from the master page. This is the Trees chapter, so don't change any of the text. The chapter title must be detached from the master page in preparation for the next exercise.

Now that the document has been synchronized, you have established consistency throughout the pages of the book. As the book grows, and documents are added, you can synchronize the book again to ensure consistency of styles and pages in those new documents.

16 Choose File > Save, and then choose File > Close to close the Trees chapter.

Creating Captions

InDesign has a powerful captions feature that allows you to automatically generate captions for images that have been placed into a document based on the metadata embedded in the image. There are photos on the first spread of every chapter in the book that need a photo credit applied. In the following steps, you'll set-up the captions and generate them for each photo.

1 Double click the 1_Trees file in the Book panel to open it. In the Pages panel, double-click page 2 to go to that page. You'll add a photo credit for this image.

2 Choose Object > Captions > Caption Setup. In order to control how a caption is created, you need to setup the parameters in this dialog box. In the Text Before field, type **Photo Credit:** followed by a space.

3 In the Metadata drop-down menu, choose Author from the list. This is the metadata that will be pulled from the image to generate the caption.

4 In the Position and Style section at the bottom of the dialog box, choose Left of Image from the Alignment drop-down menu, and set the offset to **–0.375** inches; in the Paragraph Style drop-down menu, choose Photo Credit. Click OK.

Caption Setup		

Metadata Caption

Text Before	Metadata	Text After
Photo Credit:	Author	

Position and Style

Alignment: Left of Image   Paragraph Style: Photo Credit

Offset: -0.375 in   Layer: [Same as Image]

☐ Group Caption with Image

Cancel   OK

Setting the parameters in the Caption Setup dialog box.

Metadata Explained

Metadata is information about an image or file that doesn't generally appear as part of the files content. Metadata generally describes information about a file that can be useful for a number of purposes. In the case of photos, metadata can help you find information such as the camera that was used to take the photo, when the photo was taken, and in some cases, where the photo was taken. In the case of this lesson, we used the metadata of some of the photos to generate captions for the images. Some metadata information is embedded into the photo by the camera that took the picture. Metadata can also be added by the user to identify products or people who are in the image to make it easier to find the image later on.

One of the easiest ways to add metadata to a file or image is using the Adobe Bridge application. The Adobe Bridge allows you to quickly and easily add metadata information to a photo to identify the properties of the photo.

There are two parts to generating a caption from an image. The first step is to set the parameters in the Caption Setup dialog box as you completed in the previous step. The second step is to generate the caption for each image.

5   Select the image on page 2 with your selection tool, then choose Object > Captions > Generate Live Caption. The caption should appear along the left edge of the photo and should read Photo *Credit: istockphoto.com*. Chose File > Save and then File > Close.

The caption has been automatically generated and positioned in relation to the photo.

6   Repeat steps 2 through 5 in the 2_Flowers and 3_Plants documents to create photo credit captions in those documents as well.

Live vs. Static Captions

InDesign allows you to create two different types of captions: Live Captions and Static Captions. Live Captions update dynamically whenever you make changes to the metadata from an image used to generate the Live Caption. Static captions, by contrast, only use the metadata one time when generating the caption. From there on, the caption will not update if the metadata in the image updates.

Regardless of the dynamic advantage of Live Captions over Static Captions, you can't use Live Captions all the time because of a limitation: they cannot traverse more than one line. If a Live Caption extends beyond the length of the frame that contains the caption, the text will compress to fit within the given area. Static Captions, on the other hand, can traverse more than one line, but will not update dynamically.

Creating a Table of Contents

A book needs a Table of Contents, and InDesign helps you build one by automating its creation and formatting. For the Table of Contents feature to work, however, you must prepare the files correctly. For example, you must use paragraph styles throughout the document or book, and you must also create styles to format the text in the Table of Contents itself. The TOC document in this lesson already contains these styles. In this exercise, you'll use these styles and the Table of Contents feature to generate and format a Table of Contents.

1   Double-click the TOC document in the Book panel to open it.

2   Choose Window > Styles > Paragraph Styles to open the Paragraph Styles panel. In the Paragraph Styles panel, notice that several styles begin with the prefix TOC. You will use these to style the Table of Contents text. The styles you used to style the text of the chapters have not yet been synchronized. To create a Table of Contents, you'll load those styles into the TOC document by performing another synchronization.

3   Click the Book panel menu button (⁃≡) and choose Synchronize Options to open the Synchronize Options dialog box.

4   Uncheck all the options except for *Paragraph Styles* and *Character Styles* to instruct InDesign to synchronize only these attributes. Click OK to close the dialog box.

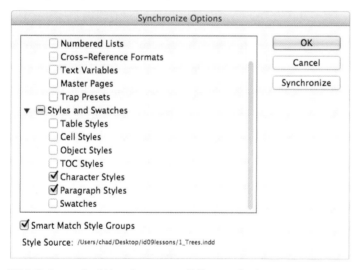

Tell InDesign exactly which attributes you would like to synchronize.

5   Make sure that the Style Source is set to the 1_Trees document in the Book panel (by clicking in the column to the left of the document name), and then Shift+click TOC and 1_Trees to select them for synchronizing.

6   Click the Synchronize styles and swatches with the Style Source button at the bottom of the Book panel. When the dialog box appears, announcing that the synchronization completed successfully, and that documents may have changed, click OK. Notice that several new styles have been imported into the TOC document during synchronization. Now you are ready to generate the Table of Contents for the book.

7   With the TOC.indd document open, choose Layout > Table of Contents. The Table of Contents dialog box appears.

8   In the area for Title in the dialog box, confirm the title is entered as *Contents*. If necessary, enter this as the title. This is the name that appears at the start of the Table of Contents.

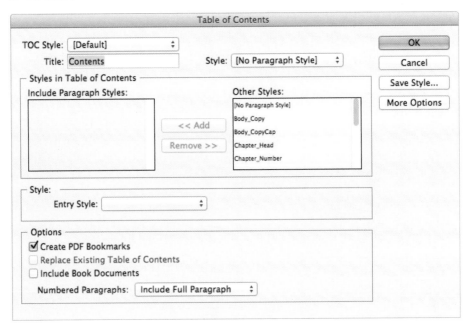

Control how the Table of Contents is styled and generated.

9 From the Style drop-down menu, choose TOC_Contents. This paragraph style defines how the title is formatted.

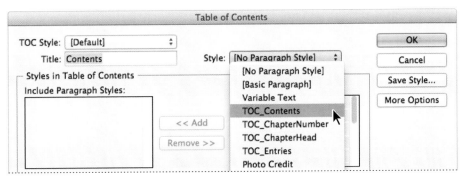

The top portion of the Table of Contents dialog box controls the title and title style of the Table of Contents.

10 The Styles in Table of Contents section is where you choose which styles in the document or book will appear in the Table of Contents. In the Other Styles list, click Chapter_Number to highlight it. Click the Add button to move the Chapter_Number style into the Include Paragraph Styles list. Highlight and click to add the Chapter_Head and Sub_Head styles as well, in that order.

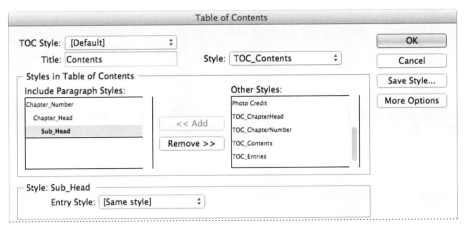

In the Styles in Table of Contents section, specify which styles InDesign uses to pull content from the document or book.

11 Now you need to define the attributes of each style's appearance. Click the More Options button at the right side of the Table of Contents dialog box to expand the Style section. If you see a Fewer Options button, you don't need to do anything, as the additional options are already displayed.

12 Click the Chapter_Number style in the Include Paragraph Styles list. The Style section below it is now labeled as Style: Chapter_Number. From the Entry Style drop-down menu, choose TOC_ChapterNumber, and from the Page Number drop-down menu, choose No Page Number.

13 Click the Chapter_Head style in the Include Paragraph Styles list, and in the Style section, set Entry Style to TOC_ChapterHead. Leave all other fields in this section at their defaults. Click the Sub_Head style next, and set Entry Style to TOC_Entries. Leave all other settings at their defaults.

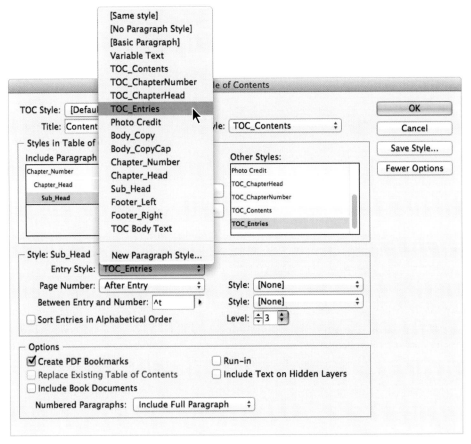

You can format the Table of Contents' elements in the Style section of the Table of Contents dialog box.

14 Click the *Include Book Documents* check box at the bottom of the dialog box to have all document files in the Book included when the Table of Contents is generated. InDesign locates text formatted with the specified styles you identified in the Include Paragraph Styles list, and the styled text is used for the Table of Contents.

15 Click the Save Style button in the upper-right corner of the dialog box. In the resulting Save Style dialog box, type **Book_TOC** in the Save Style text field, and click OK to save the settings that define how the Table of Contents is created. This saves time if you ever have to generate another Table of Contents with these settings in the future.

Clicking the Save Style button inside the Table of Contents dialog box captures the settings that you painstakingly configured for the Table of Contents. This can be useful if you have several versions of a document that each need their own Table of Contents, or if you made a mistake and later need to modify the settings.

16 Click OK in the Table of Contents dialog box to generate the Table of Contents for the book. A dialog box may appear, asking if you want to include items in overset text. Click OK. This ensures that if any of the text in the other documents is overset, it will still be included in the Table of Contents.

Overset text is text that appears in a frame that isn't big enough to display it. This can happen for several reasons; often when text is added or adjusted, it will make the text within a frame run longer than the actual frame. For this reason, you generally want to include items in overset text when creating a Table of Contents to make sure that any overset type styles to be listed as TOC entries are included.

17 The cursor changes to a loaded text cursor with a preview of the TOC text that is ready to be placed in the document. Click in the upper-left corner of the document where the margins meet. InDesign automatically creates a text frame within the boundaries of the margins and places the Table of Contents text within the frame.

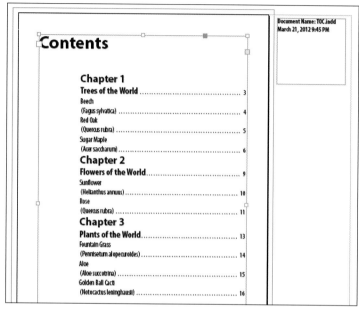

Place the loaded cursor in the upper-left corner of the document, and then click to place the Table of Contents.

18 Choose File > Save and then choose File > Close to save and close the document.

Whether you add or delete pages and documents from the book while you work, or modify the contents of your documents, you can easily update the Table of Contents to reflect these changes. Click the text frame that contains the Table of Contents text, and choose Layout > Update Table of Contents.

Building an index

Indexes are very complex components of a book. A good index is based on specific topics and can quickly direct you to the exact location of the information you need; a poorly created index is one that is confusing or unhelpful. InDesign doesn't know what you want indexed, so it can't automatically create an index for you. It can, however, make the process a lot easier. Using the Index panel, you can assemble an index with topics, references, and cross-references.

To demonstrate what's possible, two chapters of the example book have been indexed already. In this series of exercises, you'll tackle the third chapter, adding index topics to categorize the references, supplementing these with cross-references to help direct your reader to the correct topic, and finally, generating the index.

Adding topics

The most basic component of an index is its topics. Although InDesign can't help you with what to index, it makes adding the topics you choose a simple matter of pointing and clicking. Think of topics as categories into which entries will be sorted.

1   In the Book panel, double-click to open 3_Plants, the file you need to index.

2   Choose Window > Type & Tables > Index to open the Index panel.

3   Make sure the *Book* checkbox in the upper-right corner of the Index panel is checked. This tells InDesign to look in all the documents within a book for references when generating the index.

4   Click the *Topic* radio button at the top of the Index panel to switch to Topic view, and then click the Create a new index entry button (◰) at the bottom of the panel. The New Topic dialog box opens, allowing you to add the first topic.

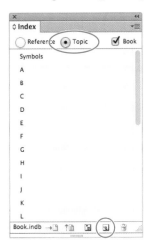

Click the Topic radio button, and then click the Create a new index entry button to begin building a topic list.

5   In the New Topic dialog box, type **Plants** in text field 1 under Topic Levels and click the Add button on the right side of the dialog box to add *Plants* to the topic list. Each letter of the alphabet appears at the bottom of the New Topic dialog box, and there is now a triangle next to *P*. If you click the triangle, the list expands and you see the word *Plants* has been added to the list of topics. In text field 1 under Topic Levels, type **Genus**, and then click Add. Click the OK or Done button. You have now added *Plants* and *Genus* to the topic list of the index.

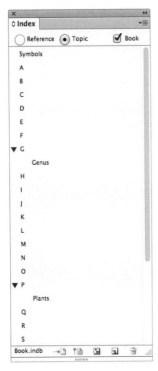

The new topics are added to the topic list of the index.

6   Click the *Reference* radio button at the top of the Index panel to switch to the Reference view, which shows each entry's page number and any cross-references that you add.

7   If the Pages panel isn't open, click on the Pages button in the dock to open it. Double-click on page 14 in the Pages panel to display page 14 and, using the Type tool (T), select the phrase *Fountain Grass* at the top of the page.

8   Click the Create a new index entry button at the bottom of the Index panel. The New Page Reference dialog box appears with *Fountain Grass* entered in the Topic Level 1 text field. Click the Add button to add the reference to Fountain Grass to the index. In order to accommodate a range of searching styles, you will add Fountain Grass as a subtopic beneath the Plants entry.

9   With the New Page Reference dialog box still open, click once in the Topic Level 1 text field, then click the down arrow icon to move Fountain Grass to the Topic Level 2 text field. Click to insert the cursor in the Topic Level 1 text field, then scroll down to the P topics in the list at the bottom of the New Page Reference dialog box. Click on the triangle next to P to expand its entries, and then double-click Plants to insert it in the Topic Level 1 text field. Click the Add button, and click OK or Done to close the New Page Reference dialog box.

New Page Reference		
Topic Levels:	**Sort By:**	OK
1 Plants	⬆	Cancel
2 Fountain Grass	⬇	Add
3		Add All
4		
Type:		
Current Page ⬍		
☐ Number Style Override	[None] ⬍	
O		
▼ P		
Plants		
Q		
R		
S		

The New Page Reference dialog box allows you to add index references for topics and subtopics within the text.

10 Repeat steps 7 to 9 for the word *Aloe* on page 15 and the phrase *Golden Ball Cacti* on page 16.

Now, in addition to the plant's name, you need to add each plant's scientific name to its Genus topic.

11 Double-click on page 14 in the Pages panel to go to that page. Highlight the scientific name *Pennisetum alopecuroides* and click the Create a new index entry button at the bottom of the Index panel. Click the down arrow icon to move the entry to the Topic Level 2 text field. Click to select the Topic Level 1 text field, then scroll down to the G topics in the list at the bottom of the New Page Reference dialog box. Click on the triangle next to G to expand its entries, then double-click Genus to insert it in the Topic Level 1 text field. Click the Add button, and click OK or Done.

12 Repeat step 11 to highlight the scientific name for each of the remaining plant names on pages 15 and 16, then add their references to the topic Genus. Click OK or Done to close the New Page Reference dialog box. Save the 3_Plants.indd document and keep the file open for the next exercise.

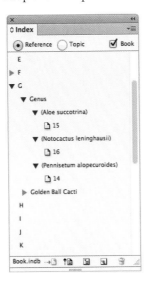

The Index Reference list shows what page each entry appears on in the documents.

Adding cross-references

Now that you've added all the necessary references to the index for the 3_Plants document, it's time to think about adding cross-references to the index. Cross-references refer a reader to a similar topic if there are no entries for the topic being looked up. For example, someone may look up the topic *grass* in the index. It does not contain a topic for grass, but the index can refer the reader to the closest thing, which would be Fountain Grass. Try adding the cross-reference now.

1 With the 3_Plants.indd document still open, choose New Cross-reference from the Index panel menu. If you see New Page Reference instead, deselect any text on the page by pressing Shift+Ctrl+A (Windows) or Shift+Command+A (Mac OS), and then choose New Cross-reference from the Index panel menu. The New Cross-reference dialog box appears.

2 In the list at the bottom of the New Cross-reference panel, scroll to the letter F and expand the topic by clicking on the triangle to its left. Double-click *Fountain Grass* to add it to the Topic Level 1 text field.

3 In the Referenced text field, type **Grass**. This tells InDesign to direct the reader to the Fountain Grass topic when the word *grass* is referenced. This places an entry in the index under the topic *Fountain Grass* that says, *See also* Grass.

4 Click the Add button to add the cross-reference to the index, and click OK or Done to close the New Cross-reference dialog box.

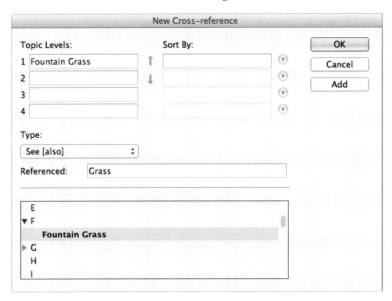

Enter the referenced word, as well as the related topic to which you will direct the reader.

5 Choose File > Save to save your work, and then close the file by choosing File > Close.

Generating the index

With all the pieces in place, you're ready to generate the index and place it within the book.

1 Open the Index file from the Book panel.

2 If the Index panel is not open, choose Window > Type & Tables > Index to open it.

3 Make sure that the Book checkbox in the upper-right corner of the panel is checked.

4 Click the Generate Index icon (⊟) at the bottom of the Index panel.

5 In the resulting Generate Index dialog box, leave the settings at their defaults. It's important that the *Include Book Documents* option is checked. Click OK to close the dialog box and generate the index. If a dialog box appears, announcing that the index has been replaced successfully, click OK.

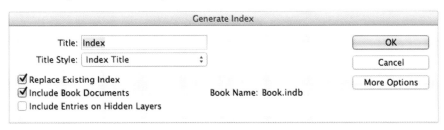

In the Generate Index dialog box, you can name the index and format it with a paragraph style.

6 The cursor changes to a loaded text cursor containing all the text that makes up the index. Click in the upper-left corner of page 18 of the Index document to place the text. InDesign creates a text frame on the page with the index text inside it.

If the entire index does not fit on the page you choose, simply flow the extra text onto the second page of the document. For more on flowing text from one frame to another, see Lesson 3, "Working with Text and Type."

7 Save and close the Index.indd file.

When you make changes to an index and need to update the existing index with new content, simply choose the Generate Index option from the Index panel menu to display the Generate Index dialog box. Within that dialog box is a check box called Replace Existing Index. When that check box is turned on, InDesign replaces the current index with the new index content.

Creating PDFs and printing from the Book panel

Now that you are finished working on your book, you may want to send the files to a coworker or client as proof of progress or for review. Because not everyone has InDesign, you can convert the InDesign documents to a file type that can be easily shared. InDesign's Book panel simplifies the process of creating PDF files and printing so you can easily share the project.

Creating PDFs

Creating a PDF from a book file is quick and easy in InDesign, and the results can be read by anyone with Adobe Reader, a free download is available at *get.adobe.com/reader*. InDesign CS6 allows you to create PDF files for print output or for interactive output. You will now export the InDesign book as a PDF.

1 Click in the open area below the list of documents in the Book panel to ensure that no documents are selected. From the Book panel menu, choose Export Book to PDF.

2 In the resulting Export dialog box, name the file **id09_book.pdf**, navigate to your desktop, choose Adobe PDF (Print) from the Save as type drop-down menu, and click Save.

3 In the Export Adobe PDF dialog box, choose High Quality Print from the Adobe PDF Preset drop-down menu. Enable the Bookmarks and Hyperlinks check boxes at the bottom of the dialog box so that the TOC text in the resulting PDF will provide clickable links to the corresponding page in the document. Click Export. A Generating PDF dialog box appears with status bars showing the progress of the PDF file creation.

The High Quality Print preset generates a PDF file that is fairly large in size. If you need a smaller PDF, choose the Smallest File Size setting from the Adobe PDF Preset drop-down menu. This setting presents an additional dialog box indicating that the transparency blend space is different from the document's blend space. Simply click OK and proceed as usual.

Printing

The Book panel also simplifies the process of printing the book, should you want a hard copy. Although the steps are few, keep in mind that printing the entire book—six files—will take some time.

1 Click in the open area below the list of documents in the Book panel to ensure that no documents are selected.

2 From the Book panel menu, choose Print Book. InDesign opens the standard print dialog box from which you can print all the pages from all documents of the book simultaneously.

For more on printing from InDesign CS6, see Lesson 10, "Preflighting, Printing and Creating PDFs from InDesign."

3 Click Cancel to close the Print dialog box.

4 From the Book panel menu (·≡), choose Save Book, then from the Book panel menu again, choose Close Book to close the project.

Congratulations! You've just finished working in your first InDesign book file.

Self study

Work with other text variables available in InDesign to find out other ways in which they can be used. The Running Header variable, for instance, allows you to define a paragraph style within the document, whose content will appear where the Running Header variable is placed. This can save considerable time when working with long documents.

Create your own paragraph styles for the Table of Contents to change its appearance. Get creative by changing the fonts and paragraph spacing, and then choose Update Table of Contents to see the changes.

Add additional references to the index. Practice creating index references and cross-references and then regenerate the index to apply the recent entries. With index copy, you can customize the appearance of the text by using paragraph styles. You can change these settings by clicking on the More Options button in the Generate Index dialog box.

Review

Questions

1   What feature in InDesign allows you to ensure that paragraph and character styles have a consistent appearance across multiple files?

2   What is the key requirement for creating a Table of Contents in InDesign?

3   How do you update an existing index within InDesign?

4   How can you make a PDF file of all pages within a Book file?

Answers

1   The synchronize options feature in a Book ensures consistent styles and appearance.

2   Paragraph styles must be used to format text throughout the document.

3   Choose Generate Index from the Index panel menu and make sure that the *Replace Existing Index* checkbox is checked.

4   Choose Export Book to PDF from the Book panel menu.

What you'll learn in this lesson:

- Preflighting your document

- Packaging your document for distribution

- Creating and customizing a PDF file

- Printing a proof

Preflighting, Printing and Creating PDFs from InDesign

Designing your document is only half the job. You still need to deliver it, whether to a commercial printer, the Web, or colleagues and coworkers. To help you, InDesign offers multiple methods for proofing and packaging your files, as well as flexible export controls to PDF.

Starting up

Before starting, make sure that your tools and panels are consistent by resetting your preferences. See "Resetting the InDesign workspace and preferences" in the Starting up section of this book.

You will work with several files from the id10lessons folder in this lesson. Make sure that you have copied the id10lessons folder onto your hard drive from the Digital Classroom DVD. See "Loading lesson files" in the Starting up section of this book. This lesson may be easier to follow if the id10lessons folder is on your desktop.

For this lesson, you need either Adobe Acrobat or Adobe Reader to view the PDF files you will create. If necessary, you can download the free Adobe Reader at *get.adobe.com/reader*.

See Lesson 10 in action!

Use the accompanying video to gain a better understanding of how to use some of the features shown in this lesson. The video tutorial for this lesson can be found on the supplied DVD.

The project

To sample the PDF and print-related controls offered by InDesign, you will prepare a car ad for delivery to multiple customers. You'll preflight the document using the InDesign Preflight feature and then package the document to send to a printer or other user. Finally, you will generate a PDF file of the complete project.

Package inventory

Before you send your files to a printer or other service provider, in order to print your job professionally, it's important that you check the file for common errors that can occur during the design phase of your project. If your files aren't prepared to the required specifications, your job could be delayed or, even worse, reproduced incorrectly. The InDesign CS6 Live Preflight feature enables you to check all the mechanics of your file to ensure that everything is in working order. You can even define custom Preflight profiles in CS6 that will preflight your document to your or your printers' specific needs.

For example, say you're planning to submit an ad for the new IDCS6 sports car to a newspaper. In this exercise, you'll use Package to see the Package Inventory of the file, and then you'll define a Preflight setting to see how well your ad complies with the newspaper's specifications.

1   Choose File > Open, navigate to the id10lessons folder, and select CarAd.indd. Click Open.

2   Choose File > Package. InDesign analyzes the document, and displays a summary of its findings in the Package Inventory dialog box. For more information on a specific category, click its name in the list on the left side of the dialog box.

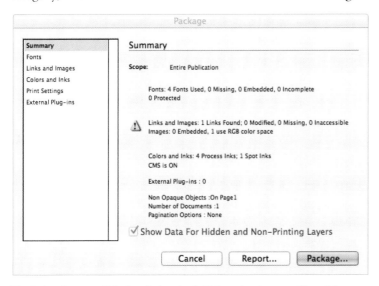

The Package Inventory dialog box displays detailed information about your file, and flags potential errors that could cause problems.

3   From the list on the left side of the dialog box, choose Fonts. The right side of the dialog box now lists all the fonts used in your document as well as their format and status. If the status is OK, the font is loaded onto your system and recognized by InDesign. A status of Missing indicates that the font cannot be found. Because this lesson file was created using fonts installed with InDesign, all your fonts should say OK.

4   Choose Links and Images from the list on the left side of the dialog box. This section displays information about the images that are used within your document. At the top of this dialog box is a caution icon (⚠), indicating that InDesign found a potential problem, specifically that one of the images uses the RGB color space. Most printing companies require images to be submitted in the CMYK color space; ask your printer for their specifications prior to sending your files.

You can fix this error manually by opening the RGB file in Adobe Photoshop and converting it to CMYK. In addition, you can carefully check the color conversion options set within InDesign to ensure that when output, the colors would convert properly based on your printers specifications.

The Links and Images section also indicates the state of your images, linked or unlinked, as well as the actual versus effective resolutions of your images.

Actual versus effective resolution

The resolution of an image is indicated by the number of pixels per inch (ppi) that make up the image—a seemingly simple concept that can be a bit complicated. As a general rule, the higher the resolution of an image, the higher its quality. Most images that you see when browsing the Internet are 72 ppi or 96 ppi, which is the standard screen resolution of most monitors. For high-quality printing, however, image resolution should generally be around 300 ppi.

To further complicate things, the Package window's Links and Images section lists two different numbers at the bottom: actual ppi and effective ppi. Actual ppi is the actual resolution of the file that you are placing into InDesign. The effective ppi is the resolution of the image after it has been scaled in InDesign. For example, if you place a 300-ppi image in your document and then scale it 200 percent, the effective resolution becomes 150 ppi. As you increase the size of images in InDesign, the effective resolution decreases. The effective resolution is the number that you should pay most careful attention to, as it determines the quality at which the image is output.

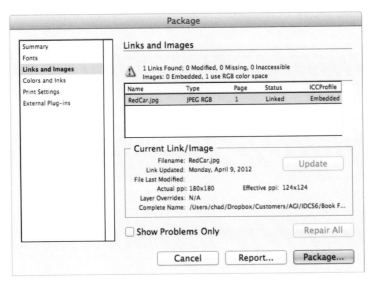

The Links and Images section of the Package Inventory dialog box.

5   Select Colors and Inks in the Package list to see which ink colors the document uses. This file uses a color called Pantone 187 C. Any color besides cyan, magenta, yellow, or black is considered a spot color or plate. You'll learn more about these later in the "Separation Preview" section. Click the Cancel button to close the Package dialog box.

For more information on Pantone colors, see Lesson 7, "Using Color in Your Documents."

Keep the file open, as you'll need it for the next part of the lesson. Later in this lesson you'll complete the packaging process and send it to the newspaper that is running the ad. Before doing this, you'll Preflight the InDesign file to ensure that it meets the proper specifications.

6 Choose File > Save As. Navigate to the id10lessons folder and type **CarAd_work.indd** in the Name text field. Click Save.

Preflight checks

Like a pilot checking over their plane prior to takeoff, Preflight assesses your document, then reports potential problems—missing fonts, missing images, RGB (Red, Green, Blue) images, whether interactive elements are contained in the document and more—that could prevent a printer from outputting your job properly, or hinder a customer's ability to view your file accurately. You can set up different profiles for all the intended destinations of your documents. For example, you could define a Preflight profile for all the documents you create that will end up as just PDFs on the Web, which are not intended for high-end output. You could define the profile to look for images with a resolution over 100 ppi. Whenever a photo was placed that had a higher effective resolution than 100 ppi, an error would appear in the Preflight panel. You can also see the Preflight status in the bottom-left area of your document window. In this exercise, you will define a new profile in the InDesign CS6 Preflight panel, and then check your document against the profile.

1 Choose Window > Output > Preflight. The Preflight panel opens. Right now, the Preflight profile is set to Basic, which looks only for broken or missing links to images, inaccessible URL links, missing fonts in the document, or overset text. You will now define a new profile that will look for RGB images in the document.

The Preflight panel in InDesign CS6.

2   From the Preflight panel menu (▾≡), choose Define Profiles.

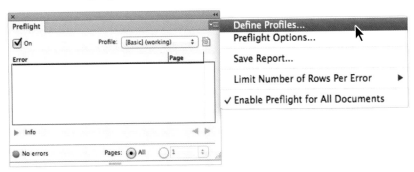

Define Profiles is located in the Panel menu of the Preflight panel.

3   The Preflight Profiles dialog box opens. You cannot change the default Basic profile, so you will define a new one that looks for RGB color in your document. In the Profiles section on the left, click on the plus sign (✚) at the bottom to create a new profile.

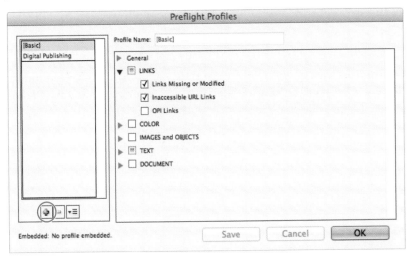

Make a new profile by clicking on the plus sign.

4   In the Profile Name text field at the top, select the text New Preflight Profile, then type **CMYK**.

5 In the Profile definition area, open the triangle next to Color by clicking on it. Now open the triangle next to Color Spaces and Modes Not Allowed. Check the box next to *Color Spaces and Modes Not Allowed*. Now check *RGB*.

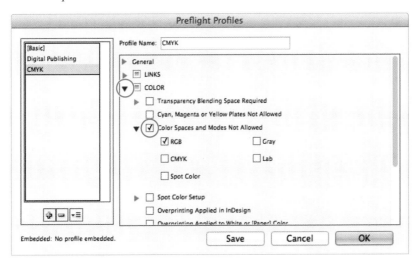

Click on the triangle next to Color Spaces and Modes Not Allowed, then choose RGB.

6 Click Save, then click OK. You have now defined a new preflight profile.

7 Change the profile in the Preflight panel from Basic to the new CMYK profile you have just made. Notice that the bottom-left area of your document and the Preflight panel now state that there is one error.

8 Expand the triangles to see the error that InDesign has found from within the Preflight Error window. Click on the triangle next to Color, and then click on the triangle next to *Color space not allowed*. The Prefight profile you have just built will now give you an error message for any RGB color that might find its way into your document. To fix this issue, you would need to open the problem image in Photoshop and change the color space to CMYK. But that is only if you are sending a Package to a printer. When exporting a PDF file, certain PDF settings would automatically change the color space of the RGB images to CMYK.

The Preflight panel showing you that the red car has a color that is not allowed in this document.

Creating a preflight profile benefits you because that profile exists on your computer but if you send this document to another user, they will not have the benefit of being able to use this profile. That is unless you embed the profile into the active InDesign document so that it can be used by any user on any computer.

9 Click on the embed selected profile button (🖻) located directly to the right of the Profile drop-down menu to embed the profile into the document. The selected CMYK profile now contains the word (embedded) next to it.

Embedding the preflight profile makes the profile available to anyone who opens the document.

10 Switch the profile back to Basic and close the Preflight panel.

11 Choose File > Save.

Packaging your document

When you need to send your InDesign document out for review, alterations, or printing, you must be sure you're sending all the necessary pieces. Without the font and image files used by the document, your coworkers or service provider can't accurately see and reproduce the file as you intended. To avoid this frustrating scenario, turn to the InDesign Package feature. Package gathers all the document elements the recipient needs into one folder and even enables you to include an instruction file. In this exercise, you will use Package to collect the car ad's fonts and graphics.

1 Choose File > Package. InDesign automatically runs Package Inventory and displays a warning if it finds problems. You've already seen the information in this dialog box earlier in this lesson, so simply click the Package button to proceed.

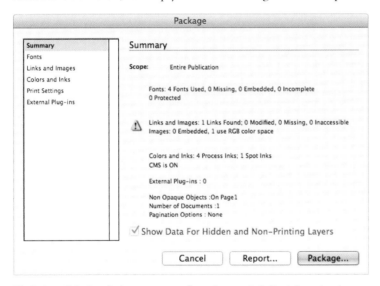

The Package dialog box displays a summary of your document including information about links, fonts, and color.

2 The Printing Instructions window allows you to enter contact information and basic instructions for your project. When packaging a file to send to another user, this information could be helpful and could assist the output provider in properly processing your job. Fill in the information, if desired, and then press the Continue button.

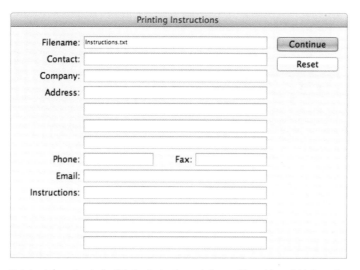

Entering information in the Printing Instructions window could provide useful information to the person who will be receiving your packaged file.

3   The Package Publication (Windows) or Create Package Folder (Mac OS) dialog box opens; here you choose what to include in the file Package, what to call it, and where to save it. Make sure the first three options are checked: *Copy Fonts*, *Copy Linked Graphics*, and *Update Graphic Links in Package*. All others should be unchecked. Type **CarAd Folder** in the Folder Name (Windows) or Save As (Mac OS) text field, choose Desktop from the Save in (Windows) or Where (Mac OS) drop-down menu, and click the Package button.

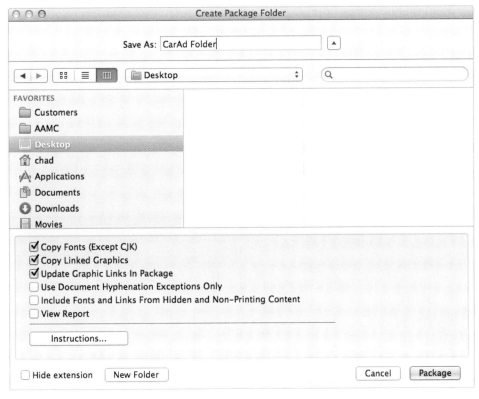

Use the Package Publication Folder dialog box to tell InDesign which files to gather and where to save them.

Package Options

Copy Fonts (Except CJK)—Copies all fonts used in the document into the resulting package with the exception of Chinese, Japanese, and Korean fonts.

Copy Linked Graphics—Copies all graphics used in the document into the resulting package folder.

Update Graphic Links In Package—When graphics are copied to the package folder, the graphics in the packaged InDesign document will be linked to the graphics that were copied to the package folder instead of the original location of the graphics.

Use Document Hyphenation Exceptions Only—These options prevent reflow from occurring if someone opens this document on a computer that contains different hyphenation settings.

Include Fonts and Links from Hidden and Non-Printing Content—This option will package content in your document that is found on hidden layers and will include content that has been marked as non-printing. With this option unchecked, those elements will not get included in the package.

View Report—Will display the Printing Instructions report after the package has been completed.

4   In response to the Font Alert dialog box that details the legalities of giving your fonts to a printer or service provider, click OK to begin packaging the files. If you don't want to see this alert in the future, click the *Don't show again* checkbox before you click OK.

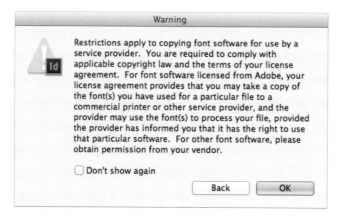

The font warning dialog box explains some of the legalities of sharing fonts with other users.

5   When the dialog box closes, a small progress window appears, displaying the status of the packaging process. Once it has finished, close your CarAd_work.indd file.

6 In the Windows Explorer or Finder, navigate to the desktop, and double-click the CarAd folder. Inside, you'll find a copy of the document file, an instructions file, a Fonts folder with all the fonts used in the job, and a Links folder that contains all the graphics—all in one easy-to-send Package.

When the Package process is complete, all the project's elements are displayed together in the CarAd folder.

Now that all the files required to reproduce your job have been copied to the location you specified and are contained within their own folder, you can send this folder to another person to review, or to your printer or service provider to output your job. To ensure the integrity of the files and speed the transfer, compress the packaged folder before sending. The compressed file can then be shared through e-mail, uploading them to an FTP server, or using a service such as Adobe's SendNow or another service such as DropBox.

Creating an Adobe PDF

The Package feature collects all your data files, but the recipients still must have InDesign to read the document. But what if they don't?

The answer is to send a PDF file. PDF (Portable Document Format) is a common format that can be viewed and printed from any computer platform—Mac, Windows, Linux, and others—that has the free Adobe Reader program installed. A PDF file is an excellent way to make your project available for a wide range of users, and InDesign CS6 makes the process of creating a PDF file of your project very easy. In the following steps, you will create a PDF file of your CarAd_work.indd file so that other people can see your progress and provide feedback on changes that might need to be made before this project is sent to a printer for production.

PDFs can also be used for presentation purposes. PDFs generated in InDesign can contain sound, movies, animations, and hyperlinks to name a few.

1. In InDesign, choose File > Open Recent > CarAd_work.indd to open your work file.

2. Choose File > Export. In the resulting Export dialog box, name the file **CarAd.pdf**, choose Desktop from the Save in (Windows) or Where (Mac OS) drop-down menu, and select Adobe PDF (Print) from the Save as type (Windows) or Format (Mac OS) drop-down menu. Click Save.

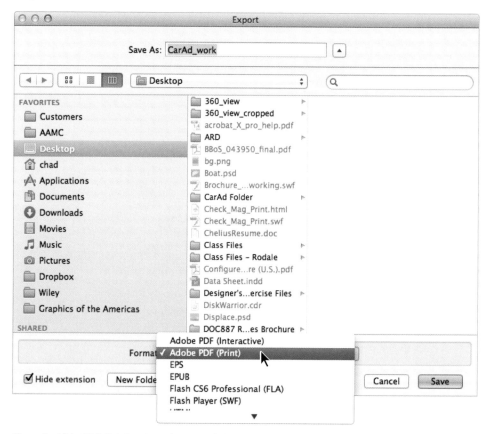

Choose the Adobe PDF (Print) option in the Export dialog box.

3. The Export Adobe PDF dialog box appears. From the Adobe PDF Preset drop-down menu at the top of the dialog box, you can choose settings that control the PDF file's size and quality, among other options. Because you will send the car ad to several people for general review, choose the [*Smallest File Size*] option from the Adobe PDF Preset drop-down menu.

PDF presets are a way of saving favorite settings for the final generated PDF file. If you own Adobe Acrobat 7.0 or a more recent version, InDesign CS6 shares these settings with Acrobat Distiller, which is included with Acrobat. Likewise, if you create a custom setting within Distiller, you'll see those settings in the Adobe PDF Preset drop-down menu when you export a PDF file from within InDesign CS6.

4 Click the Hyperlinks checkbox near the bottom of the Export Adobe PDF dialog box. Activating the Hyperlinks option makes any hyperlinks created in the InDesign document clickable hyperlinks in the resulting PDF document. Also click the *View PDF after Exporting* checkbox so that the resulting PDF file opens in Acrobat after the export.

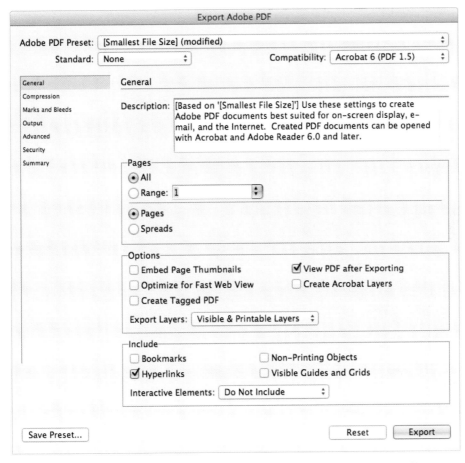

The Export Adobe PDF dialog box allows you to customize the PDF file you create from your InDesign file.

5 Click the Export button. InDesign displays a warning that your document's transparency blend space doesn't match the destination color space. This is because the Smallest File Size setting converts colors to RGB and the InDesign document is CMYK. Because your PDF file is for viewing purposes only, this is not a concern. Click OK to begin generating the PDF file.

6 When the PDF export is finished, it should automatically open in Adobe Acrobat or Adobe Reader. If not, double-click the CarAd.pdf file on your desktop to open it. Hover your cursor over the *www.idcs6.com* link, and the cursor changes to a hand. Click on the link to go to the web site specified in the ad. If you receive a message warning you that the document is trying to connect to a website, choose Allow.

The exported PDF file can contain interactive elements that are included in your InDesign file.

7 Choose File > Close to close the PDF file.

Separation preview

Designed primarily to produce print layouts, InDesign supports both traditional methods of printing color: the four-color process (CMYK) model and spot colors as well as the RGB color model. In the four-color process model, cyan, magenta, yellow, and black inks (C, M, and Y, with black as the K) combine in various values to reproduce numerous colors. A printing press uses a separate plate for each of these four colors, laying the ink down on the substrate in separate layers. Spot colors are pre-mixed inks that match standard color values. To ensure the green in your company's logo matches across all your print jobs, for example, you could choose a specific green spot color to ensure consistency.

Probably the most widely used spot color system is the Pantone Matching System, which is also called PMS, or simply Pantone colors. As a companion to the system it developed, Pantone Inc. also offers a swatch book so you can see how the colors reproduce on paper. All the Creative Suite applications have the Pantone library built in, so you can add spot colors to your document easily. Spot colors each require their own plates as well.

All Pantone colors have CMYK equivalents that enable you to reproduce the color using the standard process colors as well, should you need to conform to CMYK-only printing requirements, or reduce the number of plates.

Printing a Pantone color as a CMYK color may cause it to look different from the spot version of that Pantone color. This is because of the limited gamut, or color range, that process colors are able to reproduce. Pantone offers a Process Color Simulator guide that compares the printed spot color against the printed process color and is indispensable when you reproduce spot colors as four-color process.

In the printing industry, printers charge customers for each plate that has to be produced for the printing job. You want to be sure that unnecessary colors are not mistakenly sent to the printer, as extra colors increase your cost and can cause confusion. To prevent this added expense and frustration, the InDesign Separations Preview panel lets you view the separate plates, or separations, as the printer would see them before you send your file. Take a tour of the panel as you check the car ad's separations.

1   Choose Window > Output > Separations Preview, or press Shift+F6, to open the Separations Preview panel.

2   Click on the Separations Preview panel menu button (⁃≣) and choose *Show Single Plates in Black* to turn off that option and see each plate in its actual color.

3   Choose Separations from the View drop-down menu in the Separations Preview panel.

4   Click the visibility icon (👁) to the left of the CMYK entry to turn off the visibility of the Cyan, Magenta, Yellow, and Black plates in your document. InDesign now displays only the elements in Pantone 187 C.

All New		
Design		

$13,999	$11,999	$10,899
$13,899	$11,799	$10,599
$12,989	$11,599	$9,899
$12,899	$11,499	$9,599
$12,599	$11,499	$8,999
$12,299	$11,299	$8,899

Use the separation Preview panel to see where certain colors are used in your document.

You can tell that Pantone 187 C is a spot color because it is still visible after all the other separations have been hidden. Another way to identify a spot color in your document is to look at your Swatches panel. If any color has this icon (▣) to the right of the color name, it indicates that the color is a spot color and outputs on its own plate. Because the newspaper's specifications forbid spot colors, you must replace them in the car ad.

5   Click on the panel menu button (▾≡) in your Separations Preview panel or in the Swatches panel, and choose Ink Manager from the list. The Ink Manager lists all the plates or inks that are currently in your document.

6   In the Ink Manager, click the spot icon to the left of the Pantone 187 C plate to change it from a spot color to a process color. You now see a process color icon (❌) to the left of the Pantone 187 C plate, indicating that the color will output as process instead of spot. Click OK. Because you mapped the Pantone 187 C plate to process and you turned off display of your process colors in step 4, no colors are currently visible.

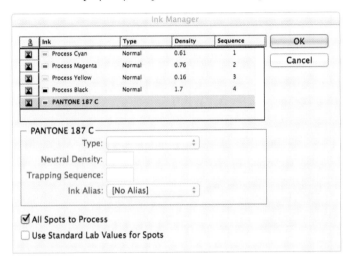

The Ink Manager allows you to control how colors will be output without having to manually modify the color in the document.

7   Click on the visibility icon to the left of CMYK to see all the colors in your document again. The red color that was Pantone 187 C is now a red made of the four process colors. If you hover your cursor over different areas of your document, you can see the ink percentages to the right of each color in the Separations Preview panel.

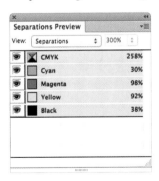

Hover your cursor over areas of your document to see the ink percentages.

8   Toggle the visibility of various separations in your Separations Preview panel to see how the colors in your document are combined to achieve other colors, called *builds.*

9   Choose Off from the View drop-down menu in the Separations Preview panel to get back to your normal viewing mode, and close the Separations Preview panel. Now your ad is properly prepared for printing in the newspaper.

Printing a proof

The best way to avoid surprises at press time is to print a proof of your document on your desktop printer. Seeing your project on paper sometimes reveals design flaws or mistakes you missed when viewing your document on screen. Printing out a version of your document on a printer is referred to as printing a proof. The term proof is used to describe any type of output that is generated prior to making plates for a printing press. In this exercise, you'll use InDesign to print a proof to your desktop printer.

1   With CarAd_work.indd open, choose File > Print to open the Print dialog box.

2   From the Printer drop-down menu at the top of the Print dialog box, choose a printer that is available on your computer.

3   Because there is only one page in your CarAd_work.indd file, leave Pages set to *All*. For multi-page documents, however, you could specify a limited range of pages to print.

4   Click Setup in the list on the left side of the Print window. On the right side, choose US Letter [8.5 × 11] from the Paper Size drop-down menu and click on the Landscape Orientation icon (⬛) to print your document in landscape orientation on standard letter-sized paper. The preview in the lower-left corner shows your page orientation and selected printer.

5   Your ad is larger than the letter-sized paper you specified in step 4, so click on the *Scale to Fit* radio button to scale your document to fit the available space. This automatically fits and centers your document on the printed page. (If you have a large-format printer, of course, you can adjust the paper size as needed and print at full scale.)

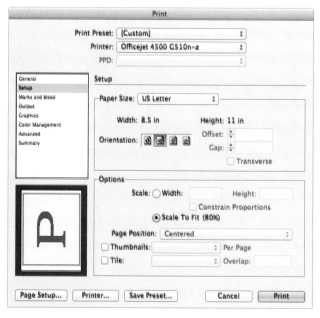

The Print dialog box enables you to control all aspects of how your page is oriented to the paper and printer.

6 In the list on the left, click Marks and Bleed. Click the *All Printer's Marks* checkbox to tell InDesign to add the appropriate trim, bleed, and color marks to your page as you would see on a printer's proof. Leave the other settings at their defaults.

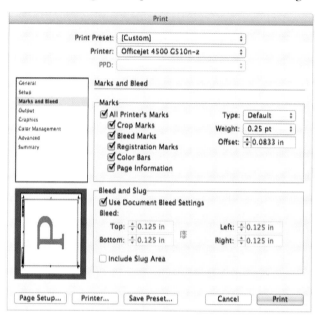

The Marks and Bleed section allows you to control the marks that are placed on your page when it is printed.

7 Click Output in the list on the left. If you are printing to a color printer that prints CMYK colors, choose Composite CMYK (or Composite RGB, if your printer doesn't print CMYK colors) from the Color drop-down menu on the right. If you are printing to a black-and-white printer, choose Composite Gray instead.

8 Click Graphics in the list on the left. In the Send Data drop-down menu of the Images section, choose the output quality of the graphics. Choose All for the best quality possible; choose Optimized Subsampling to let InDesign reduce the quality of your images slightly so the document prints faster. The higher the quality of the graphics, the more data InDesign needs to send to the printer and the longer it takes.

9 Click Print.

10 Choose File > Save to save your file, and then choose File > Close to close it.

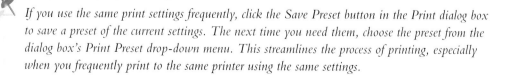

If you use the same print settings frequently, click the Save Preset button in the Print dialog box to save a preset of the current settings. The next time you need them, choose the preset from the dialog box's Print Preset drop-down menu. This streamlines the process of printing, especially when you frequently print to the same printer using the same settings.

Congratulations! You have completed this lesson.

Self study

Try the Find Font feature by choosing Type > Find Font to replace the fonts that Preflight or Package identifies as missing, with fonts you have loaded on your computer. Likewise, use the Links panel by choosing Window > Links to fix images that are missing or modified in your document. To find out more about what it means when fonts are missing, go to the Help file.

Investigate the numerous tools in InDesign CS6 that enable you to add interactivity to a PDF document when it is exported. For example, you can use the Button tool to add navigation to your exported PDF document, or you can add hyperlinks that are clickable links in the final PDF file. InDesign CS6 offers two PDF output methods, Print and Interactive. The interactive choice allows you to output a PDF file with interactive components like page transitions and animation. For more information on adding interactivity to an InDesign document, see Lesson 11, "Introduction to Digital Documents." Practice modifying the PDF settings to achieve different results in file size and other properties. When you create a configuration that you like, save it as a PDF Preset so you can easily use it again in the future.

Using the Separation Preview panel's Ink Manager, you can create an Ink Alias that maps one spot color to another. For instance, if you have two spot plates, you can map one ink to output on the same plate as the other ink. This feature is great when you realize at the last minute that you have too many spot colors in your document and need to minimize them. Practice this by creating a new document and adding at least two spot colors to your document. For more information on spot colors, check out Lesson 7, "Using Color in Your Documents."

Review

Questions

1 What command copies the active document and all the fonts and graphics used in the document into a single folder on your computer?

2 When creating a PDF file from InDesign, what's the easiest way to make sure that the settings for the PDF file are consistent every time?

3 What tool can be used to view the different ink colors that have been used in an InDesign document?

4 The Package dialog box tells you that there is a spot color used in your InDesign document and you simply want that color to output to the standard CMYK plates. What InDesign feature allows you to do this most efficiently?

Answers

1 The Package command.

2 You can save the settings as a PDF Preset.

3 The Separations Preview panel shows you all colors being used in an InDesign document.

4 The Ink Manager allows you to control the output of colors in an InDesign document with the click of a button.

- Creating a multi-state object

- Creating buttons

- Creating hyperlinks

- Using the Content tools

- Creating Alternate Layouts

- Using Liquid Layout

Introduction to Digital Documents

The term "Digital Document" can take on any number of different meanings. As technology changes and evolves and publishing embraces different mediums, you will create a variety of Digital Documents for different purposes. InDesign has become the hub for creating these digital documents.

Starting up

Before starting, make sure that your tools and panels are consistent by resetting your workspace. See "Resetting the InDesign workspace and preferences" in the Starting up section of this book.

You will work with several files from the id11lessons folder in this lesson. Make sure that you have copied the idlessons folder onto your hard drive from the Digital Classroom DVD. See "Loading lesson files" in the Starting up section of this book. This lesson may be easier to follow if the id11lessons folder is on your desktop.

In this lesson, you will create a multimedia brochure promoting a blueberry farm. You will add video, multi-state objects, and buttons that can be used when exported to various file formats.

See Lesson 11 in action!

Use the accompanying video to gain a better understanding of how to use some of the features shown in this lesson. The video tutorial for this lesson can be found on the supplied DVD.

InDesign relies on the free QuickTime Player to import video file formats. If you work on a Mac OS computer, you probably have QuickTime. If you work on a Windows computer, download QuickTime from www.apple.com/quicktime/download *and install it on your PC.*

InDesign as your Digital Publication Hub

Traditionally, InDesign has been the preferred tool for creating different types of print publications, including catalogs, brochures, flyers, newsletters, posters, etc. InDesign's powerful graphic and typographic functions make it the tool of choice for design professionals. But as technology changes, so does InDesign.

Digital mediums have gained popularity in recent years because they add features such as audio, video, and other interactivity to the experience of reading content in such a way that can't be done in the traditional print medium. Print still has its place and will continue to be used for years to come, but in the digital age, users want enhanced content that can be viewed on a computer or other devices such as smartphones and tablets. This is precisely why InDesign can export to such a variety of formats, including PDF, SWF, HTML, XML, .folio and many more.

With the demand for digital mediums that can be read on various devices, there needs to be a tool that can be used to create content for these devices. Adobe InDesign CS6 has some great new features to make the process of creating digital content easy and efficient, and because it's a tool that so many users are already familiar with, they can jump right in using InDesign to create this digital content. These new features are not limited to digital content, however; many of the new features added to InDesign CS6 will be helpful for creating traditional print-based content as well.

Interactive design considerations

It's not enough to export your document intended for print to a digital format and place it online. You must recognize that readers use online content differently, and that you'll need to make your content fit within their computer or device display so that it's clearly readable. Some simple considerations with the type and layout can be very helpful. Sans-serif fonts, such as Myriad Pro, Arial, and Helvetica, are easier to read on-screen.

Additionally, you need to adjust the layout to fit the medium. Print layouts are often designed to be tall and narrow in a portrait orientation, which does not translate well to a computer display. Online layouts work better in landscape (wide) orientation so that they can be viewed completely without scrolling. In this lesson, you'll learn how to deal with some of these challenges using some new features found in InDesign CS6.

The finished online layout.

Importing multimedia content

You can use InDesign to import a variety of media types into your layout, including FLV, F4V, MP4, SWF, MOV, AVI, and MPEG for video and MP3 for audio. However, only files exported as interactive PDFs, .folio, and certain other formats will support MOV, AVI, and MPEG; an exported SWF file will not. It's also important to remember that certain digital devices such as the iPhone® and iPad® do not currently support the Flash file format. InDesign does not support the common Windows Media file format (WMV), which is used with Windows Media Player and the Silverlight platform. You will start by importing a movie file into an existing frame.

1 Choose File > Open. In the Open dialog box, navigate to the id11lessons folder, select the id1101.indd file, and click Open. If necessary, update the links in this file.

2 Make certain that page 1 is visible; if necessary, use the page drop-down menu in the lower-left corner of the document window to navigate to page 1. Choose the Selection tool (♦) from the Tools panel and select the yellow frame in the lower-right corner.

3 Choose File > Place. In the Place dialog box, confirm that *Replace Selected Item* is selected and *Show Import Options* is not selected. Navigate to the Links folder within the id11lessons folder and select the file 1102.mp4; then click Open. The video file is placed into the layout.

Placing a video file into InDesign is the same process as placing a graphic file; however, they do appear slightly different. Notice that the video file has diagonal lines within the frame and there's a media icon in the upper-left corner of the frame. The video file that was just placed is much bigger than the frame that it was placed into. In the next steps, you will resize the video to better fit in the frame.

Media files contain diagonal lines within the frame and have a media icon located in the upper-left corner of the frame.

4 With the Selection tool active, click the yellow frame to select it. Be sure not to click the Content Grabber () within the frame as that will select the media file instead of the frame. Choose Object > Fitting > Fill Frame Proportionately to scale the media file to better fit within the frame.

For the Fitting options to work correctly, the frame must be selected with the Selection tool. If the content is selected, the multimedia may not resize correctly.

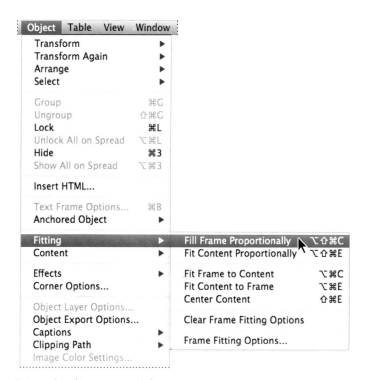

Fitting multimedia content into the frame.

5 InDesign does not provide a preview of the placed video file because no poster is chosen. Choose Window > Interactive > Media to open the Media panel, which provides options for you to control the selected media.

6   Click the Play button to preview the video, or manually drag (scrub) the playhead to preview different parts of the video. When the video displays a frame that you'd like to use for the poster, choose From Current Frame from the Poster drop-down menu. This sets the initial view of the video to the current frame.

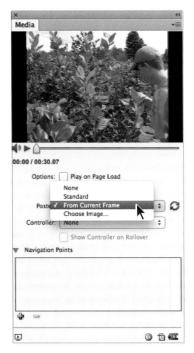

The Media panel provides a way to preview the video file and choose a poster frame.

As you can see, adding multimedia content to an InDesign layout is similar to adding still images and graphics. A little bit later, you'll add buttons to control the playback of this video file.

7   Close the Media panel, then choose File > Save As. In the Save As dialog box, navigate to the id11lessons folder and type **id1101_work.indd** in the Name text field. Click Save.

Adding a Hyperlink

What's a digital document without hyperlinks? Hyperlinks provide a way to link content from a number of different locations including to a page, an e-mail address, and a URL. To make it easy for a user to obtain more information about the Smith Blueberry Farm, you'll add a hyperlink to a web page on page 1 to provide additional information to the user.

1   Choose Edit > Deselect All. If this option is grayed out, you don't have any items selected and you can proceed to step 2.

2   In the Layers panel, click the Text and Buttons layer to make it the active layer.

3   Using the Type tool (T), click and drag to draw a text frame in the lower-left corner of Page 1. Type **Visit our web site** in the text frame.

4   Select the text and then click the Paper swatch in the swatches panel. Change the point size of the text to 24pt and change the font to Myriad Pro Regular.

5   Switch to the Selection tool and click the text frame to make it active. Open the Hyperlinks panel by choosing Window > Interactive > Hyperlinks. Click the Create New Hyperlink button (●*) to add a hyperlink to the selected frame and to display the New Hyperlink dialog box. Uncheck the Shared Hyperlink Destination check box and in the URL field type **http://www.agitraining.com**. Click OK, then close the Hyperlinks panel.

6   Choose File > Save to save your work.

Creating a Multi-State Object

A multi-state object is a great way to display multiple elements within a common area on an InDesign page. Using a multi-state object, you can create two or more object states that can display different content within each state making it a great solution for items such as slideshows. Multi-state objects will appear in exported content such as .swf files, but they also can be used with Adobe's new Digital Publishing Suite (DPS) software for producing content for digital tablet devices such as the Apple iPad®.

1   Navigate to Page 2 in the id1101_work.indd file. Open the Layers panel by choosing Window > Layers.

2   Note that there are three MSO layers that contain the content that will appear in each state of the multi-state object. Click the small square on the far right side of the MSO 1 layer to select all the content on that layer. Note that the content on this layer has been grouped together to make the process of creating a multi-state object easier.

3   Press and hold the Shift key on your keyboard and click the small square on the far right side of the MSO 2 and MSO 3 layer to select all the content on all three layers.

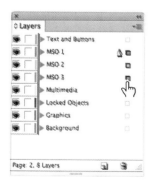

Shift+click the small square on the far right side of each layer to select all the content on each layer.

You don't need to create a separate layer for each state that will appear in a multi-state object, but it does make the process easier.

4 Open the Object States panel by choosing Window > Interactive > Object States. Click the Convert selection to multi-state object button (⬛) to convert the selected content to a multi-state object. Each set of grouped items is converted to its own individual state within the multi-state object. The multi-state object is denoted by a heavy dashed line around the boundary of the item and an icon appears in the lower-right corner indicating that it is a multi-state object.

5 In the Object Name text field at the top of the Object States panel, change the name to **Slideshow**.

6 Click the different states within the Object States panel to see the content change on the page as each state is selected. When you are finished, click back on State 1 to set it as the default state in the multi-state object, then close the Object States panel.

7 Choose File > Save to save your work.

The different states of a multi-state object

The default names for the states in the multi-state object are State 1, State 2, State 3, and so on. Although you can change the names of the states by clicking the name and typing a new name, we highly recommend you keep the names simple and not use any special or unique characters in the state names because this can cause the multi-state object to behave abnormally. In the next section, you will create buttons to provide a navigational mechanism to jump from one state to the next within the multi-state object.

Creating buttons to control multimedia content

You can add buttons to your InDesign document for controlling a variety of actions including placed multimedia content, navigating states of a multi-state object, or to help the user navigate to other pages or even an external web site.

1   Navigate to page 1 of the document. Using the Selection tool (↖), double-click the green frame located below and to the left of the multimedia file you imported on page 1 in the previous exercise. The cursor changes to an insertion point, and the Type tool (T) is selected.

2   Type **Play Movie** in the text frame.

3   Choose the Selection tool from the Tools panel, then right-click (Windows) or Control+click (Mac OS) on the text frame and choose Interactive > Convert to Button from the context menu that appears.

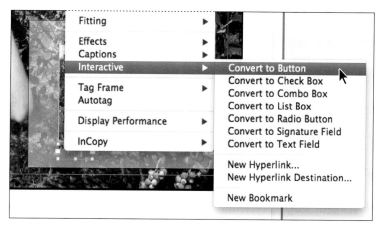

Converting an object to a button.

The Buttons and Forms panel appears. The button does not yet have any actions applied to it. You will assign actions to the button to control the movie.

4   In the Buttons and Forms panel, type **Play** in the Name text field to name the button. Leave the Event drop-down menu set to its default of On Release or Tap, which causes the action to occur after the mouse has been clicked and is then released or tapped.

5   Click the Add new action for selected event button (⊕) under Actions and choose Video for the button to control a movie. After choosing the Video action, the Video drop-down menu appears.

6 From the Video drop-down menu, choose the 1102.mp4 movie, and then ensure that the Options drop-down menu is set to Play. You have applied an action to a button, causing it to control the movie clip you imported earlier.

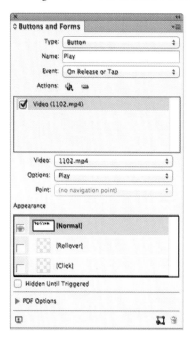

Adding an action to a button.

Button actions control the file after it has been exported to PDF, SWF (Flash), or .folio (DPS) format. The buttons do not control any actions within InDesign.

Adding buttons to control a multi-state object

The multi-state object on page 2 contains a total of 3 different states; however, there is no current way for a user of the exported file to view these states. You will now add some buttons that will allow you to navigate between the different states in the multi-state object.

1 In the lower-left corner of the document window, click the pages drop-down menu and navigate to page 2.

2 Display the Layers panel by choosing Window > Layers. Click the visibility icon (👁) next to the MSO 1 layer to hide the contents of the layer. This should hide the multi-state object on page 2. If this works, turn the visibility back on by clicking the visibility icon again, then click the Lock Layer icon directly to the right of the visibility icon to lock that layer. Click on the Text and Buttons layer to make it active.

If the multi-state object in your file is on a different MSO layer, lock it in accordance with the instructions in step 2 above, substituting your MSO layer for the other MSO.

Locking the MSO layer that contains the multi-state object.

3 Open the Buttons and Forms panel by choosing Window > Interactive > Buttons and Forms. Then, display the sample buttons panel by clicking the panel menu in the Buttons and Forms panel and choosing Sample Buttons and Forms.

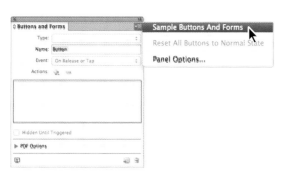 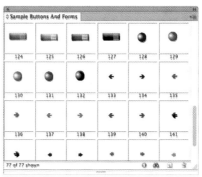

Opening the Sample Buttons and Forms panel.

4 Drag buttons 143 and 144 from the Sample Buttons and Forms panel onto the green bar on the right side of page 2. Position them side by side, centered on the green bar toward the bottom of the page.

5   Using the Selection tool, resize each button by dragging one of the handles to enlarge them as shown in the figure below. Close the Sample Buttons and Forms panel.

Resize the buttons and position on the right side of page 2.

6   Make sure that the Buttons and Forms panel is still open. If it's not, choose Window > Interactive > Buttons and Forms.

7   Select the left button that you dragged onto page 2 in step 4. In the Buttons and Forms panel, notice that this button already has an action assigned to it called Go To Previous Page. This might be useful for certain projects, but not for this one. Click the Delete selected action button (⊜) to remove it from the selected button. When the dialog box appears asking if you want to delete the selected action, click OK.

8   With the left button still selected, click the Add new action for selected event button (⊕), and choose Go To Previous State from the drop-down menu. In the Object drop-down menu, choose Slideshow from the list and click the Stop at First State check box. Finally, change the name of the button to Previous by typing the word **Previous** in the Name text field.

9   Using the Selection tool, select the right button. Click the Delete selected action button (⊜) to remove the action, then click the Add new action for the selected event button (⊕), and choose Go To Next State from the drop-down menu. In the Object drop-down menu, choose Slideshow from the list and click the Stop at Last State check box. Change the name of the button to Next by typing the word **Next** in the Name text field.

You have now added buttons to page 2 to control the multi-state object on that page.

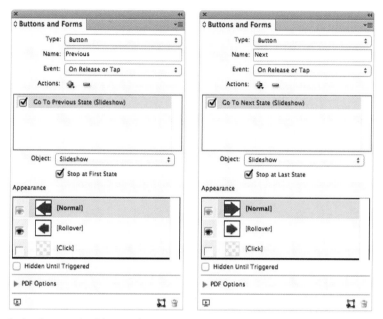

Setting the properties of the arrow buttons to control the multi-state object.

Creating page transitions

You can make the viewing experience of a file more interesting by adding transitions that are applied when navigating between the pages of a document. These transitions will be visible when the InDesign document is exported to an Interactive PDF file or to a .swf file.

1 Click the Pages button (⌗) in the dock on the right side of the workspace to open the Pages panel. Double-click on page 2 to make it the active page.

2 Choose Window > Interactive > Page Transitions to open the Page Transitions panel, or click the Page Transitions button (▥) in the panel dock.

3   In the Page Transitions panel, choose Comb for Transition, Horizontal for Direction, and for Speed, choose Medium. Note the icon that appears next to the page 2 icon in the Pages panel, indicating that the page has a transition applied to it. Note that the transition you apply to a page will appear when navigating TO that page. So applying a transition to page 1 isn't necessary unless you navigate back to page 1 from another page.

Applying a page transition for when the document is viewed as an Interactive PDF or SWF file.

4   Open the Preview panel by choosing Window > Interactive > SWF Preview and click the Set Preview Document Mode button (⬚) button in the lower-right corner of the Preview panel, then click the Play Preview button (▶) to preview the animation.

5   Click the Go to Next Page (▶) and Go to Previous Page (◀) buttons at the bottom of the Preview panel to see the page transitions. Note that no transition appears when going back to page 1 because no transition was applied to that page.

Previewing the page transitions in the Preview panel.

6   Collapse or dock the Preview panel and Choose File > Save.

Creating animations

InDesign CS6 has the ability to apply animations to objects within your document that will animate when exported to the .swf format. This provides numerous opportunities for enhancing what can be done with interactive documents in InDesign.

1   Double-click on page 1 in the Pages panel to make it the active page.

2   Using the Selection tool (⬉), click on the frame at the top of the page that says Blueberry Picking Guide. Right-click on the frame and choose Fitting > Fit Frame to Content. This reduces the size of the frame, making it easier to work with.

3   With the Blueberry Picking Guide frame still selected, click on the Animation button (●˙) to display the Animation panel. If the Animation button isn't available, choose Window > Interactive > Animation to display the Animation panel.

4   From the Preset drop-down menu, choose Fly in from Top. The preview area at the top of the Animation panel displays a proxy of how the animation will appear, and a motion path appears above the selected frame on the page indicating the path that the animation will follow.

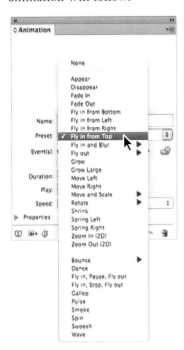

The Animation panel allows you to specify how the selected object will be animated on the page.

The motion path indicates the length and direction that the frame will be animated.

5   Set the duration to **1.5 seconds** and leave the remaining choices at their defaults.

6   Next, click on the text frame on page 1 that reads Smith Blueberry Farm to select the frame.

7 In the Animation panel, choose Fly in from Right from the Preset drop-down menu. Leave the other setting at their defaults.

When you have multiple animations in a document, you can control the order that they will appear using the Timing panel.

8 Choose Window > Interactive > Timing. The timing panel lists all the animations at the bottom of the panel and allows you to change their order and set properties. Click on the Blueberry Picking Guide entry at the bottom of the Timing panel and drag down so it appears as the second item. Now, the Smith Blueberry Farm text will appear first, then the Blueberry Picking Guide text.

The Timing panel allows you to change the order that animations appear in the document.

9 To preview your document, click on the Preview Spread (⊡) button in the lower-left corner of the Timing panel. This will open the SWF Preview panel and show you the animations in action!

10 Collapse the Preview and Animation panels and save the document.

PDF Forms

If you've used any previous version of InDesign, you might have noticed that the Buttons and Forms panel has a new name. This is because InDesign CS6 adds the ability to author PDF-based forms directly within InDesign.

Using the InDesign tools that you're already familiar with, you can create visually interesting forms and then define InDesign frames as a check box, combo box, list box, radio button, signature field, or text field. In addition, frames can be converted to buttons with PDF actions that can print a form, clear a form, or submit a form.

For users who regularly need to create PDF-based forms, this is a huge improvement from having to add this functionality directly inside of Adobe Acrobat.

Previewing your document

InDesign CS6 has a Preview panel that allows you to preview your interactive elements without the need to export the document. In the next steps, you'll use the Preview panel to see the interactive elements in your document.

1   Double-click page 1 in the Pages panel to make page 1 the active page.

2   Click the Preview Spread button (⊡) in the lower-left corner of the Buttons and Forms panel to display the SWF Preview panel. You can also access the SWF Preview panel by choosing Window > Interactive > SWF Preview. Feel free to detach the Preview panel from the panel dock and make it larger to make it easier to view.

3   Click the Set Preview Document Mode button (⬚) in the lower-right corner of the SWF Preview panel to make it active, then click the Play Preview button (▶) in the lower-left corner of the SWF Preview panel to preview the document. Notice immediately that the animations appear in the document.

4   Move your cursor over the hyperlink in the lower-left corner of page 1 and click it. The hyperlink should appear in your default browser (provided you have Internet access). Next click the Play Movie button to preview the movie.

5   Click the Go to Next Page button in the lower-left corner of the SWF Preview panel, the page transition that you applied to page 2 earlier in the lesson appears. Move your cursor over the arrow buttons that you inserted onto page 2 earlier in this lesson. Your cursor becomes a pointer finger (☝). Click the left and right arrow buttons to navigate through the states of the multi-state object to see the slideshow that you've created. When you are finished, click the Clear Preview button (■) to stop previewing the page.

6   Close the Preview panel or dock it in the panel dock. Close the Buttons and Forms panel, then choose File > Save to save your work and then close this file.

The Preview panel allows you to preview and test your interactive document without exporting the file to a .swf file.

Although the SWF Preview panel suggests that this slideshow will only appear when exported to flash, the new Adobe DPS tools permit the use of a multi-state object with buttons for use on digital tablet devices as well.

Exporting your document

Once you've added interactive elements in InDesign, you'll want to export that document to various formats such as Interactive PDF, .SWF, and the new Adobe DPS .folio format for interactive magazines. In this section, you'll learn how to export an InDesign document to Interactive PDF and the .SWF format.

Creating an interactive PDF

To export an interactive PDF, you can use the id1101_work.indd file that you created earlier in this lesson. If you haven't created that file yet and would like to follow along creating an interactive PDF, simply open the id1101_export.indd file.

1   Choose File > Export. The Export dialog box opens.

2   In the Export dialog box, choose Adobe PDF (Interactive) from the Save as type drop-down menu, and type **Blueberries.pdf** in the Name text field to name the PDF file. Choose a location to save this file, such as the current lesson folder. Click the Save button, and the Export to Interactive PDF dialog box appears.

3 In the Pages section, click All, if necessary, to export all pages to PDF. Also make sure that the Pages radio button is enabled and that the *View After Exporting* and the Embed Page Thumbnails checkboxes are checked.

4 In the Page Transitions drop-down menu, choose From Document to use the page transitions that are specified in the Page Transitions panel within InDesign.

5 In the Forms and Media section, be sure that the *Include All* radio button is selected so that all the interactive elements defined in the InDesign document are included in the final PDF file.

6 In the Image Handling section, choose JPEG (Lossy) for compression, Medium for JPEG Quality, and 72 for Resolution (ppi).

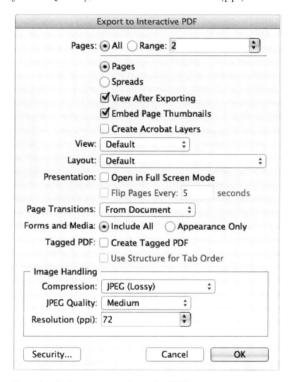

Exporting the document as an interactive PDF.

7 Click OK to create the PDF file. The PDF should open in either Adobe Reader or Adobe Acrobat Standard or Pro, whichever application you have installed. If you are running the Mac OS and the PDF opens in Preview, close the file and launch Adobe Reader or Adobe Acrobat on your computer and open the file you just exported by choosing File > Open.

8 In Acrobat, move the cursor over the Play Movie button in the lower-right corner of page 1, and click it to play the movie. The movie plays and then stops when it is completed. You may need to approve playing the video in a Manage Trust dialog box, depending upon the version of Acrobat or Adobe Reader you are using.

9 Continuing to work in Acrobat, choose View > Full Screen Mode. The document displays in a presentation format, without any menus or tools. Press the right arrow key on the keyboard to advance to the next page. Notice that the page transition is displayed as you navigate from page 1 to page 2. Use the left arrow key on the keyboard to return to page 1. Press the Escape (or Esc) key to return to the normal viewing mode.

You will notice that some of the interactive features that have been added throughout this lesson, do not work in an interactive PDF file. Some of these features include the animations as well as the multi-state objects. This is a current limitation of exporting these elements to an Interactive PDF from InDesign. For more information on some of these limitations and for some tricks to overcome them, see the sidebar "Interactive PDF or Flash?"

10 In Acrobat, choose File > Quit (Windows) or Acrobat > Quit Acrobat (Mac OS) to leave Acrobat and return to InDesign. Leave the file open for the next section.

Creating a SWF file

Next, you'll export an InDesign document to the Flash .swf format that can be used on a web page or even within another interactive file.

1 In InDesign, choose File > Export. The Export dialog box opens.

2 In the Export dialog box, choose Flash Player (SWF) from the Save as type drop-down menu, and type **blueberries.swf** in the Name text field to name the file. Choose a location to save the file, such as the current lesson folder. Click Save, and the Export SWF dialog box opens.

3   In the Export SWF dialog box, click on the General button at the top of the dialog box and make sure that Pages is set to All and that Scale is set to 100 percent. Also make sure that *Generate HTML File*, *View SWF after Exporting*, and *Include Interactive Page Curl* are selected. Keep all other settings unchanged.

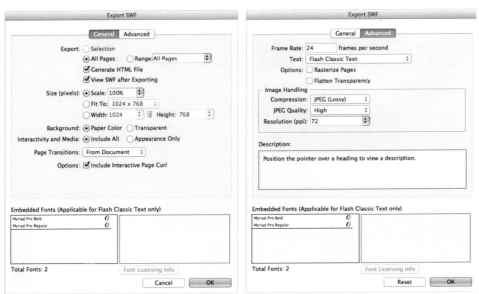

The General and Advanced windows of the Export SWF dialog box control how the final SWF file is generated.

4   Click OK to generate the SWF and accompanying HTML file. The .swf file will open in your default web browser.

5   Notice that the Headline text animations animate on the page. Click the Play Movie button to see the movie play.

6 Move the cursor over the lower-right corner of the first page. Notice the page curl that appears as you move the cursor in this area of the page. Click once to navigate to the second page. Note that the page transition defined in the InDesign document is used. To use the interactive page curl, click and drag to the left as if you were flipping the pages of a magazine.

SWF files created from InDesign can include an interactive page curl for changing pages.

7 On the second page of the document, position the cursor over the right-facing arrow and click the button to navigate to the second state of the slideshow. Click both the left- and right-arrow buttons to navigate from one page to the next.

8 Position the cursor in the upper-left corner of the second page. As the interactive page curl displays, click and drag to the right to navigate back to page 1.

9 Close the browser window.

After exporting a document to the SWF file, you will have an HTML file, a SWF file, and possibly a Resources folder. The Resources folder will contain any external content that may be required to view the document, such as audio or video. It's important that when uploading this content to a Web server that you include all the files, including the Resources folder, so that anyone viewing the web page will see it properly and in its entirety.

Interactive PDF or Flash?

When working with multimedia content, Adobe InDesign CS6 contains two very powerful formats in which you can export interactive content: Flash and Interactive PDF. The tricky part about these formats is that not all the interactive features export to both formats. For example, animations that you create in InDesign will not directly export to an interactive PDF file even though Interactive PDF files support Flash.

Adobe InDesign CS6 contains several components specific to the Flash (.swf) file format that can be used to create animations and effects within InDesign. As of this writing, these animations are Flash-specific and will not directly export to the PDF format but will export to the .swf format.

For starters, multi-state objects like the one you created earlier in this lesson will function when exported to the .swf format. In addition, the Page Transitions panel provides one transition that will function only in the .swf format, which is the Page Curl effect.

When it comes to creating animations in InDesign CS6, you'll notice two panels to help you do this: the Animation panel, and the Timing panel. Use the Animation panel to apply preset animation effects to objects in an InDesign layout and to customize the properties of those effects as well. Then, use the Timing panel to control the order of those animations when exported to the .swf format.

Interactive PDF files do support the use of buttons, movies, and placed .swf files. The fact that you can distribute these files to anyone who has the free Adobe Reader, makes the interactive PDF file format a great choice for reaching a broad audience.

A little-known trick when working with .swf files and interactive PDF files in InDesign, is that you can create the animations in InDesign, export to .swf and then reimport the .swf files into InDesign and the animation will work in an interactive PDF file. In addition, some features such as Go to Next View and Open file, work in an interactive PDF file but not in a .swf file. Understanding these nuances will save you time and frustration when working with these two formats.

New layout features

In this growing digital age, the need for designers to repurpose layouts at different sizes and at different specifications is becoming more and more common. For example, let's say you create a layout for a project at 8.5″ × 11″ and now the customer needs a similar project for use in European countries at A4 size (8.3″ × 11.7″). Often times, however, the new size is more dramatic. For instance, maybe that 8.5″ × 11″ project now needs to become poster size at 17″ × 22″. With the advent of digital tablet devices, the need to create projects at multiple sizes has grown exponentially as each tablet has different dimensions and each tablet has two orientations—portrait and landscape. Multiply those two orientations by the number of tablet devices on the market and you have a lot of layouts to create. Traditionally, your approach to this problem probably would be to duplicate the InDesign file and start reworking it for the new size resulting in several InDesign files and a lot of extra time.

InDesign CS6 offers several new features that makes repurposing layouts much easier. Regardless of whether you are designing for print or for digital, these new features are bound to make creating and repurposing projects easier for you, the designer.

Auto-Size Text Frames

New in InDesign CS6 is the ability to define a text frame so that it automatically resizes based on the specifications that you define. This can save you quite a bit of time by preventing you from resizing frames whenever text is overset. If you know in advance how you want a text frame to behave if it becomes overset, this feature can be a huge benefit.

1 Open the id1102.indd file from the id11lessons folder that you copied to your hard drive at the beginning of this lesson. If necessary, update the links in this file. This is an 8.5″ × 11″ flyer that was created and we will be working with it throughout this exercise.

2 With the Type tool active (T), select the text "Feather Ridge" at the top of the page. We want to change the name of the ski slope for this flyer, so type **Endless Mountain** to replace the text in this frame.

Notice that the text is overset because there is more text than will fit within the frame. The obvious solution at this point is to make the frame larger to accommodate the text. But what if you could save some time and have this occur automatically? You'll do exactly that in the next steps.

3 Press Ctrl+Z (Windows) or Command+Z (Mac OS) several times to return the text to its original appearance. Click the frame that contains the name of the ski slope with your Selection tool (⬉), and choose Object > Text Frame Options.

4 Click the Auto-Size tab at the top of the dialog box to make it active. Currently the Auto-Sizing drop-down menu indicates that it is off.

5 From the Auto-Sizing drop-down menu, choose Width Only. Then in the Auto-Sizing proxy, choose the right-most option to cause the text frame to grow to the left when overset text exists. Click OK to close the dialog box.

6   Using the Type tool (T), select the text "Feather Ridge" at the top of the page and type the words **Endless Mountain**. Notice that now, instead of the text becoming overset, the frame grows automatically to accommodate the text contained within the frame.

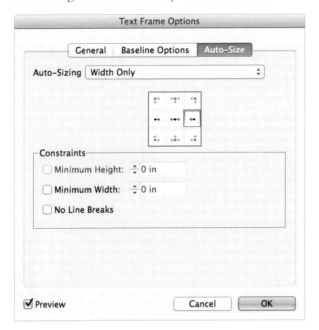

Setting the Auto-Sizing properties for the selected text frame.

7   Choose File > Save As. In the Save As dialog box, change the name to **id1102_work** and click OK to save a working version of the file.

Flexible Width Text Frames

Often times when redesigning a page with different specifications, you might want to add more columns to a text frame depending on how large the frame becomes. Again, InDesign CS6 adds a new feature that allows this to occur automatically based on the settings that you define.

1   With the id1102_work file still open, select the text frame in the middle of the page that begins with the text "A Seasonal Paradise." Drag the right handle of the frame over to the right margin. Notice that the frame expands and the text reflows to fill the frame. Although this may work for certain designs, we want the text to flow automatically into two separate columns.

2   Press Ctrl+Z (Windows) or Command+Z (Mac OS) to undo the resizing of the frame.

3   With the frame still selected, choose Object > Text Frame Options to open the Text Frame Options dialog box. Make sure that the General button at the top of the dialog box is enabled.

4 In the Columns drop-down menu, choose Flexible Width. You'll notice that when you choose this option, the Maximum field becomes editable. This field allows you to define the maximum width of the frame before an additional column is automatically added.

5 Change the value in the Maximum field to 2.5″ and change the Gutter to .25″. Click OK.

Choosing the Flexible Width option defines how big a frame can be before it will add columns to the text frame.

6 Using the Selection tool (⭠), drag the right handle of the text frame over to the right margin of the page. Notice this time that an additional column is added to the frame because of the specifications that we defined in step 5. Feel free to make the frame even larger to see the results, but then undo back to the 2 column appearance.

7 Choose File > Save to save your work.

Layout adjustments

InDesign has contained the Layout Adjustment feature for many versions now and has helped many designers simplify the process of modifying layouts for different purposes. InDesign CS6 takes this feature to a brand new level with its Liquid Layout feature. Liquid Layout offers multiple options for controlling how a layout is resized when the page size changes.

Liquid Layout

1 With the id1102_work file already open, choose Layout > Liquid Layout. Choosing this options does two things, it opens the Liquid Layout panel, and it activates the Page tool (◻).

There are four different Liquid Page Rules to choose from: Scale, Re-Center, Object-based, and Guide-based. After choosing Layout > Liquid Layout, the default Page Rule becomes Scale. In the next several steps, you will experiment with the different Page Rules and then apply one of the Page Rules in the next section.

2 Verify that the Page tool is active and that Scale is chosen from the Liquid Page Rule drop-down menu in the Liquid Layout panel. Drag any of the handles that appear in the corners and sides of the page to resize the page. Note that the objects scale to reflect the new page size. Note that when you let go of the mouse, the page returns to its original size. This is by design to make the experimentation process easier when working with Liquid Layout. To make your adjustment "stick," press and hold the Alt key (Windows) or Option key (Mac OS) before releasing the mouse button. If you do this however, press Undo to return to the original page dimensions.

Using the Page tool, drag the handles to resize the page.

3 In the Liquid Layout panel, change the Liquid Page Rule to Re-center and drag the handles to see the behavior of this rule. Notice that all the content is recentered on the page based on the new size. Resizing the page to a smaller size isn't much benefit with this Liquid Page Rule, but could be helpful when resizing the page to a larger size. Let go of the mouse to return to the original page size.

4 In the Liquid Layout panel, change the Liquid Page Rule to Object-based. Drag one of the handles to resize the page. You need to perform an additional step to make this method work. Release the mouse button.

5 With the Object-based page rule, you need to define the objects that you want to scale and maintain position. With the Page tool still active, click the photo of the snowboarder in the lower-right corner of the page. In the Liquid Layout panel, click the Auto-fit check box to make the photo auto-fit within the frame, then enable the Height and Width check boxes to allow the frame to scale in both directions. Finally, enable the Bottom and Right check boxes to pin the bottom-right of the frame to its current location.

6 Drag the handles to resize the page. Note that the photo of the snowboarder grows as you resize the page and its location is pinned to the bottom right of the page. Release the mouse button to return the page to its original size.

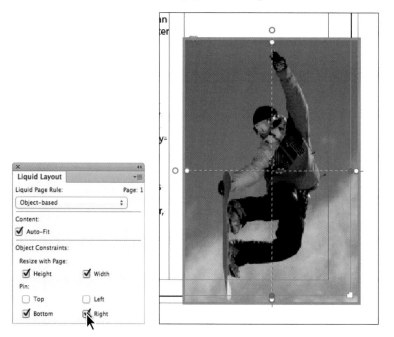

Defining properties for the Object-based page rule (left) and the visual indicators that appear on the selected object (right).

7 In the Liquid Layout panel, change the Liquid Page Rule to Guide-based. The Guide-based Page Rule requires that you drag out a guide to define objects that should resize with the page.

8 Click the ruler on the left side of your screen and drag out a guide so that it is positioned in such a way that it intersects through the photo on the bottom-left of the page, the main text frame on the page, and the "Endless Mountain" text frame. Any object that the guide pierces will expand when the page is resized in a horizontal direction. Vertical guides control horizontal resizing and horizontal guides control vertical resizing.

9 Click and drag the page handles with the Page tool active to resize the page. Notice that the objects that are pierced with the guide resize but the other items do not. Release the mouse button to return the page to its original size.

10 Choose File > Save to save the file.

You will have to experiment with your own project to determine which Liquid Page Rule will best suit your needs. Now that you understand how these page rules work, proceed to the next section where you will apply a Liquid Page Rule in conjunction with another new InDesign CS6 feature.

Alternate Layouts

When creating projects that require more than one version of a layout, it can be cumbersome and time-consuming to make sure that changes to one layout get updated in all the other layouts. This leaves a lot of room for human error that can be costly in several ways. InDesign CS6 introduces a new feature called Alternate layout that allows you to create multiple versions of a layout and makes it easy to maintain changes from one layout to another. In this exercise, you will create a poster size version of the flyer that you've been working with.

1 Make sure that the id1102_work file is open in InDesign and make the Selection tool (▶) active.

2 Open the Pages panel by choosing Window > Pages.

3   In the Pages panel menu (⁃☰), choose Create Alternate Layout.

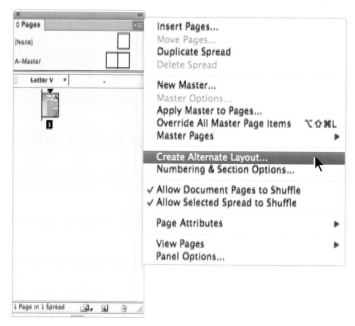

Creating an Alternate Layout.

4   In the Page Size drop-down menu, choose Custom.

5   In the Custom Page Size dialog box, type **Poster** in the name field, and set the width to **17″** and the Height to **22″**. Click the Add button, then click OK.

6 Back in the Create Alternate Layout dialog box, click the portrait button (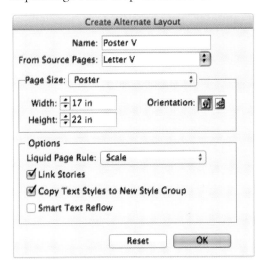) to set the orientation to portrait and change the page rule to Scale by choosing it from the Liquid Page Rule drop-down menu. Click OK.

Specifying the parameters of the Alternate Layout.

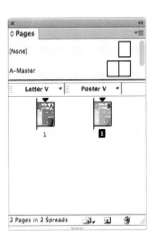

The Pages panel reflects the alternate layouts.

7 Open the Pages panel, and notice that there are now two versions of the layout, one at the original flyer size and one at the new poster size. Double-click each alternate layout to see each version in the document window. Choose File > Save.

Linked Content

There's more than meets the eye when creating Alternate Layouts. When the Alternate Layout was created, the Link Stories option was chosen. This caused the alternate layout to create links to the text in the original layout. The graphics also are linked to the original layout. This makes the process of updating content across multiple layouts very efficient.

1 In the id1102_work document, double-click page 1 of the Letter V layout in the Pages panel to make that the active page.

2 Click the Split Layout View button (▮▮) in the lower-right corner of the document window. This view allows you to compare two different alternate layouts or the same layout at a different magnification.

Activating the Split View option to compare layouts.

3 Click in the view to the left to make it active. In the Pages panel, double-click page 1 of the Letter V layout, then press Ctrl+0 (Windows) or Command+0 (Mac OS) to fit the layout in the window. Zoom in on the text that reads "A Seasonal Paradise".

4 Click in the view to the right to make it active. In the Pages panel, double-click page 1 of the Poster V layout, then press Ctrl+0 (Windows) or Command+0 (Mac OS) to fit the layout in the window. Zoom in on the text that reads "A Seasonal Paradise."

5   Click back in the view to the left (the Letter V layout), and using the Type tool (T) change the text "A Seasonal Paradise" to **A Winter Wonderland**. You will immediately notice that the text in the Poster V layout has a modified link icon in the upper-left corner of the frame to indicate that the text is out of date. This is because the Poster V layout is linked to the Letter V layout.

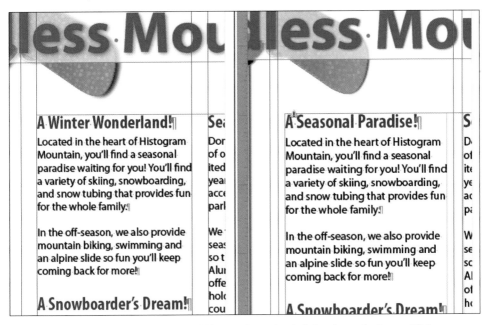

When text is modified in the parent layout, the child layout indicates that the link to the text has been modified.

6   To update the text in the Poster V layout, select the Selection tool (⬆) and click once on the modified link icon (⚠). The text change is now updated in the Poster V layout.

7   Click the Close Split Layout View button (▬) at the bottom-right corner of the document window to close Split Layout View.

8 Choose File > Save to save your work. Leave this file open for the next part of the lesson.

Alternate Layouts and Tablet Publishing

Alternate layouts are also useful when using InDesign to create layouts to be viewed on a tablet device such as an iPad.

Tablets include two orientations—horizontal and vertical. You can use alternate layouts to design how a page will look in either orientation, and use the liquid layout feature to reduce the amount of time required to create each orientation.

These are only useful if distributing publications using Adobe's Digital Publishing Suite, which is not an ideal solution for most publishers because it has a high cost per publication distributed, and also has additional fees charged to the publisher for every copy downloaded. Some competitive offerings are starting to emerge at lower prices, such as the Digital Publishing System from Aquafadas (*www.aquafadas.com*). Whether using Adobe, Aquafadas, or another vendor, you can create content using InDesign and distribute it onto various tablets using their services, for a fee.

Alternate Layouts for Tablet Devices

Let's say you started with an InDesign document that was built for the portrait orientation of a tablet device. Now you wanted to create a landscape version for that device, you could do the following:

1 Go to the panel menu of the Pages panel, and choose Create Alternate Layout.

2 Change the orientation to landscape but keep the same size. You could also at this point choose a liquid page rule to let InDesign attempt to reorganize the page elements to fit the new layout. Click Ok.

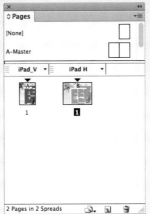

Clockwise from upper-left: The Portrait layout, the landscape layout, and the Pages panel showing the Alternate Layouts that made them.

You now will have an alternate layout of your document. Even if Alternate layout required some minor adjustments to the positioning of objects on the layout, you'd still be much further along than you would have been by staring over with a new document.

The other benefit to using Alternate Layout, is that the content is linked together. Both text and images will update in all Alternate Layouts when a modification to one of them is made providing for even more time savings in the long run.

The Content tools

As you've seen in the previous section, when you create an Alternate Layout, you can link the graphics and stories so that when an item is modified in one layout, it can easily be updated in another layout. But what if you need to add content after the Alternate Layout has been created? Adobe InDesign CS6 includes some new tools to assist you in this situation. The Content Collector tool, Content Placer tool, and Content Conveyor allow you to pickup content from one layout and easily place it in another. In this exercise, you will learn how to use these tools.

1   With the id1102_work.indd file still open on your computer, go to the Pages panel, and double-click page 1 of the Letter V layout to make it active. Press Ctrl+0 (Windows) or Command+0 (Mac OS) to fit the page to the window.

2   Choose File > Place and choose the SSI.ai file located in the Links folder of the id11lessons folder. Click Open.

3   With the loaded graphics icon, click and drag in the lower-left corner of the page to place the graphic within the width of the photo already on the page.

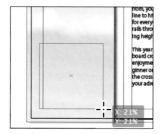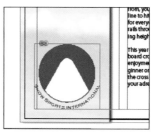

Click and drag to place the graphic in the lower-left corner of the page on the Letter V layout.

4   In the Pages panel, double-click page 1 of the Poster V layout to make that page active. Press Ctrl+0 (Windows) or Command+0 (Mac OS) to fit the page to the window. Notice that the graphic does not appear in this layout.

5   Double-click page 1 of the Letter V layout to make it active.

6 Select the Content Collector tool (🖿) from the Tools panel and click the graphic in the lower-left corner of page 1 of the Letter V layout. Notice that the graphic now appears in the Content Conveyor at the bottom of the screen. Using this tool, you can click as many elements as you wish (graphic or text elements) and collect them for reuse in the Content Conveyor.

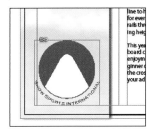 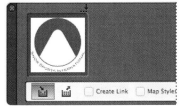

The graphic from the page picked up with the Content Collector tool and loaded into the Content Conveyor.

7 Double-click page 1 of the Poster V layout to make the page active. Press Ctrl+0 (Windows) or Command+0 (Mac OS) to fit the page to the document window.

8 Switch to the Content Placer tool (🖿) by selecting it at the bottom of the Content Conveyor, or by clicking and holding the Content Collector tool and choosing it from the drop-down menu.

9 Click the Create Link check box at the bottom of the Content Conveyor panel, then click to place the graphic in the lower-left corner of page 1 of the Poster V layout. Switch to the Selection tool and resize the graphic appropriately for the larger Poster V layout.

10 Because we created a link between these two layouts for this graphic, when you update the parent element (the one on the Letter V layout), the child element (the one on the Poster V layout) will update. Unfortunately, this includes the sizing as well. Fortunately, we can control that. With the graphic selected on the Poster V layout, go to the Links panel and choose Link Options from the panel menu.

11 In the Link Options dialog box, you can control which properties will get updated when updating the link. Click the Size and Shape check box to enable this option. By choosing this option, you are telling InDesign that if the parent object is modified, don't update the size on the child element when the link is updated, but update all the other properties. Click OK.

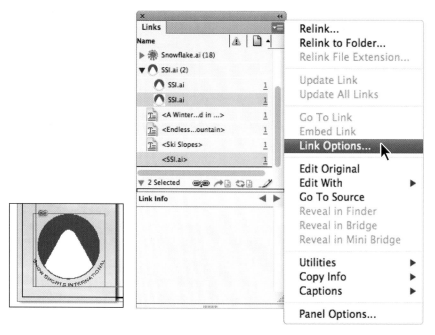

Controlling which properties get updated when updating the child element.

12 Choose File > Save to save your work. Then choose File > Close to close the document.

Creating PDF Forms

InDesign CS6 has added the ability to export to a PDF file with fillable form fields that were created in InDesign. This saves a large amount of time as the form fields don't need to be created directly in Adobe Acrobat as they have in the past. There are several different types of form fields that InDesign allows you to define including Check Box, Combo Box, List Box, Radio Buttons, Signature Fields, and Text Fields. In this lesson, you'll use a few of these field types to make a fillable PDF form.

1 In InDesign, choose File > Open and navigate to the id11lessons folder and select the file id1103.indd and open the file.

2 Choose Window > Layers to open the Layers panel. Then click on the Form Field Layer to make it the active layer. Note that there is Form Appearance layer that is locked and contains static information about the form and a Form Fields layer where you'll be creating form fields that users can type in to enter data. The document has been setup this way for convenience and although isn't necessary, it can be helpful when creating a PDF form with multiple fields.

3   Open the Buttons and Forms panel by choosing Window > Interactive > Buttons and Forms.

4   Click on the frame for the First Name field using the Selection tool, and choose Text Field from the Type drop-down menu in the Buttons and Forms panel.

To save time, the frames have already been created to indicate where PDF form fields are needed. These frames can be drawn using the Type tool, Rectangle tool, or Rectangle Frame tool. Any of these frame types will work when creating fillable PDF fields.

5   In the Name text field, type **first_name** to give the field a unique name and in the Description field, type **Please enter your first name here**. The text entered in the Description field will provide a tool-tip in the final PDF form. Leave the remaining settings at the defaults.

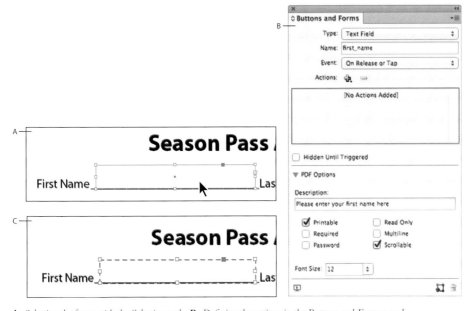

*A. Selecting the frame with the Selection tool. **B.** Defining the options in the Buttons and Forms panel.*
C. The frame appearance changes when Form properties have been defined

When defining the name for a form field, it's good practice to avoid spaces and unique characters. Although a basic form will still work when spaces are used in the name, if any advanced programming will be done to the form later on, spaces and unique characters could cause problems.

6   Click on the frame for the Last Name field using the Selection tool, and choose Text Field from the Type drop-down menu in the Buttons and Forms panel.

7 In the Name text field, type **last_name** to give the field a unique name and in the Description field, type **Please enter your last name here**.

8 Repeat steps 6 and 7 for the Address, City, Zip, Phone, and E-mail fields. Although you may be tempted to define the Zip and Phone fields as a number, this is not possible directly in InDesign. In addition, Zip and Phone fields can't be defined as number fields because they often require "-" as the contents which are not considered numerals. If desired, you could modify these fields directly in Acrobat to contain the correct data.

9 Choose File > Save As and name the file id1103_work.indd. Click OK.

Adding a Combo Box

A Combo Box provides a drop-down menu with predefined options for a user to choose from. This is especially useful to the form designer as it provides control of the choices that the user has to choose from and can prevent the entry of invalid data.

1 Click on the frame for the State field using the Selection tool, and choose Combo Box from the Type drop-down menu in the Buttons and Forms panel.

2 In the Name text field, type state to give the field a unique name and in the Description field, type **Please choose your state from the list**.

Now you will enter the choices that will become available in the State drop-down menu.

3 In the List Items field, type Massachusetts, then click the plus sign (⊕) to add it to the list of choices for the drop-down menu.

4 Repeat step 3 for the following states: New Hampshire, Vermont, Connecticut, Rhode Island, New York, New Jersey, Pennsylvania, and Maryland.

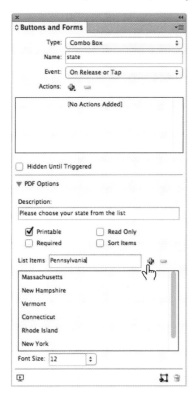

The Buttons and Forms panel makes it easy to add choices to a Combo Box list.

5 All the added items are now listed in the order in which they were created. To sort them alphabetically, click the Sort Items checkbox.

If you leave one of the items selected when creating the Combo Box list of items, it will become the default selection in the form. If you don't want any item set as the default, click on the current selected item in the list again to deselect it.

6 Choose File > Save to save your work.

Creating a Submit button

Now that your form is created, users will be able to fill in the field to provide their information to the recipient. They would be able to print the form, but there's no convenient way to submit the form via e-mail. In this section, you will create a submit button that will submit the form to the intended recipient when clicked.

1   With the id1103_work.indd file still open, click on the Submit button frame using the Selection tool.

2   In the Buttons and forms panel, click on the Convert to Button (⬤) button. This converts the standard frame, to a button object. In the name field, type **submit**, and in the Description field, type **Click the submit button to send your completed form to Feather Ridge**.

3   Uncheck the Printable checkbox to prevent the Submit button from printing if the form is printed.

The button has been created, but it doesn't do anything yet. You need to tell the submit button where to submit the form.

4   Click on the plus sign in the Actions section of the Buttons and Forms panel and choose Submit Form.

5   In the URL field, type **mailto:** followed by the e-mail address of the recipient. In this example we used a fictitious e-mail address of **mailto:info@featherridge.com**.

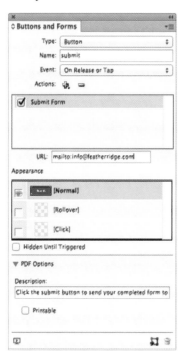

Creating a submit button so that the form information can be submitted electronically.

6   Choose File > Save to save your work.

Creating the PDF Form

The last step in the process is creating an actual PDF form that users can open using Adobe Acrobat or Adobe Reader. Using these applications, the form can be filled out and submitted.

1   With the id1103_work.indd file still open, choose File > Export.

2   Choose a location to save the PDF file and in the Format drop-down menu, choose Adobe PDF (Interactive) and click the Save button.

3   In the Export to Interactive PDF dialog box, make sure that the View after Exporting checkbox is enabled, and make sure that the Include All radio button is enabled in the Forms and Media section. Leave the other setting at their defaults and click OK.

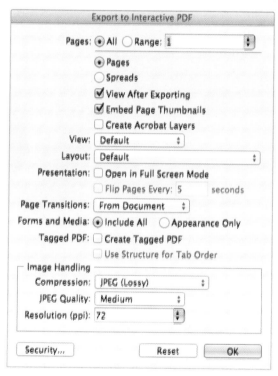

The Export to Interactive PDF dialog box controls how the resulting PDF form will be created.

The resulting PDF form should open in your default PDF application. Preferably Adobe Acrobat or Adobe Reader. The form can now be filled in and submitted to the recipient.

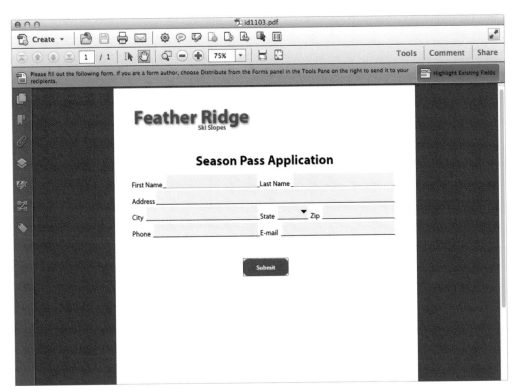

The final PDF form.

Congratulations, you have completed Lesson 11!

Self study

1 Experiment with the Flexible Width and Auto-Size options in the Text Frame Options dialog box to control how text frames behave when content is added or frames are resized.

2 Create additional Alternate Layouts for the snowboarding flyer and experiment with the Liquid Page Rules to see the results.

3 Practice using the Content Collector, Content Placer, and Content Conveyor to reuse content between alternate layouts.

Review

Questions

1 Will animations created in InDesign export to an interactive PDF file?

2 How can you prevent a text frame from becoming overset when text doesn't fit?

3 When creating an Alternate Layout, is content automatically linked to the source layout?

4 When using Liquid Layout, how do you make the new page size "stick" without the page reverting back to its original size?

Answers

1 Not directly. However, you can export the animation as a .swf file and reimport the .swf file into InDesign and Export to interactive PDF where the animation will appear correctly.

2 You can use the Auto-Size options in the Text Frame Options dialog box to control how a text frame resizes when text doesn't fit.

3 Graphics are automatically linked, but text stories are only linked if the Link Stories check box is enabled in the Create Alternate Layout dialog box.

4 Pressing and holding the Alt key (Windows) or Option key (Mac OS) will allow you to retain the page size change when using the Page tool with a Liquid Layout rule.

Lesson 12

What you'll learn in this lesson:

- Preparing documents for conversion to ePub
- Style Mapping
- Setting export order
- Object export options
- Adding CSS formatting
- Generating ePub digital book files

Creating Digital Books

This lesson covers the capabilities for creating digital books by generating ePub digital book files using InDesign CS6.

Starting up

Before starting, make sure that your tools and panels are consistent by resetting your preferences. You'll use InDesign's Advanced workspace for this lesson. Choose Window > Workspace > Advanced and then choose Window > Workspace > Reset Advanced. For more details on this process, see "Resetting the InDesign workspace and preferences" in the Starting Up section of this book.

You will work with several files from the id12lessons folder in this lesson. Make sure that you have copied the id12lessons folder onto your hard drive from the Digital Classroom DVD or downloaded from the location specified in your ebook if you are reading a digital version of this book. See "Loading lesson files" in the Starting Up section of this book for details. This lesson may be easier to follow if the id12lessons folder is on your desktop.

See Lesson 12 in action!

Use the accompanying video to gain a better understanding of how to use some of the features shown in this lesson. The video tutorial for this lesson can be found on the included DVD.

The project

In this lesson you will create a digital book file using InDesign to generate an ePub document. ePub is the digital book format used to freely distribute digital book files across all major electronic devices such as the nook or iPad and serves as the foundation for the format used on Kindle devices. For this lesson you will work with a document that is being created for both print and digital versions. You will take the completed version that was prepared for printing and modify it for use on digital devices.

You will discover how to control settings which affect the export process, and how organizing a book for reading on a digital device may require different organization and structure to the InDesign document.

About the ePub format

ePub is the format used for most electronic books today. It is maintained by an international standards group, the IDPF. The official specifications for the ePub format are found online at: *www.idpf.org.*

An ePub file is a group of files that have been bundled together into a compressed file folder that is given the ePub name. The contents of an ePub need to be arranged in a specific way so that digital readers like the nook, iPad, Sony Reader and others can understand and display the contents. The Kindle digital reading devices use their own file format which is a modified version of the ePub file format, making ePub the starting digital file format for distribution on most every digital reading device.

If you were to crack-open an ePub file, inside you would find HTML files along with a CSS file describing how to format the book. The HTML files may also reference images, multimedia, and in some cases fonts, all which could also be included within the ePub file.

You can make ePub files using Adobe InDesign and share them with readers, or sell them online. When selling them online, some stores may add Digital Rights Management to protect against unauthorized copying and distribution, but this is something that occurs with the book reseller or distributor, and is not part of Adobe InDesign.

Preparing your InDesign document for ePub conversion

InDesign documents require some adjustments prior to exporting them to ePub. If you don't prepare the file before exporting, the files may not display as intended, with images or text appearing in the incorrect sequence, or some items not appearing at all.

Using styles

Using paragraph, character, and object styles helps keep your documents looking consistent when converting to a digital format such as ePub. All text should be styled, and styles should apply consistently. Styles become even more important when converting to a digital format, as each set of text formatting must use a style name, and if you haven't assigned a style name, InDesign must create a style to identify the text and formatting. If you've already styled the text, InDesign uses your existing style name and attributes—which is both faster and more efficient.

Styles in the Paragraph styles panel should not contain any overrides. Overrides are manual adjustments or changes that you may have applied to individual pieces of text after applying a style. Instead you should always use Character styles when formatting individual characters within a paragraph. These individual character styles can then be translated into the digital version of your document. If you manually adjust the formatting of individual characters and words, without creating or using a Character style, these formatting changes may not convert to the digital document.

1 Choose File > Open. In the Open dialog box, navigate to the id12lessons folder, select the file id1201.indd, and then click Open. If a dialog box appears asking if you want to update modified links, press Update Links. The document should open to the first page. If necessary, double-click the page 1 icon in the Pages panel to navigate to this page.

2 Choose the Text tool (T) from the Tools panel, then click to place the cursor in the word By in the line By The Brothers Grimm.

3 Click the Paragraph Styles button along the right side of the document window or choose Type > Paragraph Styles. Note the plus sign (+) which appears next to the paragraph style name. This indicates that the text was changed after the style was applied to it. InDesign refers to this as a style override.

You should remove style overrides before converting to an ePub. You can do this by creating a character style that accounts for the formatting changes. By creating a character style, InDesign can easily convert these attributes into a digital document.

4 Click the Character Styles button along the right side of the document window or choose Type > Character Styles.

5 Double-click to select the word By in the line By The Brothers Grimm, then click the Italic Character Style to apply the Character Style to this word.

6 Switch to the Paragraph Style panel for a moment and notice the plus sign is no longer displayed, as the character style and paragraph style work together to describe all the text in this line.

7 Repeat this process on page 3, applying the Italic character style to the word By.

Export style tagging: Defining how InDesign styles convert to ePub styles

If you intend to use specific style names in the Cascading Style Sheet (CSS) for your ePub, you can specify how InDesign character styles and paragraph styles are identified when you create an ePub. You can specify how individual styles are converted to CSS styles as part of their InDesign style definition, or you can specify how all styles are converted.

To specify how an individual style is converted to a CSS style, start by selecting a style in either the character or paragraph style panel menu, then use the panel menu to choose the Style Options command. In the Style Options dialog box, use the Export Tagging option to specify the CSS style to apply when creating the ePub by choosing the CSS style (tag) to be used from the Tag option.

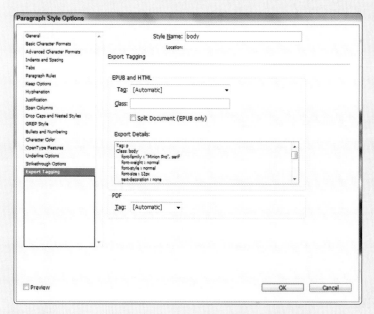

Specify how individual InDesign styles convert to CSS styles in an ePub using the Tag drop-down menu in the Export Tagging section of the Style Options dialog box.

To specify how all InDesign styles convert to CSS styles used in an ePub, choose Edit all Export tags from either the Paragraph styles or Character styles panel.

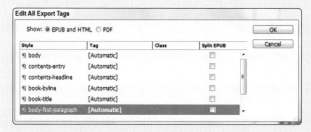

In the Edit all Export Tags dialog box, you can specify the CSS styles to use for all the document styles in a single location.

Controlling Object Export Settings

To control the positioning or spacing of objects on a page that will be converted to ePub, you may use the Object Export Options. This is especially useful if you have one item that should be positioned or controlled differently from all other elements. For example, if you have one image that is to be positioned in the center of the layout, while all other images are to be flush along the left side of the layout. You can use the Object Export Options to adjust the one item that varies from all the others.

1　Navigate to the fourth page of the document.

2　Choose the Selection tool (⤢) from the Tools panel, then click to select the picture of the bird.

3　Choose Object > Object Export Options. Click the Alt Text tab and from the Alt Text Source drop-down menu, choose Custom and type **Picture of a Bird**. The Alt text helps visually impaired readers to understand the picture, as the text can be read to them.

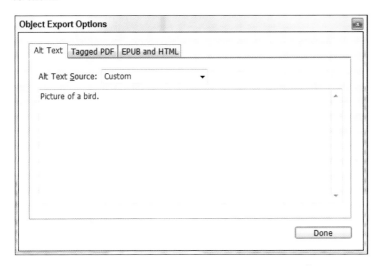

Entering Alt text to assist visually impaired readers understand the contents of an image.

4   Click the EPUB and HTML tab, and then click to enable Custom Layout, and click the Align Center icon so the image will align to the center when it is exported to ePub.

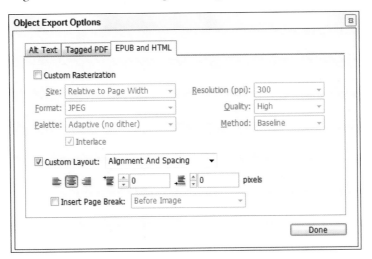

Using Object Export Options to control the positioning of an individual image when the document is converted to ePub.

5   Click Done.

Adding interactive links

Digital books can include hyperlinks to enhance the reading experience. You can use InDesign to add hyperlinks to different parts of the same document, or to web addresses on the Internet. Some of this linking can be done automatically for you, such as creating a table of contents with hyperlinks, while others you can add or modify on your own. You'll start by adding a hyperlink to a website, and then create an interactive table of contents that links to the start of each fairy tale in the book.

Adding hyperlinks

Adding hyperlinks involves selecting text and indicating to InDesign where the text should link to when it is clicked after the document is exported to an ePub file. The hyperlinks are not active within the InDesign file itself.

1   Navigate to page 3 of the document, containing the book title and byline.

2   Open the Hyperlinks panel by choosing Window > Interactive > Hyperlinks.

3   On page 3, use the Type tool to select the words Digital Classroom.

4   In the Hyperlinks panel, at the top of the panel in the URL section, place the cursor after the *http://* and enter **www.DigitalClassroom.com** then press the Enter or Return key on your keyboard. The hyperlink is added to the document.

5   Choose File > Save As to save your work. Add **_work** to the file name so the file name becomes id1201_work.indd.

Creating an interactive Table of Contents

A table of contents is important for readers to navigate to a section of a book. You do not want to manually create links to each of the chapters in a book, or in this case, each of the individual stories. Here you will have InDesign create the table of contents for you, and add hyperlinks to the location of the stories.

The table of contents can also appear in the built-in navigational controls available within e-reading devices and software. To enable this, you will create a table of contents style. Later, when exporting to ePub, you will have InDesign use this style to automatically generate an interactive contents file for digital readers along with the table of contents that appears at the start of the book.

1   Navigate to page 2 of the document. A blank page is displayed. You will add the table of contents to this page.

2   Choose Layout > Table of Contents Styles, then click New to create a new style. A style is necessary for creating a table of contents that appears within the built-in navigation controls of digital reading devices.

3   In the TOC Style text box, enter the name **ePub TOC**, confirm the Title is Contents and from the Style drop-down menu, choose contents-headline to apply this style to the word Contents when it appears at the top of the automatically generated table of contents.

4   In the Styles in Table of Contents section, locate the Other Styles list and scroll to the chapter-headline style. Click this style, then click the << Add button to add this to the list of styles included in the table of contents.

All text using the style chapter-headline will be added to the table of contents.

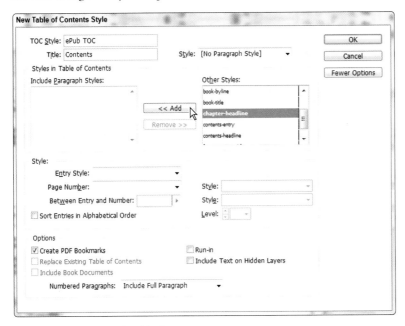

Adding a style to include in the table of contents.

5   Continuing to work in the New Table of Contents Style window, confirm the chapter-headline style is selected in the Include Paragraph Styles list, then make the following adjustments:

- For Entry Style choose contents-entry. This is a style that was created for you to use in this document.

- For Page Number choose No Page Number as the digital version of the book will not have specific page numbers, and the hyperlink will take the reader to the start of the selected story, regardless of its location.

- For Level confirm that 1 is selected, indicating that each story will be the top-most item in the table of contents.

If you do not see the Page Number or Level options, click the More Options button in the upper left side of the New Table of Contents Style dialog box.

6   Click OK to save the style, then choose OK to close the Table of Contents Styles dialog box.

7   Choose Layout > Table of Contents. From the TOC Style drop-down menu, choose the ePub TOC style you created in the previous steps, then click OK. The cursor becomes loaded, ready to place text into the layout.

8   Click the loaded cursor near the upper-left corner of the page, where the two margin guides intersect. The table of contents is placed into the page. While the text may appear to be normal text, InDesign will add hyperlinks for you at the time to document is exported. The TOC style you created will also be used in the next part of this lesson to automatically create the interactive table of contents at the time you generate the ePub file.

9   Choose File > Save As. In the Save As dialog box, navigate to the id12lessons folder and type **id1201_work.indd** in the File name text field. Click Save.

Adding document metadata

Information that describes the document and its content is referred to as metadata. Digital book readers use metadata to display information such as the author, book title, and copyright status. Here you will enter metadata about this document.

1   Choose File > File Info. The File Information dialog box is displayed.

2   In the File Information dialog box, enter the following information:

- For Document Title type **Grimms Fairy Tales**
- For Author type **The Brothers Grimm**
- From the Copyright Status drop-down menu choose Public Domain
- Click OK to save the metadata.

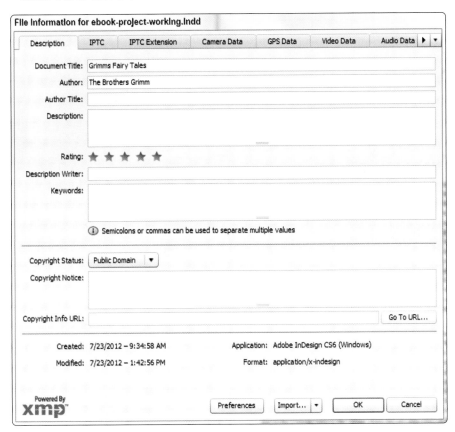

Enter document metadata in the File Information dialog box for InDesign to automatically include this information when generating an ePub.

Creating an ePub

As you prepare to export your book to the ePub format, you will want to identify which items should be part of the digital version of the book, and the sequence in which they will export.

Specifying Object Export Order

The page layout for your InDesign document doesn't always translate perfectly to digital books. If you were to convert this book directly to ePub, you would find that images may appear in wildly different locations in the book, or that certain content may not appear at all in the ePub. For example, master page items are not included in digital book files created from InDesign, and images and non-linked text frames may not appear in the order in which they need to flow within the book.

On its own, InDesign doesn't do an effective job of determining how text and graphics should be positioned on a digital page when files are converted to ePub. Fortunately you can provide some guidance to help create digital files that more closely match your desired layout. With some guidance from you, InDesign can produce a more logically structured digital book file. One way to help with this is to use the Articles panel to organize content into the sequence in which it should appear in a digital book.

1   Choose Window > Articles. The Articles panel opens. You will use the Articles panel to specify which items in the document will be converted to the digital version of the document in the ePub format, and the order in which they appear in the digital layout. Items that are not contained in the Articles panel will not be exported.

2   Continuing to work on the second page of the document, use the Selection tool to click and drag the entire text frame containing the Table of Contents into the articles panel. The New Article window appears. Enter the name **Contents** and confirm Include when Exporting is checked, and then click OK.

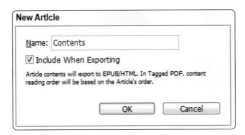

Adding an item to the Articles panel to specify its export order when creating an ePub.

You started adding items on the second page and not the first because in this publication the first page will be used as the cover, and you will specify this at the time you generate your ePub file. If the cover was created separately, you would start adding items to the Articles panel at the first page of the InDesign document.

3   Navigate to page 3. Using the Selection tool, click and drag the text box containing the book title into the articles panel. The New Article window appears. Enter the name **Body Text** for the Article Name and confirm the checkbox is selected for Include when Exporting, and then click OK.

You can also use the Articles panel to arrange the digital version of a book in a different sequence than the book layout within InDesign. For example, you may have a copyright page at the start of a book layout you created for a print version, but prefer to place this at the end of the layout for the digital version. Using the Articles panel you can reorganize the content for the digital version, placing the copyright page, or any other content, in a different sequence within the layout.

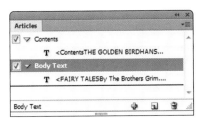

The Articles panel after adding the Body Text article.

4   Navigate to page four and continuing to use the Selection tool, click on the text frame containing the headline for the story *The Golden Bird*. If text threads are not already visible, choose View > Extras > Show Text Threads. Because this text frame is linked to the text frame added to the articles panel, it will be included in the ePub export. When a text frame is placed in the Articles panel, the content of all linked text frames is exported to ePub.

Using anchored objects to control object placement

On page 4 of the document, notice the picture of the golden bird. Unless you add this image to the articles panel, it will not be included in the ePub you are creating. You can add the image to the articles panel, but the only options are for adding it before or after each article or between each story. This image needs to appear in the middle of the article—not at the start or end. For images to export with text in the middle of an article, they need to be attached, or anchored, to the text. Here you will anchor the image to the related story so that it exports in the correct location.

1   Using the selection tool, click to select the image of the golden bird. Notice the solid blue square along the top edge of the frame, near the top-right corner. You will use this to anchor the image to the story.

2 Move your cursor over the solid blue square. Click and hold on the solid blue square, and while continuing to press on the mouse or track pad, drag the cursor so it is located slightly to the left of the word The in the story title *The Golden Bird*.

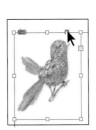

Anchoring the image to text (left) and after it is anchored (right).
Anchor images to text frames so they export in the correct location

3 Save your document by choosing File > Save.

You can also use anchored objects for separate text frames that relate to text surrounding them but are not part of a text flow, such as a sidebar or pull-quote.

Specifying the cover

You can create a separate cover image using a program like Photoshop, and add the cover at the time you are exporting, or you can use the first page of the InDesign file as the cover. For this example you will use the first page as the cover.

1 Navigate to the first page of the document.

2 Using the Selection tool, click to select the image of the fairy. Shift+click to also select the text under the image containing the title of the book.

3 With both the text and image selected, choose Object > Group to have these items treated as one element by InDesign.

4   Choose Object > Object Export Options and click the EPUB and HTML tab. Click the Custom Rasterization option and specify that the group should be rasterized (converted to a picture) at a fixed size with a resolution of 300 ppi in a JPEG format with high quality settings using the baseline method, then click Done.

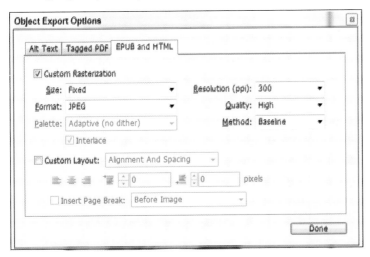

Specifying the image conversion settings for the book cover.

5   Click and drag the grouped items to the bottom of the Articles panel. Name the new article **Cover** and click OK.

6   In the Articles panel, click and drag the Cover article to the top of the list of articles. When exporting, you will specify to InDesign that this group of items on the first page will be used as the cover image for the book.

ePub export settings

You are now ready to export your document to the ePub file format.

1   Choose File > Export. The Export dialog box opens. Choose EPUB from the Save as type (Windows) or Format (Mac) menu at the bottom of the dialog box, confirm you are saving the file in a location you can easily access such as the Desktop, then click Save. The EPUB Export Options dialog box appears. The dialog box has three separate sections you can select along the left side: General, Image, and Advanced. You will work through these three sections to specify how your ePub file will be created.

2   In the General section, for Version: choose EPUB 3.0.

New devices sold since 2011 support this standard and most older devices have had software updates to allow ePub files created using this standard to display. While 3.0 supports having audio and video files embedded into the digital book, older devices typically ignore these elements if they were created as purely reading devices. Many of the more modern reading devices are multipurpose, and can be used for reading and also support multimedia content. Keep the EPUB Export Options dialog box open.

3 In the Setup section, for Cover choose Rasterize First Page.

This causes the first page of the document to be turned into an image, which will be used to represent the cover of the book. The cover of the book is displayed when the book is placed into most digital reader's libraries.

4 For TOC Style, choose ePub TOC. This is the Table of Contents style you created earlier in this lesson. It calls for all text using the chapter-headline style to be added to the interactive table of contents, with links to the location where each story starts.

5 For margins, enter 10 pixels for all four sides. The margins are placed around the edge of the book, allowing space between the text and the side of the reader. Note that many reading devices use their own margins and will ignore this value, but it's worth entering it here for those readers using software or a device that would otherwise place the text right against the edges of the container displaying the book.

6 From the Content Order drop-down menu select Same as Articles Panel. This causes InDesign to use the order you specified in the Articles panel to determine the ePub export order.

While it is possible to convert an InDesign book to ePub without using the articles panel, by choosing the Based on Page Layout option, the results are typically quite poor. Unless you have a document containing no images and one long text flow, the Based on Page Layout option is not advisable.

7 Under the Text Options settings:

- Leave the Place Footnote After Paragraph option unchecked. This is useful if your document contains footnotes, so they are located closer to their location in the document. This document contains no footnotes.

- Check to select the Remove Forced Line Breaks option. This causes InDesign to remove any extra line breaks that may have been added for a print layout. When converting to a digital format, these line breaks disrupt the reading experience, as each user may have a different screen width and resolution, and all line breaks are different. This is unlike a printed version where all readers see the same document with the same line breaks.

- Set Bullets to Map to Unordered Lists

- Set Numbers to Map to Ordered Lists

- Deselect (uncheck) the View EPUB after Exporting option so that you can control which viewer is used to test and review your ePub.

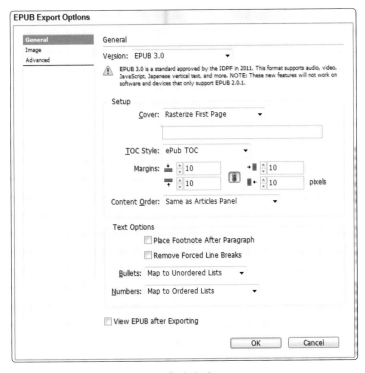

Setting the ePub general Export Options for the book.

8   Click the Image tab along the left side of the dialog box and review these settings:

- Select the Preserve Appearance option from Layout to make certain images are cropped just as they are within the layout. If this is deselected, full-size images are used within the layout.

- Set Resolution (ppi) to 150 for images to retain enough resolution if they are zoomed-in or viewed on modern devices with higher resolution displays.

- Select Fixed from the Image Size drop-down menu to keep images the same size, regardless of the size of the display. If you prefer to allow images to adapt to the display size, choose Relative to Page.

- For Image Alignment and Spacing, click the Align Left button and set the space of 6 pixels before and after all images.

- Do not select the option to Insert Page Break before or after the image. You may find this option useful with books that use an image to separate each chapter, but the images in this book do not need to sit on their own page.

- Select Settings Apply to Anchored Objects to apply these image settings to any anchored images such as the picture of the Golden Bird.

- For image conversion, choose JPEG because all images in this book use a variety of colors and shades which lend themselves well to the JPEG format. For other books, you may wish to select Automatic when there are a variety of image types, such as pictures and illustrations.

- For JPEG Options, choose High for the Image Quality and select Baseline for Format Method. These options control how the images will appear after converted to the JPEG format for use in the ePub.

- Do not select the Ignore Object Export Settings. This option is used if you need to override the Object Export Settings that have been set for specific images. It is preferable to keep this deselected and set the export options for individual images as needed, and then control all others here. Most of the controls available in this section can be accessed for each individual image, or for grouped objects, by choosing Object > Object Export Settings

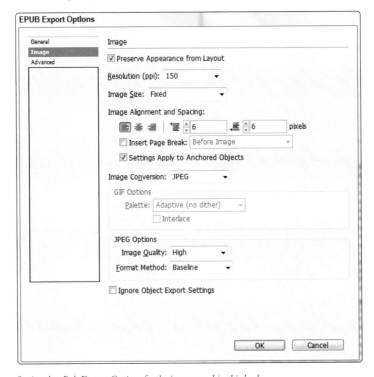

Setting the ePub Export Options for the images used in this book.

9 Click the Advanced tab along the left side of the dialog box.

- From the Split Document drop-down menu, select Do Not Split. This option could be used to break the document into sections at each of the chapter titles.

- For EPUB Metadata enter your name as the publisher and keep the Unique ID produced by InDesign. For books, the ISBN is typically placed in this Unique ID field.

- For CSS Options:

  - Select the Include Style Definitions option for InDesign to define the style of text formatting when the ePub is generated.

  - Deselect the Preserve Local Overrides option so that only text with styles applied is formatted in the ePub.

  - Deselect the option to Include Embeddable Fonts because many ereaders cannot use fonts embedded by InDesign, and books with fonts embedded fail validation tests and cannot be sold on most digital books stores.

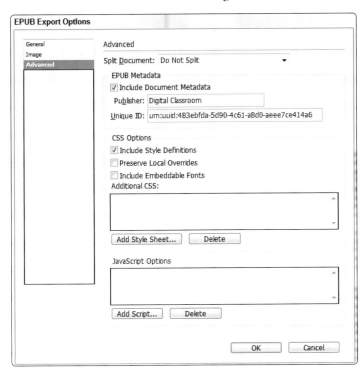

The Advanced ePub settings control whether metadata is included in the file and whether InDesign creates a cascading style sheet (CSS) to apply formatting and styling to the contents of the ePub. If a CSS file is not generated, or if styles are not defined by InDesign, the ePub must be edited later using a text editor to add the CSS rules.

10 Click OK to generate the ePub from your InDesign document. Depending upon the speed of your computer, this may take a minute or two for it to complete. Longer documents may take several minutes to complete.

Testing your ePub

After generating your ePub, you can view it to confirm that all the contents exported and are displaying as you expected them to appear.

ePub viewers

There are many ePub viewers using different viewing "engines" to display ePub files: Adobe Reader Mobile SDK (RMSDK) and WebKit. Along with reading devices that support the ePub format, there are also the Kindle devices which use their own file format. It's quite possible that your ePub files will look different across many devices. For this reason, it is useful to understand ways to test your ePub files to confirm they will look acceptable on the majority of devices. You'll start by gaining an understanding of the two primary ePub reading engines that power most ePub readers:

Adobe Reader Mobile SDK (RMSDK) is licensed by Adobe to device makers for displaying digital books. It provides Adobe Digital Rights Management (DRM) for ePub files to limit them from being copied without permission. On computer desktops, Adobe Digital Editions behaves similarly to RMSDK, making Adobe Digital Editions a good option for testing to see how a book will display within RMSDK devices. You'll find RMSDK used in Adobe Digital Editions, the Sony Reader, and the nook among other devices.

To test your book using the Adobe Reader, go to *adobe.com* and download Adobe Digital Editions. After downloading Adobe Digital Editions, open the ePub file you created using the Adobe Digital Editions software. Confirm the cover displays as expected, and the hyperlinks along the side of the document function properly. These hyperlinks were created using the TOC style you included when generating the ePub.

The ePub file being viewed using Adobe Digital Editions.

WebKit is the other major ePub viewing engine. It powers many readers including Chrome, Safari, iPhone/iPad/iPod Touch, and Android. WebKit is also a popular mobile web browser, and is used on many smartphones sold today. Readers that use WebKit include the desktop version of the nook reader, Apple's iBooks, Bookworm, and Ibis reader.

If you are using the Firefox web browser, you can find an ePub viewer for testing ePubs right within your Mac or Windows computer here: *https://addons.mozilla.org/en-us/firefox/addon/epubreader/*.

The ePub file being viewed using the Firefox ePub plugin.

ePub validation

Formal ePub validation is required if you plan to sell your ePub file through various online stores. This confirms the ePub file meets that standards for ePub files.

There are two options for validating an epub:

- Online validation is an option using the International Digital Publishing Forum validator available at *http://validator.idpf.org/*. This supports files that are 10 MB or smaller.

- Download and install the epubcheck validation tool on your own computer. It is available at *http://code.google.com/p/epubcheck/*

Not all files generated from InDesign are valid, as InDesign includes options to add items to an ePub that are not supported, and earlier versions of InDesign failed to include other required items. It is often necessary to extract and edit the contents of an ePub file to manipulate its contents in order to make it fully valid. This process is beyond the scope of this lesson, as it can involve code editing and requires some knowledge of HTML and CSS.

Kindle conversion

While Kindle devices use their own file format, most Kindle books start as ePub files. You can then convert your books to the Kindle format. The easiest way to convert ePub files to the Kindle format is to use the Kindle Previewer. Opening an ePub using the Kindle Previewer automatically converts it to the Kindle format. The exact web address to download the previewer is quite long, and it's easier to simply use a search engine such as Bing or Google to search for Kindle Previewer. The correct link is located on the *Amazon.com* site. The full link for downloading the previewer is *http://www.amazon.com/gp/feature.html?ie=UTF8&docId=1000765261*.

Distributing ePub files

Once you create an ePub, you can distribute the file through a traditional publisher or on your own by establishing accounts with the largest ePub resellers such as Apple, Barnes & Noble, Amazon. These services will add Digital Rights Management to your files if you request, making it so that the files are less likely to be copied illegally.

To self-publish on Amazon, visit Kindle Direct Publishing at *http://kdp.amazon.com/*. For self-publishing on Barnes & Noble visit *http://pubit.barnesandnoble.com*. To publish via iTunes, establish an account with Apple here *http://itunes.com/sellyourbooks*. In all cases you will want to validate your ePub before distribution.

Congratulations! You have completed this lesson.

Self study

1   Convert the ePub file from this lesson using the page layout instead of the Articles panel. Note the differences in the structure and organization of the ePub file.

2   Create an ePub file without using a TOC and notice what is different about the file.

3   Add a video file and convert the document to an ePub. Test the file using both a Webkit and Adobe Reader-based engine.

Review

Questions

1   Is the ePub file format used by all digital book reading devices?

2   What is the purpose of the Articles panel?

3   What can be controlled using Object Export Settings?

4   Does InDesign automatically generate a table of contents for all ePub files?

Answers

1   No, the ePub format is an industry standard used by many major book readers such as the iPad and nook, but not the Kindle. The Kindle uses a format that starts with ePub files, but converts them to its own format.

2   The Articles panel controls the sequence in which items are exported into an ePub document.

3   You can use Object Export Setting to specify how individual images will export and whether grouped content, including text and images, should be converted to a single item and turned into an image (rasterized).

4   No, InDesign only generates a table of contents if you have first created a table of contents style, and then specified the use of that style in the ePub export dialog box.

Lesson 13

What you'll learn in this lesson:

- Content Collector
- Linked content
- Liquid layouts
- PDF forms
- Alternate layouts
- Primary text frame
- ePub enhancements

Adobe InDesign CS6 New Features

This lessons provides an overview of capabilities added to InDesign CS6.

Starting up

This lesson is designed for existing InDesign users to get an understanding of what's changed within this version of InDesign, or new users who may be working with one version of InDesign at home and another in the office, and want to know the differences. There are no specific lesson files used for this lesson.

About the new features in InDesign CS6

Adobe InDesign CS6 is the eighth version of InDesign, and the software has been available for more than a decade. InDesign has a well-established way of performing most basic tasks, and the fundamentals of working with the software have not changed much over the recent versions. If you were to be placed in front of a computer using InDesign CS4, CS5, or CS6, you would likely feel right at home for creating most basic documents. The recent updates to InDesign have focused on minor improvements to the software to improve efficiency and more recently on digital publishing. We've updated every chapter in the InDesign CS6 Digital Classroom to reflect changes in the InDesign CS6 software. Most of the new features are targeted at more experienced or advanced users, and the chapters that focus on advanced features and digital publishing contain the most significant updates from previous versions of this book. Here you will discover the new capabilities of InDesign CS6 that impact most users.

About the Digital Publishing Suite

Along with generating digital documents for open standards such as PDF and ePub, Adobe is also trying to establish their own proprietary format for distributing digital documents. This format includes a per-issue fee that is paid to Adobe for every publication that is created, and requires content to be distributed, in part, through Adobe servers. These documents are created using the Adobe Digital Publishing suite of tools that expand the capabilities of InDesign.

While these tools may be used by some publishers, there is a high per-issue cost for documents created and distributed using the Adobe Digital Publishing Suite. These costs are compounded by additional fees that Adobe charges based upon the number of downloads a publication receives. Because these fees put the digital publishing suite beyond the reach of many publishers, we have focused in this book only on the new features that pertain to the widest group of users and do not require paying any additional fees to distribute the content you create within InDesign. As very large magazines are exploring options for digital document distribution, the Digital Publishing suite is one of several options they are exploring. The ways for creating and distributing digital documents are still in their infancy, and several software companies, including Adobe, are working to develop possible solutions for publishers to create and distribute content across the variety of devices that are also rapidly evolving.

Content Collector

The Content Collector tool, Content Placer tool, and Content Conveyor allow you to pickup content from one layout and easily place it in another.

Using the Content Collector tool (⊞) found in the Tools panel you can place items in the Content Conveyor located by default at the bottom of the InDesign workspace. Using the Content Collector tool, you can collect graphics or text frames by clicking on them. Once they are collected, you can reuse them.

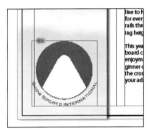

The graphic from the page picked up with the Content Collector tool and loaded into the Content Conveyor.

The Content Placer tool (⊞) is located at the bottom of the Content Conveyor, or in the Tools panel by clicking and holding on the Content Collector tool. When using the Content Placer tool, clicking the Create Link checkbox at the bottom of the Content Conveyor panel, any update the parent element will cause the child element to also be updated. You can learn more about using the InDesign CS6 Content Collector tool in Lesson 11.

Linked content

If you are familiar with the Place and Link option added in a previous version of InDesign, then the Linked Content feature will appear familiar to you. The new Linked Content feature is really an enhanced version of the Place and Link feature. Using the Selection tool you can select content to be duplicated in other parts of a layout and choose Edit > Place and Link and then click to place a copy of the original content elsewhere in the layout. Updates to the original text or image are reflected in the copies that are made in this way.

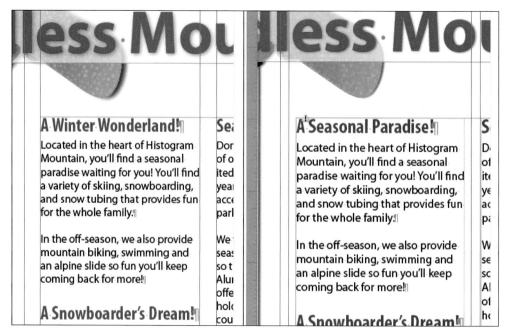

When text is modified in the parent layout, the child layout indicates that the link to the text has been modified.

You can also use the Content Placer tool to place linked content. When using the Content Collector tool, click the Create Link option before placing content on the page for the original item to be linked to the copy. You can learn more about Linked Content in Lesson 11.

You can also link duplicated content within the same document by clicking the Create Link option in the Content Collector tool.

Liquid layouts

Liquid Layout offers multiple options for controlling how a layout is resized when the page size changes Access Liquid Layout by choosing Layout > Liquid Layout to open the Liquid Layout panel.

There are four different Liquid Page Rules you can use:

• Scale

• Re-Center

• Object-based

• Guide-based.

The Liquid Layout panel is used in conjunction with the Page tool (⌖). After choosing Liquid Layout, use the page tool to drag the handles at the corners and sides of the page to resize the page and preview how the page will look at a different size. Releasing the mouse causes the page to return to its original size. This makes it easier to experiment with different layouts. Pressing the Alt key (Windows) or Option key (Mac OS) before releasing the mouse causes the layout adjustment to be maintained. You can still use Edit > Undo to return to the original page dimensions.

Using the Page tool, drag the handles to resize the page.

The Scale Liquid Layout option causes all objects on a page to increase or decrease in size as the page itself is scaled.

The Recenter Liquid Layout option causes all the page content to be recentered on the page based on the new size.

The Object-based Liquid Layout rule requires that you define which objects you want to scale and which you want to maintain position. Select individual objects and use the Liquid Layout panel to specify how they each object is to be treated.

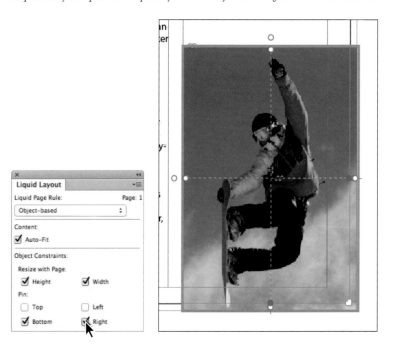

Defining properties for the Object-based page rule (left) and the visual indicators that appear on the selected object (right).

The Guide-based Liquid Layout rule uses ruler guides to define objects that should resize with the page Any object that has guides touching them are adjusted when the page is resized. Vertical guides control horizontal resizing and horizontal guides control vertical resizing.

You can learn more about Liquid Layouts in Lesson 11.

Alternate layouts

Alternate layouts make it easier to create projects with more than one version of a layout. Alternate layouts in InDesign CS6 make it so that changes to one layout get updated in all related layouts.

Using the Pages panel and Window > Pages lets you access the Pages panel menu (▾≡) where you choose the option to Create Alternate Layout.

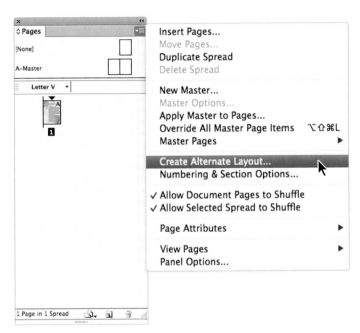

Creating an Alternate Layout.

You can choose options and use Liquid Layout features to specify how the new layout will appear.

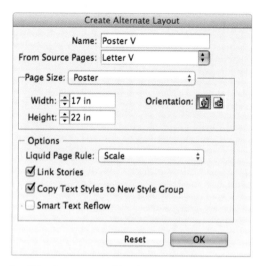

Specifying the parameters of the Alternate Layout.

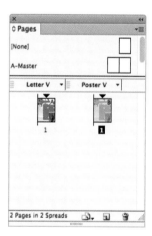

The Pages panel reflects the alternate layouts.

When you use Alternate Layouts the Pages panel displays two versions of the layout. You can double-click either alternate layout to inspect them.

Learn more about alternate layouts in Lesson 11.

PDF forms

Most forms are becoming web based, and are created using HTML and can display in any web browser on any device. PDF forms require the Adobe reader and tend to only display well on desktop and laptop computers, making them less useful for sharing to a large audience. But for users that require a form to look a certain way, such as a form that needed approval from a regulatory agency, there is still a need for PDF forms.

Adobe has added capabilities for creating PDF forms into InDesign CS6. Previously the look of the form could be designed using InDesign, but any PDF forms interactivity or PDF forms fields were added later using Adobe Acrobat.

There are several types of form fields that you can create using InDesign including Check Box, Combo Box, List Box, Radio Buttons, Signature Fields, and Text Fields.

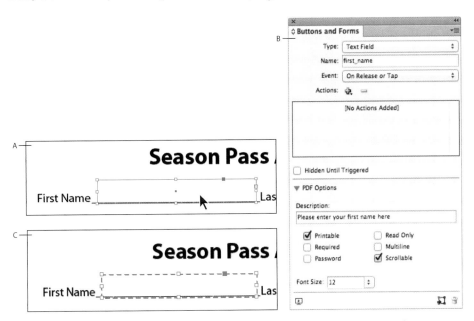

A. Selecting the frame with the Selection tool. **B.** *Defining the options in the Buttons and Forms panel.*
C. The frame appearance changes when Form properties have been defined

Primary text frame

When creating a master page you can specify a primary text frame. A primary text frame is useful if you have one frame containing the majority of the text on a page, and the master page applied to that document page is subject to change.

If a different master page is applied to a document page that uses a primary text frame, the text automatically flows from the old primary text frame into the new primary text frame. Additionally, primary text frames can be worked with on a document page more easily, as they are automatically overridden and do not require any additional adjustments before using them in your layout.

You can designate a text frame on any master page as a primary text frame by clicking to select the frame and then clicking the primary text frame symbol located near the top of the left edge of a text frame. There is only one master text frame per master page.

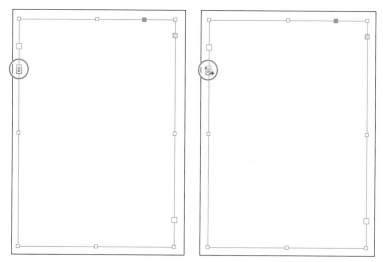

A master text frame before being converted to a primary text frame (left) and after being converted to a primary text frame (right). Designate a primary text frame on a master page to more easily adjust text layout when a new master page is applied to a document page.

ePub enhancements

InDesign CS6 includes a number of updates that improve support for ePub. The most notable is InDesign's support for the ePub 3.0 standard. This includes the ability to include multimedia content within an ePub. Many of the ePub enhancements for InDesign CS6 are not visible when creating a document, and impact only the options available when exporting an InDesign file to the ePub format. You can learn more about creating ePub files from InDesign in Lesson 12.

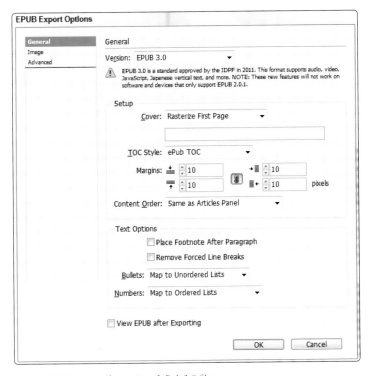

InDesign CS6 supports the creation of ePub 3.0 files.

Congratulations, you have discovered the new capabilities of InDesign CS6.

Index

A

Acrobat, 384, 406, 411–412
actual resolution, 350
Add Documents dialog box, 322
adding
  cross-references to indexes, 342–343
  graphics to layouts
    contact sheets, 180
    display quality, adjusting, 181
    fitting, 172–176
    importing using Adobe Bridge, 176–178
    Mini Bridge used for placing multiple graphics, 178–181
    multiple, 178–181
    object styles, 181–184
    overview, 168
  images to master frames, 73–75
  rules to paragraphs, 89–90
  text
    to documents, 78–79
    to master frames, 73–75
  text variables to documents, 318–321
  topics to an index, 339–342
  words to dictionary, 99–100
Add to Autocorrect List dialog box, 102
adjusting
  creative effects for objects, 293–294
  display quality, 181
  fill opacity, 273–274
  radial gradient direction, 274–276
  text size, 81
Adobe Acrobat, 384, 406, 411–412
Adobe Bridge
  applications, 176–178
  metadata, 331
Adobe Digital Publishing Suite, 375, 386, 438
Adobe Digital Rights Management, 432
Adobe Flash files (.swf)
  creating, 388–390
  interactive PDF files versus, 391
  viewing, 389–390
Adobe Flash Player, 6–7
Adobe InDesign CS6
  graphics. *see* graphics
  help resources, 44–45

navigating documents
  changing magnification, 22–24
  overview, 20
  Pages panel, 20–22
new features and improvements
  Alternate Layouts, 397–406, 443–444
  Combo Box, 408–409
  Content Collector tool, 404–405, 439–440
  Content Conveyor tool, 404–405
  Content Placer tool, 404–405, 439–440
  ePub enhancements, 447
  layouts, 391–406, 443–444
  Linked Content, 400–403, 440
  Liquid Layout, 395–397, 402, 441–442
  Live Corner Effects, 257–259
  overview of, 438
  PDF forms, 384, 406–412, 445
  primary text frame, 66, 74, 446
overview, 9–10
panels. *see* panels
resetting workspace and preferences, 4
review, 46
self study, 46
starting
  Macintosh OS, 3
  Windows OS, 3
styles. *see* styles
system requirements
  Macintosh OS, 2
  overview, 2
  Windows OS, 2
tools. *see* tools
type. *see* type
workspace. *see* workspace
Adobe InDesign CS6 Digital Classroom
  book series, 7
  fonts used in book, 3
  lesson files, loading, 4
  overview, 1
  resources for educators, 7
  video tutorials
    setting up for viewing, 6
    viewing with Adobe Flash Player, 6–7
Adobe Mini Bridge, 178–181

Adobe Photoshop files, importing layered, 196–198
Adobe Reader Mobile SDK, 432
advanced document features
  books, creating from multiple files
    document order, 322–325
    overview, 321–322
    pagination, 322–325
  indexes, building
    adding cross-references, 342–343
    adding topics, 339–342
    generating, 343–344
    overview, 338–339
  overview, 317–318
  PDFs
    creating, 344–345
    printing from Book panel, 345
  review, 346
  self study, 346
  slug area, 319
  synchronizing attributes across book files, 325–330
  Tables of Contents, creating, 333–338
  text variables, adding, 318–321
  trim area, 319
Align away from Spine button, 54
alignment
  frame, 267
  text
    horizontal, 84
    within table cell, 221–222
    vertical, 111–112
Allow Master Item Overrides option, 63
alpha channels
  applying selections, 311–313
  versus clipping paths, 309
  using graphics with, 186–189
Alternate Layouts, 397–406, 443–444
Alternating Pattern drop-down menu, 214–216
Anchored Object Options dialog box, 194
anchored objects
  description of, 191–195
  object placement controlled using, 425–426
Android, 433
animation, 383–384

answers, review
  advanced document features, 346
  color, 283
  digital books, 435
  digital documents, 413
  document delivery, 368
  effects, 316
  essential skills, 46
  graphics, 200
  master pages, 76
  styles, 159
  tables, 251
  text, 135
Apple iBooks, 433
Apple iPad, 402, 433
Apple iPhone, 433
Apple iPod Touch, 433
Apple Mac OS
  starting InDesign CS6, 3
  system requirements, 2
  unlocking files on, 5
Apple Safari, 433
applications
  Adobe Bridge, 176–178
  Microsoft Word, 70, 72, 129–132
applying
  color
    to frames, 254, 256–257
    to multiple objects, 277–278
    to text, 254–256, 262–265
  creative effects
    to fills, 289–290
    opacity, 287–288
    to strokes, 289–290
    to text, 289–290
  effects to graphics, 42–44
  master pages to multiple pages, 75
  path selection, 314–315
  styles
    character, 30–32, 142–143
    object, 32–33, 154–155
    paragraph, 29, 141
    table, 249–250
Apply Master dialog box, 71, 75
Articles panel, 424–425, 428

attributes
  character
    baseline shifts, 83
    character spacing, 82–83
    font and type styles, 80–81
    line spacing, 82
    overview, 80
    size adjustment, 81
  frame, copying with Eyedropper tool, 276–277
  paragraph
    drop caps, 92
    hanging indents, 88
    horizontal text alignment, 84
    overview, 84
    rules above and below paragraphs, 89–90
    spacing before and after paragraphs, 84
    tabs, 85–88
    Tabs panel, 85–87
    text color, 90–91
  synchronizing across book files, 325–330
Autocorrect feature, 98, 102–103
auto fitting graphics, 175–176
autoflow, semi-, 115–116
automatic page numbering, 53–55
automatic spelling correction, 102–103
auto-size text frames, 112, 392–393
Auto-Sizing drop-down menu, 392

B

background, removing image, 189–191
Balance Ragged Lines command, 26
Based on Page Layout option, 428
baseline grid, 120–123
baseline shift, 83
Bevel and Emboss settings, 43, 294–295
binding, 48
bleed, 48
Bleed and Slug section, 50
Bleed option, 14
blending mode, 305–308
Body style, 27
bold type style, 81
Book Page Numbering Options dialog box, 324–325
Book panel, 345

books. *see also* advanced document features
  creating from multiple files
    document order, 322–325
    overview, 321–322
    pagination, 322–325
  digital
    ePub. *see* ePub
    hyperlinks added to, 420
    interactive links added to, 420–423
    metadata, 423
    self-study, 435
    table of contents, interactive, 421–422
  indexes
    adding cross-references, 342–343
    adding topics, 339–342
    generating, 343–344
    overview, 338–339
  synchronizing attributes across files of, 325–330
  Table of Contents, creating, 333–338
book series, 7
Bookworm, 433
border, table, 213–214
bounding box, wrapping text around, 185–186
Bridge
  applications, 176–178
  metadata, 331
buttons
  Align away from Spine, 54
  Clear Preview, 385
  Close Split Layout View, 401
  Constrain Proportions for Scaling, 188
  Create New Hyperlink, 375
  Delete selected action, 380
  Go To Link, 164–165
  Go to Next Page, 385
  Make All Settings the Same, 186
  Mode, 14–15
  multimedia content controlled using, 377–378
  multi-state objects controlled using, 378–381
  Object Styles, 183
  Pages, 18
  Paragraph Formatting Controls, 80, 84, 140
  Play Preview, 385
  portrait, 399

Preserve Styles and Formatting from Text and Tables, 131
Preview Spread, 384
Reject Change, 105–106
Relink, 164, 166
Remove Styles and Formatting from Text and Tables, 131
Right-Justified Tab, 87
Save Preset, 367
Save Style, 337
Screen Mode, 43
Set Preview Document Mode, 385
Specify Attributes to Change, 31
Specify Attributes to Find, 93
Spine, 54
Split Layout View, 400
Stroke, 181
submit, 409–410
Switch to Compact Mode, 177
Wrap Around Bounding Box, 39, 186
Wrap Around Object Shape, 64, 189, 191
Buttons and Forms panel, 379–380, 384, 407

C

Calendar Event style, 29
caps, drop, 92
captions, 330–332
Cascading Style Sheet (CSS) style, 418, 431
Cell Options dialog box, 221–222, 236–237
cells
    graphics, placing in, 239–242
    header, defining, 230–235
    merging, 230
    text
        alignment within, 221–222
        formatting within, 222–226
        inset within, 221–222
    type too large for, 232
cell styles
    applying, 246–247
    creating, 243–245
    overview, 138
    resetting, 219–220
Cell Styles panel, 220
centralized user dictionary, 100
Change Format Settings dialog box, 31–32

channels, alpha
    applying selections, 311–313
    versus clipping paths, 309
    using graphics with, 186–189
character attributes
    baseline shifts, 83
    character spacing, 82–83
    font styles, 80–81
    line spacing, 82
    overview, 80
    size adjustment, 81
Character Formatting Controls, 80, 140
characters. *see also* text
    spacing, 82–83
    special, 54, 107–109
character styles
    applying, 30–32, 142–143
    defining, 142–143
    document conversion to ePub, 417
    overview, 138
Character Styles panel, 30, 142–143
checking spelling
    automatically correcting, 102–103
    overview, 98
    while typing, 100–101
Check Spelling dialog box, 98
Choke, feathers, 298
Chrome, 433
classified page, 71–72
Clear Preview button, 385
clipping path
    graphics, 186–189
    imported files that use transparency, 309–310
Clipping Path dialog box, 312
Close Split Layout View button, 401
CMYK (cyan, magenta, yellow, black) color model, 280, 363
collapsed mode, 17
collected content, 123
color
    default, resetting, 256
    frames, applying to, 254, 256–257
    gradients
        direction of, 274–276
        fill opacity, 273–274
        linear, 270–271

radial, 274

saving, 272–273

new swatches, creating and saving, 260–265

one-click edits of

applying to multiple objects, 277–278

Eyedropper tool, 276–277

updating, 278–279

overview, 253–254

review, 283

self study, 283

spot

colorizing grayscale images, 281–282

saving, 280–282

separation preview, 363

strokes

applying to text, 262–265

dashed, 267–269

text

applying to, 254–256

changing, 90–91

tint reduction, 265–266

colorizing grayscale images, 281–282

color models, 363

color stop, 269, 275

column guides, 72

columns

dimensions of, 236–239

flexible, 118

formatting, 214–217

formatting text by, 227–228

number of in text frame, 117–119

spanning, 119

splitting, 119

in text frame, 118

Column Strokes tab, 215

Combo Box, 408–409

commands

Balance Ragged Lines, 26

Place, 168

Redefine Style, 186

compression, folder, 359

conferences, 45

Constrain Proportions for Scaling button, 188

contact sheet, 180

Content Collector tool, 404–405, 439–440

Content Conveyor tool, 404–405

Content Grabber, 171

Content Indicator, 36, 38, 171

Content Placer tool, 404–405, 439–440

contextual menu, 31

Contour Options, Text Wrap panel, 313

Control panel, 20, 61, 69, 80, 84

converting

tables to text, 208–209

text to paths, 302–305

text to tables, 208–209

Convert Table to Text dialog box, 208–209

Copy Fonts option, 358

copying

frame attributes with Eyedropper tool, 276–277

lesson file to hard drive, 5

table information, 204–207

video tutorial to hard drive, 6

Copy Linked Graphics option, 358

corner effects, 257–259

Corners, feathers, 298

correcting spelling automatically, 102–103

cover image, 426–427

Create Alternate Layout dialog box, 399

Create New Hyperlink button, 375

Create Outlines option, 302

Create Package Folder dialog box, 357

creating

books from multiple files

overview, 321–322

pagination, 322–325

buttons to control multimedia content, 377–378

cell styles, 243–245

centralized user dictionary, 100

classified page, 71–72

drop caps, 92

Flash files, 388–391

indexes, 343–344

master pages, 51–52

PDF files, 344–345, 359–362

tables

converting tables to text, 208–209

converting text to tables, 208–209

copying and pasting information, 204–207

new, 202–204

creative effects. *see also* effects

adjusting for objects, 293–294

Bevel and Emboss, 294–295
drop shadow, 290–292
fills, applying to, 289–290
opacity, applying, 287–288
overview, 286
strokes, applying to, 289–290
text, applying to, 289–290
cropping images, 35
cross-reference, index, 342–343
CSS (Cascading Style Sheet) style, 418, 431
customizing
Links panel, 167–168
page size, 48–51
cyan, magenta, yellow, black (CMYK) color
model, 280, 363

D

dashed stroke, 267–269
defining
character styles, 142–143
document order, 322–325
header cells, 230–235
object styles, 152–154
pagination, 322–325
text variables, 55–56
Delete selected action button, 380
delivery, document
actual versus effective resolution, 350
overview, 347–348
package inventory, 348–351
packaging documents, 355–359
PDF files, creating, 359–362
Preflight checks, 351–355
printing proofs, 366–367
review, 368
self study, 368
separation preview, 363–365
Detect Edges feature, 311
dialog boxes
Create Alternate Layout, 399
Create Package Folder, 357
Edit all Export Tags, 418
Effects, 43
Export Options, 427
Export to Interactive PDF, 411
File Information, 423

Find/Change, 30–32, 93, 96, 108–109
Font Alert, 358
Frame Fitting Options, 62, 175–176
Generate Index, 343–344
Gradient Options, 272–273
Grids Preferences, 121
Image Import Options, 187–189, 197
Import Options, 72, 130, 210
Insert Pages, 65–66
Insert Table, 203–204
Link Options, 406
Load Styles, 51, 125, 148–149
Master Options, 52, 59–60
Microsoft Word Import Options, 69, 113,
129–132, 210
Missing Font, 133
New Book, 322
New Cell Style, 244
New Color Swatch, 260–261, 263–264,
280–281
New Cross-reference, 342–343
New Document, 49
New Glyph Set, 109
New Hyperlink, 375
New Object Style, 153–154, 184, 296
New Page Reference, 340–341
New Paragraph Style, 124, 140, 224, 233
New Style Group, 151–152
New Table Style, 248
New Text Variable, 55–56
New Topic, 339–340
New User Dictionary, 100
New Workspace, 19
Numbering & Section Options, 67
Object Styles Options, 155–156
Open a File, 59
Package Inventory, 349–350
Package Publication Folder, 357
Panel Options, 167
Paragraph Rules, 89–90
Paragraph Style Options, 146–147
Place, 26, 71, 372
Place InDesign Document, 198–199
Preferences, 102
Print, 345, 366–367
Save As, 422

Step and Repeat, 62–63
Style Mapping, 132
Style Options, 418
Swatch Options, 278–279
Synchronize Options, 328
Table of Contents, 334–338
Table Options, 213–218, 234–235
Text Frame Options, 54, 58, 110–112, 118,
    153, 393
Type Preferences, 106
dictionary
    adding words to, 99–100
    centralized, creating, 100
digital books
    ePub. *see* ePub
    hyperlinks added to, 420
    interactive links added to, 420–423
    metadata, 423
    self-study, 435
    table of contents, interactive, 421–422
DigitalClassroom.com, 44
digital documents
    Alternate Layouts, 397–406
    animation, 383–384
    Content Collector tool, 404–405, 439–440
    Content Conveyor tool, 404–405
    Content Placer tool, 404–405, 439–440
    design considerations, 370–371
    ePub conversion of, 417–420
    Flash files
        creating, 388–391
        viewing, 389–390
    hyperlinks added to, 374–375
    interactive PDF files
        creating, 386–388
        viewing, 387–388
    multimedia content
        creating buttons to control, 377–378
        importing, 371–381
    multi-state objects
        adding buttons to control, 378–381
        creating, 375–376
    overview, 369–370
    page transitions, 381–382
    PDF Forms, 384, 406–412
    popularity of, 370

previewing of, 382, 385
    review, 413
    self study, 413
    text frames, 392–394
Digital Publishing Suite, 375, 386, 438
Digital Rights Management, 432
directional feathering, 298
Direct Selection tool, 171, 281–282, 304–305
display quality, adjusting, 181
docked panels, 16
documents
    advanced features for
        books, creating from multiple files,
            321–325
        indexes, building, 338–344
        overview, 317–318
        PDFs, 344–345
        review, 346
        self study, 346
        slug area, 319
        synchronizing attributes across book files,
            325–330
        Tables of Contents, creating, 333–338
        text variables, adding, 318–321
        trim area, 319
    delivering
        actual versus effective resolution, 350
        overview, 347–348
        package inventory, 348–351
        packaging documents, 355–359
        PDF files, 359–362
        Preflight checks, 351–355
        printing proofs, 366–367
        review, 368
        self study, 368
        separation preview, 363–365
    digital
        design considerations, 370–371
        ePub conversion of, 417–420
        Flash files, 388–391
        hyperlinks added to, 374–375
        interactive PDF files, 386–388
        multimedia content, 371–381
        multi-state object, 375–376
        overview, 369–370
        page transitions, 381–382

previewing of, 382, 385
review, 413
self study, 413
ePub conversion of, 417–420
master pages
automatic page numbering, 53–55
basing on other master pages, 59–60
creating, 51–52
custom page sizes, 48–51
formatting, 52
layout pages, 64–75
overriding items, 60–64
overview, 47–48
planning documents, 48
review, 76
self study, 76
text variables, 55–58
navigating
magnification, changing, 22–24
overview, 20
using Pages panel, 20–22
styles, importing from, 125, 147–149
text, adding, 78–79
document window, 11–13
double-arrow icon, 16
drag-and-drop text editing, 106–107
dragging objects, 58
drawing tools, 260
drop caps, 92
Drop Caps and Nested Styles dialog box, 92
drop shadow effect, 290–292
DVD video icon, 6
DVD video tutorials
setting up for viewing, 6
viewing with Adobe Flash Player, 6–7
Dynamic Spelling feature, 98, 100–101

E

Edit all Export Tags dialog box, 418
editing. *see also* adjusting
color
applying to multiple objects, 277–278
Eyedropper tool, 276–277
updating, 278–279
drag-and-drop, 106–107
Story Editor, 103–106, 229

tables
borders, 213–214
column formatting, 214–217
fills, 217–219
overview, 211
row formatting, 214–217
row height, 211–212
Track Changes, 104–106
educators, resources for, 7
effective resolution, 350
effects
blending modes, applying to objects
Multiply blending mode, 307–308
overview, 305–306
Screen blending mode, 305–307
converting text to paths, 302–305
creative
adjusting for objects, 293–294
Bevel and Emboss, 43, 294–295
drop shadow, 290–292
fills, applying to, 289–290
opacity, 287–288
overview, 286
strokes, applying to, 289–290
text, applying to, 289–290
feathering
Gradient Feather tool, 301–302
overview, 298–301
graphics, applying to, 42–44
imported files that use transparency
applying alpha channel selection, 311–313
applying path selection, 314–315
overview, 309–310
object styles with, 296–298
overview, 285–286
review, 316
self study, 316
Effects button, 42
Effects dialog box, 43, 290–295, 299–300
Effects panel, 273, 287–289, 306–308
emboss settings, 43, 294–295
ePub
anchored objects used to control object
placement, 425–426
Cascading Style Sheet (CSS) style for, 418,
431
cover image, 426–427

creating, 416, 424–431
description of, 416
distributing files, 434
document conversion to, 417–420
enhancements to, 447
export settings, 427–431
export style tagging, 418
files, 416
Kindle conversion, 432, 434
metadata, 431
multimedia content, 447
Object Export Options, 419–420, 430
Object Export Order, 424–425
table of contents style, 428
testing, 432–434
validation, 434
viewers of, 432–434
Export Adobe PDF dialog box, 345, 360–361
Export dialog box
ePub files, 427
Flash files, 388
PDF files, 344–345, 360, 386
Export Options dialog box, 427
export style tagging, 418
Export SWF dialog box, 388–389
Export to Interactive PDF dialog box, 411
Eyedropper tool, 276–277

F

favorite settings, 360
Favorites tab, 176
feathering
directional, 298
Gradient Feather tool, 301–302
overview, 297–298
features
advanced document
books, creating from multiple files, 321–325
indexes, building, 338–344
overview, 317–318
PDFs, 344–345
review, 346
self study, 346
slug area, 319
synchronizing attributes across book files, 325–330

Tables of Contents, creating, 333–338
text variables, adding, 318–321
trim area, 319
new
Alternate Layouts, 397–406, 443–444
Combo Box, 408–409
Content Collector tool, 404–405, 439–440
Content Conveyor tool, 404–405
Content Placer tool, 404–405, 439–440
ePub enhancements, 447
layouts, 391–406
Linked Content, 400–403, 440
Liquid Layout, 395–397, 402, 441–442
Live Corner Effects, 257–259
overview of, 438
PDF forms, 384, 406–412, 445
primary text frame, 66, 74, 446
File Information dialog box, 423
files
book, synchronizing attributes across, 325–330
ePub, 416
Flash
creating, 388–391
viewing, 389–390
imported, that use transparency
applying alpha channel selection, 311–313
applying path selection, 314–315
overview, 309–310
lesson, loading, 4
multimedia, 168
multiple, creating books from
document order, 322–325
overview, 321–322
pagination, 322–325
PDF
creating, 344–345, 359–362
interactive, 386–388
Photoshop, importing layered, 196–198
unlocking, 5
Fill Frame Proportionally option, 172, 176
Fill icon, 255–256
fills
applying effects to, 289–290
opacity, 273–274
tables, 217–219
Fills tab, 217

Find/Change
    applying object styles using, 297–298
    dialog box, 30–32, 93, 96, 108–109
Find Font dialog box, 134
finding
    missing fonts, 133–134
    missing images, 162–163
    text to change, 92–97
Firefox, 433
Fit Content Proportionally option, 172
Fit Content to Frame option, 172
Fit Frame to Content option, 172
fitting images within existing frame, 172–174
Fitting options, 172, 373
fixed row height, 236–237
fixing missing fonts, 133–134
Flash documents, 371
Flash files (.swf)
    creating, 388–391
    viewing, 389–390
Flash Player, 6–7
flow, text
    manual, 113–114
    overview, 27–28
    semi-autoflow, 115–116
folder compression, 359
font
    in Control panel, 80
    missing
        finding and fixing, 133–134
        overview, 133
        warning, 3
    styles, changing, 80–81
    used in book, 3
Font Alert dialog box, 358
footer, page, 57–58
formatting
    master pages, 52
    in tables
        columns, 214–217
        header cells, defining, 230–235
        merging cells, 230
        paragraph styles, saving, 222–226
        resetting cell styles, 219–220
        rows, 214–217
        Story Editor, 229
        text, formatting by column, 227–228

text, formatting within cell, 222–226
text alignment, 221–222
text inset, 221–222
text
    headlines, 123–124
    overview, 24–27, 123
    placing, 69–71
    styles, applying, 123–124
    styles, importing from other documents,
        125, 147–149
    styles, redefining, 125–127
forms, PDF, 384, 406–412, 445
forums, 45
four-color process model, 363
frame
    image
        adding images and text to, 73–75
        alignment, 267
        copying attributes with Eyedropper tool,
            276–277
        fitting images within existing, 172–174
        positioning graphics within, 36–38
    placeholder, 61–63
    text
        adding images and text to, 73–75
        automatic sizing of, 112
        changing number of columns in, 117–119
        color, applying to, 254–257
        creating, 78–79
        elements of, 114
        linking with semi-autoflow, 115–116
        multiple, 79
        options for, 110–112
        primary, 66, 74, 446
        repositioning of, 79
        sizing of, 112
        threading text between, 114–115
Frame Fitting Options dialog box, 62, 175–176
Full Screen Mode, 388
fx symbol, 301

G

Generate Index dialog box, 343–344
generating indexes, 343–344
Global Light effect, 294
globally updating styles, 146–147
Global Regular Expression Print. *see* GREP

glyphs, 107–109
Glyphs panel, 109–110
Google Chrome, 433
Go To Link button, 164–165
Go to Next Page button, 385
gradient
    direction of, adjusting, 274–276
    fill opacity, adjusting, 273–274
    linear, 270–271
    overview, 269
    radial, 274
    saving, 272–273
Gradient Feather tool, 301–302
Gradient Options dialog box, 272–273
Gradient panel, 270–276
Gradient Swatch tool, 274–275
graphics
    adding to layouts
        contact sheets, 180
        display quality, adjusting, 181
        Mini Bridge used for placing multiple
            graphics, 178–181
        multiple, 178–181
        object styles, 181–184
        overview, 168
    adding to master frames, 73–75
    background, removing, 189–191
    colorizing grayscale, 281–282
    effects, applying, 42–44
    fitting
        Auto Fitting, 175–176
        within existing frame, 172–174
        options for, 172
    importing
        with Adobe Bridge, 176–178
        InDesign layouts, 198–199
        layered Photoshop files, 196–198
    layers, 40–42
    Links panel
        customizing, 167–168
        overview, 163–164
    locating missing, 162–163
    overview, 161–162
    placing
        multiple, 178–181
        overview, 34–35
    positioning within frames, 36–38

review, 200
self study, 200
using in tables, 239–242
wrapping text around
    alpha channels, 186–189
    anchored objects, 191–195
    bounding boxes, 185–186
    clipping paths, 186–189
    overview, 39
    removing image background, 189–191
Graphics layer, 40–42
grayscale images, colorizing, 281–282
GREP
    characters used in, 97
    description of, 97
    finding and changing text using, 94–97
GREP styles, 138, 157–158
grid, baseline, 120–123
Grids Preferences dialog box, 121
groups, organizing styles into, 151–152
guides
    liquid, 14, 442
    margin, 13
    ruler, 13

H

Hand tool, 23, 37–38
hanging indent, 88
hard drive
    copying lesson file to, 5
    copying video tutorial to, 6
header cell, defining, 230–235
Headers and Footers tab, 234–235
Heading style, 25
headline, 123–124
height, row, 211–212
help resources, 44–45
horizontal text alignment, 84
HTML files, 416
hyperlinks
    digital books, adding to, 420
    digital documents, adding to, 374–375
Hyperlinks panel, 420

I

Ibis reader, 433

iBooks, 433

icons
  Character Formatting Controls, 80
  double-arrow, 16
  DVD video, 6
  Fill, 255–256
  Missing Link, 164
  padlock, 42
  paintbrush, 179
  Stroke, 255–256
  Stroke indicator, 263
  style source, 329
  visibility, 36, 38, 206, 379

image frame
  adding images and text to, 73–75
  alignment, 267
  copying attributes with Eyedropper tool,
      276–277
  fitting images within existing, 172–174
  positioning graphics within, 36–38

Image Import Options dialog box, 187–189,
    197

images. *see also* graphics
  adding to master frames, 73–75
  background, removing, 189–191
  caption generated from, 32
  colorizing grayscale, 281–282
  cover, digital books, 426–427
  cropping of, 35
  fitting within existing frame, 172–174
  locating missing, 162–163
  order of, 73
  selecting of, 39
  using object styles for, 181–184

importing
  file types, 26
  graphics with Adobe Bridge, 176–178
  layered Photoshop files, 196–198
  layouts as graphics, 198–199
  multimedia content, 168, 371–381
  styles from other documents, 125, 147–149
  tables, 209–211
  text
    columns, changing number of, 117–119
    flowing text manually, 113–114
    from Microsoft Word, 70, 129–132
    overview, 112

semi-autoflow, 115–116
  threading between frames, 114–115

Import Options dialog box, 72, 130, 210

inches, 294

Include Fonts and Links from Hidden and
    Non-Printing Content option, 358

indent, hanging, 88

InDesign CS6
  graphics. *see* graphics
  help resources, 44–45
  navigating documents
    changing magnification, 22–24
    overview, 20
    Pages panel, 20–22
  new features and improvements
    Alternate Layouts, 397–406, 443–444
    Combo Box, 408–409
    Content Collector tool, 404–405, 439–
        440
    Content Conveyor tool, 404–405
    Content Placer tool, 404–405, 439–440
    ePub enhancements, 447
    layouts, 391–406
    Linked Content, 400–403, 440
    Liquid Layout, 395–397, 402, 441–442
    Live Corner Effects, 257–259
    overview of, 438
    PDF forms, 384, 406–412, 445
    primary text frame, 66, 74, 446
  overview, 9–10
  panels. *see* panels
  resetting workspace and preferences, 4
  review, 46
  self study, 46
  starting
    Macintosh OS, 3
    Windows OS, 3
  styles. *see* styles
  system requirements
    Macintosh OS, 2
    overview, 2
    Windows OS, 2
  tools. *see* tools
  type. *see* type
  workspace. *see* workspace

InDesign CS6 Digital Classroom, Adobe
    book series, 7

fonts used in book, 3
lesson files, loading, 4
overview, 1
resources for educators, 7
video tutorials
    setting up for viewing, 6
    viewing with Adobe Flash Player, 6–7
indexes
    cross-references, adding, 342–343
    generating, 343–344
    overview, 338–339
    topics, adding, 339–342
Index panel, 339–340
initial caps, 92
Ink Manager, 364–365
inline objects, 191
In Port, 114
in-product help, 44
Insert Pages dialog box, 65–66
Insert Table dialog box, 203–204
inset, text, 110–111, 221–222
inventory, package, 348–351
iPad, 402, 433
iPhone, 433
iPod Touch, 433

J

JPEG format, 430
jump, story, 122–123

K

kerning, 82–83
keyboard shortcuts
    cutting, 240
    guides, showing and hiding, 15
    layout pages, adding, 64
    magnification, increasing and decreasing, 23, 184
    Pages panel, opening, 52
    pasting graphics in tables, 240
    selecting all type, 141
    Text Frame Options dialog box, opening, 110
    toggling between modes, 15, 43
    viewing, 11
Kindle, 432, 434

L

layered Photoshop files, importing, 196–198
layers, 40–42
Layers panel, 34, 205–206, 249–250
Layout menu, 64
layout pages
    applying to multiple pages, 75
    creating classified page, 71–72
    images, adding, 73–75
    numbering options, 67–68
    overview, 64–66
    section options, 67–68
    text, adding, 73–75
    text, placing formatted, 69–71
layouts
    adding graphics to
        contact sheets, 180
        display quality, adjusting, 181
        fitting, 172–176
        importing using Adobe Bridge, 176–178
        Mini Bridge used for placing multiple graphics, 178–181
        multiple, 178–181
        object styles, 181–184
        overview, 168
    adjustments, 395–406
    Alternate, 397–406, 443–444
    importing as graphics, 198–199
    importing file types into, 26
    liquid, 395–397, 402
    new features, 391–406
    online, 371
    repurposing, 391–392
    size of, 391
leading, 82
lesson files
    access to, 3
    loading, 4
line spacing, 82
Link badge, 163–168
Linked Content, 400–403, 440
linked stories, 123, 400
linking text frames, 116
Link Options dialog box, 406
Links panel, 163–168
liquid guide, 14
liquid layout, 395–397, 402, 441–442

Liquid Layout panel, 395–397, 441
lists, 88
Live Captions, 332
Live Corner Effects, 257–259
loading lesson file, 4
Load Styles dialog box, 51, 125, 148–149
locating
    missing fonts, 133–134
    missing images, 162–163
    text to change, 92–97
locking
    layers, 41
    master item, 63–64

M

Mac OS
    starting InDesign CS6, 3
    system requirements, 2
    unlocking files on, 5
magnifying documents, 22–24, 184
Make All Settings the Same button, 186
manual text flow, 113–114
margin guides, 13
Master Options dialog box, 52, 59–60
master pages
    automatic page numbering, 53–55
    basing on other master pages, 59–60
    creating, 51–52
    custom page sizes, 48–51
    formatting, 52
    layout pages
        applying to multiple pages, 75
        creating classified page, 71–72
        images, adding, 73–75
        numbering options, 67–68
        overview, 64–66
        section options, 67–68
        text, adding, 73–75
        text, placing formatted, 69–71
    overriding items
        locking, 63–64
        overview, 60–61
        placeholder frames, 61–63
        setting text wrap, 63–64
    overview, 47–48
    planning documents, 48
    review, 76

self study, 76
    text frame on, 66
    text variables
        defining, 55–56
        page footers, 57–58
menus
    Alternating Pattern, 214–216
    contextual, 31
    Layout, 64
    Special Characters, 54
    Styles drop-down, 67–68
merging cells, 230
metadata, 330–331, 423, 431
Microsoft Windows OS
    starting Adobe InDesign CS6, 3
    system requirements, 2
Microsoft Word, importing text from, 70, 72, 129–132
Microsoft Word Import Options dialog box, 69, 113, 130–132, 210
Mini Bridge, 178–181
Mini Bridge panel, 287
Missing Font dialog box, 133
missing fonts
    finding and fixing, 133–134
    overview, 133
    warning, 3
missing images, locating, 162–163
Missing Link icon, 164
Mode button, 14–15
models, color, 363
Mozilla Firefox, 433
multimedia content
    creating buttons to control, 377–378
    ePub, 447
    importing, 168, 371–381
multiple files, creating books from
    document order, 322–325
    overview, 321–322
    pagination, 322–325
multiple graphics, placing, 178–181
multiple objects, applying colors to, 277–278
multiple pages, applying master pages to, 75
Multiply blending mode, 305, 307–308
multi-state objects
    adding buttons to control, 378–381
    creating, 375–376

N

navigation, document
  magnification, changing, 22–24
  overview, 20
  using Pages panel, 20–22
nested styles, 144–145
New Book dialog box, 322
New Cell Style dialog box, 244
New Color Swatch dialog box, 260–261,
    263–264, 280–281
New Cross-reference dialog box, 342–343
New Document dialog box, 49
new features and improvements
  Alternate Layouts, 397–406, 443–444
  Combo Box, 408–409
  Content Collector tool, 404–405, 439–440
  Content Conveyor tool, 404–405
  Content Placer tool, 404–405, 439–440
  ePub enhancements, 447
  layouts, 391–406
  Linked Content, 400–403, 440
  Liquid Layout, 395–397, 402, 441–442
  Live Corner Effects, 257–259
  overview of, 438
  PDF forms, 384, 406–412, 445
  primary text frame, 66, 74, 446
New Glyph Set dialog box, 109
New Hyperlink dialog box, 375
New Object Style dialog box, 153–154, 184,
    296
New Page Reference dialog box, 340–341
New Paragraph Style dialog box, 124, 140,
    224, 233
New Style Group dialog box, 151–152
New Table Style dialog box, 248
New Text Variable dialog box, 55–56
New Topic dialog box, 339–340
New User Dictionary dialog box, 100
New Workspace dialog box, 19
Next Page marker, 122
Noise, feathers, 298
Nook, 433
numbering, page
  automatic, 53–55
  setting options, 67–68
  table of contents, 422
Numbering & Section Options dialog box, 67

O

Object-based Liquid Layout rule, 442
Object Export Options, 419–420
Object Export Order, 424–425
objects
  anchored, 191–195, 425–426
  applying blending modes to, 305–308
  applying opacity to, 287–288
  colors, applying to multiple, 277–278
  creative effects, adjusting for, 293–294
  dragging, 58
  multi-state
    adding buttons to control, 378–381
    creating, 375–376
object styles
  applying, 32–33, 154–155
  changing, 155–156
  creating, 152–154
  document conversion to ePub, 417
  with effects, 296–298
  Find/Change used to apply, 297–298
  overview, 138
  using for images, 181–184
Object Styles button, 183
Object Styles Options dialog box, 155–156
Object Styles panel, 296
one-click color edits
  applying to multiple objects, 277–278
  Eyedropper tool, 276–277
  updating, 278–279
on-line help, 44
online layouts, 371
opacity
  applying to objects, 287–288
  fill, 273–274
  tint versus, 287
Open a File dialog box, 59
operating systems
  Mac
    starting InDesign CS6, 3
    system requirements, 2
    unlocking files on, 5
  Windows
    starting Adobe InDesign CS6, 3
    system requirements, 2
options
  Allow Master Item Overrides, 63

Bleed, 14
Create Outlines, 302
Fill Frame Proportionally, 172, 176
Fit Content Proportionally, 172
Fit Content to Frame, 172
Fit Frame to Content, 172
Fitting, 373
page numbering, 67–68
Place, 304
section, 67–68
Update Links, 163
Use Typographer's Quotes, 131
order, document, 322–325
organizing styles into groups, 151–152
Out Port, 114–115
overrides, 60–64, 126, 219–220, 417
overset text, 103–104, 329, 337
oversize text, 28

P

Package Inventory, 348–351
Package Inventory dialog box, 349–350
Package Publication Folder dialog box, 357
packaging documents, 355–359
padlock icon, 42
page numbering, 53–55
pages
    custom size, 48–51
    footers, 57–58
    guides, 13–14
    layout
        applying to multiple pages, 75
        creating classified page, 71–72
        images, adding, 73–75
        numbering options, 67–68
        overview, 64–66
        section options, 67–68
        text, adding, 73–75
        text, placing formatted, 69–71
    master
        automatic page numbering, 53–55
        basing on other master pages, 59–60
        creating, 51–52
        custom page sizes, 48–51
        formatting, 52
        overriding items, 60–64
        overview, 47–48

planning documents, 48
    review, 76
    self study, 76
    text variables, 55–58
numbering
    automatic, 53–55
    setting options, 67–68
    table of contents, 422
rulers, 53
transitions, 381–382
Pages button, 18
Pages panel, 20–22, 26, 52
Pages panel menu, 398
Page tool, 395, 397, 441
Page Transitions panel, 381–382
pagination, 322–325
paintbrush icon, 179
Panel Options dialog box, 167
panels
    accessing of, 40
    Articles, 424–425
    Book, 345
    Buttons and Forms, 379–380, 407
    Cell Styles, 220
    Character Styles, 30, 142–143
    Control, 20, 61, 69, 80, 84
    docked, 16
    Effects, 273, 287–289, 306–308
    Glyphs, 109–110
    Gradient, 270–276
    Hyperlinks, 420
    Index, 339–340
    Layers, 34, 205–206, 249–250
    Links, 163–168
    Liquid Layout, 395–397, 441
    managing, 17–18
    Mini Bridge, 287
    Object Styles, 296
    overview, 15
    Pages, 20–22, 26, 52
    Page Transitions, 381–382
    Paragraph Styles, 25, 51, 123–127, 139–141,
        222–228
    Preflight, 351–355
    Preview, 382, 385
    saving workspace, 19–20
    Separations Preview, 363–365

Stroke, 182, 264, 267–269
Swatches, 90–91, 223, 231, 256–257, 271–272
SWF Preview, 385–386
Table, 238–239
Tabs, 85–87
Text Wrap, 64, 185–186, 189, 191, 195, 312–313
Tools, 15–17, 405
Track Changes, 104–105
Pantone Matching System (PMS), 363
Paragraph Formatting Controls button, 80, 84, 140
Paragraph Rules dialog box, 89–90
paragraphs
adding rules, 89–90
changing spacing before and after paragraphs, 84
changing text color, 90–91
creating drop caps, 92
hanging indents, 88
horizontally aligning text, 84
overview, 84
Tabs panel, 85–87
using tabs, 85–88
Paragraph Style Options dialog box, 146–147
paragraph styles
applying, 29, 141
defining, 139–140
document conversion to ePub, 417
overview, 138
saving, 222–226
Paragraph Styles panel, 25, 51, 123–127, 141, 222–228
pasteboard, 11–12
pasting
graphics in tables, 240
table information, 204–207
paths
clipping
graphics, 186–189
imported files that use transparency, 309–310
converting text to, 302–305
type on, 127–132
path selection, 314–315
PDF (Portable Document Format) files

creating, 344–345, 359–362
forms, 384, 406–412, 445
interactive
creating, 386–388
saving as, 391
.swf files versus, 391
viewing, 387–388
Photoshop files, importing layered, 196–198
picas, 294
Place command, 168
Place dialog box, 26, 71, 372
placeholder frame, 61–63
Place InDesign Document dialog box, 198–199
Place option, 304
Play Preview button, 385
PMS (Pantone Matching System), 363
Portable Document Format (PDF) files
creating, 344–345, 359–362
forms, 384, 406–412, 445
interactive
creating, 386–388
saving as, 391
.swf files versus, 391
viewing, 387–388
portrait button, 399
positioning graphics within frame, 36–38
preferences, resetting, 4
Preferences dialog box, 102
Preflight panel, 351–355
prerequisites for Adobe InDesign CS6 Digital Classroom lessons, 1
Preserve Local Overrides check box, 131
Preserve Styles and Formatting from Text and Tables radio button, 131
preview
digital documents, 382, 385
separation, 363–365
Preview panel, 382, 385–386
Preview Spread button, 384
Preview viewing mode, 43
primary text frame, 66, 74, 446
Print dialog box, 345, 366–367
printing from Book panel, 345
printing proofs, 366–367
Process Color Simulator guide, 363
professional development, 7
proofs, printing, 366–367

Q

questions, review
 advanced document features, 346
 color, 283
 digital books, 435
 digital documents, 413
 document delivery, 368
 effects, 316
 graphics, 200
 master pages, 76
 styles, 159
 tables, 251
 text, 135
Quick Apply feature, 149–151
QuickTime Player, 370

R

Reader Mobile SDK, 432
Recenter Liquid Layout option, 441
Rectangle Frame tool, 61, 407
Rectangle tool, 407
Redefine Style command, 186
redefining styles, 125–127
red plus sign, 28
red square, 41
Reject Change button, 105–106
Relative to Spine checkbox, 194
Relink button, 164, 166
Remove Styles and Formatting from Text and
 Tables radio button, 131
removing image background, 189–191
resolution, actual versus effective, 350
resources
 for educators, 7
 help, 44–45
Resources folder, 390
reviews
 advanced document features, 346
 color, 283
 digital books, 435
 digital documents, 413
 document delivery, 368
 effects, 316
 graphics, 200
 master pages, 76
 styles, 159

tables, 251
text, 135
Right-Justified Tab button, 87
Roman Numeral style, 68
rows
 dimensions of, 236–239
 formatting, 214–217
ruler guides, 13, 442
rulers, page, 53
rules, 89–90

S

Safari, 433
Save As dialog box, 422
Save Preset button, 367
Save Style button, 337
saving
 gradients, 272–273
 new color swatches, 260–265
 paragraph styles, 222–226
 spot colors, 280–282
 workspace, 19–20
Scale Liquid Layout option, 441
scaling images, 35
Screen blending mode, 305–307
Screen Mode button, 43
scrolling, 22
section options, 67–68
Selection tool, 20, 27–28, 33, 60–61, 79, 380,
 394, 401, 407, 419
self study sections
 advanced document features, 346
 color, 283
 digital books, 435
 digital documents, 413
 document delivery, 368
 effects, 316
 graphics, 200
 master pages, 76
 styles, 159
 tables, 251
 text, 135
semi-autoflow, 115–116
seminars, 45
separation preview, 363–365
Separations Preview panel, 363–365
Set Preview Document Mode button, 385

shift, baseline, 83
shortcuts, keyboard
  cutting, 240
  guides, showing and hiding, 15
  layout pages, adding, 64
  magnification, increasing and decreasing, 23, 184
  Pages panel, opening, 52
  pasting graphics in tables, 240
  selecting all type, 141
  Text Frame Options dialog box, opening, 110
  toggling between modes, 15, 43
  viewing, 11
sizing
  images, 35, 172–174
  pages, 48–51, 81
slug area, 319
spacing
  character, 82–83
  line, 82
  paragraph, 84
spanning columns, 119
special characters, 54, 107–109
Special Characters menu, 54
Specify Attributes to Change button, 31
Specify Attributes to Find button, 93
spelling
  automatically correcting, 102–103
  checking
    overview, 98
    while typing, 100–101
  dictionary
    adding words to, 99–100
    centralized, creating, 100
  drag-and-drop text editing, 106–107
  overview, 98
  Story Editor, 103–106
Spine button, 54
Split Layout View button, 400
splitting columns, 119
spot color
  colorizing grayscale images, 281–282
  saving, 280–282
  separation preview, 363
starting InDesign CS6
  Mac OS, 3
  Windows OS, 3

Static Captions, 332
Step and Repeat dialog box, 62–63
stops
  color, 269, 275
  tab, 85–88
stories, linked, 123, 400
Story Editor
  editing text, 103–106
  formatting tables, 229
  Track Changes, 104–106
story jump, 122–123
Stroke button, 181
Stroke icon, 255–256
Stroke indicator icon, 263
Stroke panel, 182, 264, 267–269
strokes
  applying creative effects to, 289–290
  color
    applying to text, 262–265
    dashed, 267–269
Style Mapping dialog box, 132
Style Options dialog box, 418
styles
  cell
    applying, 246–247
    creating, 243–245
    overview, 138
    resetting, 219–220
  character
    applying, 30–32, 142–143
    defining, 142–143
    document conversion to ePub, 417
    overview, 138
  document conversion to ePub, 417–420
  globally updating, 146–147
  GREP, 138, 157–158
  loading from another document, 147–149
  object
    applying, 154–155
    changing, 155–156
    defining, 152–154
    document conversion to ePub, 417
    with effects, 296–298
    Find/Change used to apply, 297–298
    overview, 32–33, 138
    using for images, 181–184
  organizing into groups, 151–152
  overview, 137–138

paragraph
  applying, 29, 141
  defining, 139–140
  document conversion to ePub, 417
  overview, 138
  saving, 222–226
Quick Apply, 149–151
self study, 159
table
  applying, 249–250
  creating, 247–249
  overview, 243
type, changing, 80–81
types of, 138
using to format text, 123–127
Styles drop-down menu, 67–68
style source icon, 329
submit button, 409–410
swatches, color, 260–265
Swatches panel, 90–91, 223, 231, 256–257,
  271–272
Swatch Options dialog box, 278–279
.swf (Adobe Flash files)
  creating, 388–391
  interactive PDF files versus, 391
  viewing, 389–390
SWF Preview panel, 385–386
Switch to Compact Mode button, 177
Synchronize Options dialog box, 328
synchronizing attributes across book files,
  325–330
system requirements
  Mac OS, 2
  overview, 2
  Windows OS, 2

T

Table of Contents
  creating, 333–338
  ePub, 428
  interactive, 421–422
Table of Contents dialog box, 334–338
Table Options dialog box, 213–218, 234–235
Table panel, 238–239
tables
  border, 213–214
  cells

    formatting text within, 219, 222–226
    header, defining, 230–235
    merging, 230
  columns
    dimensions of, 236–239
    formatting, 214–217
    formatting text by, 227–228
  creating
    converting tables to text, 208–209
    converting text to tables, 208–209
    copying and pasting information, 204–207
    new tables, 202–204
  data organization in, 88
  editing, 211–218
  fills, 217–219
  graphics, 239–242
  importing, 209–211
  overview, 201–202
  review, 251
  rows
    dimensions, 236–239
    formatting, 214–217
  self study, 251
  Story Editor, 229
  styles
    applying, 249–250
    cells, 219–220, 243–245
    creating, 247–249
    overview, 243
    paragraph, saving, 222–226
  text
    alignment, 221–222
    formatting by column, 227–228
    formatting within cells, 222–226
    inset, 221–222
Table styles, 138
tablets, 402
tabs
  for aligning text, 85–88
  Column Strokes, 215
  Favorites, 176
  Fills, 217–219
  Headers and Footers, 234–235
Tabs panel, 85–87
text
  adding
    to documents, 78–79
    to master frames, 73–75

alignment
  horizontal, 84
  within table cell, 221–222
  vertical, 111–112
baseline grid, 120–123
character attributes
  baseline shifts, 83
  character spacing, 82–83
  font styles, 80–81
  line spacing, 82
  overview, 80
  size adjustment, 81
color, applying to, 254–256
converting
  to paths, 302–305
  to tables, 208–209
  tables to, 208–209
entering, 24–26
flow
  manual, 113–114
  overview, 27–28
  semi-autoflow, 115–116
formatting, 24–26
  within cells, 222–226
  by column, 227–228
  headlines, 123–124
  overview, 24–27, 123
  placing, 26–27, 69–71
  styles, applying, 123–124
  styles, importing from other documents,
    125, 147–149
  styles, redefining, 125–127
importing
  columns, changing number of, 117–119
  flowing text manually, 113–114
  from Microsoft Word, 70, 72, 129–132
  overview, 112
  semi-autoflow, 115–116
  threading between frames, 114–115
inset, 221–222
missing fonts
  finding and fixing, 133–134
  overview, 133
  warning, 3
overset, 103–104, 329, 337
oversize, 28
overview, 24, 77–78

  on paths, 127–132
  review, 135
  self study, 135
  special characters and glyphs, 54, 107–109
  strokes, applying to, 262–265
  wrapping
    alpha channels, 186–189
    anchored objects, 191–195
    applying, 39
    bounding boxes, 185–186
    clipping paths, 186–189
    removing image background, 189–191
    setting, 63–64
text frame
  adding images and text to, 73–75
  anchored objects used to separate, 426
  automatic sizing of, 112, 392–393
  changing number of columns in, 117–119
  color, applying to, 256–257
  columns in, 118
  creating, 78–79
  elements of, 114
  flexible width, 393–394
  linking with semi-autoflow, 116
  multiple, 79
  options for, 110–112
  primary, 66, 74, 446
  repositioning of, 79
  sizing of, 112
  threading text between, 114–115
Text Frame Options dialog box, 54, 58,
    110–112, 118, 153, 393
Text tool, 20, 417
text variable
  adding, 318–321
  defining, 55–56
  page footers, 57–58
Text Wrap panel, 64, 185–186, 189, 191, 195,
    312–313
threading text between frames, 114–115
Times New Roman font, 322
tint
  opacity versus, 287
  reduction of, 265–266
tools
  Content Collector, 404–405, 439–440
  Content Conveyor, 404–405

Content Placer, 404–405, 439–440
Direct Selection, 171, 281–282, 304–305
drawing, 260
Eyedropper, 276–277
Gradient Feather, 301–302
Gradient Swatch, 274–275
Hand, 23, 37–38
overview, 10–11
Page, 395, 397, 441
Rectangle, 407
Rectangle Frame, 61, 407
Selection, 20, 27–28, 33, 60–61, 79, 380,
    394, 401, 407, 419
Text, 20, 417
Type, 25, 29–30, 33, 54, 57, 78–79, 91, 93,
    156, 231, 392–393, 401, 407
Type on a Path, 129
Zoom, 22–23, 91, 93
Tools panel, 15–17, 405
topic, index, 339–342
Track Changes, 104–106
Track Changes panel, 104–105
tracking, 82–83
training, 7, 45
transitions, page, 381–382
transparency, imported files using
    applying alpha channel selection, 311–313
    applying path selection, 314–315
    overview, 309–310
trim area, 319
trim size, 48
tutorial, video
    setting up for viewing, 6
    viewing with Adobe Flash Player, 6–7
type
    adding
        to documents, 78–79
        to master frames, 73–75
    alignment
        horizontal, 84
        within table cell, 221–222
        vertical, 111–112
    baseline grid, 120–123
    character attributes
        baseline shifts, 83
        character spacing, 82–83
        font styles, 80–81

line spacing, 82
overview, 80
size adjustment, 81
color, applying to, 254–256
converting
    to paths, 302–305
    to tables, 208–209
    tables to, 208–209
entering, 24–26
flow
    manual, 113–114
    overview, 27–28
    semi-autoflow, 115–116
formatting, 24–26
    within cells, 222–226
    by column, 227–228
    headlines, 123–124
    overview, 24–27, 123
    placing, 26–27, 69–71
    styles, applying, 123–124
    styles, importing from other documents,
        125, 147–149
    styles, redefining, 125–127
importing
    columns, changing number of, 117–119
    flowing text manually, 113–114
    from Microsoft Word, 70, 72, 129–132
    overview, 112
    semi-autoflow, 115–116
    threading between frames, 114–115
inset, 221–222
missing fonts
    finding and fixing, 133–134
    overview, 133
    warning, 3
overview, 24, 77–78
on paths, 127–132
review, 135
self study, 135
special characters and glyphs, 54, 107–109
strokes, applying to, 262–265
wrapping
    alpha channels, 186–189
    anchored objects, 191–195
    applying, 39
    bounding boxes, 185–186
    clipping paths, 186–189

removing image background, 189–191
setting, 63–64
Type on a Path tool, 129
Type Preferences dialog box, 106
Type tool, 25, 29–30, 33, 54, 57, 78–79, 93, 156, 231, 392–393, 401, 407
typing, checking spelling while, 100–101

U

unit of measurement, 294
unlocking files, 5
Update Graphic Links In Package option, 358
Update Links option, 163
updating
color, 278–279
style, globally, 146–147
Use Document Hyphenation Exceptions Only option, 358
Use Global Light effect, 293
Use Typographer's Quotes option, 131

V

variable, text
adding, 318–321
defining, 55–56
page footers, 57–58
vertical text alignment, 111–112
video tutorials
setting up for viewing, 6
viewing with Adobe Flash Player, 6–7
viewing
DVD video tutorials
with Adobe Flash Player, 6–7
setting up for, 6
Flash files, 389–390
keyboard shortcuts, 11

viewing mode, 14–15
View Report option, 358
visibility icon, 36, 38, 206, 379
volume, video tutorial, 7

W

WebKit, 432–433
width, column, 238–239
Windows OS
starting Adobe InDesign CS6, 3
system requirements, 2
Word application, importing text from, 70, 72, 129–132
workspace
description of, 11
document window, 12
guides, 13–14
modes, 14–15
resetting, 4
saving, 19–20
Workspace switcher, 12
Wrap Around Bounding Box button, 39, 186
Wrap Around Object Shape button, 64, 189, 191
wrapping text
alpha channels, 186–189
anchored objects, 191–195
applying, 39
around images, 185–195
bounding boxes, 185–186
clipping paths, 186–189
removing image background, 189–191
setting, 63–64

Z

Zoom tool, 22–23, 91, 93

John Wiley & Sons, Inc.
End-User License Agreement

READ THIS. You should carefully read these terms and conditions before opening the software packet(s) included with this book "Book". This is a license agreement "Agreement" between you and John Wiley & Sons, Inc. "WILEY". By opening the accompanying software packet(s), you acknowledge that you have read and accept the following terms and conditions. If you do not agree and do not want to be bound by such terms and conditions, promptly return the Book and the unopened software packet(s) to the place you obtained them for a full refund.

1. **License Grant**. WILEY grants to you (either an individual or entity) a nonexclusive license to use one copy of the enclosed software program(s) (collectively, the "Software") solely for your own personal or business purposes on a single computer (whether a standard computer or a workstation component of a multi-user network). The Software is in use on a computer when it is loaded into temporary memory (RAM) or installed into permanent memory (hard disk, CD-ROM, or other storage device). WILEY reserves all rights not expressly granted herein.

2. **Ownership.** WILEY is the owner of all right, title, and interest, including copyright, in and to the compilation of the Software recorded on the physical packet included with this Book "Software Media". Copyright to the individual programs recorded on the Software Media is owned by the author or other authorized copyright owner of each program. Ownership of the Software and all proprietary rights relating thereto remain with WILEY and its licensers.

3. **Restrictions on Use and Transfer.**

   (a) You may only (i) make one copy of the Software for backup or archival purposes, or (ii) transfer the Software to a single hard disk, provided that you keep the original for backup or archival purposes. You may not (i) rent or lease the Software, (ii) copy or reproduce the Software through a LAN or other network system or through any computer subscriber system or bulletin-board system, or (iii) modify, adapt, or create derivative works based on the Software.

   (b) You may not reverse engineer, decompile, or disassemble the Software. You may transfer the Software and user documentation on a permanent basis, provided that the transferee agrees to accept the terms and conditions of this Agreement and you retain no copies. If the Software is an update or has been updated, any transfer must include the most recent update and all prior versions.

4. **Restrictions on Use of Individual Programs.** You must follow the individual requirements and restrictions detailed for each individual program in the "About the CD" appendix of this Book or on the Software Media. These limitations are also contained in the individual license agreements recorded on the Software Media. These limitations may include a requirement that after using the program for a specified period of time, the user must pay a registration fee or discontinue use. By opening the Software packet(s), you agree to abide by the licenses and restrictions for these individual programs that are detailed in the "About the CD" appendix and/or on the Software Media. None of the material on this Software Media or listed in this Book may ever be redistributed, in original or modified form, for commercial purposes.

5. Limited Warranty.

(a) WILEY warrants that the Software and Software Media are free from defects in materials and workmanship under normal use for a period of sixty (60) days from the date of purchase of this Book. If WILEY receives notification within the warranty period of defects in materials or workmanship, WILEY will replace the defective Software Media.

(b) WILEY AND THE AUTHOR(S) OF THE BOOK DISCLAIM ALL OTHER WARRANTIES, EXPRESS OR IMPLIED, INCLUDING WITHOUT LIMITATION IMPLIED WARRANTIES OF MERCHANTABILITY AND FITNESS FOR A PARTICULAR PURPOSE, WITH RESPECT TO THE SOFTWARE, THE PROGRAMS, THE SOURCE CODE CONTAINED THEREIN, AND/OR THE TECHNIQUES DESCRIBED IN THIS BOOK. WILEY DOES NOT WARRANT THAT THE FUNCTIONS CONTAINED IN THE SOFTWARE WILL MEET YOUR REQUIREMENTS OR THAT THE OPERATION OF THE SOFTWARE WILL BE ERROR FREE.

(c) This limited warranty gives you specific legal rights, and you may have other rights that vary from jurisdiction to jurisdiction.

6. Remedies.

(a) WILEY's entire liability and your exclusive remedy for defects in materials and workmanship shall be limited to replacement of the Software Media, which may be returned to WILEY with a copy of your receipt at the following address: Software Media Fulfillment Department, Attn.: *Adobe InDesign CS6 Digital Classroom*, John Wiley & Sons, Inc., 10475 Crosspoint Blvd., Indianapolis, IN 46256, or call 1-800-762-2974. Please allow four to six weeks for delivery. This Limited Warranty is void if failure of the Software Media has resulted from accident, abuse, or misapplication. Any replacement Software Media will be warranted for the remainder of the original warranty period or thirty (30) days, whichever is longer.

(b) In no event shall WILEY or the author be liable for any damages whatsoever (including without limitation damages for loss of business profits, business interruption, loss of business information, or any other pecuniary loss) arising from the use of or inability to use the Book or the Software, even if WILEY has been advised of the possibility of such damages.

(c) Because some jurisdictions do not allow the exclusion or limitation of liability for consequential or incidental damages, the above limitation or exclusion may not apply to you.

7. U.S. Government Restricted Rights. Use, duplication, or disclosure of the Software for or on behalf of the United States of America, its agencies and/or instrumentalities "U.S. Government" is subject to restrictions as stated in paragraph (c)(1)(ii) of the Rights in Technical Data and Computer Software clause of DFARS 252.227-7013, or subparagraphs (c) (1) and (2) of the Commercial Computer Software - Restricted Rights clause at FAR 52.227-19, and in similar clauses in the NASA FAR supplement, as applicable.

8. General. This Agreement constitutes the entire understanding of the parties and revokes and supersedes all prior agreements, oral or written, between them and may not be modified or amended except in a writing signed by both parties hereto that specifically refers to this Agreement. This Agreement shall take precedence over any other documents that may be in conflict herewith. If any one or more provisions contained in this Agreement are held by any court or tribunal to be invalid, illegal, or otherwise unenforceable, each and every other provision shall remain in full force and effect.

Register your Digital Classroom book for exclusive benefits

Registered owners receive access to:

 The most current lesson files

 Technical resources and customer support

 Notifications of updates

 On-line access to video tutorials

 Downloadable lesson files

 Samples from other Digital Classroom books

Register at *DigitalClassroomBooks.com/CS6/InDesign*

⚏DigitalClassroom⚏

Register your book today at
DigitalClassroomBooks.com/CS6/InDesign